GREAT SLEEPS
PARIS

SANDRA GUSTAFSON

ELEVENTH EDITION

CHRONICLE BOOKS
SAN FRANCISCO

ELEVENTH EDITION
ISBN-10: 0-8118-5395-0
ISBN-13: 978-0-8118-5395-8
ISSN: 1074-505X

Manufactured in the United States of America.

Cover design by Jay Peter Salvas
Book design: Words & Deeds
Typesetting: Jack Lanning
Series editor: Jeff Campbell
Author photograph: Marv Summers

Distributed in Canada by
Raincoast Books
9050 Shaughnessy Street
Vancouver, British Columbia V6P 6E5

10 9 8 7 6 5 4 3 2 1

Chronicle Books LLC
680 Second Street
San Francisco, California 94107

www.chroniclebooks.com
www.greateatsandsleeps.com

For Anne Vafis—a great friend

Contents

To the Reader

**You, who have ever been to Paris know;
And you who have not been to Paris, go.**
> —*John Ruskin,*
> A Tour through France, 1835

**The crowds in the streets, the lights in the shops, the
elegance, variety, and beauty of their decorations, the
brilliant cafés with their vivacious groups at little tables
on the pavement soon convince me that this is no dream:
that I am in Paris . . .**
> —*Charles Dickens*

La Belle France continues to beckon visitors to her shores. Indeed, it
should not be surprising that Paris is one of the most popular travel
destinations in the world, playing host to more than 26 million visitors yearly, or nearly ten times the city's population. This number
translates into 130,000 tourism-related jobs and adds nearly 8 billion
euros to the economy. The American passion for Paris has not ebbed
despite wars, riots, occupations, differing politics, and the rise and
fall of hemlines and the dollar. Whether seen for the first time or the
tenth, Paris never leaves you, and it becomes a never-ending love affair
for most of us. Walk a block, turn a corner, in Paris there is always
something interesting, something beautiful and new, something that
has been there forever but that you never noticed until now. No matter
what time of year you visit, you will find it impossible to keep from
losing your heart to the city, with its grand boulevards, beautiful
men and women, breathtaking monuments and museums, glorious
food, famous art, and sweeping views—from place de la Concorde
up the Champs-Élysées, from the steps of the Sacré Coeur over the
entire city, and standing at Trocadéro looking across the fountains to
the Eiffel Tower.

The first priority for visitors is to get a roof over their heads. Despite
Paris's reputation for high prices, there are more than fifteen hundred
hotels in all price ranges, so travelers can enjoy a pleasant stay in the
city, no matter what their budget may be. However, the French have
learned to make do with cramped quarters, sitting elbow-to-elbow in
bistros, standing nose-to-nose on a crowded métro, or inching their
way through narrow, traffic-clogged streets. This intimacy is part
of the city's charm, and it translates even to the size of hotel rooms,
which by American standards are very small.

The essence of any Parisian hotel is its individuality, and no two
are alike. You can, of course, find here the most luxurious pleasure

palaces in the world, and it is always possible to check into the Hilton or any other big-name chain hotel. But only in Paris can you sleep in a romantic hideaway in Montmartre and be served breakfast in bed while looking out the window and seeing all of Paris below, rent an eighteenth-century apartment with views of the place des Vosges (the oldest square in Paris), or check into a suite in a renovated hotel a block from the Ritz but light-years away in price.

It is certainly true that a trip to Paris will cost more today than it did a few years ago, but what doesn't? Europe—or Paris—on $30 to $40 a day is ancient history and rarely exists for any traveler. Most of those romantically threadbare hotels of our youth are thankfully gone for good. More and more smaller hotels are being renovated, adding bathrooms, fluffy towels, Internet access, and buffet breakfasts served in sixteenth-century stone-walled *caves* (or cellars). This, of course, adds up to higher prices. Yet there are still many ways to save money and maximize the buying strength of the dollar without feeling *nouveau pauvre* in the process. *Great Sleeps Paris* shows you how.

Great Sleeps Paris is a highly selective guide to the accommodations that I have discovered to be the best value in their category, be it a no-star with the shower and toilet down the hall; an antique-filled, three-star Left Bank hotel with a Jacuzzi in the marble bathroom; or an antiques-filled apartment on l'Île St-Louis with a magnificent view of Notre Dame and the Seine. The purpose of this book is to offer fail-safe advice on the best-priced accommodations for a range of tastes and needs—whether you are a first-time visitor or a Paris veteran, whether you want to be in the buzzing center of the city or on its quiet fringes. There are hotels for lovers and honeymooners, nostalgia buffs, backpackers, and families, while other options include living on a houseboat on the Seine, camping, renting an apartment, or bunking in a hostel. For students, a wealth of inexpensive beds awaits.

Each hotel listing has been included because I feel it has something special to offer. Some represent a particular style or era; others have been beautifully restored; and some are in nontourist neighborhoods where people like you and I live and work, send their children to school, get their cars repaired, eat lunch, shop, and go to the dentist. Some accommodations are basic, many are charming, and a few are starkly modern. Most are moderately priced, some are inexpensive Cheap Sleeps, and some fall into the Big Splurge category for those with more flexible budgets and demanding tastes. All have one vital feature in common: the potential for providing a memorable stay that will make you feel you have discovered your own part of Paris, one that you will savor and want to return to as often as possible.

It is important for readers to know that no hotel can purchase a listing or ask to be included in this book. I pay my own way, and I do all the research and writing for the book myself; the buck stops right here. In reviewing the hotels, I pull no punches and call the shots as I see them, good, bad, and otherwise, including giving the specifics about the best and worst rooms, so that you will know exactly what to expect when you check into your room during your Parisian holiday.

What are the guidelines I use for selecting a hotel? The two primary concerns are value for money and cleanliness, followed by location, pleasant surroundings in the room, and management attitude and service. On my visits to the hotels, which are always unannounced, I wipe my fingers across the door tops, check closets, turn on the showers, look for mold, flush toilets, spot thin towels and waxed or sandy toilet paper, open and close windows, bounce on the beds, look under them for dust, and visit the dining room where breakfast is served. I have stumbled along dimly lit corridors, climbed endless flights of stairs, and been squeezed into minuscule cage elevators that seem to have been in operation since the fall of the Bastille, all so that I can warn you about avoiding the same.

In addition to giving the value-conscious traveler the inside track to the best hotel prices in Paris, *Great Sleeps Paris* offers insider information on shopping. If you are like I am and believe the eighth deadly sin is paying full retail price for anything, then you will love the "Great Chic" shopping section (see page 314). Here I've collected my best shopping finds: from designer discount shops and big-name cosmetics sold for less than their regular retail price, to neighborhood markets, hidden boutiques, and gourmet food and wine shopping.

On my most recent trip for the eleventh edition of this guide, I inspected every hotel and shop that's listed, along with scores of others that did not make the final cut for one reason or another. In so doing, I walked hundreds of miles, wearing out my walking shoes in the process, and was asked for directions or the time of day sixty-five times. And yet, no matter what the weather, how long the day, or the personalities and moods of the people I met along the way, it never seemed like work. I loved every minute of it, and I can't wait to pack my bags and return to Paris to do it all again. I hope that *Great Sleeps Paris* shows you how to cut corners with style, so that whatever your budget, you need not give up the good life by lowering your standards. If I can help you select that special hotel that makes your stay in Paris truly memorable and sets the stage for many return visits, I will have done my job well. I wish you *bonne chance* and *bon voyage*.

Tips for Great Sleeps in Paris

Paris is planted in my heart.
> —*Endre Ady, Hungarian lyric poet*

The great advantage of a hotel is that it is a refuge from homelife.
> —*George Bernard Shaw,*
> You Never Can Tell, *1898*

1. Unless you enjoy standing in long lines in French government tourist offices or rail stations, or wandering the streets looking for a hotel, never arrive in Paris without confirmed hotel reservations.

2. Websites are good resources, but there are other excellent ways to ensure Great Sleeps in Paris. Don't forget the endangered species called "travel agents." Often they can get discounts with the hotels they deal with and pass the savings on.

3. Before reserving a particular hotel, check www.pagesjaunes.fr. Type in the hotel's address (or that of almost any Paris business or residence), and you can see one or more photos of the building. Click again, and there is a map of the surrounding area, which will give you a sense of the views you will encounter each day. Click on *Rues Commerçantes,* and you will go on a virtual tour of every business on the block.

4. Dealing directly with the hotel almost always insures the best rate. Almost every hotel listed in *Great Sleeps Paris* has discounted rates based on season and availability. Always ask for the best rates being offered for weekends, families, the off-season, and so on. When negotiating price, remember the higher the rack rate for the hotel, the more negotiating room there will usually be, especially in slow periods. If a hotel has an Internet site, *always* check it to find out about special offers. If the hotel has a toll-free 800 number, the rates quoted are usually regular or premium rates. However, special rates are sometimes available, so it doesn't hurt to inquire here either. No matter how you reserve your room, bring paper copies of your confirmations to present upon check-in.

5. Luxury does not necessarily have to be beyond your budget if you go when everyone else does not. The weather may not always cooperate in the off-season months, but there will be far fewer tourists, and hotels will be cutting deals. The two fashion weeks in mid-January, from Easter through June, September, October, and ten days around Christmas and New Year's are considered high season and the hardest times to find a hotel room in Paris. During the height of winter and summer, hotel rates are at their lowest.

6. You pay for the room, not for the number of people occupying it. Back rooms often face blank walls or dreary courtyards and are usually smaller, but they cost less and are quieter. Twin beds cost more than a double, and any room with a private shower and toilet will generally be less than one with a bathtub. If you ask for a double room, you must specify whether you want a double bed or twin beds. During major trade shows, international exhibitions, and the designer fashion shows in the fall and early spring, many hotels add a supplement.

7. Don't be surprised if your shower, either stall or over the bathtub, has no curtain. In smaller hotels, towels are usually changed only every two or three days.

8. Many hotels do not allow outside guests to visit you in your room. This is an iron-clad rule in hostels, student digs, and almost every no-star and one-star hotel in Paris.

9. If you pay a deposit, always ask about the hotel's refund policy. Some smaller hotels have draconian ideas about refunds, which may leave you out of luck if you have to cancel at the last minute or leave earlier than planned.

10. If you have booked an apartment and paid a chunk of money in advance or have a nonrefundable and nonchangeable airline ticket, seriously consider purchasing trip insurance. If you have to change dates, interrupt travel, or cancel altogether, you will be grateful for it. For further details, see Insurance, page 41.

11. Always check out the room before you check in. While most hotels cannot promise specific rooms, they should guarantee the type (twin beds or a double bed; facing front or on the back; with shower or bath). At check-in, confirm the rate and discuss the cost of any extras (such as telephone calls, both local and long distance, logging onto the Internet, and breakfast); don't wait until you're paying the bill. All hotels must clearly post their rates by the reception desk, but they are not required to list "hidden" charges they may add on later.

12. Avoid eating breakfast at your hotel if you want to save money. Instead, join the Parisians standing at the bar at the corner café or occupying a stool in a *boulangerie* or *pâtisserie*. Only a few hotels now include breakfast in their prices, and even if you do not eat it, many hotels will not deduct the charge for it, saying, "It is offered." Still, it doesn't hurt to ask to have the "offer" deducted. However, if you partake of your hotel's buffet breakfast, please do not take advantage and load your pockets and bags with enough extra food to sustain you and your family for lunch and/or snacks during the day. Hoteliers take a very dim view of this cheap trick.

13. Wash loads of clothes at the local laundromat and take your cleaning to the neighborhood dry cleaner yourself. Laundry and dry cleaning sent from the hotel can blow a budget. If you do wash out a few things, be sure they do not drip over carpeting or fabric. And please, do not hang things in the windows!

14. Notify the hotel if you expect to arrive after 6 P.M. Even if you paid the room deposit, the hotel can technically resell your room to someone else if they do not know your arrival time.

15. Change money at a bank, never at a hotel.

16. For security's sake, avoid rooms on the *rez-de-chaussée,* or ground floor. In France, the ground floor is what Americans call the first floor; the French first floor *(premier étage)* is our second floor.

17. Paris is a very noisy city both day and night, making it heaven for night owls and a nightmare for insomniacs. Traffic, sirens, motor scooters, and voices magnify on the narrow streets, echoing throughout the night. Street-cleaning crews and trash trucks start their rounds at zero-dark-hundred, jarring awake many a sleeper. If noise is a problem, ask for a room away from the street, in the back of the hotel, or facing an inner courtyard. For added insurance, buy or bring earplugs *(boules de quièss).*

18. In the winter, hotels often schedule remodeling and/or repainting. This can involve anything from adding a coat of paint or remodeling a few bathrooms to months of time-consuming cleaning and exterior repairs that require scaffolding and sheets of plastic covering the windows. Work crews at these sites arrive at dawn and leave at dusk, and at no time are they or their machines quiet or conducive to peace. Before making final reservations, ask the hotel if it, or any of the buildings immediately around it, will be undergoing repairs or renovations during your stay. If so, consider carefully whether you want to put up with the noise and new paint smells.

19. It is important to realize that a *hôtel* is not always a hotel. The word *hôtel* has more than one meaning in French. Of course, it

means a place offering lodging, but it also means a mansion or town house, like the Hôtel Lambert, or a large private home (a *hôtel particulière*). The city hall is the *Hôtel de Ville;* auctions are held at the *Hôtel des Ventes; Hôtel des Postes* refers to the general post office; and the *Hôtel des Invalides,* once a home for disabled war veterans, is now the most famous military museum in the world and the final resting place of Napoléon Bonaparte. Finally, if you are in the hospital, you are in a *Hôtel-Dieu.*

20. Traveler: Know thyself. It has often been said that all a person needs for adventure is the desire to have one. Your trip to Paris (or to any other destination) should be an adventure filled with treasured memories that last a lifetime. During any adventure, there will always be surprises. If you aren't willing to risk some unexpected turns in your plans, but insist on absolute predictability, especially in your accommodations, then I recommend you do one of two things: reserve a room at the Hôtel Ritz (01-43-16-30-30; www.ritzparis.com; double room from 880–8,500€, breakfast 45€), or invest your travel money elsewhere and stay home.

How to Use Great Sleeps Paris

You need three things to have a great trip: your passport, your money, and above all your sense of humor.
—*Mary Beth Bond, "Bon Voyage,"*
Traveler's Tales: Gutsy Women

Big Splurges and Cheap Sleeps

Most of the hotels in this guide are in the midrange price category. However, a few are higher priced and designated as "Big Splurges," and a few are true budget accommodations and designated as "Cheap Sleeps." Big Splurge hotels have amenities, ambience, services, and an overall appeal that will suit those celebrating special occasions or those with more flexible budgets and demanding tastes. Even though their rates are higher, they still offer the same good value for money as the other accommodations in this guide. All Big Splurge hotels are marked with a dollar sign ($). The index includes a separate list of these special hotels (see page 409).

Conversely, those looking to maximize their travel dollar without sacrificing cleanliness and a good night's sleep should look for the Cheap Sleep hotels, which are denoted with a cent symbol (¢) and are also listed separately in the index (see page 409). These budget-priced hotels are in safe and pleasant locations and maintain excellent quality for their price category. Those on a budget could also consider hostels or, if you qualify, student accommodations, which are listed under "Other Options" (see page 280).

Stars

Hotels throughout France are controlled by a government rating system that ranks them from no stars to four-star deluxe. The number of stars reflects a property's price range and determines its tax structure. Every hotel must display prominently the number of stars it has.

Because the number of stars has to do with the size and number of rooms, the distance from the bed to the light switch, heating and air-conditioning, telecommunication services, and whether or not there is an elevator—and it has absolutely nothing to do with the level of cleanliness, decor, attitude of management or personnel, location, or value for money—you cannot always judge the quality or even the price of a hotel by its stars. In older hotels, many of the rooms are not standardized, and they can range in size and price from a dark little cavelike cell in the back to a sumptuous suite facing a leafy garden.

However, the star ratings do act as a general guide. The hotel's rates are evaluated before they open and again every six years, unless reclassification is requested. A no-star hotel is usually mighty basic, with few, if any, private bathrooms, no elevator, and someone behind the desk who speaks limited English. Many of them, however, are spotlessly clean, well-located, and excellent budget values. A one-star hotel has minimum facilities, but again, it may be well-located and very clean. Two stars means a comfortable hotel with direct-dial phones in all rooms and an elevator in buildings of four or more stories. Three stars indicates a very comfortable hotel where rooms have most amenities, and the building has an elevator. A four-star hotel is first class all the way, usually with a restaurant and a business center, and a four-star deluxe is a virtual palace, with every service you could dream of. This book covers no-star to three-star hotels, with the exception of a handful of four-stars that were too good to leave out.

Reservations

Be prepared.

—*Boy Scout motto*

People always ask me, "Do I need advance hotel reservations in Paris?" The answer is yes, positively! In order to be assured of a room, you must reserve as far in advance as possible. Paris experiences some of the worst hotel bottlenecks in Europe, and a confirmed reservation, even on the slowest day in the low season, will save you frantic hours spent searching for a room after your arrival. It will also save you money, since without advance reservations you will probably be forced to take something beyond your budget, perhaps in a part of the city you do not like. Do not reserve for more nights than you think you will need. If you decide to leave before you intended, or if you want to switch hotels, you may not get back any money you have paid ahead, or you could be charged on your credit card for the nights you do not stay. The easiest way to reserve is to let your travel agent do all the work. However, it is not hard to do it yourself, and frankly, with the ease and speed of the telephone, email, and the Internet, you will be able to ask questions, inquire about exact rates, and arrange just what you want without going through an intermediary. In addition, the hotel may pass along to you their savings of the travel agent's commission, have special prices for reserving on their Website, or negotiate a better rate over the telephone. When you reserve, you will be asked to guarantee your booking by fax or email with a major credit card, or in a few cases, a money order in euros.

When reserving, discuss the following points:

1. Dates of stay, time of arrival, and number of persons in the party.

2. Size and type of room (double or twin beds, extra beds, adjoining rooms, suite, and so on).

3. Facilities needed: private toilet, shower and/or bathtub, or hall facilities if acceptable.

4. Location of room: view, on the street, on the courtyard, or in the back of the hotel.

5. Rates. Determine what the nightly rate will be, including the per-person City of Paris tourist tax, called the *taxe de séjour* (see "Rates: Paying the Bill," page 19, for details). Be sure to state whether or not you will be eating breakfast at the hotel (and remember you will save money if you do not).

6. Deposit required and form of payment.

7. Refund policy if you should have to cancel, and penalty if you check out earlier than planned. Request a confirmation by fax or email (print it out), and bring it with you.

Email and the Internet

Today, the French hotel industry uses email and the Internet to the same degree as you'll find in the States, and all but the smallest budget hotels have joined the electronic age. In this guide, each hotel's email and/or Internet address is given when they exist. When booking over the Internet, request a confirmation by email, print it out, and take it with you to the registration desk when checking in. This eliminates possible misunderstandings on both sides.

Fax

Faxing is still a reliable way to secure a confirmed booking because it ensures that all parties get the details correct. Insist on a confirmation fax from the hotel, acknowledging your reservation and all pertinent details. See "Staying in Touch," page 50, for information on how to send a fax to Paris.

Telephone

With the use of an international telephone card, a telephone call to Paris costs next to nothing. For the best results, call Paris during regular, local weekday business hours to avoid talking to a hotel night clerk who has no authority to negotiate prices. The best times to get anything done in Paris is between 10 A.M. and noon, and between 3 and 6 P.M. Before calling, write down all your requests and questions. The hotel will ask you to send a fax or email with your credit card number as a guarantee for your reservation. In this fax or email to the hotel, cite the details of the conversation, the name of the person with whom you spoke, and the date and time of the call. It is vital to ask the hotel to fax or email you a confirmation of your reservation in return. See "Staying in Touch," page 50, for information on how to dial Paris from the United States.

Making Your Reservation in French

Most hotels have someone on staff who speaks English. However, if you want to try your luck with French, here are a few simple phrases for making your reservation (see also the glossary, page 400).

Bonjour/Bonsoir madame/monsieur.
Hello/Good evening, madam/sir.

Parlez-vous anglais?
Do you speak English?

Je voudrais réserver ____ chambre(s) (tranquille) pour une/deux/trois personne(s) qui donne sur (le jardin/la rue/la cour) à deux lits (avec un grand lit/à un lit) avec salle de bains et WC (avec douche ou bain et WC/sans douche ou bain et WC) pour ____ nuit(s) à partir du ____ au ____ .
I would like to reserve ____ (quiet) room(s) for one/two/three person(s) that is/are on (the garden/the street/the courtyard) with two beds (one big bed) with bath and toilet (with shower or bath and toilet/without shower or bath and toilet) for ____ night(s) beginning on ____ to ____ .

Je voudrais prendre la (les) chambre(s) avec (sans) le petit déjéuner.
I would like to have the room(s) include (without) breakfast.

Quel est le tarif?
What is the price?

Quel est votre tarif meilleur? Avez-vous des prix basse-saison?
What is your best price? Do you have a low-season rate?

Voici mon numero de carte de credit.
Here is my credit card number.

Mon numéro de fax/email est _____ .
My fax/email number is _____ .

Veuillez-vous confirmer ma reservation des que possible?
Would you please confirm this reservation as soon as possible?

Merci beaucoup, madame/monsieur.
Thank you very much, sir/madame.

If you are sending a confirmation fax, you will want to add in writing:

Vous trouvez ci-joint ____ (mon carte de credit) à titre d'arrhes.
You will find attached ____ (my credit card number and expiration date) as a first-night deposit.

Auriez-vous le bonté de bien vouloir me confirmer cette réservation dès que possible? Je vous remercie de votre obligeance, et je vous prie de croire, monsieur/madame, à l'assurance de mes sentiments distingués.
Would you please be kind enough to confirm this reservation as soon as possible? Thank you for your assistance.
Yours sincerely,

Cancelling a Reservation

If you cancel a reservation before you arrive in Paris, be sure to request that the hotel confirm the cancellation in writing, either by email or fax. If you don't specifically ask for such a confirmation, you probably won't get one, and even when you do ask, it may take a telephone call on your part to get it.

Deposits

After making a reservation, most hotels will require at least a one-night deposit, even if you have been a guest there before. This is smart insurance for both sides. The easiest way to handle a deposit is with a credit card. If the hotel does not take credit cards, there are other options. You can sometimes send your own personal check, which the hotel will only cash if you are a no-show. They will return the uncashed check to you upon arrival. The next best option from your standpoint is to send the hotel an international money order in U.S. dollars. This can be converted into euros by the hotel, and it saves you from having to secure a deposit in euros on this side of the Atlantic. While this option is more convenient for you, it is added work for the hotel, costs them money to exchange, and some, especially in the lower price ranges, simply refuse. If your hotel insists on a deposit in euros, you will have to purchase them in the form of a money order or a wire transfer through your bank.

Checking In/Checking Out

The lobby is usually one of the most attractive parts of a hotel, both because first impressions are important and because it is where the owner and manager spend their day. When you arrive at your hotel, ask to see your room. This is a normal and expected practice in all hotels in France. If you are dissatisfied, ask to see another room. Keep going until you are satisfied. After approving the room, reconfirm the rate and whether or not you will be eating breakfast at the hotel. This advance work prevents any unpleasant surprises at checkout time.

In most hotels, you pay for the room, not for the number of persons occupying it. Thus, if you are alone and occupy a triple, you will pay the triple price, unless negotiated otherwise. Watch out! Most rooms are set up for two, and the few singles tend to be tiny and located on a top floor without much view or along the back facing a blank wall. Single travelers may be more comfortable in a small double. Most hotels have two kinds of double rooms: those with a double bed *(un grand lit)* and those with twin beds *(deux lits)*. If you ask for a double, you will get a room with a double bed, so when reserving, be sure to be specific about exactly what type of bed arrangement suits you.

In Paris, the hotel day begins and ends at noon. If you overstay, you can be charged the price of an extra day. If you are arriving before noon after a long international flight, the room will probably not be ready if the hotel is fully booked. If you must have your room at 8 or 9 A.M., you will have to book (and pay) for it the night before. If you think you might arrive after 6 P.M., be sure to notify the hotel; otherwise, your room can legally be given away, even if you have a deposit.

Rates: Paying the Bill

Just like French restaurant menus, hotel rates and the number of stars must be posted.

The city of Paris levies a visitor's tax on persons not liable for the resident tax. This visitor's tax, called the *taxe de séjour,* applies to all forms of paying accommodations: hotels and tourist residences, furnished flats, holiday campsites, and RV parking. The tax is charged per person, per night. The amount ranges from 0.30€ for guests staying at no-star hotels and campgrounds to 1.20€ for those patronizing four-star hotels. Some hotels charge it over and above the quoted rate, which is technically illegal, but no one seems to be looking; others include it in the total hotel rate. All *Great Sleeps Paris* listings note the specific amount for each hotel and whether or not this tax is included or extra in the daily rate. However, policies on this tax change, so to avoid confusion, be sure to inquire at the time of booking whether or not the *taxe de séjour* is included or extra. The proceeds of the *taxe de séjour* are allocated for the development and promotion of tourism in Paris.

The French government no longer tightly controls hotel prices, but they do give special authorization for hotels to increase prices by a certain percentage every year. Many hotels do this around April; others have held steady for two and three years at a time. It usually depends on the economy. Most hotels offer different rates at different times of the year, getting what they can when they can, based on the law of supply and demand. This is especially true during the fashion and trade shows, when hotels in premium Paris locations have been known to double prices—and have people fight to pay them. All rates listed in *Great Sleeps Paris* are for full price and do not reflect any special deals. Don't let the rack rates scare you: almost all hotels have special offers or discounted seasonal rates that are less than the published price. In this guide, rate descriptions tell whether or not breakfast is extra or included and, if included, whether or not the hotel will allow you to deduct it if not taken. While I have made every effort to be accurate about rates, I cannot control changes or fluctuations of the dollar against the euro, inflation, yearly percentage rate hikes, owner whims, or grand renovations that result in higher prices. So, be prepared for the prices to vary (unfortunately, usually upward).

All listings state which credit cards are accepted. The favored cards are Visa and MasterCard. American Express is third, and Diners Club a very distant fourth (thanks to their vendor charges and slow payments). In most hotels, payment is required one night in advance. Some low-priced hotels, youth hostels, and student accommodations do not accept credit cards. It is cash up front in euros only. I have yet to see one of these hotels bend on this important point, so be prepared.

The following credit card abbreviations are used in this guide:

American Express	AE
Diners Club	DC
MasterCard	MC
Visa	V

Hotel exchange rates are terrible. If you plan to pay your bill in cash, convert your money at a bank before checkout time (see "Currency Exchange and Traveler's Checks," page 39). Before leaving the hotel, go over your bill carefully, question anything you do not understand, and get a receipt marked *paid*.

Complaints

If you have a serious complaint about some aspect of your hotel stay (and this does not mean noise or mismatched colors in your room), complain directly to the manager, not to the desk clerk, who has no authority and will rarely pass on your comments to the boss. If the problem cannot be resolved at this level, then put your concerns in writing and send them to the Direction du Tourisme, 2, rue Linois, 75015, Paris; Métro: Charles-Michels. I encourage you to also let me know about any major problems you encounter. While I cannot intercede on your behalf, it is important for me to know if a hotel is no longer measuring up so that I can take up the matter with the hotel on my next visit (see "Readers' Comments," page 415).

Breakfast

Hotel breakfasts are almost always a bad buy. Hotels stand to make as much as a 200 percent profit on this meal, so they naturally encourage their guests to eat it at the hotel. It is much cheaper, and twice as interesting, to join the locals at the corner café for a *café crème* and a croissant, or to stop by a neighborhood *pâtisserie* or *boulangerie* that has a few tables and chairs and indulge in freshly baked treats. Almost every Parisian hotel charges extra for their Continental breakfast, which consists of coffee, tea, hot chocolate, bread, croissants or other rolls, butter, and jam. Some throw in a glass of juice or a piece of cheese. If you want anything beyond this (for example, an egg or fruit), it will cost dearly and is usually not worth the extra expenditure.

Many hotels are now offering a buffet downstairs for about the same price as a Continental, which they will serve in your room. An all-you-can-eat buffet—with cereals, yogurt, hard-boiled eggs, cheese, cold meat, and fruit added to the standard Continental fare—can sometimes be worth the price, especially if you plan to skip lunch. But please! Do not treat the buffet as a free feed for the rest of the day by loading up a bag with the fixings for lunch and a predinner snack. This is extremely bad form, and hoteliers will be furious if they catch you doing it.

Be aware of the "breakfast is offered" ruse. No, it isn't . . . you are paying for it in the room rate; it just has not been separately charged, and it will be virtually impossible to have it deducted, even if you do not eat it. Of course, if a hotel charges for breakfast separately, it should not be on your bill unless you eat it.

Unless otherwise noted, none of the hotels listed serve meals other than breakfast.

English Spoken

While it is fun to practice your high-school French, it is not fun to try to deal with a problem while struggling to speak it. Nearly every hotel listed in this book has someone on staff who speaks at least limited English, and many of them have staff who are fluent. The only times you will run into language difficulties are typically at budget no-star and one-star hotels. In this guide, whenever English is not spoken, or if it is very limited (such as when it's dependent on a single staff person), that will be noted in the hotel's write-up. But always remember, if you can dust off a few French phrases, smile, and display good will, you will find that the hotel staff will prove to be friendly and go out of their way to help you.

Smoking/Nonsmoking Rooms

Bon chance on this one! Statistics show that 50 percent of Parisian men are smokers, and 30 percent of Parisian women light up. I think these figures are very low, considering that three tons of cigarette butts are cleaned off the streets of Paris every day! Statistics are even higher for other countries whose residents vacation in Paris and smoke in their hotel rooms. Many hotels will say they have nonsmoking rooms "on request." What that really means is that, if you ask when reserving, the maid will open the window and spray air freshener on the day you arrive. Or, as one hotel owner seriously said to me when questioned about nonsmoking rooms, "Yes, we do have nonsmoking rooms. We always remove the ashtrays in rooms of our nonsmoking guests." If the hotel provides exclusive nonsmoking rooms, it is definitely noted under the Facilities and Services category. Fortunately, most of the hotel breakfast dining rooms are nonsmoking. The index has a list of hotels that have rooms exclusively set aside for nonsmoking guests (see page 410).

Facilities and Services

A brief summary at the end of each hotel listing states which facilities and services are offered by the hotel. They may include: air-conditioning (if in some rooms only, this is noted), bar, conference room, direct-dial telephone, hair dryer, elevator, fitness center, WiFi

Internet in lobby and/or rooms, laundry service, minibar, parking, room service, television with either French or international reception, pay-per-view television or videos, safe in office or in the room (and whether there is a charge), and exclusive nonsmoking rooms. Of course, the better the hotel, the more offerings there will be.

Tourist Attractions and Neighborhoods

Since what's outside your hotel is often just as important as what's inside, in the introductions to the arrondissements, I describe the popular tourist attractions they contain and what the neighborhoods are like. Maybe you want to be within walking distance of the Louvre, or you'd prefer to stay in a working-class neighborhood where real folks live, work, and dream. These introductions will help you decide what part of the city you would like to stay in. To figure out exactly how close your hotel is to what you want to see, consult the arrondissement maps, which label the major tourist sites and parks.

Transportation

The closest métro and RER stops are given with each hotel listing. That is not to say that taking the bus might not be a better way for you to get where you want to go. It is beyond the scope of *Great Sleeps Paris* to provide bus routes, but there are free métro and bus maps available in métro stations and detailed *Plan de Paris* (see Maps, below) at most kiosks. When in doubt, just ask at the hotel desk. You can bet that person rides either the métro or the bus to work (see also "Transportation," page 53).

Maps

There is never any ending to Paris and the memory.
—*Ernest Hemingway*

The maps in *Great Sleeps Paris* are meant to help locate this guide's recommended hotels and shops; they are not meant to replace detailed street maps to guide you as you walk about the city. On this book's maps, hotels are marked with bullets, shops with triangles, and key tourist sites and métro and rail stations are noted.

The free maps you will pick up at your hotel are worth what you paid for them: nothing. If you plan to be in Paris for more than a day, a necessary investment, and one that will last forever, is a copy of the *Plan de Paris par Arrondissement*. This Parisian "bible" offers a detailed map of each arrondissement, with a completely keyed street index, métro and bus routes, tourist sites, churches, *marchés,* theaters, and other valuable information. You do not have to speak a word of French to benefit from the *Plan de Paris par Arrondissement*, which is available at major newsstands and bookstores and costs between 10€ and 15€. All Parisians have a copy, and so should you.

General Information

When to Go

Whoever does not visit Paris regularly will never be elegant.
—*Balzac, 1815*

If you don't travel when you can, your heirs probably will.
—*Anonymous*

How wonderful it would be to drop everything and fly to Paris whenever the spirit moved us! If such romantic impulses do not quite fit into your schedule or budget, then the high and low seasons must be taken into consideration. These times of year affect not only the availability of hotel rooms and the rates but also airline fares. High season in Paris is considered to be the two fashion weeks in mid-January for *haute couture* and again in March for *pret-a-porter* (the winter and spring trade shows), Easter through June, September, October, and ten days around Christmas and New Year's. It is very important for Paris visitors to note that when fashion and large trade shows fill the city to the bursting point, many hotels add on surcharges of up to 50 percent. Dates vary slightly from year to year, so the best bet is to check with the French Government Tourist Office in New York or Los Angeles (see page 27) for the latest information. This leaves July, August, November, the first three weeks of December, and parts of January to Easter, as the best times to go to Paris. The drawback in July and August is that you will be sharing your Parisian holiday with many other tourists and very few French. Despite government pleadings and tourist demands, August is still the traditional vacation month for most Parisians, and many restaurants and shops are closed for at least a week or two, if not the entire month. The good news is that hotels are always open—and many offer lower rates—and everything is easier to come by, including métro seats, café tables, and good-natured waiters.

Holidays and Events

Holidays *(les jours fériés)* are vital dates to bear in mind when planning any trip to Paris. Banks, post offices, and most retail stores are all closed, and museums that are open may run on different schedules. In addition, banks may be closed a half day before each holiday as well as sometimes the day after. The traffic is horrendous, especially if the holiday falls on a Tuesday or Thursday, since many French take off Monday or Friday to make it a long weekend. Restaurant holiday policies vary with the rise and fall of the economy. Always call ahead to make sure—even if they say they are open, they may change their mind and be closed. Skeleton or third-string crews often man the hotel desks, and there is a laid-back attitude during a holiday period, resulting in quick excuses for things not working. It can all add up to some very frustrating times for a traveler.

January 1	New Year's Day	*Jour de l'An*
Easter Sunday and Monday		*Pâques et Lundi de Pâques et Lundi de Pâques*
Ascension Day	*Ascension*	(40 days after Easter)
Whit Monday	*Lundi de Pentacôte*	(second Monday after Ascension)
May 1	Labor Day	*Fête du Travail*
May 8	VE Day	Armistice 1945
July 14	Bastille Day	*Quatorze Juillet/Fête Nationale*
August 15	Assumption Day	*Assomption*
November 1	All Saints' Day	*Toussaint*
November 11	Armistice Day	Armistice 1918
December 25	Christmas Day	*Noël*

For motorists, the time to avoid is the last weekend in August, when Parisians return from their vacations en masse. This grand *rentrée* creates traffic snarls of world-class proportions.

Events

The two best sources for events in Paris are the weekly magazines *Pariscope: Une Semaine de Paris* and *l'Officiel des Spectacles.* They come out on Wednesday, cost less than one euro, and are sold at every kiosk in the city. These magazines provide listings for the opera, theater, films, concerts, art exhibitions, special events, naughty nightlife, TV, swimming-pool hours, and interesting guided tours. Although the magazines are in French, a non–French speaker can quickly decipher the information.

What to Bring

> **I think every wife has a right to insist upon seeing Paris.**
> —*Sydney Smith, British author (1771–1845), from letter to Countess Grey, September 11, 1835*

> **Why buy good luggage? You only use it when you travel . . .**
> —*Casey Stengel*

If you follow only one piece of advice in *Great Sleeps Paris,* let it be this: Travel light. Porters are no longer roaming airports or train stations, and bellboys are relics of the past for most hotels. You are going to have to carry your own luggage, and even if yours has wheels, less is definitely best. My travel rule of thumb is this: Take twice as much money as you think you will need and half as much clothing. Keep it simple, color coordinate your outfits, and remember, this is Paris, not Mars: you can buy something wonderful if you need to fill a gap in your travel wardrobe. For travel products and travel clothing, I think one of the best sources is Magellan's Travel Catalog (Tel: 800-962-4943, www.magellans.com).

One of the favorite pastimes of Parisians and their expatriate friends is to sit in a café along a busy boulevard and pick out the tourists. You can spot them a mile away, in their summer tank tops and shorts, a bottle of water dangling from a hook on their belts—and in winter, bundled up in parkas as if the ski slopes were just around the corner. Of course, they all wear jogging shoes, carry cameras around their neck, and the men have baseball caps . . . often turned backward.

Parisians are some of the most stylish people on earth. They are also some of the most conservative in their dress. Yes, you will see some off-the-wall outfits on bionic, buffed bodies, but you will never see short shorts and skimpy tops on any well-groomed Parisian man or woman. Big-city clothes are the call of the day, no matter what the weather may bring.

Naturally, you will leave your heavy wool coat and long johns at home when you visit Paris in August. But what kind of coat makes sense in May or June? Knowing the monthly average temperatures will help:

January	45.5°F	(7.5°C)
February	44.8°F	(7.1°C)
March	50°F	(10.2°C)
April	60.3°F	(15.7°C)
May	61–62°F	(16.6°C)
June	75°F	(23°C)
July	77°F	(25.1°C)
August	78°F	(25.6°C)
September	69–70°F	(20.9°C)
October	61.7°F	(16.5°C)
November	53°F	(11.7°C)
December	46°F	(7.8°C)

If you are going during the warm months, wear light cottons and comfortable shoes. Synthetics don't breathe and add to the heat discomfort. For winter visits, layering makes sense, and so do a lined raincoat, a set of silk long underwear, and a hat (since 70 percent of body heat goes out through your head). Jeans are universal and certainly acceptable for sight-seeing and casual dining. However, they are not considered in vogue at more expensive restaurants or if you are invited to someone's home. Men will feel comfortable wearing slacks and a nice shirt or turtleneck, along with a jacket if it is cool. Women will feel best in simple, well-tailored outfits. Gauzy, lime-green jumpsuits with sequined Eiffel Tower T-shirts, along with jogging shoes for every occasion, spell tourist and can lead to such problems as poor service or being a target of pickpockets.

When packing your bags, use every bit of space to its fullest: stuff your shoes, roll your sweaters and underwear, use plastic garment bags between layers to prevent wrinkling and pack so things will not slip and slide to one end. Pack your toiletries and cosmetics in a sealable, waterproof bag. You only need one experience with the mess caused by airplane pressure blowing off the top of your shampoo or nail polish remover to know what I am talking about.

Aside from the obvious documents, money, airline tickets, medicines, emergency telephone numbers, and clothing, the following is a list of useful items. It is by no means exhaustive, nor do I suggest you take every item on it, but it is a list of things you might consider bringing.

- Your favorite shampoo and soap
- As many moist towelettes as you can fit in, and a large bottle of antiseptic hand wash
- Packaged wipes for shoe cleaning, make-up removal, nail polish removal
- Sunscreen lotion and sunglasses
- French dictionary and/or phrasebook
- Portable radio or CD player with earphones
- Pedometer to keep track of the number of miles you walk, so you can impress your friends when you return
- First-aid kit
- Sewing kit, with a pair of decent scissors
- Travel tool kit with Swiss army knife, screwdriver, tape, stapler, packing tape, Scotch tape, string
- A few hangers you can toss out at the end of the trip. You may be surprised at the condition and scarcity of hotel hangers.
- Rubber doorstop as a security measure
- For drip-dry laundry: blow-up hangers, clothesline with clothespins, or clothespins you can hang up; and a small container of spot remover to use on tough stains before you wash your clothes in your room sink or bathtub. (However, don't pack laundry soap; it's cheap and readily available in all Paris supermarkets.)
- Adapter plug and a transformer for electrical appliances (see "Voltage," page 61), and a grounded surge protector for your computer
- A sturdy suction hook for the back of the bathroom or bedroom door
- Suction-cup magnifying mirror

- Alarm clock with lighted face
- Mosquito repellent (summer)
- Flashlight
- Reading material
- Umbrella
- Camera
- Extra batteries (including a camera battery)
- Calculator
- Lint remover roller, clothes brush
- Extra fold-up bag for shopping purchases and a few sheets of bubble wrap for wrapping breakables you might buy
- Plastic zip-lock baggies in several sizes
- Highlighter for marking maps
- Hidden money pouch
- A shoe organizer to hang over the bathroom door, useful for storing toiletries, socks, lingerie, laundry equipment, and so on in tiny bathrooms

Tourist Offices and American Embassy

The main office of the Office de Tourisme de Paris is at 25, rue des Pyramides, 75001; Métro: Pyramides; 08-92-68-30-00 (0.34€ per minute); www.parisinfo.com; open in summer daily 9 A.M.–7 P.M., in winter Mon–Sat 10 A.M.–7 P.M., Sun and holidays 11 A.M.–7 P.M. It is a one-stop shop for information on Paris and can make hotel reservations. For information on Paris and Île de France, contact Espace du Tourisme d'Île de France at La Galerie de Carrousel du Louvre, 99, rue de Rivoli, 1st; Métro: Palais Royal–Musée du Louvre; www.pidf.com; daily 10 A.M.–7 P.M.

Other convenient tourist offices are at the Eiffel Tower (April–October), Gare du Nord, and Gare de Lyon.

In the United States, the French government tourist offices are located at 444 Madison Avenue, New York, NY 10022; 212-838-7800; and 9454 Wilshire Boulevard, Beverly Hills, CA 90212; 310-271-6665. They are open Monday to Friday 10 A.M. to 4 P.M. You can send them an email at info.us@franceguide.com or surf their Website at www.franceguide.com.

In Paris, the American Embassy is at 2, avenue Gabriel, 75008; Métro: Concorde; 01-43-12-22-22; www.amb-usa.fr. Consulate/visas/passport services: 2, rue St-Florentin, 75001; Métro: Concorde. Passports and Consular: Mon–Fri 9 A.M.–12:30 P.M., 1–3 P.M. Visas: call 08-99-70-37-00 for appointment between 2 and 5 P.M.

Disabled Travelers

Paris is improving for wheelchair-bound travelers, but it still has a long way to go. Many hotels in *Great Sleeps Paris* do have rooms that have been somewhat refitted for handicapped guests, but the facilities may consist only of a wide door, a grab-bar by the tub, or just the fact that the room is on the *rez-de-chaussée* (ground floor).

L'Office de Tourisme de Paris (www.parisbienvenue.com) has some information for disabled travelers.

Both the Louvre (01-40-20-53-17; handicap@louvre.fr) and the Centre Pompidou (www.centrepompidou.fr/handicap) have group and individual programs for the disabled.

Association des Paralysés de France (13, pl de Rungis, 75013; 01-53-80-92-97; Métro: Place d'Italie; Mon–Fri 9 A.M.–12:30 P.M., 1:30–6 P.M.) publishes *Guide 98 Musées, Cinémas,* which lists museums and cinemas accessible for the disabled, and a guide to sites and restaurants.

If you speak or read French, you can get general Paris information by calling Platforme d'accueil et d'information des personnes handicapées de la Marie de Paris (0800-03-37-48) or visiting the Website www.monum.com.

An English-language guide for the disabled in Paris, *Access in Paris* by Gordon Couch and Ben Roberts (Quiller Press), is currently out of print, but it can still be purchased at Amazon.com or BarnesandNoble.com.

Very few of the métros and buses are suitable for wheelchair use. The métro line 14 and the RER Lines A and B are accessible and so are some SNCF trains. By law, taxis are obliged to pick up passengers in wheelchairs and cannot ask for a supplement for accompanying animals or wheelchairs. If you are going to and from airports, reserve with Airhop (01-41-29-01-29). They like a forty-eight-hour notice.

Neuf Orthopedio rents and sells wheelchairs, canes, and other accessories for the handicapped. They are at 9, rue Léopold Bellan, 75002; 01-42-33-83-46; Métro: Sentier; Mon–Fri 9 A.M.–6 P.M.

Other information for disabled travelers can be obtained from the following organizations in the United States:

Directions Unlimited
720 N. Bedford Road
Bedford Hills, NY 10507
Tel: 800-533-5343
A travel agency with an agent who specializes in accessible travel for the disabled.

Moss Rehabilitation Hospital
Tel: 215-456-5882
Internet: www.mossresourcenet.org
Open: Mon–Fri 9 A.M.–5 P.M.
Can refer disabled travelers to travel agents who specialize in travelers with disabilities.

Society for the Advancement of Travel for the Handicapped, Inc.
347 Fifth Avenue
New York, NY 10016
Tel: 212-447-7284
Internet: www.sath.org

Classes

In addition to being multilingual, talented, and very well qualified, the following professionals are passionate about what they do and possess an intimate, detailed knowledge of Paris, a city they have come to love and call their own through years of living and working here. Any of these classes, services, or tours are a wonderful way to enhance your trip and learn more about the fascinating City of Light.

ÉCOLE RITZ ESCOFFIER—*LES PETITS MARMITONS* AND *TOQUES JUNIORS*
38, rue Cambon, 75001 (student entrance; see map page 66)
Métro: Concorde, Opéra, Madeleine

Les Petits Marmitons du Ritz are gastronomic workshops for children ages six to twelve, and *Toques Juniors* are for budding gourmets ages thirteen to eighteen. Under the direction of a chef, *Les Petits Marmitons* spend an afternoon preparing kid-friendly dishes such as pasta sauce, crêpes, fritters, strawberry tarts, and chocolate charlotte. At the end, of course, they get to eat their creations. These classes are held on one Wednesday per month from 2:30 to 5 P.M. *Toques Juniors* have slightly more sophisticated projects and enroll for two three-hour sessions (2:30–5:30 P.M.) on consecutive days in July.

Reservations are required for all classes; call to check specific dates. English is spoken but is limited; classes are taught in French.

TEL 01-43-16-30-50; toll-free in the U.S. 888-801-1126 **FAX** 01-43-16-31-50
   EMAIL ecole@ritzparis.com **INTERNET** www.ritzparis.com
RATES *Les Petits Marmitons* 85€ per class; *Toques Juniors* 170€ per two-day
   session **CREDIT CARDS** AE, DC, MC, V

Ô CHATEAU
100, rue de la Folie Méricourt, 75011 (see map page 214)
Métro: République, Oberkampf

For a friendly, informal introduction to wines, Olivier Magny's Ô Chateau is a fun way to spend an hour or two picking up tips on basic wine appreciation. The classes are conducted by Olivier in his fourth-floor, walk-up loft apartment near République. Guests sit around tables and taste as Olivier explains how to evaluate what you're drinking. Tasting options include: Wine Two Three, a one-hour introductory tasting of three wines; Cheese and Wine Lunch, which includes one champagne and three wines, plus cheese and *charcuterie* platters; and Grand 7, a two-hour session with seven different wines. One or more tastings are offered daily.

TEL & FAX 01-44-73-97-80; cell 06-24-31-20-18; toll-free within U.S. 847-305-1615; toll-free within France 0-800-801-148
   EMAIL olivier@o-chateau.com **INTERNET** www.o-chateau.com
RATES Wine Two Three, 20€; Cheese and Wine Lunch, 65€; Grand 75€; all rates are per person **CREDIT CARDS** V

THE FRENCH SIDE.COM

Barbara Pasquet James, who is French on her father's side, is a noted American travel and food writer who has lived in Paris since 1991. She is enthusiastic and great fun, and she knows Paris and understands Parisians. Her lifelong immersion in all things French enables her to go beneath the obvious in The French Side.com, which provides seminars and concept lunches for two to eight people; these can be customized to your needs and wishes on a variety of topics. Wouldn't it be interesting to have a gourmet lunch and learn the secrets behind "Seduction and the Art of the French Woman"? For the business person she offers "Doing Business and Communicating Effectively with the French." Another topic that appeals directly to me and to readers of this guide centers around the French approach to food. She can arrange to meet a chef in his restaurant and have lunch afterward, and she offers loads of simple food tips, such as how to select the best camembert cheese. She also plans market visits, arranges cheese and chocolate tastings, and leads gastronomic walks. No matter what your interests, Barbara will make sure you have a great time and in the bargain gain a deeper understanding and appreciation of the French way of life.

TEL 01-42-64-12-03 **EMAIL** info@thefrenchside.com
   INTERNET www.thefrenchside.com
RATES 150€ for 1–3 people, 50€ per person after that; 25% deposit
   CREDIT CARDS None

PROMENADES GOURMANDES
187, rue du Temple, 75003 (see map page 86)

> **Not only did I learn a lot about cooking, but I had the opportunity to meet a wonderful person!**
> —*George Brooks, attorney-at-law*

It doesn't matter who you are—everyone from gourmet chefs to fledgling novices will learn something from the dynamic Parisian chef Paule Caillat, whose culinary heritage and love of cooking transform everything she touches. Paule was born and raised in Paris and college-educated in the States, and she gives private and group cooking lessons for lunch or dinner that are a quantum leap from the ordinary, stilted classes I have often attended. Menus are selected according to the season, student preferences, and a careful eye for product availability in your home country. Cooking with Paule means getting hands-on, from shopping at the market right through enjoying what you have prepared. On market trips, you will learn how to recognize the best ingredients, discern the different types of bread and cheese, distinguish a French apricot from one imported from Israel and know which one to buy, and select the perfect meats and fish. She will also place the products you buy into their historical and geographical context in France. Whether as part of the full-day session or booked separately, Paule also takes you on a three-hour *Promenade Gourmande* (gourmet walking tour) to visit famous bakeries, an exclusive wine store, landmark kitchen equipment emporiums, saffron producers, and much more. If you are not a serious chef but appreciate gourmet foods, join one of her three-hour gourmet walking tours in Paris, which are as much fun as they are interesting and informative.

Cooking lessons and gourmet tours in Paris are not the half of Paule and her enthusiasm about food. She can organize special events such as birthdays, anniversaries, or other celebrations. In addition, she leads small groups on excursions to areas in France that are specifically known for their exceptional food products. The trips include train travel, all meals and accommodations, and visits to points of interest. Three-month advance reservation required.

Paule is a delightful, dynamic, knowledgeable woman. If you love food and cooking, please treat yourself to one of her cooking lessons, gourmet walks, or trips. You won't regret it for a minute. As one very happy participant said, "This was the best day I have ever spent in Paris, and the highlight of my entire trip!" I agree, and so does everyone lucky enough to spend time with Paule.

NOTE: Paule takes off most of August, but during the rest of the year, to avoid disappointment, please make your reservation with her as far in advance as possible. Lunch classes are from 9 A.M. to 3 P.M.; dinner classes from 4 to 10:30 P.M.

TEL 01-48-04-56-84, cell 06-16-72-79-00 **EMAIL** info@promenades gourmandes.com **INTERNET** www.promenadesgourmandes.com
RATES half-day class (lunch or dinner) 250€ for one person, 235€ each for 2–3 persons; full-day class 350€ each for 1–3 persons; Gourmet Walking Tour (without class) 100€ per person; discounts for 4 or more. See Website for special rates and multiday programs. **CREDIT CARDS** V

Tours

A PHOTOGRAPHER IN PARIS

Christiane Michels trained as a photographer both in Paris and at her second home in the United States. Her keen eye makes her customized photo tours very special. She doesn't focus on the grand views, but on subtleties that are almost jewel-like in their intensity and charm: sidewalk cafés, street furniture, markets, and other non-stereotypical images. Her tours start when the light is best, usually in the early morning or early evening, and are conducted on foot. She also offers one- to five-day photo workshops.

Or, for a wonderful Paris memento, would you like to be photographed with Paris as the background? Whether it's your engagement or honeymoon, a trip with family or friends, Christiane's artistic approach will result in wonderful photos you will treasure for a lifetime.

TEL Not available **EMAIL** info@aphotographer.com **INTERNET** www.aphotographerinparis.com

RATES Half/full-day photo tour 85€/145€ for up to 4 people; Paris photos by Christiane: half/full day 150€/300€ (rates include CD of photos)
  CREDIT CARDS None

FAT TIRE BIKE TOURS
24, rue Edgar Faure, 75015 (see map page 230)
Métro: Dupleix (office), Bir-Hakeim (bike tour start)

Fat Tire Bike Tours offers a great way to experience Paris. All tours meet at the south leg (Pilier Sud) of the Eiffel Tower on the Champ-du-Mars and cruise the City of Light for a four- to five-hour ride. Fat Tire provides helmets, five-speed bikes, rain gear if necessary, an English-speaking guide, and a day or night of unequalled fun. All ages are welcome (as long as you can ride a bike), and bikes are sized to fit everyone from a child to his or her grandparents. Tours are limited to twenty-five riders. Fat Tire also offers day trips (reservations required) of Versailles, the D-Day beaches in Normandy, and Monet's Giverny. Prefer to walk rather than bike? Their 2½-hour guided Classic Walks cover all the Paris must-sees. They also offer tours in Amsterdam, Barcelona, and Berlin.

TEL & FAX 01-56-58-10-54 **EMAIL** info@FatTireBikeTours.com **INTERNET** www.FatTireToursParis.com

RATES Bike tour by day 24€, by night 28€, day-night combination 48€; day trips 50€ to 175€; Classic Walks 12–20€; all rates per person
  CREDIT CARDS Only for advance reservation

LA COLLECTION 1900 DE PIERRE CARDIN, CHEZ MAXIM'S
3, rue Royale 75008 (see map page 192)
Métro: Concorde

Over a sixty-year period, designer Pierre Cardin gathered one of the finest collections of Art Nouveau in the world, which he now displays above his famed Maxim's Restaurant. La Collection 1900, consisting of more than 550 Art Nouveau pieces dating from 1890 to 1914, is shown in a twelve-room replica of an elegant courtesan's apartment. The Art Nouveau masterpieces include magnificent Tiffany lamps, a Gaudí settee, Gustav Eiffel's tea service, and Sarah Bernhardt's hairbrush. Before you leave, be sure you see the public powder room.

You can also combine the tour with lunch at Maxim's (includes three courses and wine), or attend "Le Cabaret Concert," which combines the tour with a talk about the history of Maxim's followed by a piano concert. Call to check dates for both these events, as they are not available on a regular basis.

Reservations are not necessary for just a tour, but note that weekend tours are not always conducted in English. Call to check times.

TEL 01-42-65-30-47 **EMAIL** lacollection1900@maxims-de-paris.com
INTERNET www.maxims-musee-artnouveau.com
OPEN Tours run Wed–Sun; English tours are at 2 P.M., French tours at 3:15 and 4:30 P.M.
RATES Tours only 15€; lunch and tour 110€; lecture, concert, and tour 55€; all rates are per person **CREDIT CARDS** none for tour only, V for lunch or lecture

PARIS MUSE

Ellen McBreen, a graduate of New York University, can now be your private guide to the museums of Paris. As this university lecturer says, "My time with you is less expensive than a university class and a lot more fun." Ellen's 2½-hour private tours are for no more than four people and are tailored to your schedule and interests. She also specializes in art tours for children. Of course, the price includes admission not only to the museums but to the special shows, and there is no waiting on line, ever. What better way to appreciate and understand the magnificent art treasures in Paris than with this delightful muse? Because Ellen's tours are so popular, she has added 2½-hour, small-group walking tours for six to twelve people. These tours have a preset itinerary. Advance reservations are required for all tours.

TEL 06-73-77-33-52 **EMAIL** info@parismuse.com **INTERNET** www.parismuse.com
RATES Group walking tour 30€; private walking tour (2-person minimum) 90€; all rates per person **CREDIT CARDS** AE, MC, V

PARIS PHOTO TOURS

American Linda Mathieu married a Frenchman and happily transplanted to Paris. Today, she shares her love and knowledge of her adopted city on her walking tours. She will meet you in the lobby of your hotel and escort you on tours that include photography, shopping, chocolate tasting, antique hunting, or whatever else appeals.

TEL 01-44-75-83-80 **EMAIL** parisphototours@aol.com **INTERNET** www.parisphototours.com
RATES Half/full day per group (1–3 persons) 85€/145€, lunch extra
CREDIT CARDS None, euros only

PARIS WALKS
10, rue Samson, St Denis, 93200

If you are fluent in French, finding an interesting walking tour in Paris is easy. Just look in the most recent issue of *Pariscope*. For those whose French is limited, an English-language walking tour with British expatriates Oriel and Peter Caine is the solution. The Caines are licensed "blue badge" guides in France. They and a small group of assistants have put together a series of well-researched group walking tours through parts of Paris that the casual visitor is likely to miss. Their comments are both educational and entertaining, filled with little-known tidbits. The tours are given year-round and last approximately two hours. With advance notice, customized private tours (for five to six people) and family tours geared toward making Paris fun for children are available.

TEL 01-48-09-21-40 **FAX** 01-42-43-75-51 **INTERNET** www.paris-walks.com
RATES Group tours (per person), 12€ adult, 8€ student, 5€ child; customized tours (group rate), half-day 200€, full-day 350€, and you buy lunch for your guide **CREDIT CARDS** For group tours, cash only; for customized tours, V

Services

SÉGO' SPA
15, rue Beautrellis, 75004 (see map page 86)
Métro: St-Paul, Bastille

Life is stressful, even on vacation in Paris. Taking time to have a customized beauty treatment can alleviate that stress, relax tired muscles, and boost your energy. My very favorite place to relax and be pampered is at Ségolène Heurtaut's Ségo' Spa in the Marais. Ségolène says, "This is a small spa that I created. All my personality is here, and friends tell me, 'It is you. We recognize you in this place.'"

Your treatment begins the minute you walk into her soothing, pastel-colored waiting room, which faces a pretty interior courtyard centered by a tall magnolia tree. Seating is comfortable, lighting subdued, with calming music in the background. Downstairs is the pièce-de-résistance: a massive floating mattress in a pool of water. This is where you lie while being enveloped in warm chocolate, which helps to remove toxins from your body. After floating for twenty minutes or so, you will be rinsed off by the softest shower of warm water, and Ségolène's gentle massage. Trust me . . . you will want to repeat this wonderful experience as often as possible, and no, you can't eat this chocolate! Other treatments include massages, facials, waxing, and manicures, all administered by the magical, skilled hands and fingers of Ségolène. Candles are lit at dusk, and before you leave, you will be served a cup of tea. A visit to Ségo' Spa is a wonderful gift of well-being to give yourself during your trip to Paris. An added bonus for many is that Ségolène speaks fluent English.

TEL 01-42-78-90-27 **INTERNET** www.segospa.com
OPEN Mon 1–7 P.M., Tues–Sat 10 P.M.–7:30 P.M., Wed until 9 P.M. **CREDIT CARDS** MC, V

COMPUTER CONSULTANT

The last thing you want is a problem with your computer. Karl Leino is an expert computer consultant specializing in Macintosh systems, and he can also set up an Internet account in Paris for you prior to your arrival, so you will be ready to log on the moment you land. If you don't have a Mac, Karl can refer you to a PC colleague, and he also has Mac contacts in other major cities. Karl speaks fluent English, makes house calls in Paris, and is extremely patient. He also has a free monthly newsletter for anyone signing onto his Website.

TEL 06-63-82-42-88 **EMAIL** info@macserviceparis.com **INTERNET**
www.macserviceparis.com
RATES Depends on the complexity of the consultation **CREDIT CARDS** MC, V

FRANCK FANN COIFFEUR
5, rue d'Ormesson, 75004 (see map page 86)
Métro: St-Paul

Where to get your hair cut, a manicure, massage, or facial? It is always a problem in a strange city, especially if you cannot communicate very well. Relax—now you have Franck and his congenial staff ready to see to all your beauty needs. Franck is wonderful at cutting, coloring, and styling both men's and women's hair, and he speaks English. In fact, he has given me the best haircuts I have ever had. I only wish I could convince him to move to the States so I could go to him on a regular basis. He likes Miami, Florida . . . so there is hope! The other operators are all competent and professional, especially Flora, who does therapeutic massages and facials.

In French salons, all services are individually priced and tipped, from the shampoo to the blow dry. At Franck's the prices are very reasonable; it should run around 40 to 45€ for a haircut, from 47€ up for massages and facials, and from 25€ for manicures, all plus tips. Except for massages and facials, appointments are not necessary. However, it doesn't hurt to call ahead to let them know you are coming, especially if you want Franck. Whenever you go, please say hello to everyone for me . . . and encourage Franck to open a second salon in the States.

TEL 01-48-04-50-62
OPEN Mon–Sat 10 A.M.–7 P.M.
CREDIT CARDS MC, V (minimum 50€)

ZNET CYBER CAFÉ
18, rue de la Bûcherie, 75005 (see map page 108)
Métro: St-Michel

Znet offers every Web service currently out there. If you left your laptop at home and need to get plugged in, this is one of the best places in Paris, not only for the great location across the bridge from Notre Dame, but it is open every day, the keyboards are in English, and the owner speaks English. If you think you are going to become a regular, buy a card, which is good for multiple visits and less expensive in the long run than paying each time you are here. The staff is patient and helpful, but unfortunately, they do not accept credit cards.

TEL & FAX 01-44-07-20-15 **INTERNET** www.zeidnet.com
OPEN Daily 10 A.M.–10 P.M.
CREDIT CARDS None, cash only

Money Matters

There are few certainties when you travel. One of them is that the moment you arrive in a foreign country, the American dollar will fall like a stone.
—*Erma Bombeck*

If you charge big items on your credit card, carry some traveler's checks, convert as you go, and use ATMs, you will do fine. Also, remember to carry a few of your own personal checks. If you suddenly run out of money, you can use them to get cash advances, provided the credit card you have allows this. Try to have a few euros on hand when you arrive. True, you may pay a little more for this convenience, but this gets you out of the airport faster and keeps you from having to wait in line to get enough money to get into Paris. If you cannot get euros locally, you can order them by telephone or online. Contact Travelex/Thomas Cook, 630 Fifth Avenue, New York, NY 10101; 800-287-7362; www.travelex.com; Mon–Fri 8:30 A.M.–7 P.M.

The Euro

The euro has been the official currency for most of the countries of the European Union, of which France is a member, since January 2000. The euro consists of one hundred cents and comes in the following denominations: coins—1 cent, 2 cents, 5 cents, 10 cents, 20 cents, 50 cents, 1 euro, and 2 euros; and notes—5, 10, 20, 50, 100, 200, and 500 euros. At press time $1.27 bought one euro. The official Website (in French) is www.euro.gouv.fr.

Automatic Teller Machines

Automatic teller machines (ATMs) are all over Paris and take bank ATM cards, American Express, Visa, and MasterCard. There will be fees involved, but you will be getting a wholesale conversion rate that is better than you would get at a bank or currency exchange office. Naturally, the amount you can withdraw is limited depended on your account. Please—and I cannot stress this enough—do not assume your ATM card or credit card PIN (personal identification number) will automatically work in Paris. They might, but you may have to obtain a special PIN or enroll in a special program. Contact the card issuer for details; setting up an account can take several weeks, but it's free. For enrollment instructions and ATM locations by card type, contact the following:

Cirrus: 800-4-CIRRUS (424-7787), www.mastercard.com

Plus: 800-THE-PLUS (843-7587), www.visa.com

American Express: 800-CASH-NOW (227-4669),
www.americanexpress.com

Banks

Banking hours are Monday through Friday, 9:30 A.M. to 5 P.M. All banks close at noon the day before a public holiday, and all remain closed on public holidays and the day after Christmas, Easter, and Pentecost. Not all banks have foreign exchange counters. Commission rates vary, but Banque de France usually has better rates. Check with your bank at home to see if they work with banks in France; if so, you are lucky because your rate of exchange will be more favorable.

Credit Cards

For the most part, I recommend using a credit card whenever possible. It is the safest way to purchase things (eliminating the need to carry lots of cash); it provides you with a written record of your purchases; and best of all, you often get delayed billing of up to four to six weeks after you have returned home. Also, the credit-card company gives the rate of exchange on the day the receipt from the expenditure is submitted, and this can work to your advantage if the dollar is rising. Your card may also offer emergency personal check cashing, access to ATMs, and free travel insurance; check with your issuing bank to determine your benefits . . . you may be pleasantly surprised.

However, many bank-issued credit cards have now slapped on a foreign-use surcharge of 1 to 5 percent per transaction. Cards tied to airline miles are some of the worst offenders. Again, check with your issuing bank. Finally, before leaving on your trip, it is very important to notify the credit card companies whose cards you plan to use, or you could be faced with a card that won't be accepted because your issuing bank won't okay the foreign purchase.

Relatively new on the credit card scene are stored-value cards. With these, you transfer as much value (usually between $300 and $2,700) as you want onto the card, which you then use like a credit card. But the cards are not free, by a long shot. You pay an initial fee, plus another fee every time you reload the card. If you use it outside the U.S., there are ATM withdrawal fees. Visa charges less for the card, but you can only use it in places that accept Visa debit cards, and you pay a foreign exchange surcharge of up to 7 percent. Yikes! All I can say is buyer beware and read the fine print.

Take a copy of all of your credit card numbers with you, and treat it with the same importance you do your passport. Lock it up in the hotel safe—don't keep it in your wallet or purse. Save your receipts to check against the statement when it arrives. Errors are frequent.

I highly recommend carrying an American Express card simply to have access to its American Express Global Assist program (800-333-2639). This service helps with emergency medical, legal, or financial assistance while traveling—providing everything from visa requirements and prescription assistance to help with lost luggage and translations.

And remember, in Europe a MasterCard is Eurocard, and Visa is Carte Bleu. Every listing in *Great Sleeps Paris* tells you whether or not plastic money is accepted and what kind. Thankfully, most hotels accept at least one credit card.

If, heaven forbid, your cards are lost or stolen, call one of the twenty-four-hour hotlines below to report the loss as soon as possible.

In Paris:

American Express	0800-900-888, 01-47-14-50-00, 01-47-77-70-00
Diners Club	0800-22-20-73, 08-10-31-41-59
MasterCard (Eurocard)	0800-90-13-87, 01-45-67-84-84
Visa (Carte Bleu)	08-92-70-57-05

From Paris, you can call the following U.S. numbers or visit the Websites to report a lost card:

American Express	Toll-free 800-233-5432; collect 336-393-1111; www.americanexpress.com
Diners Club	Toll-free 800-234-6377; collect 702-797-5532; www.dinersclubnorth america.com
MasterCard	Toll-free 800-307-7309; collect 636-722-7111; www.mastercard.com
Visa	Toll-free 800-336-8472; collect 410-581-9994, or toll-free within France 0800-901-179; www.visa.com

Cash Advances

If you are stuck for cash, don't panic. You can use your American Express, Diners Club, MasterCard, or Visa to get cash, either by writing a personal check and presenting your card, or by going to a bank that gives cash advances for your card (see also "Wiring Money to Paris," page 40). But be warned: this is one of the most expensive ways to get money.

American Express: Cardholders can write personal checks. For more information, contact American Express Global Assist: 800-333-2639.

Diners Club: Cardholder can get cash advances of $500 a day, or $1,000 a week, at any Eurochange bank.

MasterCard or *Visa:* Available through banks displaying these card signs.

Currency Exchange and Traveler's Checks

Every time you exchange currency, someone is making a profit, and I assure you, it is not you. The worst exchange rates are at the airport and rail stations. The second-worst rates are at hotels, restaurants, shops, and most change offices that litter the tourist trails. These places should be avoided at all costs. Your best currency exchange rate will usually be at a bank (see Banks, page 37). The use of traveler's checks has been almost totally replaced by ATMs, making currency exchange much less important than it once was. However, for some, traveler's checks may be preferable because if they are lost or stolen, there is recourse to replace them, especially if you have American Express traveler's checks (0800-90-86-00). Estimate your needs carefully when changing money. If you overbuy, you will lose twice, buying and then selling.

You will not always get a better exchange rate for traveler's checks than for cash, but the real cost lies in what you spent to get the traveler's checks in the first place and the commission cost to convert them. If your bank, credit union, or automobile club offers American Express traveler's checks for no commission, by all means try to get them in euros. This eliminates your exchange problems. Otherwise, exchange your American Express traveler's checks commission-free at the American Express office in Paris (drawbacks: the exchange rates are not always the best, and the lines can be oh, so long). The office is at 11, rue Scribe, 75009; Métro: Opéra (exit rue Scribe); 01-47-77-79-50; www.americanexpress.com/france Mon–Fri 9 A.M.–6 P.M. Sat until 5 P.M.

American Express also has *bureaux de change* in terminals l, 2A, 2B, 2C, 2D and 2F at Roissy Charles-de-Gaulle Airport and at Orly sud.

Another bank with a multitude of services is Citibank, which has currency exchange, commission-free traveler's checks, international money transfers and cash advance with Visa cards. They accept Cirrus and most other ATM cards, and have English-speaking representatives. They're at 125, avenue Champs-Élysées, 75008; Métro: Charles-de-Gaulle-Étoile; 01-53-23-33-60; Mon–Fri 10 A.M.–5:30 P.M., change office closes at 5 P.M.

Travelex has offices in France and also offers many foreign exchange services, plus travel insurance, phone cards, international wires, and bank drafts. Contact them at 800-CURRENCY; www.travelex.com/usa.

A popular *bureau de change* with the Parisian locals is MULTIChange. There are several locations, but the most central, and the one that gives the same rate for dollars and traveler's checks, is at 7, rue de Castiglione, 75001; Métro: Tuileries; 01-40-15-61-16; www.multi-change.com; Mon–Sat 9:30 A.M.–6:30 P.M. Call this branch for the location nearest you.

Wiring Money to Paris

If you need to call home for money, the fastest way to refill your wallet is to have someone in the States use a moneygram. The transfer is accomplished in minutes and the sender pays the fees, which are based on the amount sent. Here is what to do:

Contact the sender in the United States, who can send the money to you either by going in person to a local Western Union office or by giving their credit card ($500 limit) over the telephone. To find the nearest Western Union office, the sender can call 800-926-9400. To send money by credit card, call 800-325-6000, Monday to Friday 6 A.M. to 4:30 P.M., MST. The Website is www.westernunion.com. Either way, the cash-strapped person in Paris will be given a ten-digit confirmation number and an address to go to in Paris to pick up the money (using a photo ID). Money transfers take less than thirty minutes. Numerous post offices in Paris provide Western Union money transfer services. Call 08-25-00-98-98 or visit www.intl.westernunion.com to find them.

Tipping

How much is too much, and what is enough? Here are a few guidelines for appropriate tipping in Paris.

By law in France, a service charge of 15 percent is added to all hotel and restaurant bills. This service charge *is* the tip. This means that when you receive your final bill at a restaurant, you don't need to tip anything more. While this eliminates the need for tips in general, there are certain times when an additional tip is appropriate.

Bars, cafés, restaurants	Leave a few extra euro cents in a bar or café, and up to 10 percent if the waiter in a restaurant has gone to extra lengths for you.
Hair salons	10 to 15 percent to anyone who has worked on you, including the shampoo girl
Hotels	Bellboys 1€ per bag; housekeepers about 6€ for a three-day stay; room service 1€
Taxis	10 to 15 percent on the metered fare, not for the supplements added for extra baggage

The bottom line on tipping in Paris is the same as anywhere else in the world: It is a matter of personal choice. If you liked the service, reward it; if not, do not feel guilty about not leaving an additional cent.

NOTE: Beware of the tipping scam. There is an increasingly common practice in restaurants of putting the entire amount of the bill, to which a 15 percent service has already been added, in the top box of the charge slip, leaving the boxes marked "tip" and "total" empty.

Do not be intimidated. Draw a line from the top figure to the total at the bottom and then write in the total figure yourself. If you are choosing to tip on top of this total (and remember you do not have to), leave it in cash. Often tips left on credit cards are not properly distributed to the waitstaff.

Insurance

No one plans on a medical crisis, either before or during a trip. Travel insurance is seldom a great bargain, but it does buy you protection and, just as importantly, peace of mind should unfortunate circumstances occur that force you to cut short your trip or cancel it altogether.

Hotel cancellations less than forty-eight hours prior to arrival can result in charges unless the room can be used by another customer. This is small potatoes and, frankly, not worth covering with an insurance policy. However, if you have prepaid a large portion of your trip, especially if you have rented a flat and paid a big chunk in advance, you would be crazy not to buy cancellation insurance. French serviced apartments, individual apartment owners, and the agencies representing them are often merciless when it comes to refunds. Their policy is very simple: no refunds after a certain date. Period.

Before your departure, check with your health-care plan to see what, if any, medical coverage you will have when you travel, and seriously consider taking out a supplemental policy to fill in the gaps. The amount you spend in supplemental insurance will be nothing compared to a foreign medical emergency for which you have to pick up the tab. If you do need medical care, many medical facilities require that you pay for your treatment in full at the time of service. Don't assume that they will file claims for you or participate in any medical plan you may belong to.

Read through your renter's or homeowner's policy to check whether it covers you in any way when you are traveling, and if it is lacking, again consider adding a floater policy for the duration of your trip, especially if you are traveling with a laptop or other expensive equipment.

Finally, if you are an American Express Card member, call 800-297-2900 to find out about their travel insurance coverage. American Express Global Assist is another helpful service for cardholders (see "Credit Cards," page 37). Below is a list of travel insurers with policies to suit many needs:

Access America, Inc.: 800-284-8300, www.accessamerica.com

Insuremytrip: www.insuremytrip.com

Medex Insurance Services: 800-732-5309, www.medexassist.com

Medjet Assist (worldwide medical transports): 800-963-3538, www.medjetassist.com

Safeware (insures laptops and electronics): www.safeware.com

Wallach & Co.: 800-237-6615, www.wallach.com

Discounts

Hotels

When booking a hotel room, it's always worth asking if any discounts are being offered, even in the middle of high season—you might get lucky. Also check hotel Websites or to call toll-free numbers to see about special package deals or lower rates. Savvy travelers check with airlines or their travel agents for package deals that include airfare coupled with a hotel at a fraction of the cost if paid for separately. Often included are airport transfers and/or car rentals. In July and August, many hotels offer a published 10 percent discount, while for others you have to ask. Some hotels give an automatic 5 to 10 percent discount to *Great Sleeps Paris* readers, and I have noted these in the listings.

The Internet is full of sites offering discounted airfares and hotel rates, and these are worth exploring. The savings can be significant.

Museums

The Paris Museum Pass is a one-, three-, or five-day French pass that covers unlimited general admission (not including special exhibitions or guided tours) to more than seventy museums and monuments, including the Louvre, Musée d'Orsay, Musée Picasso, and Versailles. It allows you to go to the head of any line, or through a special entrance, without waiting—that alone is worth the price of the pass—and you can revisit any museum as many times as you want. The passes are on sale in participating museums, main métro and RER stations, branches of FNAC, and tourism offices in Paris. The pass costs 18€ for one day, 36€ for three days, and 54€ for five days. For further information, contact interMusées at 4, rue Brantôme, 75003; 01-44-61-96-60; www.intermusees.com. To purchase a pass before leaving the United States, visit www.ticketsto.com.

In most museums, entry is free for anyone under eighteen, and reduced prices are available for those between eighteen and twenty-five. Museums are generally closed on Monday or Tuesday. Depending on the time of year and the museum, entrance on the first Sunday of the month is free, but the crowds can be lethal. Not so on Wednesday and Friday evenings at the Louvre, when most wings are open until 9:45 P.M. and you have the added pleasure of the glowing Pyramide after sunset.

If you do not have a museum pass, there are still ways to avoid the endless line at the Pyramide entrance to the Louvre. If traveling on the métro, get off at the Palais Royal–Musée du Louvre stop and use the entrance directly from the métro platform. Or, use the Porte des Lions entrance to the Denton wing. To find this, stand with your back toward the Pyramide and look across the plaza toward the Tuileries Garden. On each side of the Louvre are stairs (next to angels) that lead to the underground entrance. Another less populous entry is from the Galeries du Carrousel, the shopping mall under the museum.

If your travels will be taking you beyond Paris, consider purchasing the National Museum Pass, which is valid for one year and allows unlimited free entrance to more than one hundred museums and monuments in France, sixteen of which are in and around Paris. The pass is on sale at participating museums and monuments, and costs around 60€.

Paris City Passport

The Paris City Passport is a 5€ bargain well-spent. It is sold at tourist offices (see page 27) and offers over forty discount coupons ranging from 10 to 50 percent. The booklet is divided into six categories: culture, attractions, excursions, shopping, restaurants, and services. Each coupon is valid one time, but the booklet, which is good for one calendar year, can be shared.

Seniors

If you have reached your sixtieth birthday, in France you are a member of the *troisième age* (third age) and are eligible for a Carte Vermeil (CV). This card entitles you to a number of significant discounts, including reductions on air and rail travel as well as on the bus and métro in Paris. If you are going to be in Paris (or France) for a short time, it may not be worthwhile to get the Carte Vermeil. However, you would be surprised at the senior discounts available, especially for concerts, theater performances, and cinemas. Always ask. The answer will often be yes.

The French domestic airline, Air Inter, honors "third agers" by giving 25 to 50 percent reductions on regular nonexcursion ticket prices. On French trains, you can save between 25 and 50 percent of the cost of a first- or second-class compartment and 10 percent of an excursion ticket. These air and rail reductions are not available during all times of the year, and restrictions do apply. Other benefits include reduced entrance rates for theaters, museums, and cinemas.

The Carte Vermeil is valid for one year from June 1 to May 31 of the following year. The card cannot be purchased in the United States, but it is available at any major railway station in France. Do not expect clerks to speak English, but you won't need much French to communicate your wishes, as most of them are used to dealing with foreigners who are privy to this super deal. When you go to purchase your card, you will have to show your passport as proof of age. For more information, contact Rail Europe, 800-438-7245, www.raileurope.com; or the French Government Tourist Office in New York (see page 27); 212-838-7806. However, be prepared for frustrating waits that could speed your aging process.

Members of the AARP (American Association of Retired Persons) are entitled to discounts on some air tickets, rooms in selected major chain hotels, and some train and car rentals. Always inquire when booking a reservation. Elderhostel, another organization for seniors, operates programs throughout Europe, and many are in France. Contact them at 75 Federal Street, Boston, MA 02110-1941; 877-426-8056; www.elderhostel.org.

Students and Teachers

The best discounts for students and teachers are available with the International Student Identity Card (ISIC) and the International Teacher Identity Card (ITIC). Both are available in the United States through STA (800-226-8624; www.statravel.com), require a one-inch-size passport photo, and cost around $25. The card can also be issued in Paris through student travel agencies and at the CROUS office at 39, avenue Georges-Bernanos, 5th; Métro: Port-Royal; 01-40-51-36-00. A more convenient location is at OTU Voyage, 119, rue St-Martin, Parvis de Beaubourg, 75004; 01-40-29-12-22; www.otu.fr. To learn about additional benefits of these superb travel discount cards, see Student Accommodations in "Other Options," page 311. Anyone age twenty-six or younger, whether a student or not, can buy the Carte 12/25, which allows a 50 percent reduction on certain SNCF train travel.

Theater and Concerts

You can buy half-price tickets for selected concerts, theaters, ballets, and other shows on the day of the performance only at the Kiosque Théâtre in the eighth arrondissement. Be prepared to stand in line before the box office opens. For complete details, see page 370.

Health Matters

It is not difficult to stay healthy in Paris. The main complaints seem to be hangovers and/or exhaustion from too much late-night partying, and the usual stomach upsets caused from too much rich food. The water is safe to drink, but I always advise buying bottled water if only because it tastes better. Water from decorative fountains is not safe. Of course, it is always prudent to pack an extra set of glasses, an adequate supply of whatever medications you need, and a copy of prescriptions, perhaps translated into French.

If you need medical attention, contact one of the following:

The American Hospital   63, boulevard Victor Hugo,
                         Neuilly; Métro: Porte Maillot,
                         or bus No. 82; 01-46-41-25-25;
                         www.americanhospital.org

Hertford British Hospital (Hôpital Franco-Britannique)
                          3, rue Barbès, Levallois-Perret
                          (a suburb of Paris); Métro: Anatole-
                          France; 01-46-39-22-22

SIDA Information Service

> 0 800 840 800. Open 24 hours. Confidential AIDS information in French. English speaking counselors from 2–7 P.M. Mon, Wed, Fri.

Centre Medico-Sociale (Marie de Paris)

> 2 rue Figuier, 75004; Métro: Pont-Marie; 01-49-96-62-70; 9 A.M.– 5:30 P.M. Mon, Tue, Thur; 1:30– 5:30 P.M. Wed, Fri. Free anonymous tests for HIV, hepatitis, and other similar health problems. Also counseling.

Burns: Hôpital de St-Antoine

> 184, rue du Faubourg-St-Antoine, 75012; Métro: Faidherbe-Chaligny; 01-49-28-26-09; open 24 hours

Eyes: Hôpital des Quinze-Vingts

> 28, rue de Charenton, 75012; Métro: Bastille or Ledru-Rollin; 01-40-02-15-20. Specializes in eye problems.

Poisons: Hôpital Fernand Widal

> 200, rue du Faubourg-St-Denis, 75010; Métro: Gare du Nord; 01-40-05-48-48

Children: Hôpital Necker

> 149, rue de Sèvres, 75015; Métro: Duroc; 01-44-49-40-00

Children, Burns: Hôpital Armand-Trousseau

> 26, avenue du Dr. Arnold-Netter, 75012; Metro: Bel Air; 01-44-73-62-54

Association Française d'Acuponcture

> 3, rue de l'Arrivée, 75015; Métro: Montparnasse; 01-43-20-26-26; Mon–Thur 8:30 A.M.–12:30 P.M., 1:30–5:30 P.M., Fri 8:30 A.M.–4:30 P.M. Lists professional acupuncturists.

Homeopathic Doctors: Academie d'Homeopathie et des Médecines Douces

> 2, rue d'Isly, 75008; Metro: St-Lazare; 01-43-87-60-33; Mon–Fri 10 A.M.–6 P.M. Must have an appointment. Many pharmacies also sell homeopathic medicines.

SOS Cardiac	01-47-07-50-50; open 24 hours SOS Dentist 01-43-37-51-00; 8 A.M.–8 P.M.
SOS Doctor (SOS Médecins)	01-43-37-77-77, 08-20-33-24-24; Open 24 hours. Urgences Médicales de Paris (some English speaking doctors) 01-53-94-94-94, both make house calls 24/7. Fees start at 60€ per visit.
SOS Infirmiers (nurses)	house calls Mon–Fri 6 A.M.–midnight, Sat and Sun until 6 P.M.; 01-47-07-00-73
SOS Optique	01-48-07-22-00; www.sosoptique.com; 24-hour eyeglass repairs
SOS Help	01-46-21-46-46; daily 3–11 P.M. Bilingual crisis hotline.
Airparif	01-44-59-47-64; Mon–Fri 1 A.M.–5:30 P.M. Information about pollution levels and air quality in Paris.
Alcoholics Anonymous	01-46-34-59-65; www.aaparis.org

Pharmacies

Pharmacies are marked with a green neon cross. They are serious places where health-care advice is given out, and quality skin- and hair-care products are sold by knowledgeable personnel. The pharmacist can help with many minor medical complaints, in addition to dispensing a prescription if you need one. A system of on-duty pharmacies ensures that at least one pharmacy in each arrondissement is always open. A closed pharmacy will have a sign giving the address of the nearest open pharmacy.

Pharmacie Dhèry	84, avenue des Champs-Élysées, 75008; Métro: George V; 01-45-62-02-41; Open 24 hours.
American Pharmacy	Pharmacie Anglo-Américaine (Pharmacie Swan), 6, rue Castiglione, 75001; Metro: Tuileries; 01-42-60-72-96; Mon–Sat 10 A.M.–7:30 P.M.
Pharmacie des Halles	10, boulevard de Sébastopol, 75004; Métro: Châtelet; 01-42-72-03-23; Mon–Sat 9 A.M.–midnight, Sun 9 A.M.–10 P.M.

Pharma Presto-Night   01-42-42-42-50; open 24 hours. This
                           is a pharmacy delivery service. They
                           also transport sick pets to the vet.

To find nearest all-night pharmacy: 01-45-62-02-41

Emergency Numbers

In an emergency, dial these numbers. They are free from any phone,
including pay phones, and are staffed twenty-four hours a day.

Emergency
    from a mobile phone   112

Police   17

Fire   18

Ambulance, Paramedics   15

Medical Emergency   15

Poison   01-40-05-48-48

Drug Hot Line   0-800-14-21-52

Safety and Security

In comparison to other cities, Paris is not a dangerous place. It is
still important, however, to take the same sensible precautions you
would in any major metropolitan city in the world. Foreigners are easily spotted by their language, clothes, guidebooks, maps, and cameras.
Pickpockets usually work in pairs or larger groups. The victim seldom
knows what has happened until it's too late. A woman's handbag with
a zipper or clasp is no problem for a pickpocket if it is dangling out of
the owner's sight or lying on the floor in a restaurant or shop. A man's
wallet in an outside pocket makes for very easy pickings. Be vigilant
at ATMs. Don't let anyone come near you or ask you a question when
you are withdrawing money. Never leave anything of importance
locked in a car, and that includes the trunk.

If you are robbed or attacked, report the incident immediately at
the police station in the arrondissement where the incident happened.
Call 01-43-12-23-47 for the closest *commissariat*. Someone speaks
English Monday to Friday 9 A.M. to 5 P.M.; on the weekends there is
a duty officer to help. If you are going to file a claim with your own
insurance company, you will need this police report. In general, keep
the following advice in mind as you tour Paris:

1. Be aware of your surroundings and do not go down dark
   streets at night, especially alone.

2. Don't act lost. If you get turned around, ask directions in a
   shop, not from someone standing nearby, who may be a pickpocket just waiting for a chance such as this.

3. Carry as little money as you can, and carry it in several places. Carrying a passport is not mandatory for Americans in Paris. Wear a money belt or a neck pouch *inside* your clothing, and carry only what you need with you: some money, one credit card, and so on. Carry your purse with the strap around your neck and the clasp against your body, away from the street side. Fanny packs are magnets for thieves...they can cut and grab one in no time. If you do wear one, don't wear it on your fanny; wear it in front of you, string the strap through your belt loops, and keep only a small amount of money in it. Do not carry your valuables in your wallet, purse, or bag. These all belong in the hotel safe. Thread a safety pin through the toggle on your backpack's zipper to pin it closed.

4. Try to blend in and keep a low profile: don't wear flashy jewelry, wild colors, or prints, or speak in a booming voice. Wear dark colored shoes . . . never white jogging shoes! Unless you are a photography pro, use a small digital camera and leave the heavy camera worn on a strap around your neck at home.

5. Keep a close eye on your possessions, and do not leave packages or suitcases unattended on the métro, when making a phone call or hailing a taxi.

6. Trust your instincts: If a situation seems suspect, it probably is, so beat a hasty retreat. Beware of pickpockets, especially on the métro Line 1 between Châtelet and Charles-de-Gaulle and on Line 4 between Châtelet and Porte de Clignancourt, and in tourist areas along boulevard Haussmann, rue de Rivoli, Les Halles, the Arc de Triomphe, the Eiffel Tower, St. Michel, and Montmartre. Watch out for bands of gypsy children, who will surround you and distract your attention by fluttering papers in your face, and then strip you of your valuables before you can think to say, "Stop thief!" Another popular ruse for men is the "coin toss." Someone drops a few coins in front of you, and you instinctively lean over to help pick them up, while someone else's hand is reaching into your back pocket and grabbing your wallet. It's so fast, you will never know what happened, and may not even trace the loss of your wallet to this trick.

7. Thieves in métro stations lurk around the turnstiles and try to grab your bag as you go through, or they reach for it as the train door closes. Always avoid métro stations late at night, especially Stalingrad, Châtelet–Les Halles, Barbès-Rochechouart, Pigalle, and Anvers.

8. Be careful if you are in bars or nightclubs anywhere in Paris, but especially around Pigalle, where the term "robbery" applies to more than the prices for drinks.

9. If you are approached by someone claiming to be a law officer, insist on seeing an official badge.

10. If you are alone, don't say so to a wide audience. Also, make sure someone at home knows your itinerary, and arrange times to call to check in, just to let them know all is well.

11. Before leaving home, make two photocopies of every document that is crucial to the successful completion of your trip—such as your passport, airline tickets, hotel vouchers, credit card numbers (or the number of your credit card registry), and necessary prescriptions, including the one for your glasses. Leave one copy at home with someone you can always contact, and take the other copy with you and treat it with the same importance you do your money and passport. If your documents are lost or stolen, you have a record of your various numbers, and the process of replacing everything will be easier.

12. *Always* lock up important papers, airline tickets, traveler's checks, extra money, and so on in the hotel safe. Even if there is a charge for this, it is well worth it when you consider the cost, inconvenience, and hassle of a theft. *Never* leave anything of value in your hotel room, even in a locked suitcase.

The U.S. Department of State publishes a pamphlet called *A Safe Trip Abroad*. For a copy, write the Superintendent of Documents, U.S. Government Printing Office, Washington, DC 20402.

Hotel Security

Security in your hotel mostly pertains to theft. Note that hotel liability tends to be limited and often provides slim protection for the traveler. If an item is stolen from your room, you may have little recourse unless you can prove negligence. Here are some points to consider:

1. Avoid rooms on the ground floor and those near fire escapes.

2. Do not leave any valuables exposed in your room, even when you are sleeping.

3. When you leave your room, close and lock the windows and do not leave (or hide) any valuables. Lock them up in the hotel safe or in your individual room safe, but *never* in your suitcase. There isn't a hiding place a thief doesn't know about, and the hotel bears no responsibility if you do not do your part to protect your valuables in the places provided.

4. Valuables include more than money and jewelry. Consider camcorders, cameras, computers, personal and travel documents, cell phones, and so on.

5. If you leave luggage at the hotel after you check out, be sure the storage area is secure, and do not leave any bag containing valuables.

6. If you are a victim of a theft, insist on filing a complete report with the local police immediately. The more documentation you have, the better your chances are for compensation from your own insurance company.

Most important: If you don't absolutely need it in Paris, don't take it with you.

Lost and Found
If you have lost something in a public space or on public transport, contact the Bureau des Objets Trouvés. You must go in person with an ID to fill out a form detailing the date, time, and place where you lost the item. Very little English is spoken. Claims can take weeks. If you are leaving Paris before the claim can be processed and your lost item is (hopefully) found, you must appoint a proxy to retrieve your item. If you lost a key or diamond earring in a sewer grate or street opening, a sewer worker will try to rescue it. You will need to know the street and cross street where you lost your valuables.

Bureau des Objets Trouvés (Lost and Found)
36, rue des Morillons, 75015
Métro: Convention
Tel: 08-21-00-25-25
Internet: www.prefecture-police-paris.interieur.gouv.fr
Open: Mon–Thur 8:30 A.M.–5 P.M., Fri until 4:30 P.M.

Staying in Touch

The need to stay in touch is right up there with a safe flight, a good meal, and a comfortable bed.
—*Ann Dimon, travel writer for* the Toronto Sun

Email and the Internet
The worldwide love affair with the Internet and email has become a part of everyday life in Paris. If your laptop is WiFi compatible, you can tap into a wonderful world of wired services, and do it just about anywhere. WiFi (in Paris, pronounced "wee-fee") is all over the place: hotels, train stations, cafés . . . and, of course at McDonald's and Starbucks.

More and more hotels have Internet terminals in the lobby and provide modems in the rooms. Some charge for this, requiring you to purchase a card for so many minutes, or use a credit card to gain Internet access. Others offer it free. All *Great Sleeps Paris* listings denote what type of Internet access each hotel offers. If you are going to be in Paris for more than a few days and know you will be doing a lot of communicating via the Internet, buy a subscription card that is good for either a couple of hours or up to 250 minutes. If you have questions, let a Parisian computer expert put your mind at ease (see "Services," page 34).

If you are not coming digitally equipped, and your hotel or apartment does not have Internet access, there are cyber cafés in almost every neighborhood. A very central one that I recommend is Znet (see page 35).

Post

How quaint! Writing letters and postcards in a Paris café has become almost a nostalgic experience. For postcards, you can buy stamps at any tobacconist shop. This eliminates standing in line at the post office, and the price is exactly the same.

Every *quartier* has a post office; they are open Monday to Friday 8 A.M. to 7 P.M., Saturday until noon. I have never found one yet that did not have a long line. The main post office (52, rue du Louvre: Métro: Louvre-Rivoli; 01-40-28-76-00) is open twenty-four hours daily for *Poste Restante,* telephones, telegrams, stamps, and faxes, and for sending boxes not exceeding two kilos (4 pounds). Larger boxes have to be sent during regular post office hours. All post offices sell boxes in various sizes; the price includes the shipping, and there is no weight limit. For shipping to the U.S., you want to buy a *Colissimo* box. If you are shipping something within Europe, you will need a *Chronopost* box.

If you do not have an address in Paris, you can use Poste Restante. Mail addressed to you must have your name in block capitals, followed by the words "Poste Restante," then the main Paris post office address: 52, rue du Louvre, 75001, Paris. To get your mail, you must show your passport and pay a small fee for each letter you receive. If you have an American Express account, you can also receive mail c/o American Express, 11, rue Scribe, 75009; Métro: Opéra; 01-47-14-50-00 (main office); Mon–Fri 9 A.M.–6 P.M., Sat 9 A.M.–5 P.M.

If speed is a factor in sending parcels, then Federal Express is probably the answer. Warning: It is not cheap! For further information on shipping and FedEx, see "Getting It All Home," page 323.

Telephone

French telephone numbers have ten digits. Paris and Ile de France numbers begin with 01, and the rest of France is divided into four regional zones with prefixes 02, 03, 04, and 05. Free telephone numbers begin with 08; cell phone numbers begin with 06. If you are calling France from abroad, leave off the 0 at the beginning of the ten-digit number; dial 0+country code+area or city code+number. For instance, if you are in the United States, and the Paris number is 01-42-22-33-44, dial 011-33-1-42-22-33-44.

Don't expect your U.S. cell phone to work in France. The U.S. uses a different wireless system, so handsets that work in your home area won't work in Paris. It is beyond the scope of *Great Sleeps Paris* to go into the technical details required for bringing your own cell, but here are four options: First, buy a world phone that has a worldwide number that will ring wherever you may be. This is not a cheap deal and the expense is probably not worth it unless you are a corporate traveler who goes abroad often. Second, buy a telephone compatible with GSM, and a SIM card for each country you will be visiting (you can buy the SIM card in Paris). This is a much cheaper option, but means you will have to change the SIM card for whatever country you visit, and thus your number will change as well. If you do this, make sure your phone is unlocked. Many cell phones in the U.S. are locked so that you can only use one service. Next, rent a mobile telephone from Cellhire, www/cellhire.fr, or George V Telecom, 46, rue Pierre Charron 75008; Métro George V; 01-47-20-30-40. Prices start at 75€ for one week, minutes extra. Finally, buy an inexpensive local cell phone, load it with the cheapest usage plan that works for your stay, and when you return home, sell it on eBay to someone coming to France.

With the advent of the cell phone, public telephone booths are now regarded as dinosaurs lumbering to the tarpits! However, there may be times when using a public telephone booth may be convenient. Most public phones in Paris now require a prepaid phone card (*télecarte*), which you buy in increments or units (*unités*). To make a call, pick up the phone, insert the card into a slot on the phone, wait for the dial tone, and then start dialing the number. The amount of your call is automatically deducted from the remaining value. These cards offer several advantages: you do not need a pocketful of change; calling from a public phone eliminates the surcharges in hotels; and the card has no expiration date, so you can use what is left on your card on your next trip. Where to buy the *télecarte?* It post offices, *tabacs,* airports, and train and métro stations. Telephone books are in all post offices and hotels.

Every time you pick up a phone in Paris, it will cost you money, even if you are calling next door. If you call between a cell phone and a land line, the rates will be staggering. Always try to dial cell to cell or land line to land line to avoid this excessive rate. If you are calling abroad, especially from a hotel, the rates can be downright frightening. Even if you reverse the charges or use a telephone service such as AT&T, you will likely be hit with a surcharge, sometimes up to 100 percent of the cost of the call. Check with the hotel operator about your hotel's policy, as they all differ. To avoid the surcharge, use an international calling card that you purchase in Paris from the same places that sell the domestic *télecartes* discussed above. It is important to remember that the domestic card won't work on international calls, and vice-versa. However, you *can* buy a *télecart à puce* or a *télecart pré-payée* that is good for both domestic and international calls. Or, before leaving home, purchase an international phone card from a warehouse club (for example, Costco or Sam's Club). Some cost about $20 for four hours of talk time. These cards are simple, painless, and definitely the least expensive way to stay in touch. For further savings, call when the rates are low. Within France and Europe, the cheaper hours are Monday to Friday 7 P.M. to 8 A.M., and all day Saturday and Sunday. The cheaper rates to the United States and Canada are Monday to Friday 7 P.M. to 1 P.M., and Saturday to Sunday all day. Remember, when calling the United States, Paris is six hours ahead of Eastern Standard Time and nine hours ahead of Pacific Standard Time.

Here are some helpful numbers for domestic or international calls:

To call Paris from the United States 011+33+number

To call the United States from Paris 00+1+area code+number

To reach an English-speaking operator
AT&T	0800-99-00-11
MCI/World Phone	0800-99-00-19
Sprint	0800-99-00-87

Directory information 12

Operator 10

International information 32-12+country code (1 for United States)

Time 3699

Traffic 08-26-02-20-22

Weather
Paris	08-92-68-02-75
For France and abroad	08-99-70-12-34

France Télécom English-Speaking Customer Service
08-00-36-47-75; Mon–Fri, 9 A.M.–5 P.M.; free telephone information in English

Fax

To send a fax to Paris from the United States, dial 011+33+the number. Remember to eliminate the 0 at the beginning of the ten-digit number; for instance, if the fax number is 01-47-12-34-56, dial 011-33-1-47-12-34-56. To fax the U.S. from Paris, dial 00+1+area code+number.

Transportation

Public transportation in and around Paris is some of the best in Europe. Because it is so efficient, why would any foreign traveler willingly subject him- or herself to driving a car in this city? Isn't this supposed to be a vacation? Parking is impossible, traffic is from hell, gasoline is expensive, and the one-way streets will drive you crazy. Did you know that of Paris's 988 miles of streets, 435 miles are one way?! Behind the wheel, Parisian drivers are kamikaze pilots who take no prisoners. They think nothing of driving and parking on the sidewalk, blocking traffic on narrow streets, cutting in and out with inches to spare, and flashing their lights to indicate displeasure (honking the horn is forbidden until the moment of impact). Then there is the *priorité à droite* to get used to: this gives the right of way to the car approaching from the right, regardless of the size of the street, the traffic on it, or the safety hazard of the moment. Add to this frightening horror show the insane motorcyclists who drive on the sidewalk when the traffic is too thick for them to squeeze through it. The best reason to drive a car in Paris is to get out of town and head for the provinces.

Save yourself a great deal of aggravation by using the métro, the buses, the RER suburban railway, and your own feet to get around the city. Paris is a city that invites walking, and exploring the narrow streets or strolling along the grand boulevards is the best way to discover it. However, even as a pedestrian, you must keep up your guard. In Paris, anyone behind the wheel of a car, or traveling by any kind of wheeled conveyance—inline skates, bicycle, scooter, or motorcycle—considers the pedestrian a monumental nuisance in the effort to get from A to B in the least amount of time possible. Even when the pedestrian has a green light, don't assume that drivers will concede the right of way. By law, drivers are only required to come to a full stop at a red light. When there is a crosswalk, whether or not it has a flashing amber light or a sign saying *priorité aux pietons* (priority to pedestrians), drivers will ignore this and step on the gas.

Getting to and from the Airports
Roissy–Charles-de-Gaulle Airport
For recorded general information in English, twenty-four hours daily, call 01-48-62-22-80, or visit www.adp.fr.

A taxi is the easiest and most comfortable way to get from Roissy to Paris, but it is expensive unless there are two or more in your party. The ride into central Paris takes about fifty minutes on a good day; during rush hour, add at least thirty minutes. Taxis will take no more than three people and add at least a 1€ surcharge for every piece of luggage. Fares range between 50€ and 65€ during the day and are higher from 8 P.M. to 7 A.M. A 15 percent tip is expected. One taxi company serving Paris airports is Airportaxis: 01-48-40-17-17; www.airportaxis.com; 50€ each way, 1€ supplement for luggage; credit cards: AE, V.

A more economical way is to take the direct RER B train to Paris. There is direct access from Terminal 2. A free shuttle bus (look for the word *navette*) runs from Terminal 1 and takes passengers to Terminal 2 and the Roissy train station, where you board the Roissy RER B-line into the city, with stops at Gare du Nord, Châtelet–Les Halles, St-

Michel, Luxembourg, Port Royal, and Denfert-Rochereau. The train leaves every twenty-five minutes between 5 A.M. and 11 P.M. and costs around 9€. The train trip takes around forty-five minutes, and the shuttle between the airport terminals about fifteen.

Air France buses (you do not have to be a passenger on one of their flights to use them) leave from both terminals every twelve minutes from 5:45 A.M. to 11:30 P.M.; they take about forty-five minutes to an hour to reach Paris and cost around 12€ one way, 18€ roundtrip. The buses stop at place de la Porte Maillot/Palais des Congrès, Arc de Triomphe/Charles-de-Gaulle-Étoile at avenue Carnot, Gare Montparnasse at 113, boulevard Vaugirard, and Gare de Lyon. For information, call 08-92-35-08-20; www.cars.airfrance.com.

The RATP-operated Roissybus runs every fifteen to twenty minutes from 5:45 A.M. to 11 P.M. between the airport and 11, rue Scribe, behind place de l'Opéra, and beside the American Express office; it takes about an hour and costs around 10€ (including luggage). At Roissy–Charles-de-Gaulle airport, the bus departs for Paris from air terminals 2B and 2D, gate 11, and air terminals 2A and 2C, gate 10. Tickets are sold on the bus. Call the main RATP number (08-92-68-77-14) for information in English.

The SNCF night bus (08-91-36-20-20) has two bus routes operating nightly between the last train in the evening and the first one in the morning, roughly 11:30 P.M. and 5:30 A.M. It operates from Charles-de-Gaulle, Gare du Nord, Châtelet, Gare de Lyon and Gare d'Austerlitz. Fares vary.

There are also various shuttle services between both Roissy–Charles-de-Gaulle and Orly Airports. These take passengers door-to-door from the airport to their hotel. Advance reservations are necessary. One such company is Paris Airport Service (08-21-80-08-01), which costs 25€ for one person between 6 A.M. and 8 P.M., 40€ from 8 P.M. and 6 A.M. Always check with your hotel to see what shuttle line they use, and follow their lead. The hotel is not going to do business with a company who is not on time, or worse, doesn't show up.

Orly Airport

For information in English (6 A.M. to 11:30 P.M.), call 01-49-75-15-15 or 08-92-68-15-15; www.paris-orly.com or www.adp.fr.

A taxi to and from Orly to Paris takes twenty to forty minutes and costs between 25€ and 35€, plus 1€ for each piece of luggage.

The high-speed Orlyval shuttle train runs daily every seven minutes from 6 A.M. to 10 P.M. to RER B station Antony. It costs around 10EU and takes thirty minutes; to La Défense, 12€, fifty minutes; and to Châtelet–Les Halles, 10€, thirty-five minutes. In Paris: take the RER Line B toward St-Rémy-les-Chevreuse as far as Antony and change to the Val line to Orly Ouest or Orly Sud. For more information, call RATP information (08-92-68-77-14).

There is the Orlybus that links Orly airport to the RER Line B at place Denfert-Rochereau. Buses depart from Orly-Sud (gate H, platform 4) every fifteen to twenty minutes from 6 A.M. to 11:30 P.M.; it costs 8€ and takes thirty minutes. In Paris, the Orly bus leaves from Denfert-Rochereau RER or métro station. Tickets can be purchased on the Orlybus. For more information, call customer service (01-40-02-32-94).

Air France buses leave both terminals every fifteen minutes between 6 A.M. and 11 P.M. to the Air France air terminal at Les Invalides or Montparnasse. The fare is around 8€ one way, 12€ roundtrip, and the trip takes between thirty and forty-five minutes.

Métro and Regional Express Railway (RER)

The Paris public transportation system is made up of the RATP métro and bus routes and the RER, which connects with the Paris métro to suburban train lines. With 370 stations, the Paris métro system is one of the most efficient in the world. The system has fourteen lines, each identifiable by its number and destination. Paris and the suburbs are divided into five zones, but most visitors only go to zones 1 and 2, which cover the city center and all métro lines. Métro and RER trains run from 5:30 A.M. until 12:30 A.M.

The RER (Regional Express Railway) has five lines in Paris—A, B, C, D, and E—and is joined to the city métro network and some of the SNCF trains (France's national train system). Using a combination of the métro and the RER, you can get within walking distance of almost everything you would want to see and do in the city.

If you will be in Paris only a short time and plan on seeing a lot, the *Paris Visite* ticket is worth considering. This go-as-you-please ticket is good for one, two, three, or five days, and it is valid for the bus, metro, RER, and the SNCF trains to Disneyland Paris, Versailles, Fontainebleau, and Roissy–Charles-de-Gaulle and Orly airports. Another benefit is that it offers reductions on a few museums and tourist sites in Paris. It is available at main métro stations, any RER or SNCF station, and from the Paris Tourist Information Office. Rates depend on how many days you need and zones you travel to. Prices range from 6€ for a one-day pass to 30€ for a five-day pass. Children under twelve pay half price.

You can buy individual tickets (1.40€), but a *carnet* of ten (10.50€) is much more practical and cheaper. Either of these can be purchased at métro stations, tourist offices, or *tabacs*. If you are staying in Paris more than a few days, buy the weekly *Carte Hebdomadaire* (15.60€) valid Monday through Sunday, or the monthly *Carte d'Orange Coupon Mensuel* (50.40€), valid from the first day of the month. Both allow unlimited travel in zones 1 and 2 on the métro and buses. Always hold on to your ticket. If you are caught without it, you will be fined. To buy either type of métro pass, you must have a passport-size photo (there are photo booths in some larger métro stations). To make your purchase, go to the cashier window in almost any major métro station, or head to the RATP offices: place de la Madeleine, 75008; Métro: Madeleine; Open May–Sept only, Mon–Fri 8:30 A.M.–noon, 1–4:30 P.M., Sat 8:30 A.M.–noon, 2–4:30 P.M. The other RATP office is at 53 bis, quai des Grands Augustins, 75006; Métro: St-Michel; Open year-round Mon–Sat, same hours. For general information in English, call 08-92-68-41-14. The Website www.ratp.fr is in French only. For the most detailed Paris maps showing all streets with metro stops, consult the *Plan de Paris par Arrondissement* (see page 22).

Bus

Because the métro is so fast and efficient, visitors often overlook the buses in Paris. The routes of each bus line are generally posted at each stop. They are also listed in the back of the *Plan de Paris par Arrondissement* (see page 22), or you can pick up a free bus map, *Autobus Paris-Plan de Reseau,* at tourist offices in major métro stations, or probably at your hotel. If you have a métro ticket, or a weekly or monthly métro pass, these will all work on the bus; just show your pass to the driver.

Warning: Do not punch your weekly ticket when you board the bus; just show it. Punching it will render it unusable. You can punch your *individual* ticket, which, if you don't already have one, you can purchase from the bus driver. Always hold on to your ticket until you get off the bus. If caught without it, you will be fined.

All buses run Monday to Saturday from 6:30 A.M. to 8:30 P.M. Some continue until 12:30 A.M., and some run on Sunday. The Noctambus runs all night, but the routes are fewer. *Paris Bus, Métro, RER Routes,* a pamphlet printed by the RATP, lists several scenic bus routes and gives directions to major museums and monuments. For RATP information in English, call 08-92-68-77-14, or visit www.ratp.fr.

The Paris Montmartrobus is an inexpensive, fun way to see hilly Montmartre with the least amount of walking. The electric bus starts at the Jules Joffrin métro stop, goes up to Sacré Coeur, and then down to place Pigalle. En route, you will pass the pretty streets and corners of Montmartre that make it so famous. If you have a Carte d'Orange, you can get on and off the bus as many times as you wish without paying extra fare. Bring your camera.

Important warning: Buy your métro or bus tickets and passes from official cashiers inside métro stations or from one of the RATP offices listed above. Do not, under any circumstances whatsoever, buy from independent shysters who work the train stations claiming to be authorized RATP employees, which they are not. They are cheats out to steal your money.

River Transport—Batobus

The monuments of Paris take on a new look when viewed from a boat floating along the Seine. Batobuses cruise the river, covering central Paris in eight stops near main monuments and tourist sites. Passengers can get on and off as many times as they want during the validity of their ticket. The buses operate from February to December (closed in January) from 7 A.M. to 10 P.M. A one-day pass is 11€, two-day pass 13€, five-day pass 16€, and children under sixteen are about half price. The passes are available at Batobus stops, RATP ticket offices, and at the Office of Tourism (see page 27). For more information, call 08-25-05-01-01 or visit www.batobus.com.

Taxi

Despite the fact there are 15,000 taxis within metropolitan Paris, and 470 taxi stands, there are times when you wonder where all the taxi drivers are hiding. The challenge of finding a taxi in Paris often rivals that of New York City on a busy Friday afternoon. Add rain to that and you are better off riding public transportation or walking. Hailing a cab on a corner is difficult. It is smarter to go to a taxi stand; they are located on most major thoroughfares and at all railroad stations. Taxis are required by law to stop for you if the large white "taxi Parisien" light on top is on unless it is the driver's last half hour on duty, the passenger is less than fifty meters from a taxi stand, there are three or more in your group, or you are drunk. In other words, there is always some excuse not to stop! A glowing orange light means the taxi is not available.

Taxi drivers will take you anywhere you want to go in Paris or to either airport. They accept all handicapped passengers but are not required to take animals, other than seeing eye dogs (even though they may have their own dog riding with them in the front seat), take more than three persons, or accept an unreasonable amount of luggage. They *might* do any of these things, but the driver will probably add a supplemental charge. There is a minimum fee of 1€ for every piece of luggage, more if it is heavy or unwieldy.

Normal taxi fares are based on area and time of day. Beneath the taxi light are three little lights—A, B, and C. One of these will light up according to what tariff applies. The tariff is also shown on the meter display inside the taxi. A 15 percent tip is customary. If you want an early-morning taxi to take you to the airport, book it the night before. If you need a taxi at a specific time and don't want to chance not finding one, call ahead. If you do call a taxi, the fare starts when the driver gets the call, not when you get in. Here is a list of some of the bigger taxi companies; all take credit cards. Complaints should be made to the Bureau de la Réglementation Publique de Paris, 36, rue des Morillons, 75732 Paris Cedex 15; 08-21-00-25-25.

Airportaxis   01-48-40-17-17, www.airportaxis.com

Alpha   01-45-85-85-85

Taxi G7   01-47-39-47-39, 01-41-27-66-99

Taxis Bleu   08-25-16-10-10

Paris taxi drivers are quite honest and above-board, and they provide receipts upon request. Ask for *un reçu, s'il vous plait.*

Train

The SNCF is the acronym for the French national train system.
There are six train stations in Paris:

Gare d'Austerlitz (13th arr.)   Trains to/from the southwest of
                                France and Spain

Gare de l'Est (10th arr.)   Trains to/from Alsace and south-
                                ern Germany

Gare de Lyon (12th arr.)   Trains to/from the southeast of
                                France, the Alps, Provence, and
                                Italy

Gare du Nord (10th arr.)   Trains to/from Brussels, Germany,
                                Scandinavia, Netherlands, London
                                via the Chunnel, and other desti-
                                nations to the north

Gare Montparnasse (14th arr.) Trains to/from the west, Brittany,
                                and Bordeaux

Gare St-Lazare (8th arr.)   Trains to/from the northwest and
                                Normandy

At each station is a métro stop with the same name.

You can buy tickets at the station or call ahead to reserve your
seat, but you must pick up your ticket within forty-eight hours. Your
ticket will have your departure station printed on it. If you are under
twenty-six years old, you can save up to 50 percent on TGV fares
with the Carte12/25, but even without the card, you still get a 25
percent reduction. People over sixty also get good deals with a Carte
Vermeil (see "Seniors," page 43). You can also save considerable money
by booking at least fifteen days in advance of your travel date. Before
boarding the train you must remember to validate your ticket in an
orange *composteur;* these are located at the beginning of the platforms,
and when the conductor checks your ticket, he could fine you for not
having done it. For information, go to the ticket offices in any one of
the above listed stations, or call 08-92-35-35-35; www.sncf.fr.

Private Car and Driver or Chauffeured Limousine

For the ultimate comfort and convenience in Paris transportation, hire a private car and driver to take you where you want to go, whether it be to ride to and from the airports, to arrive unruffled for a Big Splurge dinner, or to admire Paris at night when the City of Light is at her most beguiling. I have found the following three to be reliable, on time, and very polite; they speak enough English and are especially recommended for airport transfers: Henri Rouah (06-60-44-64-65), Roland Corfmat with Take CARe (06-82-07-55-95,06-80-25-84-70; rolandcorfmat@wanadoo.fr), and JMTD (06-84-05-06-63, ask for Mario; jmtd.transport@wanadoo.fr). Prices depend on the services required.

More expensive will be a chauffeured limousine from American Limousines (01-39-35-09-99; www.aamericanlimousines.com).

Time

France is one hour ahead of Greenwich Mean Time (GMT). Time is based on the twenty-four-hour clock. To check the time and set your clock, dial 36-99. Paris is six hours ahead of Eastern Standard Time (EST) and nine hours ahead of Pacific Standard Time (PST). Daylight saving time is observed from April 1 to October 31.

Standards of Measure

France uses the metric system. Here are the conversions:

1 inch = 2.54 centimeters	1 centimeter = 0.4 inch
1 mile = 1.61 kilometers	1 kilometer = 0.62 mile
1 ounce = 28 grams	1 gram = 0.04 ounces
1 pound = 0.45 kilograms	1 kilogram = 2.2 pounds
1 quart = 0.95 liter	1 liter = 1.06 quarts
1 gallon = 3.8 liters	

How much is that in miles, feet, pounds, or degrees? Here is how to do the conversions:

Kilometers/miles: To change kilometers to miles, multiply the kilometers by .621. To change miles to kilometers, multiply the miles by 1.61.

Meters/feet: To change meters to feet, multiply the meters by 3.28. To change feet to meters, multiply the feet by .305.

Kilograms/pounds: To change kilograms to pounds, multiply the kilograms by 2.20. To change pounds to kilograms, multiply the pounds by .453.

Celsius/Fahrenheit: To change Celsius to Fahrenheit, double the Celsius figure and add 30. If the Celsius figure is below zero, double the sub-zero number and subtract it from 32.

Voltage

French electrical circuits are wired at 220 volts. You will need a transformer and an adapter plug for appliances you bring that operate on 110 volts. Things such as hair dryers and hair curling irons may have switches that convert the appliance from one voltage to another. This only eliminates the need for a transformer, not for the adapter plug. If you are planning on using a computer, be sure you have a surge protector and the adapter plug; otherwise, you could end up damaging your machine. Don't worry if you find yourself without the proper adapters or transformers. Go to the basement of the BHV department store (see page 348) and take the appliance with you. If they don't have what you need, chances are it doesn't exist.

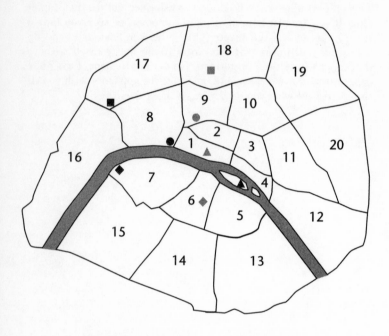

- ● Place de la Concorde
- ■ Arc de Triomphe
- ▲ Notre Dame
- ◆ Tour Eiffel
- ● Opéra
- ■ Sacré Cœur
- ▲ Louvre
- ◆ Jardin du Luxembourg

HOTEL LISTINGS BY ARRONDISSEMENT

Paris, the most popular tourist destination in the world, has more than nine million inhabitants occupying 432 square miles. Despite these numbers, it is a very compact city, bound by a ring road known as the *périphérique* and divided into twenty districts called *arrondissements*. Anything outside the *périphérique* is the *banlieu* and is considered the suburbs. The River Seine divides Paris into the Right Bank *(Rive Droite)* and the Left Bank *(Rive Gauche)*. In the late nineteenth century, Paris was reorganized and modernized by Baron Haussmann, the far-sighted planner who gave the city its wide boulevards, beautiful parks, and system of arrondissements that make up the city today. Each arrondissement has a character all its own, as well as its own mayor, city hall, police station, and central post office.

Knowing which arrondissement is which is the key to understanding Paris and quickly finding your way around. Starting with the first arrondissement, which is the district around the Louvre, the numbering of districts goes clockwise in a rough spiral. From a visitor's standpoint, the arrondissements of greatest interest are the first through the eighth, although there are interesting things to see and do in all of them. For instance, Montmartre occupies most of the eighteenth, and to attend a performance at the Opéra Bastille, you must journey to the eleventh. For mailing purposes, the Paris postal code prefix is 750, which is followed by a two-digit number indicating the arrondissement: 75001 is the code for the first, 75002 for the second, and so on. For every address in *Great Sleeps Paris,* the postal code is given.

In addition to each arrondissement being numbered, it also has a name (and in some cases, two) by which its residents often refer to it. The first arrondissement is commonly referred to as Louvre, the second as Bourse, and so on (see below). For example, Parisians might say, "I live in the sixth, Luxembourg." Some arrondissements have two sections, and each section has its own name. In this case, a resident would specify which: "I live in the eleventh, République."

First	Louvre
Second	Bourse
Third	Marais
Fourth	Hôtel de Ville
Fifth	Panthéon
Sixth	Luxembourg

Seventh	Invalides
Eighth	Élysée
Ninth	Opéra
Tenth	Magenta
Eleventh	République (northern section), Voltaire (southern section)
Twelfth	Bercy (eastern section), Reuilly (western section)
Thirteenth	Bibliothèque Nationale de France (eastern section), Italie (western section)
Fourteenth	Observatoire (eastern section), Montparnasse (western section)
Fifteenth	Vaugirard (eastern section), Grenelle (western section)
Sixteenth	Passy
Seventeenth	Ternes (western section), Batignolles (eastern section)
Eighteenth	Butte Montmartre (western section), La Chapelle (eastern section)
Nineteenth	La Villette (northern section), Buttes Chaumont (southern section)
Twentieth	Ménilmontant (northern section), Père Lachaise (southern section)

First Arrondissement

Paris began on Île de la Cité, and Parisians still regard it as the center not only of their city but of all France. Anchored in the middle of the Seine, Île de la Cité has some of the oldest and most treasured monuments of Paris. La Conciergerie is the Gothic prison where thousands, including Robespierre and Marie-Antoinette, were incarcerated during the French Revolution. Le Palais de Justice, a royal palace, became the seat of the judicial system after the French Revolution. Ste-Chapelle, located within Le Palais de Justice, has seven-hundred-year-old, breath-takingly beautiful red-and-blue stained-glass windows. The Tuileries Gardens, Musée de l'Orangerie, and Louvre Museum form the cornerstone of this regal *quartier.* In the first arrondissement you will find Les Halles, with Forum des Halles housing two hundred or more boutiques along with movie theaters, fast-food joints, and the largest métro station in the world (which has the reputation of being unsafe after dark). Two famous churches are here: St-Germain-l'Auxerrois, the Gothic church parish of French kings, and St-Eustache, the largest Gothic Renaissance church in Paris. For many, place Dauphine, with its white brick buildings, is one of the most peaceful and harmonious in the city. The palaces surrounding the moneyed place Vendôme include the famed Cartier jewelry store, the Ministry of Justice, and the world-renowned Ritz Hôtel, where room prices are within the budget of any average emir or Texas oil mogul.

RIGHT BANK
Conciergerie
Île de la Cité
Les Halles & Forum des Halles
Louvre
Musée de l'Orangerie
Musée des Arts Décoratifs
Palais de Justice
Palais Royal
place Dauphine
place Vendôme
Pont Neuf
Ste-Chapelle
St-Eustache
St-Germain-l'Auxerrois
Tuileries Gardens

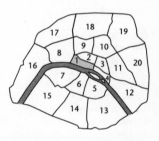

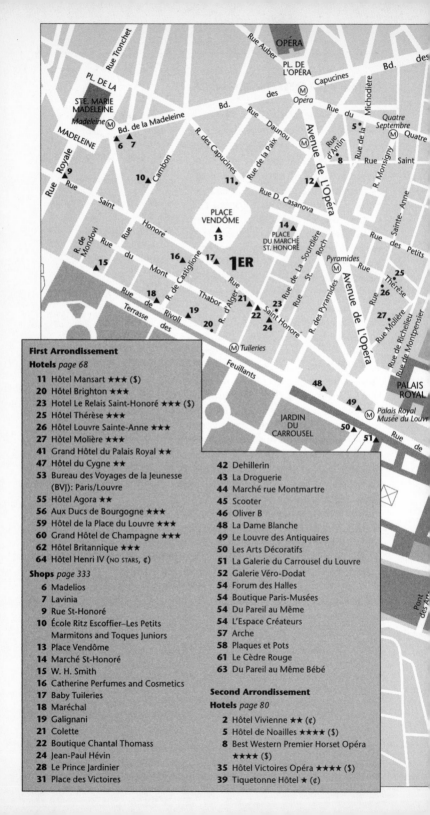

First Arrondissement

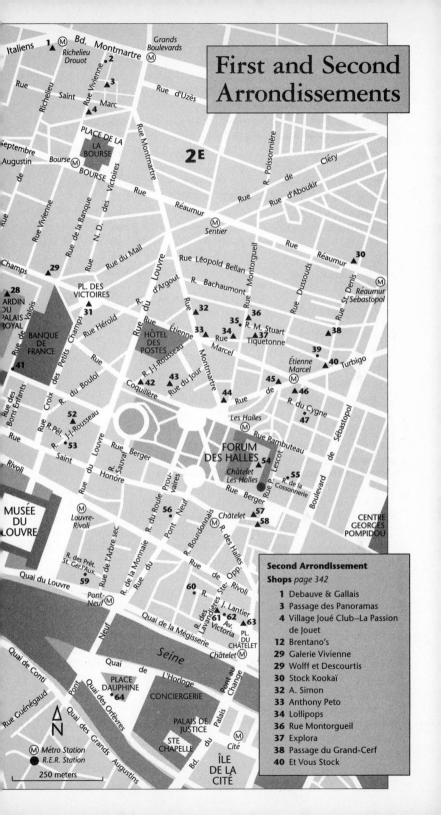

First and Second Arrondissements

Italiens ▲ 1 Ⓜ Bd. Montmartre
Richelieu Drouot
▲ 2
Rue Vivienne
▲ 3
Grands Boulevards Ⓜ

Rue
Saint
Rue d'Uzès
▲ 4 Marc

Septembre
Augustin
PLACE DE LA
LA BOURSE

2E
de Bourse Ⓜ
BOURSE

Rue Montmartre
R. Poissonnière
Cléry

Rue Vivienne
Rue de la Banque
N. D. des Victoires
Rue
Réaumur
Rue
Rue d'Aboukir
de

Champs ▲ 29
Rue du Mail
Rue Léopold Bellan
Sentier Ⓜ
Rue
Réaumur ▲ 30

▲ 28
JARDIN DU PALAIS ROYAL
PL. DES VICTOIRES ▲
▲ 31
Rue Hérold

Rue d'Argout
R. Bachaumont
Rue Montorgueil
Rue Dussouds
St. Denis
Réaumur Ⓜ
Sébastopol

BANQUE DE FRANCE
Rue des Petits Champs
HÔTEL DES POSTES
Rue Étienne
▲ 32
R. J-J-Rousseau
35 ▲ ▲ 36
33 ▲ 34 ▲ R. M. Stuart
Rue Marcel
Tiquetonne 37
▲ 38

▲ 41
Rue du Bouloi
Coquillère ▲ 42
43 ▲
Rue du Jour
Montmartre
44 ▲
Rue
Étienne Marcel
39 •
40 ▲ Turbigo
45 ▲ ▲ 46
de
R. du Cygne
47 •
Sébastopol

Rue des Bons Enfants
R. Croix des Petits Champs
52 ▲
R. Pél. J-J-Rousseau
53 •
Rue Saint
Rue du Louvre
R. Sauval
Rue Berger
Les Halles Ⓜ
FORUM DES HALLES
Châtelet Les Halles
Rue Rambuteau
R. Lescot 54 ■
R. de la Cossonnerie 55 •
Boulevard
CENTRE GEORGES POMPIDOU

MUSÉE DU LOUVRE
Rivoli
Louvre-Rivoli Ⓜ
R. des Prêt.
St. Ger.l'Aux.
Rue du Roule
Rue de l'Arbre sec
Rue Berger
Prouvaires
Rue Berger
57 ▲
58 ▲
Châtelet

Rue Honoré
Rue de la Monnaie
Pont Neuf
56 •
Rue des Halles
Opp.
de
Rivoli
Châtelet Ⓜ

Quai du Louvre
59 •
Pont-Neuf Ⓜ
Rue de la Monnaie
Rue du
R. Bourdonnais
60 •
R.
J. Lantier
61 • 62 •
Av. Victoria
▲ 63
PL. DU CHÂTELET
Châtelet Ⓜ

Quai de Conti
Pont Neuf
Quai de l'Horloge
Quai de la Mégisserie
R. des Lavandières Ste.-
Seine
Pont au Change

Quai de Conti
PLACE DAUPHINE
• 64
CONCIERGERIE
PALAIS DE JUSTICE
STE CHAPELLE
Bd. du Palais
Cité Ⓜ
ÎLE DE LA CITÉ

Quai Guénégaud
Quai des Grands Augustins
Quai des Orfèvres

△ N

Ⓜ Métro Station
● R.E.R. Station

250 meters

Second Arrondissement

Shops *page 342*

1 Debauve & Gallais
3 Passage des Panoramas
4 Village Joué Club–La Passion de Jouet
12 Brentano's
29 Galerie Vivienne
29 Wolff et Descourtis
30 Stock Kookaï
32 A. Simon
33 Anthony Peto
34 Lollipops
36 Rue Montorgueil
37 Explora
38 Passage du Grand-Cerf
40 Et Vous Stock

HOTELS IN THE FIRST ARRONDISSEMENT

OTHER OPTIONS
Student Accommodations

($) indicates a Big Splurge; (¢) indicates a Cheap Sleep

AUX DUCS DE BOURGOGNE ★★★ (56)
19, rue du Pont Neuf, 75001
Métro: Pont-Neuf; RER Châtelet–Les Halles
50 rooms, all with shower or bath and toilet

There are many appealing things about this hotel, which is affiliated with Best Western. First, the A+ location puts guests in the heart of Paris. Next, children under twelve are free, the entire hotel is equipped with high-speed Internet, and the traditional, air-conditioned rooms are very clean. Two floors are exclusively nonsmoking, all have double windows, and bathrooms have good mirror and sink space. The sunny lobby has comfortable seating with a daily selection of newspapers and magazines, a marble fireplace flanked by bookshelves, and an interesting collection of black and white prints of the Ducs de Bourgogne. The well-loved English hat rack with its collection of vintage hats has been moved to the breakfast area downstairs. The owner originally had it in the lobby as a place for guests to hang their coats, but it was too fragile for this purpose. Rather than dispose of it, he went to the flea market and bought a collection of fanciful *chapeaux*. Soon the hat rack became the symbol of the hotel, and no one would think of hanging a coat on it. Finally, the staff, headed by friendly Nathalie

Dupont, the manager, is always ready to help. Always ask her about special off-season and promotional rates.

TEL 01-42-33-95-64; toll-free in the U.S. and Canada 800-528-1234 (Best Western) **FAX** 01-40-39-01-25 **EMAIL** mail@hotel-paris-bourgogne.com
INTERNET www.hotel-paris-bourgogne.com, www.bestwestern.fr
FACILITIES & SERVICES Air-conditioning, conference room, direct-dial phone, elevator, hair dryer, laundry service, minibar, public parking across the street, tea and coffee maker, TV with international reception, office safe (no charge), 2 floors nonsmoking, WiFi
RATES Single 110–165€, double 165–215€, junior suite 245€, extra bed 25€, children under 12 free; *taxe de séjour* included **CREDIT CARDS** AE, DC, MC, V
BREAKFAST Buffet 12€ per person

GRAND HÔTEL DE CHAMPAGNE ★★★ (60)
17, rue Jean-Lantier, at 13, rue des Orfèvres, 75001
Métro: Châtelet (exit rue de Rivoli, *nos impairs*, or Bertin Poirée); RER Châtelet–Les Halles
43 rooms, all with shower or bath and toilet

Hidden on a small corner near the River Seine and the Châtelet métro stop, the family-owned Grand Hôtel de Champagne appeals to travelers looking for an ideal spot to begin exploring the Louvre, the islands, St-Michel, and St-Germain-des-Prés.

If you look carefully in the sitting area off the reception, you will see 1562 carved in one of the original wooden pillars; this is the date that the building was constructed, making it the oldest structure on rue Jean-Lantier. Before its present charmed transformation, it served as a residence for members of the tailor and shoemaker guilds, an inn during the Empire period, and until 1854, a Christian girls' school.

Different themes are carried out in each of the forty-three rooms and suites, with the colorful interiors running the gamut from masculine modern to frankly feminine. All rooms on the first floor are nonsmoking. Room 203 is a well-coordinated room with romantic rose wall covering and dancing ladies and gentlemen framing the door; the dancing ladies also form the trim on the bed coverlet. Number 405 has a nautical motif with a sailing theme carried out in the seascape painting over the bed, on the ship brass lanterns as lights, a mirrored port hole, and aqua blue fabrics. Number 403 is a popular choice featuring a burgandy bedcovering accented by deep orange pillows and ruffles. Rooms 502, 504, and 505 have terraces. Frankly, the only thing going for 502 is the balcony. I don't like the low cross beams, the open rack that subs for a closet, or the lack of tub in the bathroom.

Management is justifiably proud of its buffet breakfast served downstairs. Designed to appeal to lumberjack appetites, it includes fresh fruit, juices, a variety of breads and rolls, several selections of meat and cheese, pâté, eggs, and cereals. After this meal, you won't need to eat until dinnertime.

Also under the same ownership is Hôtel de la Motte-Picquet (see page 175) in the seventh arrondissement.

TEL 01-42-36-60-00; toll-free from U.S. 800-44-UTELL
   FAX 01-45-08-43-33 **EMAIL** champaigne@hotelchampaigneparis.com
   INTERNET www.hotelchampaigneparis.com
FACILITIES & SERVICES Air-conditioning, direct-dial phone, elevator (to
   most floors), hair dryer, laundry service, minibar in suites, TV with
   international reception, room safe (no charge), first floor nonsmoking, free
   WiFi in lobby
RATES Single 126–176€, double 168–220€, triple 177–237€, suites 220–
   420€; *taxe de séjour* 1€ per person, per day **CREDIT CARDS** AE, DC, MC, V
BREAKFAST Buffet downstairs or Continental in room, 15€ per person

GRAND HÔTEL DU PALAIS ROYAL ★★ (41)
4, rue de Valois, 75001
Métro: Palais Royal–Musée du Louvre
85 rooms, all with shower or bath and toilet

The minimalistic lobby and reception areas are softened by fake but realistic orchid and lily floral arrangements in this modern choice midway between the Bourse (stock exchange) and the Louvre. All eighty-five blue-and-yellow rooms are virtually the same. They face outward, display exceptionally high housekeeping standards, and have bare hardwood floors, simple blue-and-white bedspreads and curtains, luggage and closet space, and functional bathrooms with stall showers or tub/shower combinations and sink space. Toiletries are limited to a sliver of soap. You'll find no cable TV, no safe, no minibars, and no unpleasant surprises. Instead you can count on a decent, clean hotel room that is modestly priced for the area.

TEL 01-42-96-15-35 **FAX** 01-40-15-97-81 **EMAIL** h-palais-royal@wanadoo.fr
   INTERNET www.grandhotel-palaisroyal.com
FACILITIES & SERVICES Air-conditioning, direct-dial phone, elevator, hair
   dryer, French TV, 2 handicapped rooms, WiFi
RATES Single 140€, double 150€; extra bed 30€; *taxe de séjour* included
   CREDIT CARDS MC, V
BREAKFAST Buffet 10€ per person

HÔTEL AGORA ★★ (55)
7, rue de la Cossonnerie, off rue Pierre Lescot, 75001
Métro: Etienne-Marcel; RER Châtelet–Les Halles
30 rooms, all with shower or bath and toilet

The decor at the Hôtel Agora is an eclectic, clever pastiche of flea-market nostalgia and appealing hand-me-downs. The rooms are not large, nor are the bathrooms, but if you want something different in an active, animated section of Paris, read on.

The location, in the midst of a Les Halles block of touristy shops on a pedestrian street, is hardly inspiring. A short flight of stairs leads to a reception room with lacy green plants and a breakfast room with some of the owner's antique furnishings and a photo of an Italian film star (who must have stayed here in leaner times).

The hallways are painted a gloomy battleship gray, but the rooms are whimsically individual, mixing the old with the new in a way that comes together. Number 52 has a balcony with views of St-Eustache, Les Halles, and the tip of the Centre Pompidou. Number 31, with twin beds, features an armchair covered in a leopard print, a fireplace, and a gold-framed headboard with hand-painted flowers. In No. 64, you will have a rooftop view of St-Eustache Church, sleep in a double bed, and use a small bathroom with a mini corner shower and wash basin. The least expensive room, number 66 on the top floor, is a sweet single with a slat park chair and a white bedspread with appliquéd floral hearts. Room 61 is the biggest and will hold three, but I think it is better for two. It is dominated by a nineteenth-century painting of a woman and a mixture of similar-era art scattered on the walls. A Tunisian wood sculpture looms over the twin beds. It can combine with No. 62, a twin with two dormer windows, to make a family suite. The warm mustard-colored No. 51 is one of my favorites. Besides its tiny terrace, I like the entryway with its large oval mirror, the marble fireplace, and the gold scrolled piece of wood that forms a backdrop for the bed.

TEL 01-42-33-46-02 **FAX** 01-42-33-80-99 **EMAIL** hotel.agora.f@wanadoo.fr
   INTERNET www.hotel-paris-agora.com
FACILITIES & SERVICES Direct-dial phone, elevator (starts 1st floor), hair dryer
   available, TV with international reception, office safe (no charge)
RATES Single 70–118€, double 98–148€, triple 135€; *taxe de séjour* 0.78€
   per person, per day **CREDIT CARDS** AE, MC, V
BREAKFAST Continental 10€ per person

HÔTEL BRIGHTON ★★★ (20)
218, rue de Rivoli, 75001
Métro: Tuileries
63 rooms, all with shower or bath and toilet

The Hôtel Brighton dates from the end of the nineteenth century and takes its name from the friendship that developed between Great Britain and France during the reign of Queen Victoria. Overlooking the Tuileries Gardens and many of the most beautiful Parisian monuments, it is also only a short walk from the Louvre, place Vendôme, wonderful shopping, the Opéra, and the Seine.

The hotel has undergone a complete redecoration and the results are impressive, indeed. Naturally those rooms with the million-dollar views of Paris are the most expensive; however, all are nice and have the advantage of space, which is very hard to come by in most Parisian hotels. Number 401 is a large superior double on the back. The room includes a leather-topped desk, a comfortable reading chair, luggage space, and a marble, double-sink bathroom large enough to hold a table and small stool in addition to the regular bathroom fixtures. Another choice on the back is No. 403, with a double brass bed and armchair. The long, narrow marble bathroom is light and has a shower over the tub. Also on the back is No. 305, with a working-size desk, big bathroom, and a small balcony with a peek at the Louvre. These rooms are nice if you are willing to sacrifice a view, but frankly, when staying here, I want a room with a view, because they are nothing short of spectacular, encompassing almost all of Paris from the Arc de Triomphe and La Defense to the Eiffel Tower, Invalides, Notre Dame, and more. Yes, there is some noise, but double windows and air-conditioning buffer most of it. Take No. 309, for example: it's a large room with vintage furniture, leather armchair, mirrored dresser with a tulip light, good desk, and a huge bathroom with a separate tub, stall shower, and enclosed toilet. Number 410, a huge, blue junior suite, has one entire wall of closet space and a work table facing the Tuileries, Louvre, Eiffel Tower, and Museé d'Orsay, which makes it difficult to concentrate on desk matters when this spectacular view is at your fingertips.

Also under the same ownership are the Hôtels de la Place du Louvre (page 73), Mansart (page 77), Parc Saint-Séverin (page 124), and d'Orsay (page 179).

TEL 01-47-03-61-61 **FAX** 01-42-60-41-78 **EMAIL** brighton@espritfrance.com
   INTERNET www.esprit-de-france.com
FACILITIES & SERVICES Air-conditioning, direct-dial phone, elevator, hair
   dryer, laundry service, minibar, TV with international reception, room safe
   (no charge), WiFi in lobby
RATES Single or double 163–217€, junior suites 255€; extra bed 29€; *taxe de
   séjour* included **CREDIT CARDS** AE, DC, MC, V
BREAKFAST Continental 9€, buffet 15€ per person

HÔTEL BRITANNIQUE ★★★ (62)
20, avenue Victoria, 75001
Métro: Châtelet; RER Châtelet–Les Halles
39 rooms, all with shower or bath and toilet

The history of this hotel goes way back. In 1870–71, it was run by a Quaker mission to aid war victims. During World War I, it was where war casualties recuperated. Today it is a gracefully restored, sound choice between Châtelet and Hôtel de Ville. In the refashioning of the hotel several years ago, the owners wisely kept many original parts. The winding stairway with polished banister and the carved reception counter are two examples of how the old can blend beautifully with the new. Granite hallways lined with red print carpet lead guests to their rooms, which are behind eggplant-purple doors. Best choices are on the top three floors, just high enough to escape the brunt of the street noise; they have more light and avoid blank-wall views on the back. For a street-side balcony, ask for something on the fifth floor. The rooms, though small, are professionally decorated in soft colors with tone-on-tone wallpaper, faux marble accents, and print fabrics. For more space, reserve the suite (No. 12), done in yellow and burgundy. In addition to the bedroom, the sitting area has a comfortable sofa bed with a pretty tapestry of grapes hanging over it. Three windows let in lots of light and the double-mirrored closet provides ample unpacking room.

Classical music soothes early morning diners in the pretty breakfast room. A buffet is laid out here, or you can have a Continental breakfast sent to your room for the same price. The sunken, mirrored lounge, with eye-level windows on the street, is accented with some lovely old heirlooms. Be sure to notice the birdcage, the early record player, and the intricately detailed model of an old sailing vessel.

TEL 01-42-33-74-59 **FAX** 01-42-33-82-65 **EMAIL** mailbox@
hotel-britannique.fr **INTERNET** www.hotel-britannique.fr

FACILITIES & SERVICES Air-conditioning, bar, direct-dial phone, elevator, hair dryer, minibar, terrycloth robes in all rooms, TV with international reception, room safe (no charge), WiFi

RATES Single 144€, double 173–198€, junior suite 253–293€; lower rates depend on season and availability; *taxe de séjour* included

CREDIT CARDS AE, DC, MC, V

BREAKFAST Buffet or Continental in room 15€ per person

HÔTEL DE LA PLACE DU LOUVRE ★★★ (59)
21, rue des Prêtres-St-Germain l'Auxerrois, 75001
Métro: Pont-Neuf, Louvre-Rivoli
20 rooms, all with shower or bath and toilet

The name of the hotel gives you a hint. From the front door, the Louvre is only a five-minute stroll, the quais along the Seine a block away, and all the Left Bank has to offer is just a few minutes across the Pont Neuf to St-Michel. The hotel is imaginatively done from start to finish. Portions of the original stone walls are artistically exposed to the dramatically modern entry. Murals on curving walls lead to a tented sitting area with a purple chamois wall covering highlighted by black and tangerine leather and chrome furniture. A multicolored curtain hangs above the front window, which faces the St-Germain-l'Auxerrois Church across the street.

All of the rooms are named for famous artists whose work hangs in the Louvre. The brilliant pink, third-floor Picasso Room has a view of the church, marble-top bedside tables, a corner desk, mirrored wardrobes, and a wonderful upstairs bathroom with a skylight. If you check into the rather dull green-and-white Kandinsky double, you will have good luggage space and a salmon-colored tile bath with gray monogrammed towels and plenty of shelf space. The Robert Delaunay Room on the second floor has a good view of the church and the side of the Louvre.

There are two rooms I would avoid. The Francis Picaba is a two-room suite that has a sleeping loft and a bathroom ceiling so low over the tub-shower combination that anyone over five feet could not stand upright. Same for the Jackson Pollack—the shower is comfortable for short people only.

Breakfast is served in the original fourteenth-century stone-walled *cave* in the basement.

This hotel is under the same management and ownership as the Hôtels Brighton (page 71), Mansart (page 77), Parc Saint-Séverin (page 124), and d'Orsay (page 179).

TEL 01-42-33-78-68 **FAX** 01-42-33-09-95 **EMAIL** hpl@espritfrance.com
INTERNET www.esprit-de-france.com

FACILITIES & SERVICES Air-conditioning, bar, direct-dial phone, elevator, hair dryer, minibar, TV with international reception, room safe (no charge), WiFi

RATES Single 103–137€, double 137–163€, triple 172€; *taxe de séjour* included **CREDIT CARDS** AE, DC, MC, V

BREAKFAST Continental 12€ per person

HÔTEL DU CYGNE ★★ (47)
3, rue du Cygne, 75001
Métro: Étienne-Marcel; RER Châtelet–Les Halles
20 rooms, 18 with shower or bath and toilet

Reliable two-star hotels in this corner of Les Halles are very scarce, so I was happy to find the Hôtel du Cygne, located in a seventeenth-century building on a short, pedestrian-only street leading off the busy boulevard de Sebastopol. The owners, Mme. Elaine Gouge and her daughter, Isabelle, have taken this old hotel and made it livable and appealing on almost every count. The pretty tiled entryway leads to a homey sitting room with a yellow leather armchair and comfortable sofa. The charming, partially skylighted breakfast area has cushioned chairs, a collection of old Paris photos, a potted palm, and a swan *(cygne) jardinière*—the symbol of the hotel. The century-old mountain floor clock from the Savoie region is just for looks because guests objected to its chimes ringing in the middle of the night.

New carpeting in the halls and rooms plus some smart new baths have improved the overall appeal. The rooms, which subscribe to the Laura Ashley style of decorating, are excellent value for the price. In fact, some three-star hotel rooms can't begin to compare with the twenty here, almost all of which have a desk and chair, luggage rack, bedside tables with good lights, and decent towels in the bathrooms. Mme. Gouge told me she couldn't find curtains or bed skirts to go with the pretty bed quilts so she bought the material and made them herself. The twin-bed nests have bathtubs; the single- and double-bed rooms come with showers. Room 135, with a bright Provençal theme and original beams, is the biggest. The divided room has the beds on a platform mezzanine, and below, a sitting area with a sofa bed, table, and chairs. If you are willing to walk up one flight of stairs (from the third to the fourth floor), you can enjoy the quiet, quaint, and romantic No. 41, which is under the eaves, with windows along the mansard roof; it has a shower and a marble desk. Single travelers should book Room 11, which faces out and has a wicker armchair, or Nos. 21 or 31, which have new bathrooms, but avoid Room 38, which has no closet or drawer space, and No. 18 unless you are willing to walk up a flight of stairs to the shower and toilet.

TEL 01-42-60-14-16 **FAX** 01-42-21-37-02 **EMAIL** contact@hotelducygne.fr
INTERNET www.hotelducygne.fr

FACILITIES & SERVICES Direct-dial phone, no elevator (4 floors), hair dryer, TV with international reception, room safe (no charge)

RATES Single 60€ without bath, 95€ with bath; double 105–13€; triple
155€; *taxe de séjour* included **CREDIT CARDS** MC, V
BREAKFAST Continental 8€ per person

HÔTEL HENRI IV (NO STARS, ¢, 64)
25, place Dauphine, 75001
Métro: Pont-Neuf
20 rooms, 2 with shower and toilet, 2 with shower only

Four hundred years ago, King Henri IV's printing presses occupied this narrow townhouse on Île de la Cité's pretty place Dauphine.
Today, it is a twenty-room hotel that has been touted in every budget
guide to Paris, becoming a mecca for the seriously thrifty and anyone else eager for a romantically threadbare hotel adventure in Paris.
Despite improvements, such as hall linoleum, new wallpaper in a few
rooms, and showers installed in four rooms, all guests must continue
to be philosophical about both the accommodations and the plumbing. Remember, you cannot pour a quart into a pint . . . which here
means that short of gutting the building and starting over, not much
can be done to modernize or even upgrade. The rooms, which passed
their prime decades ago, could be a shock to some: the furniture looks
like leftovers from a garage sale, the lighting is dim, the mattresses
are spongy, most of the bedspreads have seen better days, and the
exposed pipes gurgle and sputter all day and all night. On the other
hand, it is so cheap, so perfectly located, and so quiet, and the owners
(M. and Mme. Balitrand and their son, François, who now runs it) are
so friendly that thousands of young-at-heart guests continue to flock
here from around the world and reserve many months in advance.

TEL 01-43-54-44-53
FACILITIES & SERVICES None. No elevator (4 floors); office open for
reservations 8 A.M.–7 P.M.
RATES Single 28–29€, double 34–58€, triple 55–73€, shower 3€; *taxe de
séjour* 0.30€ per person, per day **CREDIT CARDS** None, cash only
BREAKFAST Included (hot beverage, bread and butter)

HÔTEL LE RELAIS SAINT-HONORÉ ★★★ ($, 23)
308, rue Saint-Honoré, at corner of rue de la Sourdiére, 75001
Métro: Tuileries
15 rooms, all with shower or bath and toilet

The charming seventeenth-century building is in the heart of one
of the most luxurious shopping quarters in Paris. In addition to the
fabulous boutiques, the Tuileries Gardens, the Louvre, and the famed
Hemingway bar at the Ritz Hôtel on the elegant place Vendôme are
within a few minutes' walk from the hotel door. Around the corner is
the Marché Saint-Honoré, filled with restaurants and bars and hosting
a colorful outdoor market twice a week.

Large streetside picture windows in the lobby invite guests to sit
for a while and enjoy the passing parade of fashionistas and fashion
victims. Upstairs, huge ceiling beams painted in bright yellow,

raspberry orange sorbet, or vibrant blue set the color cues for the fifteen individually decorated rooms, which are fanciful harmonies of fabrics, furnishings, and artwork. One of my favorites is No. 502, a grand two-room suite done in blue and white with eight framed photos of Chinese porcelain. Three small windows let in light, yet assure quiet. Number 1, in hot coral, has a small walk-in closet and a good bathroom with a tub-and-shower combination. Breakfast is served in your room. You select the type: either the "classic" with assorted French pastries or the nutritrionally more correct "vitality" with cereal, yogurt, and fruit. With both, fresh orange juice and unlimited hot drinks are included.

Also under the same ownership is Le Relais Montmartre (see page 277).

TEL 01-42-96-06-06 **FAX** 01-42-96-17-50 **EMAIL** relaissainthonore@wanadoo.fr
INTERNET www.relaissainthonore.com
FACILITIES & SERVICES Air-conditioning, direct-dial phone, elevator, hair
dryer, laundry services, magnifying mirrors, minibar, room safe (no
charge), TV with international reception, free broadband Internet
RATES Single or double 196€, junior suite 290€, suite 330€; *taxe de séjour*
included **CREDIT CARDS** AE, DC, MC, V
BREAKFAST "Classic" or "vitality" served in room 12€ per person

HÔTEL LOUVRE SAINTE-ANNE ★★★ (26)
32, rue Ste-Anne, 75001
Métro: Palais Royal–Musée du Louvre, Pyramides
20 rooms, all with bath or shower and toilet

The owners, Claude and Bernie Terrazzoni, do a great job in maintaining their hotel close to the Louvre. Each air-conditioned room is color-coordinated in soft peach with blue or green accents, and the marble bathrooms have towel warmers and stretch tubs. All the spotless rooms can be recommended, but if it is a view of Sacré Coeur you are after or a balcony, those rooms are on the fifth floor. On the ground level there is a handicapped room with a proper shower and seat, plus plenty of maneuvering room for a wheelchair. In the morning, a hot buffet breakfast, including bacon and eggs with potatoes, is served in a stone room brightened by yellow-and-blue tablecloths. The reception staff, headed by Mounira, complements the excellent quality of the hotel in every way.

TEL 01-40-20-02-35 **FAX** 01-40-15-91-13 **EMAIL** contact@louvre-ste-anne.fr
INTERNET www.louvre-ste-anne.fr
FACILITIES & SERVICES Air-conditioning, direct-dial phone, elevator (to
most floors), hair dryer, 1 handicapped-accessible room, laundry service,
minibar, TV with international reception, room safe (no charge), free WiFi
RATES Single 107–122€, double 128–138€, superior 138–184€; *taxe de
séjour* included **CREDIT CARDS** AE, DC, MC, V
BREAKFAST Buffet 10€ per person

HÔTEL MANSART ★★★ ($, 11)
5, rue des Capucines, at place Vendôme, 75001
Métro: Opéra, Madeleine
57 rooms, all with shower or bath and toilet

If everything at the Ritz appeals except for the price (upward of $750 per night for a double, breakfast extra), consider staying at Hôtel Mansart, named after the architect of Louis XIV, who designed the place Vendôme, Versailles, and the dome on Les Invalides. The hotel used to be the Hôtel Calais, a rambling wreck totally devoid of style, with labyrinth halls, creaking floors, and turn-of-the-century plumbing. Not anymore! A stunning transformation has been achieved.

By not making any structural changes other than adding spectacular new bathrooms, the owners kept the spirit of the building intact. You will still find long hallways, high ceilings, marble fireplaces, stained-glass windows, well-loved period furnishings, and in some cases, slightly sloping floors. No two rooms are alike, but all reflect the same high level of style and good taste. Some favorites include No. 603, a top-floor choice done in blue and gray with a mirrored armoire, marble bedside tables, and a tile bathroom with double sinks. Room 400 is a large, twin-bedded room with good work space, plenty of light, and a bathroom large enough to accommodate a long tub and a marble-top table. Number 505, a sunny, rear room with twin beds, has a separate stall shower in addition to a stretch-out bathtub that is perfect for luxurious bubble baths. Rooms 506, 507, and 508 have their own terraces. Number 502, facing the street, is enormous, with a fireplace, built-in armoire, large round table with chairs, and a writing desk. A showcase room is No. 204, overlooking place Vendôme. This room is done in royal blue with gold carpeting, and its high ceilings, collectable furniture, and a lovely oil painting over the marble dresser are reminiscent of hotels on the Grand Tour of Europe that our grandmothers stayed in decades ago. A similar room is No. 203, with a corner view of place Vendôme. It has a half-canopied queen-size bed, a round table that could easily seat six, and a large leather-top desk. You must go up a few steps to the bathroom and dressing area, but the bathroom, lighted by three windows, has a separate stall shower and a long tub. Other rooms with place Vendôme views are Nos. 404 and 406.

The stark simplicity of the lobby is created by an interesting mixture of geometric wall designs based on the gardens at Versailles. Antique chairs and love seats and tiny glowing ceiling lights complete the room by elegantly mixing in a touch of the contemporary with the past. A Continental breakfast is served in a formal room with arched stained-glass windows, suede-cloth-covered chairs, and tables draped with damask cloths. Everything works together throughout this impressive hotel and adds up to a smart address in a fine location.

Four other hotels are in the same Esprit de France group: Hôtels Brighton (page 71), de la Place du Louvre (page 73), Parc Saint-Séverin (page 124), and d'Orsay (page 179).

TEL 01-42-61-50-28 **FAX** 01-49-27-97-44 **EMAIL** mansart@espritfrance.com
  INTERNET www.esprit-de-france.com
FACILTIES & SERVICES Air-conditioning, bar, direct-dial phone, elevator (to
  most floors), hair dryer, minibar, TV with international reception, room
  safe (no charge), WiFi
RATES 1–2 people 145–315€; children under 12 free; extra bed 18€; *taxe de
  séjour* included **CREDIT CARDS** AE, DC, MC, V
BREAKFAST Buffet or Continental in room 15€ per person

HÔTEL MOLIÈRE ★★★ (27)
21, rue Molière, 75001
Métro: Palais Royal–Musée du Louvre, Pyramides
32 rooms, all with shower or bath and toilet

The Molière is a sedate, midcity choice. The faux-finished, pillared
lobby boasts a stylish Art Nouveau beaded lamp on the reception desk
and groupings of tan club chairs. Toward the back is another sitting
area with a low sofa padded with double cushions and a table filled
with an assortment of magazines and daily newspapers. Just beyond
is the breakfast room, with glass-top tables and gold metal–tipped
chairs, overlooking a small interior garden. The mirrored elevator has
a bust of Molière and a trompe l'oeil painting of his books.

The rooms, which are above average in size and layout, are tastefully done in a rather formal French style. The amount of living
space is exceptional; the views, even along the back, are pleasant;
and the location puts guests within walking distance of many of the
tourist "musts" of Paris. If you are looking for space, book No. 56, a
three-room suite with two bedrooms and a sitting room done in soft
mauve. Generally speaking, it is in good condition, but hopefully
the comfortable sofa will be recovered and the desk sent to the refin-
isher before you check in. The double bedroom has a brass bed with
matching dressing table, marble bedside tables, a walk-in closet with
wide shelves and double hanging space, and a tango-size bathroom.
Finally, there is a small single bedroom that would be perfect for a
child. Similar in size and layout is No. 67, on the top floor with views
of surrounding rooftops. Less grand, but no less comfortable, is No.
41, a double with a new bathroom that has a magnifying mirror, large
tub, and sink space. The bedroom, with a brass bed and a mirrored
armoire, has good living space. Room 42, also with a new bathroom,
is another good choice if you want twin beds. Number 43 is a pleasant
single with a large working desk and a stall shower.

TEL 01-42-96-22-01 **FAX** 01-42-60-48-68 **EMAIL** info@hotel-molière.fr
  INTERNET www.hotel-molière.fr
FACILITIES & SERVICES Air-conditioning, bar, direct-dial phone, elevator, hair
  dryer, laundry service, minibar, TV with international reception, room safe
  (no charge), WiFi
RATES Single 148–155€, double 155–175€, triple 190€, suite 275€; extra
  bed 22€; *taxe de séjour* included **CREDIT CARDS** AE, DC, MC, V
BREAKFAST Buffet 12€ per person

HÔTEL THÉRÈSE ★★★ (25)
5–7, rue Thérèse, 75001
Métro: Palais Royal–Musée du Louvre
43 rooms, all with shower or bath and toilet

Hôtel Thérèse occupies a perfect location in the heart of the elegant Right Bank, close to the Louvre, Palais Royal, and shopping along rue St. Honoré. When Sylvie de Lattre (who also owns Hôtel Verneuil, see page 190) purchased it, she spent months renovating it from top to bottom in her unique and graceful style. Now gleaming from her remarkable effort, it is a success by all accounts and provides a sleek, contemporary address for the discerning traveler. The small downstairs bar and library is furnished in brown leather, dark burgundy colors accented with a flourish of eggplant, indirect lighting, and potted orchids. The sitting room, imaginatively painted in deep mustard, has comfortable armchairs and displays pieces from the owner's interesting art collection. The stairway to the sixth floor is used as exhibition space for her collection of 1890 photographs of Roman statues. The breakfast room serves as the focal point for her collection of Chinese tea caddies. Seating is on brown wicker chairs with white cushions secured with a big bow in back. All of the rooms are exceptional and again demonstrate her remarkable use of colors: plum with yellow, soft green with vanilla and chocolate. The deluxe and superior rooms are naturally the most popular because they offer more living space, either twins or king-size beds, spacious marble bathrooms with separate stall showers, and often a window. Lower rates in August and frequent promotions on the Website keep the demand for Hôtel Thérèse high.

TEL 01-42-96-10-01 **FAX** 01-42-96-15-22 **EMAIL** info@hoteltherese.com
INTERNET www.hoteltherese.com
FACILITIES & SERVICES Air-conditioning, bar, conference room, direct-dial phone, elevator (to most floors), hair dryer, Internet in lobby, laundry service, robes in deluxe rooms, TV with international reception, room safe (no charge), WiFi
RATES All rooms for 1 or 2 people: classic 136€, superior 171€, deluxe 220€, club room 266€; *taxe de séjour* included **CREDIT CARDS** AE, DC, MC, V
BREAKFAST Buffet 12€ per person

Second Arrondissement

RIGHT BANK
Bourse
passages
place des Victoires
rue Montorgueil shopping
  street

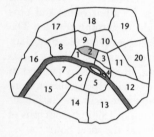

The second arrondissement is known as the area of finance (around the stock exchange, or Bourse) and the rag trade (Sentier), between boulevard Sepastapol and boulevard de Bonne Nouvelle. It makes up for its small size with the beautiful Victorian shopping *passages* and the boutiques around place des Victoires. The second is within walking distance to the Marais, Centre Georges Pompidou (Beaubourg), the Palais Royal, and the Louvre Museum. The southern half around rue Montorgueil has some of the best food markets and shops in Paris. The seedy northern section around rue d'Aboukir should definitely be avoided, and so should most of rue St-Denis, home of Paris hookers and other assorted netherworld characters.

HOTELS IN THE SECOND ARRONDISSEMENT
(see map page 66)

($) indicates a Big Splurge; (¢) indicates a Cheap Sleep

BEST WESTERN PREMIER HORSET OPÉRA ★★★★ ($, 8)
18, rue d'Antin, 75002
Métro: Opéra
54 rooms, all with shower or bath and toilet

The Best Western Premier Horset Opéra offers its guests unrestrained luxury in fifty-four individually decorated rooms in the central business district of Paris. No creature comfort has been spared, from 24-hour room service and light meals served in the attractive bar to pay-for-view television and high-speed Internet throughout. If you did not bring your own laptop . . . no problem. The hotel has one to loan you. The rooms vary in size, but none are less than 20 meters square, which is a rarity anywhere in Paris. Beautiful hand-embroidered wall hangings serve as backdrops behind the bed and over the long, comfortable working desk, and these set the vibrant color tones used in the coordinating Pierre Frey fabrics. The marble bathrooms are generous, with plenty of sink space and excellent showers. On each floor are two connecting rooms, two that face a quiet courtyard and seven overlooking a small side street.

Also under the same ownership are Au Manoir Saint-Germain-des-Prés (page 138) and Hôtel Left Bank St-Germain (page 152).

TEL 01-44-71-87-00; toll-free in Canada and the U.S. 800-528-1234 (Best Western) **FAX** 01-42-66-55-54 **EMAIL** reservation@hotelhorsetopera.com
   INTERNET www.horsetopera.com
FACILITIES & SERVICES Air-conditioning, bar serving light meals, direct-dial phone, elevator, hair dryer and magnifying mirror, laundry service, minibar, room safe (no charge), 24-hour room service, TV with international reception and pay-for-view, WiFi and computer to loan, 12 nonsmoking rooms
RATES Single 245€, double 275€; extra bed (child only) 23€; *taxe de séjour* 1.50€ per person, per day; see Website for special offers
   CREDIT CARDS AE, DC, MC, V
BREAKFAST Buffet or Continental served in room included

HÔTEL DE NOAILLES ★★★★ ($, 5)
9, rue de la Michodière, 75002
Métro: Opéra, Quatre-Septembre
59 rooms, all with shower or bath and toilet

If you are allergic to gilt and cherubs, you will appreciate this postmodern hotel, which owner Martine Falck has turned into a smart, Zen-inspired site with different bold color schemes of gray, black, chocolate brown, and midnight blue distinguishing each floor. To make sure that all aspects of the hotel were in their proper alignment in the universe, three different artists and mediums were consulted, along with a Feng Shui expert. The pleasing results are evident to anyone. The street entrance leads into a wide-spaced reception room with designer chairs and tables overlooking a full bar (with a 6:30–9 P.M. happy hour nightly and live music on Thursday evenings) and an atrium garden. To one side is a sitting room with a fireplace, changing art exhibitions, and a massive marble table with a dramatic floral display. This is flanked by two wrought-iron sculptures that represent good luck.

All 59 rooms and suites can be recommended, from the twelve rooms that open onto their own garden to the smart suites to the smallest room. Rooms have all the twenty-first-century perks: halogen lighting, built-ins, WiFi Internet access, adequate desk space, fluffy duvets, smart bathrooms, room service, and a Shiatsu masseuse on call. Room 305, with a wooden backdrop behind the bed and a state-of-the-art bathroom, is let as a standard double. It has an inside view but is light and very pleasant. For more space, reserve No. 210, a superior double. It doesn't have as much seating space as some others, but it has a large bathroom with double sinks and a separate enclosed toilet. I like No. 307, a junior suite with a bright red wool cocoon chair that envelopes you and lets you momentarily sink into your own world, far away from the stress and strife of daily life. There is a king-size bed, two televisions, and a view overlooking the hotel atrium garden. The Phillipe Stark–designed bathroom has a floating square sink, separate shower, and stretch tub.

The fifth and sixth floors are outfitted with brown leather–lined walls. The rooms are large on these floors and have a distinctly masculine feel. Most have light and feature sleek bathrooms with Japanese-style opaque sliding doors dividing the bathroom and bedroom. Added bonuses for many are the free hotel sauna, usage of L'Usine (the fitness center across the street) for a moderate charge, the exclusive nonsmoking rooms in three garden rooms and the entire fifth and sixth floors, and the attractive promotional rates on the weekend and in low season.

TEL 01-47-42-92-90; toll-free in the U.S. 800-344-1212 (Golden Tulip Hotels) **FAX** 01-49-24-92-71 **EMAIL** goldentulip.denoailles@wanadoo.fr **INTERNET** www.paris-hotel-noailles.com

FACILITIES & SERVICES Air-conditioning, bar, conference room, direct-dial phone, elevator, use of fitness across from the hotel, free hotel sauna, hair dryer, laundry service, minibar, Shiatsu masseuse on call, TV with international reception, room service, room safe (no charge), two floors of nonsmoking rooms, WiFi

RATES Single 200€, double standard room 215€, double superior room 255€, junior suites 410€; *taxe de séjour* included **CREDIT CARDS** AE, DC, MC, V

BREAKFAST Buffet 15€ per person

HÔTEL VICTOIRES OPÉRA ★★★★ ($, 35)
56, rue Montorgueil, 75002
Métro: Etienne-Marcel, Sentier; RER Châtelet–Les Halles
24 rooms, all with shower or bath and toilet

Located on the lively rue Montorgueil market street, the Hôtel Victoires Opéra draws an artful mix of fashionistas and stylish minimalists who appreciate the dynamite location and personalized service offered each guest. Admittedly, rooms are not large, but they are crafted with built-ins and all the amenities one would expect in a four-star hotel in central Paris. Brown striped and soft gray linen walls contrast smartly with soft yellow or aubergine accent colors, all of which sets off the owner's collection of Modigliani black-and-white drawings that grace each room. Marble tiled baths offer Roger & Gallet toiletries, heavy towels, and plenty of light. A pumpkin-colored hallway leads to the arched breakfast room decorated in purple-covered armchairs. Excellent promotional rates throughout the year make this hotel even more appealing to its many repeat guests.

TEL 01-42-36-41-08 **FAX** 01-45-08-08-79 **EMAIL** hotel@VictoiresOpera.com
   INTERNET www.hotelVictoiresOpera.com
FACILITIES & SERVICES Air-conditioning, direct-dial phone, elevator, hair dryer, laundry service, minibar, room safe (no charge), TV with international reception, WiFi
RATES 1–2 people: standard 214€, superior 244€, deluxe 275€, junior suite 335€; *taxe de séjour* 1.20€ per person, per day **CREDIT CARDS** AE, DC, MC, V
BREAKFAST Buffet 12€, Continental in room 18€, per person

HÔTEL VIVIENNE ★★ (¢, 2)
40, rue Vivienne, 75002
Métro: Richelieu-Drouot, Grands Boulevards
45 rooms, 30 with toilet, all with shower or bath

The picture on the reception desk was taken at the hotel in 1917. The little girl in the photo was born in this hotel, which her parents owned along with a restaurant next door. The present owner, Claudine Haycraft, bought the hotel from the family over thirty years ago. Since then, she has slowly redone it, making it a popular budget destination in this part of Paris. She recently bought the noisy bar next door and was able to expand the reception and sitting areas and add a modern breakfast room with an interesting collection of black-and-white Paris photos. The friendly desk staff is aided by Leika, the house dog, and Romeo, a cat everyone loves. The plain rooms are kept spotlessly clean by a team of career housekeepers. All twin-bedded rooms have been redone; bathrooms are functional, and ten rooms have the added plus of balconies. Best rooms in the house? I think No. 14, which faces the street and is large enough to feel comfortable in for more than overnight; No. 6, a double on the street with two windows opening onto a balcony; and No. 34, in bright Provençal gold and blue with a balcony, a tiled bathroom, and plenty of light.

TEL 01-42-33-13-26 **FAX** 01-40-41-98-19 **EMAIL** paris@hotel-vivienne.com
FACILITIES & SERVICES Direct-dial phone, elevator (to most floors), hair dryer, TV with international reception, office safe (no charge), 10 nonsmoking rooms, free WiFi in lobby
RATES Single 57–87€, double 72–107€; extra bed is 30 percent of room rate; children under 10 are free; *taxe de séjour* 0.78€ per person, per day
   CREDIT CARDS MC, V
BREAKFAST Continental 8€ per person

TIQUETONNE HÔTEL ★ (¢, 39)
6, rue Tiquetonne, 75002
Métro: Étienne-Marcel; RER Châtelet–Les Halles
46 rooms, 30 with shower and toilet, no bathtubs

Anyone looking for an old-fashioned, budget-minded family hotel that offers basic, clean rooms in central Paris will hit pay dirt here. The vintage hotel has been run for more than half a century by Mme. Sirvain, who is accompanied by her niece Marie-Jo, and the hotel dog, Verdi, a strapping German shepherd who surveys the scene from a command post in the lobby.

All the doubles have showers, but only some singles do, and with limited success. For example, in No. 34, you enter the pink-papered room through the bathroom, red curtains hang at the windows, and furniture consists of a bed and a hard chair . . . but it is clean and sunny. There is nothing wrong with No. 20, provided you can live in a room with an orange chenille bedspread, red curtains, and floral wallpaper in peach, pink, and green. Furnishings include a small table with a laminated top displaying sailing ships and two hard chairs. The bathroom has a shelf over the sink and a curtain shielding the enclosed tile shower. Number 30, an inside double with a shower and toilet, demonstrates an attempt to color coordinate the aqua blue chenille spread with the blue trim on the curtains.

Rock-bottom prices insure popularity in a part of Paris that is ani-mated, active, and very much alive almost around the clock. So book early, but don't plan on a room in August, often a week in spring, and during the week between Christmas and New Year's; at these times, the family shuts the hotel and goes on their own vacations.

TEL 01-42-36-94-58 **FAX** 01-42-36-02-94
FACILITIES & SERVICES Elevator, reception open 7:30 A.M.–midnight
RATES Single 30–50€, double 50€ (double beds only); hall shower 6€; *taxe de séjour* included **CREDIT CARDS** MC, V
BREAKFAST Continental 6€ per person (no croissants)

Third Arrondissement

This area includes the northern parts of the revitalized Marais, a thirteenth-century swampland that later became the residential suburb of the French nobility. Later still it fell from favor, and until it was rescued by Minister of Culture André Malraux in the 1960s, it was the worst slum in Paris. The magnificent seventeenth-century *hôtels particulieres* (private mansions) have been turned into museums, the most famous of which is the Musée National Picasso/Hôtel de Salé. The Musée des Arts et Métiers, occupying the medieval abbey of St-Martin-des-Champs, has a fascinating collection of industrial and scientific objects displayed on the abbey's altars, apses, and choir stalls. The Musée Cognacq-Jay showcases the mostly French Rococo collection of Ernest Cognacq, founder of La Samaritaine department store, and his wife, Louise Jay.

RIGHT BANK
French National Archives
Marais
Musée Carnavalet (City of Paris Museum)
Musée Cognacq-Jay
Musée des Arts et Métiers
Musée National Picasso (Hôtel Salé)

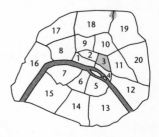

HOTELS IN THE THIRD ARRONDISSEMENT

Austin's Arts et Métiers Hôtel ★★★	**88**
Golden Tulip Little Palace ★★★	**88**
Hôtel du Petit Moulin ★★★★ ($)	**89**
Hôtel du Séjour (NO STARS, ¢)	**90**
Paris-France Hôtel ★★	**91**

OTHER OPTIONS
Apartment Rental Agencies
Kudeta Home	**290**

($) indicates a Big Splurge; (¢) indicates a Cheap Sleep

Third and Fourth Arrondissements

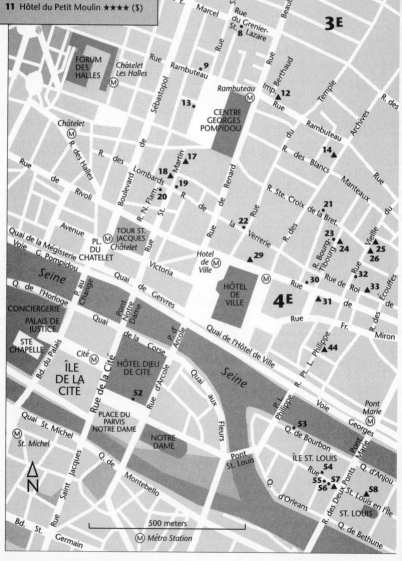

500 meters

Ⓜ *Métro Station*

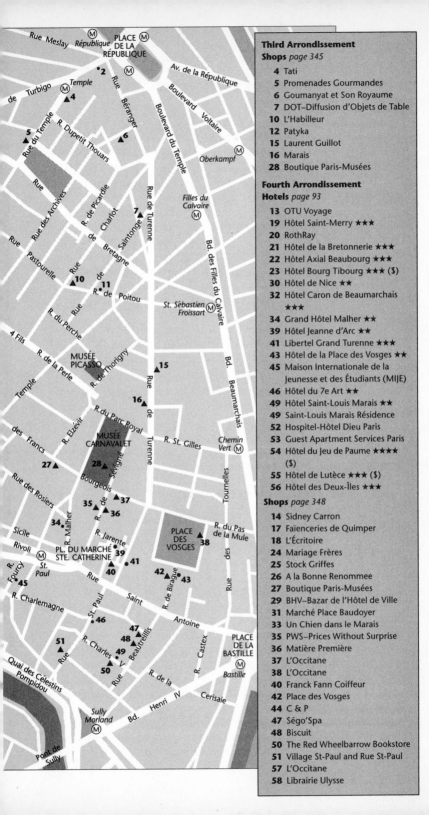

AUSTIN'S ARTS ET MÉTIERS HÔTEL ★★★ (3)
6, rue Montgolfier, 75003
Métro: Arts et Métiers
29 rooms, all with shower or bath and toilet

For a three-star family-owned hotel with more than its share of charm and facilities, this place is great. If it were in a more centrally located, touristy area, it would cost half again as much. However, this area is rapidly becoming gentrified and is considered very "in" with many Parisians. A spacious living room done in warm gold and deep brown is a welcoming beginning. The twenty-nine soundproofed rooms have every comfort. Faux finishing and fabric-covered walls in the bedrooms form the background for the cream-colored furnishings, with either red or yellow and blue coordinated spreads and curtains. Bathrooms are nice, especially those with a glass-enclosed shower stall. The best rooms face front; those along the back might be a bit calmer, but the tradeoff is a view of peeling buildings and metal grates.

Also under the same ownership is Austin's Saint-Lazare, a three-star hotel on rue d'Amsterdam, across from Gare St-Lazare. While the hotel is nice, the neighborhood is not recommended, unless you want to be in the shadow of one of Paris's largest rail stations.

TEL 01-42-77-17-61 **FAX** 01-42-77-55-43 **EMAIL** austins.amhotel@wanadoo.fr
   INTERNET www.austinshotel.com
FACILITIES & SERVICES Direct-dial phone, elevator, hair dryer, TV with
   international reception, office safe (no charge), free WiFi
RATES Single 101€, double 140€; *taxe de séjour* included
   CREDIT CARDS AE, DC, MC, V
BREAKFAST Buffet downstairs or Continental in room 7€ per person

GOLDEN TULIP LITTLE PALACE ★★★ (1)
4, rue Salomon de Caus, 75003
Métro: Réaumur-Sébastopol, Strasbourg–St-Denis
53 rooms, all with shower or bath and toilet

Overlooking the green Arts et Métiers Square, this hotel has an impressive facade with carved stones, scrolled balconies, and marble columns that is reminiscent of the roaring twenties. Inside, fabric-covered walls and drapes frame the entrance to the restaurant. The mosaic-tile bar, famous for its original stained-glass windows and floral-patterned ceiling, overlooks a well-tended garden. The comfortable sitting room is furnished with back-to-back sofas and barrel armchairs. The fifty-three rooms have built-ins that allow for more space, and they are decorated in blends of pale lavender and rose and with artwork by Gustav Klimt. They have all the three-star necessities, including WiFi and bathrooms with toiletries, heated towel racks, and a lighted magnifying mirror, and they are kept scrupulously clean by head housekeeper Maria and her team. Best bets are those on the top floor with a balcony, especially No. 64, done in purple with burgandy accents. Number 65 has no view, but is quiet and has the illusion of more space thanks to a hallway leading into the room. Number 74, a single, boasts A+ balcony views of the Arts et Métiers, Eiffel Tower, and Montparnasse. The hotel restaurant serves lunch from Monday to Friday, and dinner Monday to Thursday, but consider eating here only if you are desperate.

TEL 01-42-72-08-15; toll-free in U.S. 800-344-1212 (Golden Tulip Hotels)
  FAX 01-42-72-45-81   **EMAIL** info@littlepalacehotel.com
  INTERNET www.littlepalacehotel.com
FACILITIES & SERVICES Air-conditioning, bar, direct-dial phone, elevator, hair dryer, laundry service, minibar, TV with international reception and pay-per-view movies, room safe (no charge), WiFi
RATES Single 142€, double 158€, suite (1–3 persons) 230€; *taxe de séjour* included **CREDIT CARDS** AE, DC, MC, V
BREAKFAST Buffet 12€ per person

HÔTEL DU PETIT MOULIN ★★★★ ($, 11)
29/31, rue de Poitou, 75003
Métro: St-Sébastien Froissart
17 rooms, all with shower or bath and toilet

The Hôtel du Petit Moulin is the first Parisian hotel designed by a famous couturier, and from its opening in 2005, it has had an enormous impact and become an unqualified success. When Nadia Murano and Denis Nourry asked Christian Lacroix to collaborate with them on their two-year hotel project, he readily accepted their proposal, stating that he had now rediscovered his childhood dream of designing a personal and intimate hotel in the "colors of the times, putting ambiences together so different from the prevailing look-a-like style of the classic hotel chains."

Of his creation, M. Lacroix says, "It is like *couture,* where the harmony is created from a puzzle of inspirations, where the feeling of the moment is nourished with elements of the past, where modernity lives in the tradition of the present."

The hotel is made up of two buildings, located on the eclectic, trendy edge of the Marais. Not long ago, one of the buildings was a bakery that dated from Henri IV and was considered the oldest in Paris. Local legend also has it that Victor Hugo bought his daily bread here. The frontage is now listed as part of the French heritage by the Historic Monuments. The original, Venetian-style glass ceiling of the bakery has been restored. Its soft almond green is highlighted on the reception desk, and its rich wine colors are carried out on heavy taffeta drapes. Optical black-and-white polka-dot carpeting leads guests through the lawn green corridors to black lacquered doors with M. Lacroix's signature room numbers in shiny brass.

The mazelike design of the rooms sets a quirky, individual mood. Each one is different, decorated in relation to its orientation, the height of its ceiling, its view, and its location. Three of them (Nos. 202, 204, and 205) have framed drawings of Lacroix's sketchings. Throughout, beams mix with pebbled cement surroundings, boldly colored computer-composed plasticized wall coverings compete with gaudy fabrics and leather, floors range from wood to tile to carpet, and the meticulous coordination of elements extends even to the light switches and the color of the pen you use to fill out your room service order. The unique upholstered chairs—over sixty in all—mix brocade, velvet, fake fur, and bright modern graphics. The exceptionally comfortable beds are covered in thick, white duvets with a colorful throw at the foot of each one. Slate bathrooms contain state-of-the-art fixtures. The elevator is lined with collages of antique engravings, and the bar resembles a fanciful street café, with a zinc bar, traditional bistro tables, and seating in shades of bright yellow and pink. In other words, the entire hotel is a stunning visual cornucopia typical of Christian Lacroix.

TEL 01-42-74-10-10 **FAX** 01-42-74-10-97 **EMAIL** contact@hoteldupetit moulin.com **INTERNET** www.hoteldupetitmoulin.com

FACILITIES & SERVICES Air-conditioning, bar, bathrobes and slippers, direct-dial phone, elevator, hair dryer, laundry services, minibar, room safe (no charge), 24-hour room service, TV with international reception, WiFi and laptop to loan

RATES Comfort 180€, superior 250€, deluxe 350€, junior suite 280€; extra bed 40€; *taxe de séjour* included; lower rates August and sometimes Internet promotions **CREDIT CARDS** AE, DC, MC, V

BREAKFAST Continental 15€ per person

HÔTEL DU SÉJOUR (NO STARS, ¢, 8)
36, rue du Grenier-St-Lazare, 75003
Métro: Rambuteau, Étienne-Marcel
20 rooms, 8 with shower and toilet, 4 with shower only

If the bottom line is saving money, then visitors who do not mind a theatrically run-down, five-story walk-up will definitely be interested in this clean Cheap Sleep for their Paris sojourn. The building has been a hotel for three hundred years and is, and probably always will be, a quantum leap from modern. You enter from the street and walk up steps with a black rubber strip anchoring the laminated woodlike covering. Jean and Maria, the owners for over ten years, speak enough "hotel English" for most American guests to get by, and they have been making improvements on a cautious basis, starting with new mattresses, hall toilets, and some paint. In the past year or so, they added several showers and double windows. Singles or pairs can snooze in No. 20, a top-floor perch with a sink. The floor is uneven, but there is plenty of light. Duos can go for Nos. 12 or 13; No. 12 has a bare floor. Room 3 is a sunny double facing out with only a sink. If there are two of you, and you each plan on bathing, definitely go for a room like No. 10 or 15, each of which has its own shower, toilet, and sink. Though showerless rooms are cheaper at first glance, once you add in the extra cost for the shared hall showers, you will end up spending more.

TEL & FAX 01-48-87-40-36
FACILITIES & SERVICES Some nonsmoking rooms

RATES Single 35€, double 45–58€; shower 4€ per person; *taxe de séjour*
   included **CREDIT CARDS** None, cash only
BREAKFAST Not served

PARIS-FRANCE HÔTEL ★★ (2)
72, rue de Turbigo, 75003
Métro: Temple, République
46 rooms, all with shower or bath and toilet

This hotel opened its doors in 1910 marking the end of the Belle
Epoque in Paris. All that remains today of its gilded past are the
original tiles on the main ground floor. As anyone on a budget knows,
trying to find a decent two-star hotel in Paris is no easy task, and now
more than ever, it requires leaving tourist central to find one. While
hardly in the thick of things, this neighborhood does have some appeal.
Thrifty shoppers will be happy to know there is a Monoprix and a
small branch of Tati just up the street. Also within walking distance
are the Musée des Arts et Métiers, two métro stops, and two excellent
bus lines (Nos. 80 and 84) for further excursions. The rooms have
that decor-by-Kmart look, televisions are pitched on the ceiling, the
chairs are hard, and management has not invested in shower curtains.
However, the rooms are clean, have enough space for you and some
luggage, and won't jar your senses with wild, mismatched colors and
patterns. Some rooms on the sixth through eighth floors have views of
the Church of Ste-Elisabeth across the street, but no matter your room,
you will hear her chimes. A Continental breakfast is served cafeteria-
style downstairs or in your room for the same price.

TEL 01-42-78-00-04 **FAX** 01-42-71-99-43 **EMAIL** parisfrancehotel@
   wanadoo.com **INTERNET** www.paris-france-hotel.com
FACILITIES & SERVICES Direct-dial phone, elevator (to most floors), hair dryer,
   TV with international reception, room safe (10€ per stay), Internet in
   lobby and WiFi throughout
RATES Single 72€, double 86–109€, triple 134€; extra bed 25€; *taxe de séjour*
   included **CREDIT CARDS** AE, MC, V
BREAKFAST Continental 6€ per person

Fourth Arrondissement

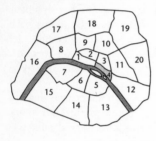

The fourth arrondissement stretches from the Marais through the ancient Jewish Quarter on the rue des Rosiers to the Île St-Louis in the middle of the Seine. It is an area perfectly suited to exploring on foot, lending itself to discovery at almost every turn. Its immense charm arises from a wonderful mixture of past and present. Notre Dame Cathedral, the geographical and spiritual heart of France, sits majestically on the Île de la Cité. In front of the cathedral is a bronze plaque (Kilometer Zéro) from which all distances in France are measured. Legend has it that if you stand on the plaque, make a wish, and twirl on your heel, your wish will come true.

Place des Vosges, with its historic pink-brick town houses set above wide arcade walkways, is the oldest square in Paris and one of the most beautiful. Victor Hugo resided here at No. 6. Not too far away is the architecturally controversial modern art museum, the Centre Georges Pompidou (also known as the Beaubourg), which logs more visitors each year than the Eiffel Tower.

L'Île St-Louis is one of the most desirable, and admittedly expensive, places to reside in Paris. The island is a capsule of all that is Parisian, with interesting shops, art galleries, boutiques, Baroque mansions, lines for the famous Berthillon ice cream, and lovely views along the romantic quais. To capture the enchantment of Paris, stay on Île St-Louis. But be forewarned: you may never want to leave! Many people like being on the island because they are only steps away from Notre Dame Cathedral, Ste-Chapelle, and the Conciergerie; within walking distance of the Latin Quarter, St-Germain-des-Prés, the Marais; and close to all the excitement and nightlife around the Bastille Opéra. Only a few feel isolated and frustrated by its narrow streets, weekend crowds, and lack of easy parking. Personally, I love it, but I am biased because this is where I lived the first year I spent in Paris.

HOTELS IN THE FOURTH ARRONDISSEMENT
(see map page 86)

OTHER OPTIONS
Apartment Rental Agencies

Student Accommodations

($) indicates a Big Splurge

GRAND HÔTEL MALHER ★★ (34)
5, rue Malher, 75004
Métro: St-Paul

31 rooms, all with shower or bath and toilet

When the good-value awards are presented, the Grand Hôtel Malher is always a winning two-star, thanks to its many three-star features and excellent three-generation, family-run management. The lobby is dominated by a lovely gold mirror and two square black leather chairs and matching sofa attractively arranged against a backdrop of centuries-old stone walls. Fresh flowers soften the setting. Breakfast is served in a seventeenth-century vaulted wine cellar with Paris regional maps and a hanging tapestry.

Rooms with twin beds face the street; those facing the interior court have double beds. Rooms 30, 32, and 62 are standard doubles on the back with space and good light in the bathroom. Other good choices are on the sunny top floors in rooms with balconies. Room 34, a pine furnished twin with a little balcony, faces front and has a big bathroom with two windows. Room 44, in orange, is similar, but the minibar takes up space where a chair should be. Number 64, a suite, is ideal for a couple with one child; it has a double and a twin bed and an extra-large sink area in the gray tiled bathroom. Pamela and Didier Fossiez are your gracious hosts, and your stay with them should be delightful. They also offer very good lower rates in the off-season.

TEL 01-42-72-60-92 **FAX** 01-42-72-25-37 **EMAIL** ghmalher@yahoo.fr
   INTERNET www.grandhotelmalher.com
FACILITES & SERVICES Direct-dial phone, elevator, fans, hair dryer, minibar, TV
   with international reception, office safe (no charge)
RATES Single 120€, double 130–140€, junior suite 185€; *taxe de séjour*
   included **CREDIT CARDS** AE, DC, MC, V
BREAKFAST Continental 8€ per person

HOSPITEL-HÔTEL DIEU PARIS (52)
1, place du Parvis Notre-Dame de Paris, 75004
Galerie B-2, 6ème étage
Métro: Cité; RER St-Michel Notre Dame
14 rooms, all with shower or bath and toilet

Wanted: A quiet, comfortable hotel room on the doorstep of Notre Dame Cathedral, only seconds away from all the fun and frolic going on around place St-Michel and the Left Bank. Impossible? *Mais non!* Not if you check into the Hospitel-Hôtel Dieu Paris, located within the walls of Paris's oldest and most prominent hospital: L'Hôpital Hôtel Dieu Paris. Originally opened to serve relatives of patients, the fourteen rooms in this historical monument are now open to anyone. Frankly, I had my doubts when I first heard about it—I could just imagine the depressing rooms with linoleum floors and institutional furnishings, all smelling like Lysol. How wrong I was. Actually, the hotel has a great deal going for it. In addition to the dynamite location, its contemporary rooms, done with Art Deco overtones and in vibrant primary colors, are blissfully quiet and several are exclusively non-smoking. The tiled baths are above average; it is, of course, absolutely spotless; and above all, the low prices are amazing for this expensive, touristy section of Paris. Reception is open from 7 A.M. to 10 P.M. daily, and room service for hot meals is available daily between 7 A.M. and 8 P.M. Because the hotel is situated on the sixth floor under a mansard roof, there are no real windows, only skylights—but they are ample and let in plenty of light and sunshine, and from the even-numbered rooms, you can see the tower of Notre Dame. The closet and drawer spaces are not geared to long stays, and you might see a few hospital patients in bathrobes en route to your elevator. Sometimes in the morning, hot water problems occur. When I asked how a hospital could possibly run out of hot water, I was told, "We are on the top floor. You have to expect these infrequent inconveniences." So, forewarned is forearmed for French logic, and if you can live with these possible downsides to this hotel, it is a real value.

NOTE: To locate the hotel within the hospital, enter directly through the door just beside the main door. The entrance is marked. The hotel is located on the sixth floor of Building 2 (look for Galerie B-2, *6ème étage*).

TEL 01-44-32-01-00 **FAX** 01-44-32-01-16 **EMAIL** hospitelhoteldieu@wanadoo.fr
   INTERNET www.hotel-hospitel.com
FACILITIES & SERVICES Direct-dial phone, elevator, hair dryer on request, two handicapped-accessible rooms, TV with international reception, room service, room safe (no charge), several nonsmoking rooms
RATES Single 95€, double 107€; extra bed 12€; *taxe de séjour* included
   CREDIT CARDS MC, V
BREAKFAST Continental 9.50€ per person

HÔTEL AXIAL BEAUBOURG ★★★ (22)
11, rue du Temple, 75004
Métro: Hôtel-de-Ville
39 rooms, all with shower or bath and toilet

Dark woods, liberal use of eggplant, plum, deep brown, and honey colors, and stylized floral arrangements set the minimalistic tone in Véronique Turmel's hotel. The breakfast room is an interesting blend of classic and modern, mixing fifteenth-century stone walls with brown linen stretch covers on armless chairs. Black doors with buffed silver handles lead to the subdued rooms. Number 62 on the top floor is one of the biggest standard rooms, with a large bed but only stools for seating. It has a street view and a compact sandy-gray marble and tile bath with a heated towel rack. Room 64 is a smaller version of No. 62, but it has a more interesting view of the top of the Hôtel de Ville and the BHV department store. If you can live with some street noise, No. 17, in eggplant tones and black furniture, has more space, a bit of character thanks to its beams, a writing desk and two chairs, and a bathroom with a long tub and decent counter space. Even the television has a bigger screen. Avoid No. 16, a tight fit for one person and an impossible squeeze for two because the room is big enough only for a double bed and two leather-covered stools—leaving no place for your luggage.

TEL 01-42-72-72-22 **FAX** 01-42-72-03-53 **EMAIL** info@axialbeaubourg.com
   INTERNET www.axialbeaubourg.com
FACILITIES & SERVICES Air-conditioning, direct-dial phone, elevator, hair dryer, laundry service, minibar, TV with international reception, room safe (no charge), free WiFi in lobby
RATES Single 115–133€, double 165–175€; *taxe de séjour* included
   CREDIT CARDS AE, DC, MC, V
BREAKFAST Buffet 12€ per person

HÔTEL BOURG TIBOURG ★★★ ($, 23)
19, rue du Bourg-Tibourg, 75004
Métro: Hôtel-de-Ville
30 rooms, all with shower, bath, and toilet

The Hôtel Bourg Tibourg, owned by the Costes family and designed by Jacques Garcia, is a testament to over-the-top opulence befitting a château, not a hotel with some rooms so small that tables and chairs are not viable options, and crawling over the bed to get from one side of the room to the other will become part of your daily aerobic workout. However, despite its lack of space, the hotel has a visually rich Moorish quality, and it certainly does not stint on rich fabrics, fringes, and frills. This is especially evident in the ground-floor sitting area, which incorporates a heavy tapestry-covered high-back settee, dark cocoa armchairs, and a massive wrought-iron chandelier hanging over thick hemp carpeting. An enviable framed collection of prints of early French fashions and tradespeople lines one wall. Tucked around the corner by the atrium garden is a fringed chaise lounge and floor lamp. The elevator hides behind a brass-studded suede-covered door.

As I've indicated, the rooms are all very small, and if you like the Ali Baba school of decorating, quite well done, especially No. 54, which is enveloped in velvet hanging behind and over the bed and on the closet doors. Double windows opening onto a tiny balcony slightly expand the sense of space. The bathroom includes a tub and the latest in free-standing sinks. Number 51, a mini-single, also has drapes that match the backdrop behind the bed and the covering of the narrow closet. There is no work space or chair, so when not in bed, you can relax in the stretch bathtub framed in mosaic tiles. Number 21 is a slightly larger single on the back facing a wall. It is a quiet, corner choice, with a small table and an extra chair. Breakfast is served on round tables in a small seventeenth-century stone cellar downstairs highlighted by a wrought-iron chandelier with massive jade green shades and twelve candles. In addition to the hotel's visual bang, it has a central Marais address and is popular with artists and style groupies eager to experience the luster of luxe.

TEL 01-42-78-47-39 **FAX** 01-40-29-07-00 **EMAIL** hotel@bourgtibourg.com
   INTERNET www.hotelbourgtibourg.com
FACILITIES & SERVICES Air-conditioning, direct-dial phone, elevator, hair dryer, laundry service, minibar, TV with international reception, room safe (no charge), WiFi
RATES Single 150€, double 200€, deluxe 250€, suite 350€; *taxe de séjour* included **CREDIT CARDS** AE, DC, MC, V
BREAKFAST Continental 12€ per person

HÔTEL CARON DE BEAUMARCHAIS ★★★ (32)
12, rue Vieille-du-Temple, 75004
Métro: Hôtel-de-Ville, St-Paul
19 rooms, all with shower or bath and toilet

Named after the boisterous author of *The Marriage of Figaro* and *The Barber of Seville*, the Caron de Beaumarchais is close to place des Vosges, interesting shopping in the Marais, the Jewish Quarter, and the Bastille Opéra. The beautifully restored hotel, which opened for business in June 1993, is run by father and son owners Étienne and Alain Bigeard. Between them they have all the credentials necessary to run a fine, small hotel. Service and attention to guests' needs are dwindling commodities in today's hotel market, but not here. Every time I have been in the hotel, guests could not say enough about the care and consideration extended to them during their stay, and this is backed up by the many glowing letters I have received from contented readers who have stayed here.

The downstairs lobby features a wood-burning Louis XVI fireplace that is lighted on cold evenings, a rare, 1792 piano-*forte,* copies of eighteenth-century murals, an antique game table laid out with authentic old playing cards, and a tiny atrium garden off to one side. Breakfast, served until noon, includes freshly squeezed orange juice, assorted pastries, fresh fruit, and yogurt and is served in a comfortable room that lends itself to lingering while thumbing through the collection of guidebooks left here for everyone's use. If guests prefer, a Continental breakfast will be brought on a tray to their rooms. A café au lait and the *Herald-Tribune* can also be brought to your room for a small charge.

The nineteen bedrooms are small, but effective design and elegant eighteenth-century decor overcome this. No detail has been overlooked in providing a coordinated look. The Gustavian III–style furniture was made specially for the hotel. Original pages from *The Marriage of Figaro* are framed and hang in each room. Hand-painted and signed ceramic tiles highlight the bathrooms, where even the color of the soap in the soap dish has been taken into consideration. All rooms are air-conditioned and soundproofed, and six have balconies with tables and chairs. In operating the hotel, the family strives to re-create a typically French atmosphere where guests feel at home and want to return. They achieve their goal with great success.

TEL 01-42-72-34-12 **FAX** 01-42-72-34-63 **EMAIL** hotel@caronde
  beaumarchais.com **INTERNET** www.carondebeaumarchais.com
FACILITIES & SERVICES Air-conditioning, direct-dial phone, elevator, hair dryer,
  magnifying mirrors, minibar, robes, TV with international reception,
  office safe (no charge), free WiFi
RATES 1–2 persons 142–162€; extra bed 16€; *taxe de séjour* included
  CREDIT CARDS AE, MC, V
BREAKFAST Continental 10€ per person and available until noon

HÔTEL DE LA BRETONNERIE ★★★ (21)
22, rue Ste-Croix-de-la-Bretonnerie, 75004
Métro: Hôtel-de-Ville
29 rooms, all with shower or bath and toilet

A stay in this captivating hotel will make you feel like an inhabitant of old-world Paris. Set in a restored seventeenth-century town house in the heart of the picturesque Marais, it is just minutes from Beaubourg, place des Vosges, the Musée National Picasso, the banks of the Seine, and Notre Dame. High praise goes to management for providing a warm welcome to the many returning guests, who rightfully consider this one of the best small hotels in Paris.

Quality and taste are evident from the minute you enter the comfortable cross-beamed lobby and vibrant red sitting room, with a large hanging tapestry and tapestry-covered armchairs. The twenty-two rooms and seven suites are individually decorated, and all are recommended. For a special treat, reserve No. 25 with modern British colonial wicker and a four-poster metal bed. Bathroom touches include a deep tub and an inset sink with plenty of space for all the cosmetics one could possibly need. The suites are not only stunning but great value, especially No. 5, which has two rooms and two bathrooms done in soft rose and green. Unfortunately, the view is not much. Number 28 is another beautiful two-room suite with a double bathroom to die for . . . just wait until you sink into the massive oval tub. Room 35 is also wonderful; magnificently done in pale yellow and green with enviable antiques, it consists of a bedroom, a separate sitting room, and one of the most beautiful three-star marble baths in Paris. For something smaller but just as appealing, try Room 14 or 29, both with a four-poster canopy bed, or No. 4, an inside room with a half-tester drape over the bed and a nice table with two upholstered chairs. Breakfast is served in the arched, stone-walled *cave* (cellar), with colorful dried floral arrangements complementing the rich French red decor.

Also under the same ownership is the Hôtel Chopin (see page 208).

TEL 01-48-87-77-63 **FAX** 01-42-77-26-78 **EMAIL** hotel@bretonnerie.com
　　INTERNET www.bretonnerie.com
FACILITIES & SERVICES Direct-dial phone, elevator, hair dryer, laundry service, minibar, TV with international reception, room safe (no charge), free Internet in lobby
RATES 1–2 persons: classic 116€, charming 149€; 3–4 persons: charming 174€, junior suite 180–205€; *taxe de séjour* 1€ per person, per day
　　CREDIT CARDS MC, V
BREAKFAST Continental 10€ per person

HÔTEL DE LA PLACE DES VOSGES ★★ (43)
12, rue de Birague, 75004
Métro: Bastille
16 rooms, one apartment, all with shower or bath and toilet

Renovating a hotel in Paris can be a trying experience thanks to mountains of red tape, building constraints, and historical conservation demands, not to mention expense. The determined owners of this prime Marais hotel are forging ahead and slowly redoing it. Their philosophy ("Buy the best and cry only once") is evident in the quality materials used in new rooms, which also prove the adage small is beautiful. Masterful attention to detail is apparent, from the nonallergic quilts on top-of-the-line beds to the lighted alcoves beside the bed that replace the need for side tables. It is the Marais, so naturally the new rooms have heavy beams, exposed stone walls, and hardwood floors. You don't have to travel light to stay in one of these rooms: the beds were specially designed to be high enough to slide a regulation suitcase underneath, and an armoire provides shelf and hanging space. The five-star marble bathrooms have state-of-the-art shower heads and six wall massage jets. If a bathtub is important, the only one in the hotel is in the penthouse, and it will be a Jacuzzi. In this room, guests also have a great Bastille view. What about the other rooms? They, too, are small with little or no seating, but they are well-maintained so that guests do not feel second class by staying in one.

The hotel also has a huge apartment called The Loft. The apartment takes its name from one of the sleeping areas, which is up a dangerous twisting staircase in a mezzanine space hardly tall enough for a child to stand upright in. The apartment is located in a building next to the hotel, and while it has all the amenities—washer and dryer, closet space, and enough space to house a small army—I found it cold and starkly impersonal.

TEL 01-42-72-60-46 **FAX** 01-42-72-02-64 **EMAIL** contact@hpde.net
　　INTERNET www.hotelplacedesvosges.com
FACILITIES & SERVICES Bar, direct-dial phone, elevator (starts 1st floor), fans, hair dryer, laundry service, TV with international reception, room safe (no charge), free WiFi
RATES 1–2 persons: older rooms 120€, new rooms 140€, top-floor room with bath 207€; free extra bed for a child; *taxe de séjour* included
　　CREDIT CARDS AE, DC, MC, V
BREAKFAST Continental 8€ per person, served anytime

HÔTEL DE LUTÈCE ★★★ ($, 55)
65, rue St-Louis-en-l'Île, 75004
Métro: Pont Marie
23 rooms, all with shower or bath and toilet

Île St-Louis is a small island, a mere six blocks long and two blocks wide, in the middle of the Seine. Every day and night, and especially on the weekends, crowds of tourists and Parisians surge down the main street, browsing through the boutiques and art galleries or stopping for ice cream at the famed Berthillon. Lovers of this unique part of Paris check into either the Lutèce or the Deux-Îles, both owned by husband-and-wife team Roland and Elisabeth Buffat. Stepping inside the Hôtel de Lutèce from the island's main street, you are welcomed by bouquets of fresh flowers and a large stone fireplace surrounded by soft couches and armchairs. Overlooking a miniature atrium garden is the breakfast room, which is lined with a fine collection of antique sepia prints.

The rooms at the Lutèce are not large by any standard, but they are nicely decorated in soft, tawny colors and ruby carpets and have the requisite exposed beams and pretty rooftop views (that is, if you are lucky enough to secure a top-floor room). For a slight increase in space, reserve the double-bedded duplex, up ten steps off the landing between the third and fourth floors; it faces the court, so it will be very quiet. Because the hotel exudes charm from top to bottom, it is booked months ahead, so you should reserve as far in advance as possible.

The following hotels are under the same ownership: Hôtel des Deux-Îles (page 101), Hôtel Henri IV (page 75), and Galileo Hôtel (page 194).

TEL 01-43-26-23-52 **FAX** 01-43-29-60-25 **EMAIL** lutece@
  hotel-ile-saintlouis.com **INTERNET** www.hotel-ile-saintlouis.com
FACILITIES & SERVICES Air-conditioning, direct-dial phone, elevator (to
  most floors), hair dryer, laundry service, minibar, TV with international
  reception, room safe (no charge), free WiFi
RATES Single 150€, double 195€, triple 215€; *taxe de séjour* 1€ per person,
  per day **CREDIT CARDS** AE, MC, V
BREAKFAST Continental 12€ per person

HÔTEL DE NICE ★★ (30)
42 bis, rue de Rivoli, 75004
Métro: Hôtel-de-Ville
23 rooms, all with shower or bath and toilet

When I first walked into the Hôtel de Nice, I was blinded by the use of turquoise everywhere: on the stairs leading to the reception, on the doors to the rooms, even on the wood trim and around the light switches in the hall. But after awhile, I was so busy looking at the pleasantly cluttered hotel, I forgot all about this blast of color. The main sitting room, which also serves as the reception and breakfast room, has a certain *grand-mère*'s parlor look, complete with oriental rugs on the floors, paisley prints tossed over tables and chairs, and a portrait of Lady Diana Cooper mixed in with the eclectic collection of artwork and a variety of green plants.

The rooms are as generously flossy as the public areas, and of course, no two are alike. The all face out onto rue de Rivoli or the square Bourg Tibourg. Noise can be a nuisance, especially if your room faces the rue de Rivoli, a major thoroughfare in this part of Paris. Floral bedspreads, tartan cushions, Indian elephant fabric curtains, mismatched antique chairs, and old prints pasted onto the bathroom door sum up the look in No. 11. The bathroom has a tub-and-shower combination, good towels, and some sink space. Room 16 is a favorite, and no wonder when the two windows on rue de Rivoli frame views of the towers of Notre Dame, the Bastille, and the Hôtel de Ville. Number 5, a tight double, is a study in mustard yellow with limited negotiating room around the foot of the bed. It is saved by a balcony overlooking the leafy square below. No, it isn't the Paris hotel for the masses, but if you like a hopscotch of colors in quirky surroundings, book now.

TEL 01-42-78-55-29 **FAX** 01-42-78-36-07 **EMAIL** contact@hoteldenice.com
   INTERNET www.hoteldenice.com
FACILITIES & SERVICES Direct-dial phone, hair dryer, elevator (starts 1st floor), TV with international reception, office safe (no charge)
RATES Single 75€, double 105€, triple 130€, quad 145€; *taxe de séjour* included **CREDIT CARDS** MC, V
BREAKFAST Continental 7€ per person

HÔTEL DES DEUX-ÎLES ★★★ (56)
59, rue St-Louis-en-l'Île, 75004
Métro: Pont Marie
17 rooms, all with shower or bath and toilet

The Hôtel des Deux-Îles is a beautiful seventeenth-century mansion owned by decorator Roland Buffat and his wife, Elisabeth. This hotel displays their touches at every turn, from the lobby with its atrium garden and antique birdcage to the Louis XIV tiled bathrooms. The snug breakfast area downstairs has a big fireplace and several secluded nooks with soft overstuffed sofas, making it a perfect place to start your Paris day. The rooms are very small, but they are well done. The very essence of Paris can be viewed from the top-floor windows.

NOTE: The hotel is scheduled for renovations in 2007. The dates, details, and possible rate increases were not available at press time, but given the decorating talents of the Buffats, it will be wonderful, and the prices will be fair.

The Buffats also own Hôtel de Lutèce (page 99), Hôtel Henri IV (page 75), and Galileo Hôtel (page 194).

TEL 01-43-26-13-35 **FAX** 01-43-29-60-25 **EMAIL** hotel.2iles@free.fr
   INTERNET www.deuxiles-paris-hotel.com
FACILITIES & SERVICES Air-conditioning, direct-dial phone, elevator, hair dryer, laundry service, TV with international reception, room safe (no charge), WiFi
RATES Single 150€, double 170€; *taxe de séjour* 1€ per person, per day
   CREDIT CARDS AE, MC, V
BREAKFAST Continental 11€ per person

HÔTEL DU JEU DE PAUME ★★★★ ($, 54)
54, rue Saint-Louis-en-l'Île, 75004
Métro: Pont Marie
30 rooms, all with bathtub, shower, and toilet

At the beginning of the seventeenth century, Louis XIII decided to build a royal tennis court patterned after those in England. The result was the Jeu de Paume, which existed on this site for more than one hundred years. After several other owners and years of neglect, it was completely refashioned in 1988 and now is a stunning, secluded hotel of impressive caliber. Many original features remain, including the dramatically high-pitched, open cross-beamed roof that once accommodated the gallery spectators. This open area is the focal point of the hotel and lends itself well to deep-seated chairs and sofas nicely placed throughout.

An artful glass elevator whisks guests to the beautifully executed rooms, which are not lavish, but all boast themed decorating and comfortable furnishings. All have hardwood floors, Pierre Frey fabrics, fresh flowers, and full marble bathrooms with Annick Goutal toiletries. Some have private terraces. Room 6 is a blue and yellow ground-floor single opening onto the garden. In addition to a marble bath with gold and silver fixtures, the room itself has plenty of work and living space. Number 205 is a large twin with two windows also overlooking the garden. Number 12 is a junior suite on two levels. In the downstairs sitting room, the mirrored wall reflecting the stone floor gives a sense of space. Here you will find a sofabed, television, table and chairs, and a small bathroom with a shower. Upstairs, you have double windows with a view of the garden, twin beds, a large walk-in closet, and an Italian tile bathroom with a marble sink set into a wooden console. The location in the heart of Paris on l'Île St-Louis is ideal in every respect. In fact, it simply does not get any more romantic, or Parisian, than this.

TEL 01-43-26-14-18 **FAX** 01-40-46-02-76 **INTERNET** www.jeudepaume hotel.com
FACILITIES & SERVICES Bar, billiard room, conference room, direct-dial phone, elevator, fans, small equipped gym, hair dryer, laundry service, minibar, room service for light snacks, sauna, TV with international reception, room safe (no charge), WiFi in lobby
RATES Single 175–245€, double 265–295€, triple 415€, junior suite 520€; dog 12€; *taxe de séjour* 1.15€ per person, per day
　　CREDIT CARDS AE, DC, MC, V
BREAKFAST Continental 18€ per person

HÔTEL DU 7E ART ★★ (46)
20, rue St-Paul, 75004
Métro: St-Paul, Bastille
23 rooms, all with shower or bath and toilet

The theme of this hotel is "yesterday's and today's movies." If you are a movie buff, especially if you love old films, you must at least drop by to admire the hotel's fabulous collection of film posters. For instance, the sitting room displays an irreverent takeoff on the Last Supper with Marilyn Monroe as the central figure and twelve male film stars, ranging from Laurel and Hardy to Elvis and Frankenstein, sitting and gesturing along the laden table.

The rooms are not posh, nor are they large, but they do have funky character…and at least one or two framed film posters. Room 27, a back double with a miniature bathroom squeezed into a closet, sports a *L'Est d'Eden* with James Dean, *Les Trafiquants de la Nuite (The Long Haul)* starring Victor Mature and Diana Dors, and *Ne Me Quitter Jamais (Never Let Me Go)* with Clark Gable and Gene Tierney. Room 21, with beige grass-cloth walls and brown paisley quilted spreads on twins, can fit three, but I think it's better for two. Posters here include *The Swan* with Grace Kelly and *Niagara* with Marilyn Monroe, Joseph Cotten, and Jean Peters. From a nostalgic standpoint, my favorite in this room is *Scandle en Floride,* featuring Ronald Reagan and Shirley Temple. Number 18 is a real hoot, with *How to Marry a Millionaire,* starring Marilyn Monroe, hanging over the bed, and on the adjacent walls, Maureen O'Hara and Charles Laughton in *Quasimoto* and Charlie Chaplin in *The Kid.* In the bathroom, posters are imposed on some tiles and the shower curtain continues the film theme. If you can't live without your own bit of film memorabilia or collectable kitsch, check out the small boutique and the front window display—almost everything is for sale.

TEL 01-44-54-85-00 **FAX** 01-42-77-69-10 **EMAIL** Hotel7art@wanadoo.fr
FACILITIES & SERVICES Air-conditioning, bar, direct-dial phone, no elevator (4 floors), hair dryer available, laundry room for guests, TV with international reception, room safe (no charge)
RATES 1–2 persons 80–135€; extra bed 20€; *taxe de séjour* included
    CREDIT CARDS AE, DC, MC, V
BREAKFAST Continental 7€ per person

HÔTEL JEANNE D'ARC ★★ (39)
3, rue de Jarente, 75004
Métro: St-Paul, Bastille
36 rooms, all with shower or bath and toilet

The Hôtel Jeanne d'Arc sits on a quiet street leading into the Marais. Discovered long ago by astute, wallet-conscious travelers, the hotel offers spotless rooms with a minimum of snags and tears. Sometimes it is hard to account for different types of decorating tastes, and I admit to being baffled about a few of the choices in the public areas of this hotel. My prize for the most bizarre mirror on the Continent goes to the one done by a local artist that hangs near the reception and defies rational description. Fortunately, the rooms do not keep pace with the unusual decoration elsewhere, and they are actually quite plain by comparison.

Rooms 11 or 12 are good bets if there are two of you. Number 60, with its sloping eaves and rooftop views, is a good choice for parties of three, and Nos. 53 and 63 for parties of four. If you are alone, request No. 41, all in pink with an open closet, sunny rooftop view, and a compact blue bathroom with a stall shower. Recent improvements include new stairway carpeting and halls repapered in textured orange. Repeat customers comprise the bulk of the clientele, so book early if this one appeals to you.

TEL 01-48-87-62-11 **FAX** 01-48-87-37-31 **EMAIL** information@ hoteljeannedarc.com **INTERNET** www.hoteljeannedarc.com

FACILITIES & SERVICES Direct-dial phone, elevator, TV with international reception, office safe (no charge)

RATES Single 60–84€, double 84–98€, triple 117€, quad 147€; free baby bed; *taxe de séjour* included **CREDIT CARDS** MC, V

BREAKFAST Continental 8€ per person

HÔTEL SAINT-LOUIS MARAIS ★★ (49)
1, rue Charles V, 75004
Métro: St-Paul, Bastille
19 rooms, all with shower or bath and toilet

For a peaceful stay on a quiet Marais street, look no further than Jean-Michel Tournu's completely redone Hôtel Saint-Louis Marais. In redoing the hotel, he carefully respected the building and its historical past, keeping the tiled floors, heavy beamed ceilings, and rough stone walls. Antique pieces of furniture add interest in the well-coordinated rooms; bathrooms have space, and many offer extra-long tubs. If stairs are a problem, ask for No. 1 on the ground floor, which is done in rich French red with gold accents. The closet space is excellent. In addition to the appealing surroundings and Great Sleeping prices, guests are made to feel right at home by the friendly attitude of Jean-Michel and his staff.

NOTE: For another type of Parisian experience, consider reserving one of the dozen or more apartments the hotel manages in this dynamic part of the city (see Saint-Louis Marais Résidence, page 294). Also under the same ownership are the Hôtel Saint-Louis Opéra (see page 211) and Hôtel Saint-Louis Bastille (see page 220).

TEL 01-48-87-87-04 **FAX** 01-48-87-33-26 **EMAIL** slmarais@noos.fr **INTERNET** www.saintlouismarais.com

FACILITIES & SERVICES Direct-dial phone, no elevator (4 floors), hair dryer, room safe (no charge), TV with international reception, WiFi

RATES Single 99€, standard double 115€, superior double140€, triple 150€, junior suite 160€; *taxe de séjour* 0.78€ per day, per person **CREDIT CARDS** AE, DC, MC, V

BREAKFAST Buffet 10€ per person

HÔTEL SAINT-MERRY ★★★ (19)
78, rue de la Verrerie, 75004
Métro: Châtelet, Hôtel-de-Ville; RER Châtelet–Les Halles
11 rooms, 1 suite, all with shower or bath and toilet

The former presbytery of the seventeenth-century Gothic church of St-Merry is now the most unusual hotel in Paris, and it qualifies as its own tourist attraction! It is the labor of love of former owner M. Crabbe, who for more than forty years worked to create a true Gothic masterpiece. His immense pride in his achievement is well deserved, and the results are spectacular.

The hotel is located on a pedestrian walkway, and the entrance is through a short hallway with exposed beams and stone steps leading up to the lobby and reception area. Each room in the hotel is different and showcases a collection of authentic Gothic church and castle memorabilia mixed with custom-made pieces. All the back rooms share a common wall with the church, and wherever possible this stone wall has been kept visible. Room 9 contains a carved stone flying buttress, which flows from the floor to the ceiling over the bed. Others have rough red tiles from the Château de l'Angeres in the Loire Valley, hand-carved mahogany pews, converted confessionals serving as headboards, and impressive eight-lamp chandeliers. All of the windows in the hotel are stained glass, and the balcony rails still bear the St-Merry Church crest. Since each room is unique, room rates vary accordingly, depending on the plumbing and the level of Gothic detailing.

For years M. Crabbe worked on Room 20, the Gothic Suite, and it is finally completed. It isn't just a hotel suite—it is an experience! The approach is through an entry hall and up seventeen steps into a huge, pitched-roof room with cross beams, a baronial dining table seating six, skylights, a ten-foot clock, a fireplace, a wall of carved wooden shelves, and a large sofabed where you can view the big-screen television. The bedroom is equally dramatic, with a view of the church. Even the bathroom is fabulous, with an ornately carved door depicting the three wise men, Mary, Joseph, and baby Jesus.

While you are here, please don't miss visiting the St-Merry Church adjoining the hotel. It has a beautiful choir and the oldest church bell in Paris, cast in 1331.

NOTE: M. Crabbe has recently sold the hotel, and I am not the only longtime loyalist who hoped this day would never come. The new owner has another hotel in the neighborhood that is not covered in *Great Sleeps Paris* because I think it offers absolutely no value and is not well maintained. Those of us who admire M. Crabbe and his marvelous achievement at the Hôtel St-Merry sincerely hope the new proprietor will properly care for this unique, historic hotel and not let it fall by the wayside.

TEL 01-42-78-14-15 **FAX** 01-40-29-06-82 **EMAIL** hotelstmerry@wanadoo.fr
INTERNET www.hotelmarais.com

FACILITIES & SERVICES Direct-dial phone, no elevator (4 floors), fans, hair dryer, laundry service, TV in suite, room safe (no charge)
RATES 1–2 persons 160–230€, suite (2–4 persons) 335€–407€; *taxe de séjour* included **CREDIT CARDS** MC, V
BREAKFAST Continental in rooms only, 11€ per person

LIBERTEL GRAND TURENNE ★★★ (41)
6, rue de Turenne, 75004
Métro: St-Paul, Bastille
41 rooms, all with shower or bath and toilet

   The Libertel/Accor hotel group has many smart lodgings in various price categories scattered throughout Paris. All are done from top to bottom with coordinated colors and furnishings. Libertel Grand Turenne offers forty-one rooms done in blues, greens, or soft reds with attractive accent pieces and pretty prints on the walls. The first and second floors are devoted entirely to nonsmokers. There are several categories of rooms. However, for best value for money, stick with the basics. A case in point: No. 603, a top-floor superior double, has a big bathroom with windows and a tub, but the slanted wall makes it awkward for a tall person. The hotel location, only a five-minute walk from place des Vosges, offers visitors a convenient base for exploring one of the most interesting *quartiers* in Paris. From here it is a pleasant stroll to the Musée National Picasso, Île de la Cité, Île St-Louis, the Bastille Opéra, and all the wild and woolly nighttime fun in the eleventh arrondissement. In addition, many restaurants listed in *Great Eats Paris* are close by.

TEL 01-42-78-43-25 **FAX** 01-42-74-10-72 **EMAIL** H2760@accor.com
   INTERNET www.accorhotels.com
FACILITIES & SERVICES Direct-dial phone, elevator, hair dryer, laundry service, minibar, some tea and coffee makers, TV with international reception, office safe (no charge), 2 floors nonsmoking, WiFi
RATES 1–2 persons 176€, suite 245€; *taxe de séjour* included
   CREDIT CARDS AE, DC, MC, V
BREAKFAST Buffet 14€ per person

Fifth Arrondissement

The fifth is named the Latin Quarter for the students who came during the Middle Ages to study at the Sorbonne, which was founded in 1253 and remains a center of student life to this day, though not much Latin is spoken here anymore. The arrondissement stretches from the colorful street *marché* on rue Mouffetard to the dome of the Panthéon, then beyond to the Seine and through the botanical wonders of the Jardin des Plantes (opened by Louis XIV's doctor for the king's health). This ancient, interesting, and exhilarating part of Paris is crisscrossed with networks of narrow, curved streets lined on both sides with bookshops, restaurants, and cafés that surge with action twenty-four hours a day. It is youthful, cosmopolitan, bohemian, and fun. Even though St-Michel has lost its penniless chic, it is still the soul of the Latin Quarter. Crowds of all ages and types gather daily around the St-Michel fountain to flirt, eat, drink, argue, pose, and watch the sidewalk entertainment. The area around place de la Contrescarpe is where Hemingway lived when he was a starving writer new to Paris. You can see two of his addresses: 39, rue Descartes, a studio; and 74, rue de Cardinal-Lemoine, where he lived with his wife, Hadley. Also of interest in the fifth is the Musée Rodin, the twelfth-century Église St-Julien-le-Pauvre, the Manufacture des Gobelins (tapestry workshops), and the Cluny baths—which form part of the Musée du Moyen Age (known as the Musée de Cluny) and are regarded as the most important Roman ruins in Paris.

LEFT BANK
Jardin des Plantes
Latin Quarter
Manufacture des Gobelins
Musée de Cluny
Musée Rodin
Panthéon
rue Mouffetard
Sorbonne

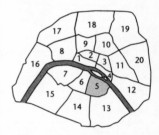

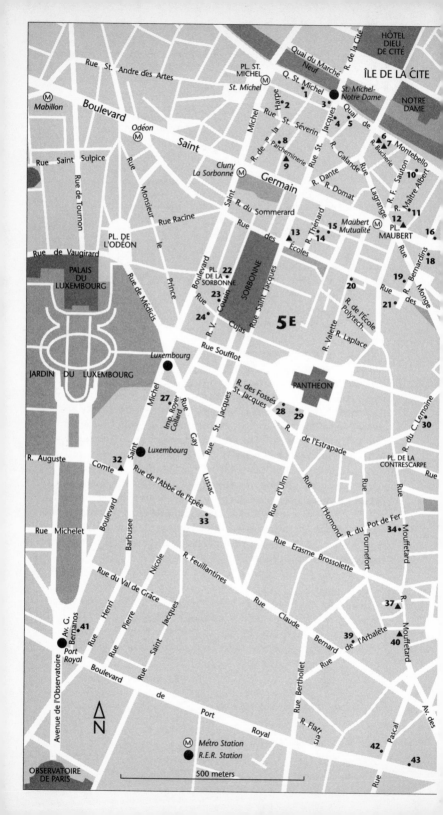

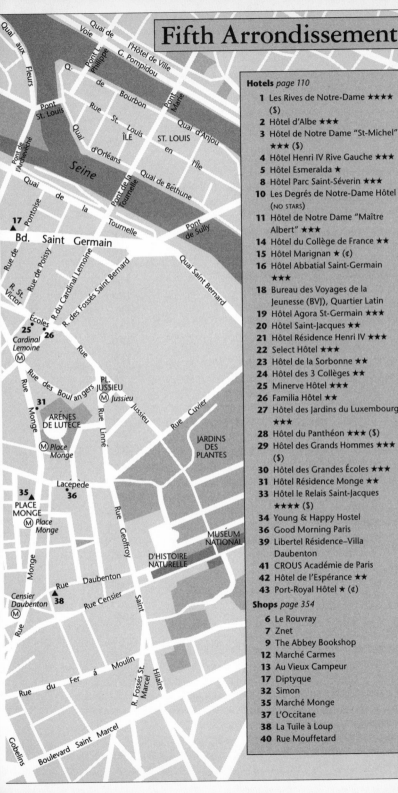

Fifth Arrondissement

Hotels *page 110*

1 Les Rives de Notre-Dame ★★★★ ($)
2 Hôtel d'Albe ★★★
3 Hôtel de Notre Dame "St-Michel" ★★★ ($)
4 Hôtel Henri IV Rive Gauche ★★★
5 Hôtel Esmeralda ★
8 Hôtel Parc Saint-Séverin ★★★
10 Les Degrés de Notre-Dame Hôtel (NO STARS)
11 Hôtel de Notre Dame "Maître Albert" ★★★
14 Hôtel du Collège de France ★★
15 Hôtel Marignan ★ (¢)
16 Hôtel Abbatial Saint-Germain ★★★
18 Bureau des Voyages de la Jeunesse (BVJ), Quartier Latin
19 Hôtel Agora St-Germain ★★★
20 Hôtel Saint-Jacques ★★
21 Hôtel Résidence Henri IV ★★★
22 Select Hôtel ★★★
23 Hôtel de la Sorbonne ★★
24 Hôtel des 3 Collèges ★★
25 Minerve Hôtel ★★★
26 Familia Hôtel ★★
27 Hôtel des Jardins du Luxembourg ★★★
28 Hôtel du Panthéon ★★★ ($)
29 Hôtel des Grands Hommes ★★★ ($)
30 Hôtel des Grandes Écoles ★★★
31 Hôtel Résidence Monge ★★
33 Hôtel le Relais Saint-Jacques ★★★★ ($)
34 Young & Happy Hostel
36 Good Morning Paris
39 Libertel Résidence–Villa Daubenton
41 CROUS Académie de Paris
42 Hôtel de l'Espérance ★★
43 Port-Royal Hôtel ★ (¢)

Shops *page 354*

6 Le Rouvray
7 Znet
9 The Abbey Bookshop
12 Marché Carmes
13 Au Vieux Campeur
17 Diptyque
32 Simon
35 Marché Monge
37 L'Occitane
38 La Tuile à Loup
40 Rue Mouffetard

HOTELS IN THE FIFTH ARRONDISSEMENT

OTHER OPTIONS

($) indicates a Big Splurge; (¢) indicates a Cheap Sleep

FAMILIA HÔTEL ★★ (26)
11, rue des Écoles, 75005
Métro: Cardinal Lemoine, Maubert-Mutualité

30 rooms, all with shower or bath and toilet

Many hotels on rue des Écoles are run by foreign managers for absentee owners residing in other countries. As a result, service, cleanliness, and upkeep are often drastically reduced because no one at the hotel has any stake in it or really cares. You will find none of this at the Familia Hôtel. M. and Mme. Gaucheron, who owned the hotel for a decade, have now turned the operating duties to their son, Eric, whose hands-on management and high-energy enthusiasm keep him on top of things every minute. Speaking rapid-fire French, Spanish, or English, he never stops doing whatever is necessary to ensure that all guests are looked after properly. His wife, Sylvie, also helps whenever she is not busy with their young son, Charles, who is the apple of his grandfather's eye and adored by all the staff at the hotel.

The family is constantly on the lookout for ways to improve the hotel, and as a result the hotel is a two-star in price only—certainly not in guest amenities. One very successful project involved chipping away years of plaster and paint from the walls to expose the original stone from 1850, which now serves as a perfect backdrop for Eric's collection of original tapestries. Many rooms also have exposed walls; others have frescoes of famous Parisian landmarks. Room 62 has the Canal St-Martin painted over the twin beds, No. 43 has the famed Pont Neuf in sepia tones, and No. 25 highlights the place des Vosges. I like No. 52, with the Pont Alexandre III and the Eiffel Tower gracing one wall and its little outdoor terrace with a view of Notre Dame, and No. 17 with its Palais du Luxembourg mural. The same artist painted the mural of old Paris along the front entry and all the doors leading to the bedrooms.

The rooms are all very well done and are on a rotating schedule for maintenance and improvements, which guarantees nothing ever extends beyond its due date. Some rooms will have new mattresses one year, others a new marble bathroom, while still others will be repainted and recarpeted. Many have parquet or ceramic tiled floors, a boon for allergy sufferers. Adding to the overall appeal are double-glazed windows and expensive touches like special Canadian cherry-wood closet doors and reproduction antique furnishings designed specifically for the hotel. If you want a bird's-eye view of Notre Dame Cathedral, ask for a front room on the fifth or sixth floors. For a room with a balcony, you want something on the second or fifth floors, facing the street. Motorists can reserve one of the hotel's five parking spaces. Staying at the Familia puts guests only a few minutes from St-Germain-des-Prés, the islands, and all the famous cafés in the Latin Quarter. Métro connections are good, and so is bus transportation.

If the Familia is booked, don't worry. The family now owns the Minerve Hôtel next door (see page 129), which they completely renovated into a very smart three-star.

TEL 01-43-54-55-27 **FAX** 01-43-29-61-77 **EMAIL** hotelfamilia@wanadoo.fr
  INTERNET www.hotel-paris-familia.com
FACILITIES & SERVICES Direct-dial phone, hair dryer, elevator, minibar, TV
  with international reception, office safe (no charge), WiFi throughout (free
  in lobby)
RATES Single 74€, double 85–116€, triple 134€, quad 147€; *taxe de séjour*
  0.78€ per person, per day; 5 parking places 20€ per day
  CREDIT CARDS AE, DC, MC, V
BREAKFAST Continental 6€ per person, in room, dining room, or on your
  balcony

HÔTEL ABBATIAL SAINT-GERMAIN ★★★ (16)
46, boulevard St-Germain, 75005
Métro: Maubert-Mutualité
43 rooms, all with shower or bath and toilet

The Abbatial Saint-Germain offers comfort, convenience, and location. True, the rooms are generally small by American standards, but they are the norm in this popular section of Paris, and they are carefully cleaned by a team of housekeepers headed by Maria, who has spent over a quarter century working here. The spirit of the nineteenth-century building is evident from the original cross beams along the halls, tapestry-covered furniture, and white antiqued or wood grain bedroom furnishings. The plaster plaques of nymphs and cherubs that hang in almost every room, and the rooms decorated in fiery orange, seem a little too much, but to each his own. The rooms decorated in blue and gold are less vivid. The fifth- and sixth-floor rooms have balconies with views of Notre Dame and the Panthéon, and the sunny street-side rooms are soundproofed with double-glazed windows. Single Great Sleepers should avoid No. 28 and its view of the fire escape on the inner courtyard. Also under the same ownership is the Hôtel Agora St-Germain (see below).

TEL 01-46-34-02-12 **FAX** 01-43-25-47-73 **EMAIL** resa@
  abbatial-paris-hotel.com **INTERNET** www.abbatial.com
FACILITIES & SERVICES Air-conditioning, direct-dial phone, elevator, hair
  dryer, laundry service, minibar, public parking across the street, TV with
  international reception, room safe (no charge), WiFi
RATES Single 120€, standard double 150€, superior double 190€, triple
  205€; *taxe de séjour* included **CREDIT CARDS** AE, DC, MC, V
BREAKFAST Buffet or Continental 10€ per person

HÔTEL AGORA ST-GERMAIN ★★★ (19)
42, rue des Bernardins, 75005
Métro: Maubert-Mutualité
39 rooms, all with shower or bath and toilet

The Agora St-Germain continues to represent a success story for both owners and guests. The customized rooms with pretty silk wall coverings and marble-tile bathrooms are beautifully maintained. Several have balcony views of St-Nicholas de Chardonnet, which is the only church in Paris that still conducts services in Latin. An interior garden with a bubbling fountain gives the marble floored sitting area and lobby more dimension, making it a pleasant place to linger and read the daily newspapers. A Continental breakfast is served in a stone-walled dining room with baskets of flowers and linen napkins on each table. The friendly owners, Pascale and Michèle Sahuc, and their staff see to the wishes of every guest. Firmly recommended by all who have stayed here, this haven for weary travelers is less than five minutes away from good restaurants (see *Great Eats Paris*) and close to all the charm and excitement of this part of the Left Bank. Also under the same ownership is the Hôtel Abbatial St-Germain on boulevard St-Germain (see page 112).

TEL 01-46-34-13-00 **FAX** 01-46-34-75-05 **EMAIL** agorastg@club-internet.fr
    INTERNET www.agorasaintgermain.com
FACILITIES & SERVICES Air-conditioning, direct-dial phone, elevator, hair dryer, laundry service, minibar, TV with international reception, room safe (no charge), WiFi
RATES Single 130€, double 165–185€, triple 195€; *taxe de séjour* included
    CREDIT CARDS AE, DC, MC, V
BREAKFAST Buffet 10€ per person

HÔTEL D'ALBE ★★★ (2)
1, rue de la Harpe, 75005
Métro: St-Michel; RER St-Michel-Notre-Dame
45 rooms, all with shower or bath and toilet

This is the perfect site for Latin Quarter night owls and other urbanites who consider 11 P.M. the shank of the evening and the crack of dawn bedtime. Rue de la Harpe is just off place St-Michel, the twenty-four-hour, nonstop, pulsating hub of this *quartier*. The street itself is lined with restaurants and cafés geared to tourists out for a good time. So, I must warn you, while this hotel has a good location, good value, and is the best on the street, it is going to be very noisy unless you use earplugs, sleep with the double-glazed windows tightly shut, and keep the air-conditioning on in a room on the top two floors. Above-average closet space and tiled bathrooms complement well-maintained, spotless, color-coordinated rooms. Best choices are the corner rooms with three windows, but remember that they will be noisy. If there are four of you, look elsewhere; there aren't any quads. An ultra-modern lounge sleekly furnished in marble, chrome, and wood serves as a gallery for the owner's collection of art prints. The bright modern breakfast room faces the street and plays relaxing classical music while you enjoy a morning croissant and *café au lait*.

TEL 01-46-34-09-70 **FAX** 01-40-46-85-70 **EMAIL** albehotel@wanadoo.fr
    INTERNET www.hotelalbe.fr
FACILITIES & SERVICES Air-conditioning, direct-dial phone, hair dryer, elevator (to most floors), laundry service, minibar, TV with international reception, room safe (no charge), 4 floors exclusively nonsmoking, WiFi
RATES Single 135€, double 160–170€, triple 180€; *taxe de séjour* included
    CREDIT CARDS AE, DC, MC, V
BREAKFAST Buffet 12€ per person

HÔTEL DE LA SORBONNE ★★ (23)
6, rue Victor Cousin, 75005
Métro: Cluny–La-Sorbonne; RER Luxembourg
39 rooms, all with shower or bath and toilet

Experienced proprietors, continuing improvements, and a friendly crew headed by Frédéric Lopez have turned this once dumpy dowager into a popular two-star. It is owned by a husband-and-wife team who have several other wonderful three-star hotels on the Left Bank, and when I heard they had acquired Hôtel de la Sorbonne, I knew it would be a winner. The hotel is located in a small courtyard off the street. There is no lobby, but a pretty breakfast room with a bulldog guarding a gas-log fireplace is a welcome place to sit during the day. Upstairs the rooms have all been repainted and updated with simple prints and fabrics, faux woods, and wrought-iron light fixtures. The only choices I do not recommend are the eight rooms similar to No. 31, which have bathrooms so small that you cannot shut the door once you are inside. Despite the sixteen-stair climb to reach Nos. 61 and 62, these rooms are the most popular, thanks to their Panthéon views and new bathrooms; if you are tall, however, the mansard roof lines could be a problem.

Also under the same ownership: Hôtel des Grands Hommes (page 117), Hôtel du Panthéon (page 120), Hôtel Résidence Henri IV (page 125), and Jardin de l'Odéon Hôtel (page 163).

TEL 01-43-54-58-08 **FAX** 01-40-51-05-18 **EMAIL** reservation@
hotelsorbonne.com **INTERNET** www.hotelsorbonne.com
FACILITIES & SERVICES Direct-dial phones, elevator (to most floors), hair dryer,
French TV, office safe (no charge), WiFi in lobby
RATES Single or double 110–130€; *taxe de séjour* included **CREDIT CARDS** AE,
MC, V
BREAKFAST Continental 8€ per person

HÔTEL DE L'ESPÉRANCE ★★ (42)
15, rue Pascal, 75005
Métro: Censier-Daubenton, Gobelins
38 rooms, all with shower or bath and toilet

Baubles, bangles, and beads—and then some—describes the effusive frilly decor and the effervescent owner, Mme. Ellen Aymard, awaiting you at this hotel. Fortunately, you are not sleeping in her downstairs lobby, which is loaded with bowers of oversized fake flowers, Yugoslavian colored crystal, a doll collection, and an extensive array of hand-crocheted pillow covers, doilies, and lamp throws. Add to this a gurgling fountain and reproduction eighteenth-century furniture, and some might need blinders to get to their rooms, which are all quite nice and tame by comparison. The color scheme revolves around coordinated yellow and soft-rose florals. Cleanliness is always stressed. The bathrooms are all nice, and most have heated towel racks. At night you will always find a candy on your pillow. Room 11 is a double with a private garden and a large bathroom suitable for the handicapped.

If you want quiet, book No. 21, a double on the back with its own balcony. I think No. 35 is too crowded for three, and the ugly sofabed looked uncomfortable. Breakfast is served in a room overlooking a garden terrace, or on the terrace weather permitting. The location is an interesting one, close to rue Mouffetard and within easy transportation to most Left Bank and Latin Quarter points of interest.

TEL 01-47-07-10-99 **FAX** 01-43-37-56-19 **EMAIL** hotel.esperance@wanadoo.fr
  INTERNET www.hoteldelesperance.com
FACILITIES & SERVICES Direct-dial phone, elevator to each half-floor (some steps required), fans, hair dryer, TV with international reception, office safe (no charge)
RATES Single 72–82€, double 80–90€, triple 105€; *taxe de séjour* included
  CREDIT CARDS AE, DC, MC, V
BREAKFAST Continental 7€ per person

HÔTEL DE NOTRE DAME "MAÎTRE ALBERT" ★★★ (11)
19, rue Maître Albert, 75005
Métro: Maubert-Mutualié; RER St-Michel-Notre-Dame
34 rooms, all with shower or bath and toilet

Walk along the Seine, turn onto a winding, cobblestone street lined with century-old buildings, and suddenly you will come to this quintessential Parisian hotel. The traditional Pierre Deux–designed fabrics go hand in hand with the Asian mirrored screen that reflects the antique furnishings, polished beams, and collection of French porcelain in the reception and sitting areas. The garden breakfast room, filled with an attractive mixture of blooming flowers and green plants, is one of the nicest places in Paris to start your day. Framed prints of teacups, teapots, and flower bouquets on the marble-top tables add more color. Oriental-style rugs and red-and-green-checked tissue-covered walls lead to the pleasing, well-planned rooms, which reflect the same standards of high quality and elegant coziness. This is an ancient building, so *small* is the operative word when it comes to room size. However, comfort is never compromised, and you can expect lovely coordinated quarters, marble bathrooms, and all the beams and stone walls this part of Paris is known for.

Also under same ownership is the Hôtel de Notre Dame "St-Michel" (see page 116).

TEL 01-43-26-79-00 **FAX** 01-46-33-50-11 **EMAIL** hotel.denotredame@ libertysurf.fr **INTERNET** www.hotel-paris-notredame.com
FACILITIES & SERVICES Air-conditioning in some rooms on 5th floor, bar, minibar, direct-dial phone, elevator, hair dryer, TV with international reception, room safe (no charge), WiFi
RATES 1–2 persons 155–165€; *taxe de séjour* 1€ per person, per day
  CREDIT CARDS MC, V
BREAKFAST Continental in room or breakfast room, 8€ per person

HÔTEL DE NOTRE DAME "ST-MICHEL" ★★★ ($, 3)
1, quai St-Michel, 75005
Métro: St-Michel; RER St-Michel–Notre-Dame
26 rooms, all with shower or bath and toilet

Hôtel de Notre Dame offers twenty-six beautiful rooms, all with the latest bathrooms and bold color plans. Reserve one of the eighteen rooms with a view, and you will look out across the *bouquinistes* (second-hand booksellers) lining the quays along the Seine and to the great western facade of the famed cathedral. Unless the windows are tightly shut and you are using earplugs, you will go to sleep and wake with the sounds of Paris, but for many of us, the majestic view will be worth it.

Entrance to the hotel is through a mirrored ground-floor hall and up a short flight of steps. The sitting room and breakfast area off the reception area have picture windows facing Notre Dame Cathedral and the river. Warm dark woods show off the gold tartan-covered walls and form a backdrop for the comfortable seating, inviting you to linger for hours and watch *tout* Paris surge by.

The rooms are decorated with an attractive mix of antiques and reproductions. If space is a prime concern, opt for No. 61, a two-story duplex. When you walk in, *voila!* The river and Notre Dame are in full view. Upstairs there is a glass partition and a rooftop window with more views. In No. 63, it's more of the same. However, in No. 62, under a pitched roof, the windows are high, and unless you are right in front of them, you won't have the view. I love the contemporary bathroom in No. 32, plus its bedroom windows allow you to lie in bed and gaze at the cathedral. In No. 34, the bathroom is bigger, but the view of Notre Dame not as full. In No. 53, you can still see the church but not from bed; the new marble bathroom has a heated towel rack and good light. You definitely do not want to stay in Room 25 or 55, both of which face a back airshaft and noisy fan.

Also under same ownership is Hôtel de Notre Dame "Maître Albert" (see page 115).

TEL 01-43-54-20-43 **FAX** 01-43-26-61-75 **EMAIL** hotel.lenotredame@
libertysurf.fr **INTERNET** www.paris-hotel-notredame.com
FACILITIES & SERVICES Air-conditioning, direct-dial phone, elevator (starts
1st floor; stairs to reception), hair dryer, minibar, TV with international
reception, room safe (no charge), WiFi in lobby
RATES 1–2 persons 150€ (without view), 200€ (with view), duplex for 2–3
persons 245€; *taxe de séjour* 1€ per person, per day **CREDIT CARDS** AE, DC,
MC, V
BREAKFAST Continental 7€ per person

HÔTEL DES GRANDES ÉCOLES ★★★ (30)
75, rue du Cardinal-Lemoine, 75005
Métro: Cardinal-Lemoine, Place Monge
51 rooms, all with shower or bath and toilet

It is unanimous—everyone *adores* this hotel.

Once found, this hotel address is one that its loyal followers whisper only to a select few. Nestled in a beautiful garden and hidden from the world by towering wooden doors opening off the street, it is definitely one of the most romantic havens of peace and quiet in Paris. The grandmotherly owner, Leonore LeFloch, and her receptionist, Marie, treat their guests like family members. As you can imagine, reservations for this very special hotel are essential months in advance.

Two facing houses make up the hotel. In both, the rooms are decorated with a feminine touch, and there is no ruffle, crocheted table or bed throw, or pretty flowered fabric that wouldn't earn a Laura Ashley seal of approval. Almost all of the rooms in both buildings look out onto the large tree-shaded garden with trellised roses, singing birds, spring daffodils, and summer wildflowers. Tables and chairs are placed here, making it a lovely spot for reading and sipping a cool drink. When you look out of your window between April and October, you will imagine you are in a French country village, not in the middle of Paris.

The hotel is an uphill climb from the métro, but once there you are close to place de la Contrescarpe, which played such an important part in Hemingway's Paris. You can also walk to rue Mouffetard, famous for its colorful daily street *marché,* some good places to eat (see *Great Eats Paris*), and inexpensive clothing stores geared to cute young things.

TEL 01-43-26-79-23 **FAX** 01-43-25-28-15 **EMAIL** Hotel.Grandes.Ecoles@ wanadoo.fr **INTERNET** www.hotel-grandes-ecoles.com

FACILITIES & SERVICES Direct-dial phone, elevator (to most floors), fans, hair dryer, no TV, office safe (no charge), hotel is entirely nonsmoking

RATES 1–2 persons 105–130€; extra bed 20€; parking 30€; *taxe de séjour* included **CREDIT CARDS** MC, V

BREAKFAST Continental 8€ per person

HÔTEL DES GRANDS HOMMES ★★★ ($, 29)
17, place du Panthéon, 75005
Métro: Maubert-Mutualité; RER Luxembourg
31 rooms, all with shower or bath and toilet

The Hôtel des Grands Hommes is a popular three-star choice, thanks to the personal management of the owner, Corinne Brethous-Moncelli. The hotel faces the Panthéon—the final resting place of many of France's great, including Voltaire, Rousseau, Victor Hugo, Alexandre Dumas, and Pierre and Marie Curie. In addition to its knockout location, it has historical significance: it is where André Breton invented the electric typewriter in 1919. The rooms have benefited from a recent redecoration using Greek and Roman classical themes and bold color schemes that mix eggplant with brown, and azure blue with verdant green. The gracious formal lobby is decorated in peach colors with faux marble finishes and outfitted with plenty of soft seating, a small corner bar, and an atrium garden filled with blooming plants. While all the rooms are very nice, I would request one of the spacious front rooms with a balcony on the fifth and sixth floors, where you can have breakfast and gaze onto the Panthéon across the street and see Sacré Coeur gleaming in the distance. Not only do the rooms on the back have no view, but some are so tightly fitted that you can hardly get around the bed.

Also under the same ownership is the Hôtel du Panthéon next door (page 120), the Hôtel Résidence Henri IV (page 125), Hôtel de la Sorbonne (see page 114), and Jardin de l'Odéon Hôtel (page 163).

TEL 01-46-34-19-60 **FAX** 01-43-26-67-32 **EMAIL** reservation@ hoteldesgrandshommes.com **INTERNET** www.hoteldesgrandshommes.com

FACILITIES & SERVICES Air-conditioning, bar, conference room, direct-dial phone, elevator, hair dryer, minibar, TV with international reception, room safe (no charge), 10 nonsmoking rooms, free WiFi in lobby

RATES Standard single or double 185–215€, superior single or double 225–255€, triple 245–275€, suite 365–395€; excellent rates in low season; *taxe de séjour* included **CREDIT CARDS** AE, DC, MC, V

BREAKFAST Buffet or continental in room 12€ per person

HÔTEL DES JARDINS DU LUXEMBOURG ★★★ (27)
5, Impasse Royer-Collard, 75005
Métro: Cluny–La Sorbonne; RER Luxembourg
26 rooms, all with shower or bath and toilet

On his first trip to Paris in 1885, Sigmund Freud lived at this address, which was then the Hôtel de la Paix. When he noticed that the curtains around his bed were green, he applied chemical tests to make sure they did not contain arsenic.

Freud is long gone, as are the green curtains. In their place is this charming boutique hotel with casually elegant guest quarters, the best of which overlook the quiet street. The lobby is filled with personal touches that set the tone for the rest of the hotel. In one corner, a park bench is lined with colorful pillows; in another is a mirrored hat and coat rack. A cloisonné table holds a selection of magazines, and kilim rugs scattered on hardwood floors add color. The intimate breakfast room has marble-top bistro tables, each with its own brass reading light. Some of the rooms are a bit tight, so if you require space, book a superior or the sixth-floor minisuite, which has a tip-of-the-Eiffel-Tower view. Two other good bets are No. 24—a twin with rooftop and sky views that is nicely turned out with brown fabric walls that blend with the blue-and-green color scheme—and No. 25, a double with a nice bathroom and a peek at the Eiffel Tower. There is one handicapped room, which unfortunately is dark because the one window opens onto the wall of the hotel atrium garden. Next to the hotel, there are also two ground-floor superior rooms with separate entrances. They do have space, but they have absolutely no privacy from the street-facing windows unless you keep the curtains permanently drawn. For security, the windows do not open, which means the only fresh air comes from the transom over the door. Another minus is the lack of closets; instead, there is only a movable clothes rack.

TEL 01-40-46-08-88 **FAX** 01-40-46-02-28 **EMAIL** jardinslux@wanadoo.fr
INTERNET www.les-jardins-du-luxembourg.com

FACILITIES & SERVICES Air-conditioning (not in 2 rooms next to hotel), honor
bar, direct-dial phone, hair dryer, elevator, laundry service, minibar,
sauna (free), TV with international reception, room safe (no charge),
1 handicapped room, WiFi
RATES Single or double 140–150€; *taxe de séjour* included **CREDIT CARDS** AE,
DC, MC, V
BREAKFAST Buffet or Continental in room 10€ per person

HÔTEL DES 3 COLLÈGES ★★ (24)
16, rue Cujas, 75005
Métro: Maubert-Mutualité; RER Luxembourg
44 rooms, all with shower or bath and toilet

This three-generation family hotel takes its name from the three
colleges on the Montagne–St-Geneviève: La Sorbonne, founded in the
thirteenth century; the fifteenth-century Collège St-Barbe, the oldest
private school in France; and the prestigious Collège de France. The
hotel is in a good Left Bank neighborhood between the Sorbonne
and the Panthéon, and within easy walking distance to a multitude
of restaurants and shops. The small, off-white lobby has a California
look, with modern chairs, large green plants, and bleached wooden
floors. The pocket-size rooms have all the necessities: luggage racks,
desks and chairs, full-length mirrors, wall-mounted television sets, and
fitted bathrooms. What they are missing is extra space. The best from
a size standpoint are on the top floor. Number 62 looks onto the dome
of the Sorbonne Observatory and St-Etienne du Monde church, which
has the ashes of the writer Pascal and a shrine to Sainte Geneviève, the
Patron Saint of Paris. Room 63 has a sloping roof and Panthéon view,
and it sleeps two or three nicely. Room 54 is a corner double with a
white matlesée bedspread accented with two brick orange throw pillows. Numbers 46 or 56, both with showers, are nice selections for
the single traveler. The glass-roofed lounge off the lobby showcases a
large, central tree that's surrounded by rattan chairs.

TEL 01-43-54-67-30 **FAX** 01-46-34-02-99 **EMAIL** hotel@3colleges.com
INTERNET www.3colleges.com
FACILITIES & SERVICES Direct-dial phone, elevator, hair dryer, laundry service,
TV with international reception, room safe (no charge), Internet in lobby
RATES Single 72–120€, double 94–101€, large 6th-floor rooms for 1–2
persons 120€, 3 persons 140–160€; *taxe de séjour* included
CREDIT CARDS AE, DC, MC, V
BREAKFAST Continental 8€ per person

HÔTEL DU COLLÈGE DE FRANCE ★★ (14)
7, rue Thénard, 75005
Métro: Maubert-Mutualité, Cluny–La Sorbonne; RER St-Michel-Notre Dame
29 rooms, all with shower or bath and toilet

Well-placed in the heart of the Latin Quarter and across the street
from the Collège de France, this is an outstanding Great Sleeping value
for a two-star hotel. The immaculate rooms are uniformly done. The
best ones are on the top floors; they have wooden beams and paneling,

glimpses of Notre Dame Cathedral, and in summer are equipped with portable fans. One room on the second floor and some on the fifth have a balcony. If you want connecting rooms, they will be on the first or second floors. If sunshine is a priority, request a room ending in 3. Room 62 is the largest and most requested, probably due to the two floor-to-ceiling windows opening onto a small balcony, where you can see the Collège de France. The bathrooms are modern, with hair dryers, large towels, and space for more than just a toothbrush. The lobby and breakfast room feature rust red fabrics, which goes well with the collection of healthy green plants, and a statue of Joan of Arc guards the entryway. Jean Marc, the very personable owner, and his excellent staff have proven their motto: "If you are a client once, you will always be one." The popularity of this little hotel is reflected in its guest register, which can fill up months ahead, so plan accordingly.

TEL 01-43-26-78-36 **FAX** 01-46-34-58-29 **EMAIL** hotel.du.college.de.france@
wanadoo.fr **INTERNET** www.hotel-collegedefrance.com
FACILITIES & SERVICES Direct-dial phone, fans, elevator (to most floors), hair
dryer, TV with international reception, room safe (no charge), free WiFi
RATES Single 85€, double 95–115€; extra bed 20€; children under 14 are
free; *taxe de séjour* included **CREDIT CARDS** AE, MC, V
BREAKFAST Continental 8€ per person

HÔTEL DU PANTHÉON ★★★ ($, 28)
19, place du Panthéon, 75005
Métro: Maubert-Mutualité; RER Luxembourg
36 rooms, all with shower, bath, and toilet

The elegent Hôtel du Panthéon is a converted eighteenth-century town house that faces the imposing place du Panthéon in the fifth arrondissement. The métro is about five blocks away, but if you love this part of Paris, you know that almost everything is within walking distance. From the ground up, the hotel benefits from the impeccable taste and preservationist sensibilities of the gracious owner, Corinne Brethous-Moncelli, who also owns Hôtel des Grands Hommes next door (see page 117), Hôtel Résidence Henri IV (see page 125), Hôtel de la Sorbonne (see page 114), and Jardin de l'Odéon Hôtel (see page 163).

The large entry leads to the attractive lounge, which has a small atrium garden to one side and a panoramic view of the Panthéon. The Continental breakfast is served on glass-topped tables under stone arches in the house's original cellar or in the privacy of your room. Guests will feel at home immediately in any one of the thirty-six rooms, harmoniously decorated with antique furniture, perfectly coordinated fabrics, textile-covered walls, nicely framed artwork, and floor-length curtains from fourteen-foot ceilings. Several with canopy beds are romantic choices for honeymooners. The twenty-three front rooms facing the Panthéon, some with sweeping views beyond to Sacré Coeur, are naturally in demand, especially the five with balconies on the fifth floor. However, if you need absolute silence and calm, the attractive, but viewless, back rooms will guarantee this. The bathrooms are spacious, many with free-standing sinks, separate stall showers, and enclosed toilets.

TEL 01-43-54-32-95 **FAX** 01-43-26-64-65 **EMAIL** reservations@
  hoteldupantheon.com **INTERNET** www.hoteldupantheon.com
FACILITIES & SERVICES Air-conditioning, bar, conference room, direct-dial
  phone, elevator, hair dryer, laundry service, magnifying mirrors, minibar,
  porter, TV with international reception, room safe (no charge), free WiFi
  in lobby and some rooms
RATES 1–2 persons 225–255€, triple 285€; *taxe de séjour* included
  CREDIT CARDS AE, DC, MC, V
BREAKFAST Buffet or Continental 12€ per person

HÔTEL ESMERALDA ★ (5)
4, rue Saint-Julien-le-Pauvre, at quai de Montebello, 75005
Métro: St-Michel; RER St-Michel–Notre-Dame
19 rooms, 16 with shower or bath and toilet

Warning: This hotel is not for perfectionists!

The Esmeralda is an unconventional hideaway directly across the Seine from Notre Dame Cathedral. It has been owned for years by Madame Bruel, a sculptor and writer who lived in England and studied at Oxford. She and her former husband owned the first Bateaux Mouches that now take tourists up and down the Seine. After a bitter divorce, she bought the Esmeralda because she could see her beloved Seine from many of the windows. She told me most of the rooms at the time were occupied by "permanent residents," all of whom shared one bathroom! She has made some improvements since then. Notice I said *some*. This is a hotel people either love or absolutely hate. For some, its faded charm with a definite past holds great appeal, especially when sitting by one of the large windows and looking across the Seine to Notre Dame bathed in moonlight.

Maybe it does not have the most modern accommodations in town, but it does have one of the best Left Bank locations and some of the most interesting guests. The lack of embellishments, which might disappoint some, is the lure that brings others back again and again. This is a hotel with character for people with character.

No two rooms are alike, and they definitely are light-years away from modern. Just like the unique owner, they flout convention and are eccentric to the core. Some are the size of a walk-in closet; others have chandeliers, marble fireplaces, and picture-perfect postcard views of Notre Dame Cathedral over the gardens of St-Julien-le-Pauvre, Paris's oldest church. All the rooms are reached by passing through a stone-walled lobby and climbing up a circular flight of ancient stairs. Some of the floors slant, many areas need more than just a coat of paint, and others have only a nodding acquaintance with the housekeeper. It is also noisy. But its many cult followers do not care because just being at the Esmeralda spells Paris for them. Be sure to bring earplugs and reserve way in advance.

TEL 01-43-54-19-20 **FAX** 01-40-51-00-68

FACILITIES & SERVICES Direct-dial phone, no elevator (4 floors), office safe (no charge)

RATES Very small single 42€, 1–2 persons 88€, triple 97€, quad 125€; *taxe de séjour* included **CREDIT CARDS** None, cash only

BREAKFAST Continental 7€ per person

HÔTEL HENRI IV RIVE GAUCHE ★★★ (4)
9–11, rue Saint-Jacques, 75005
Métro: Cluny–La Sorbonne, Maubert-Mutualité; RER St-Michel–Notre-Dame
23 rooms, all with shower or bath and toilet

The wonderful Hôtel Henri IV Rive Gauche, the latest jewel in the crown of owners Roland and Elisabeth Buffat, proves that style does not have to come with high price tags. The sophisticated design and great value of their other hotels are both clearly evident in this venture. The brick-floor lobby is done in soft sea green, accented by an antique Portuguese-tile wall and comfortable dark brown–leather armchairs. The halls are covered in the same soft green, with linen-textured walls adding interest above the wainscoting. The tasteful rooms repeat the same putty and white colors on the stucco walls and wicker furnishings. All have luggage and closet space, a comfortable chair, desk space with high-speed Internet lines, and attractive bathrooms with tub-and-shower combinations and heated towel racks. I like the rooms on the higher floors, not only because they are light and airy, but because some have views of the top of Notre Dame Cathedral or the St-Séverin Church. Some of the rooms facing the interior hotel courtyard have small balconies.

Also under the same ownership are Hôtel de Lutèce and Hôtel des Deux-Îles, both on Île St-Louis (pages 99 and 101), and Galileo Hôtel (page 194).

TEL 01-46-33-20-20 **FAX** 01-46-33-90-90 **EMAIL** info@hotel-henri4.com
INTERNET www.hotel-henri4.com

FACILITIES & SERVICES Air-conditioning, direct-dial phone, elevator, hair dryer, Internet in lobby, laundry service, minibar, TV with international reception, room safe (no charge), WiFi

RATES Single 149€, double 167€, triple 188€; *taxe de séjour* 1€ per person, per day **CREDIT CARDS** AE, DC, MC, V

BREAKFAST Continental 11€ per person

HÔTEL LE RELAIS SAINT-JACQUES ★★★★ ($, 33)
3, rue de l'Abbé de l'Épée, 75005
Métro: RER Luxembourg
22 rooms, all with shower, bath, and toilet

A beautiful Louis XV furnished salon with Aubusson tapestries and a marble fireplace flanked by bookcases set the regal tone at this lovely boutique hotel, which is on the road that pilgrims once took on their way to Santiago de Compostela in Spain. The theme of the hotel celebrates the grace and beauty of the castles of the Loire Valley, while the hotel itself reflects the meticulous care that the Bonneau family has put into making sure that their guests are pampered with a combination of the traditions of the past and the luxurious amenities of the present. The stunning collection of photographs of the Loire hanging in the common areas and the glass-roofed breakfast room are the work of the family patriarch, who was named the best French photographer of the year in 1961.

In keeping with the theme, each room is named after a château in the Loire and furnished in one of four traditional styles: Louis XV, Louis XVI, Empire, and Portuguese Manuelian. Room 402 ("Château Usse") is done in the last, with handmade twisted dark mahogany wood offsetting the lace linens on the four-poster bed. The stunning desk was originally a type of office trunk used for traveling from castle to castle. Number 203, Château Beaugency, decorated in soft aqua, is Louis XVI. The customized gold-trimmed furnishings include a console cabinet containing a television, safe, and minibar. Château Blois, and two others like it, are Empire. Room 503, Chenonceaux, is a luxuriously livable two-room suite. In the large sitting room you will have an entire wall of closet space, plank floors, DVD player, flat-screen television, a bathroom with shower, and a balcony with a view of the Panthéon. The bedroom features heavy Damask silk curtains, a second television, and full marble bathroom with Jacuzzi bathtub. Most of the other bedrooms face out, but the few that do not instead face walls that have been painted to resemble country garden themes. The bathrooms are beautifully done in marble with plenty of mirrors, excellent light, bathrobes and slippers in most, and all the towels and toiletries you would expect.

TEL 01-53-73-26-00, toll-free in the U.S. 800-44-UTELL **FAX** 01-43-26-17-81
   EMAIL hotel-relais@wanadoo.fr **INTERNET** www.relais-saint-jacques.com
FACILITIES & SERVICES Air-conditioning, bar, business center, conference room, direct-dial phone, elevator, hair dryer, handicapped room, laundry service, minibar, trouser press, TV with international reception, 24-hour room service, room safe (no charge), all rooms are nonsmoking, WiFi
RATES 1–2 persons privilege 160€, prestige 190–245€, deluxe 255€, suite 480€; *taxe de séjour* 1.40€ per person, per night **CREDIT CARDS** AE, DC, MC, V
BREAKFAST Buffet 17€, Continental 14€, per person

HÔTEL MARIGNAN ★ (¢, 15)
13, rue de Sommerard, 75005
Métro: Maubert-Mutualité, Cluny–La Sorbonne; RER St-Michel-Notre-Dame
30 rooms, 13 with shower or bath and toilet, 6 with toilet and sink, 11 with sink only

The Marignan lives up to the three Cs of all lower-priced accommodations: it is clean, convenient, and cheap, especially from October through February (but not between Christmas and New Year's) when rooms booked for three nights or more are 25 percent less than the published prices. The hotel is usually jammed year-round with a frugal crowd of students, backpackers, and professors. A spirit of camaraderie prevails in this busy spot, making it impossible to feel lonely for long. The linoleum-lined rooms are above average for a one-star. Mattresses are good, more than a third of the rooms have full facilities, and there is space, but don't look for views from the back singles or much in the way of reading lights. Breakfast, which is generous by one-star standards (cheese, fruit salad, and orange juice along with bread and jam, but no croissant), is included in the rate and cannot be deducted. Guests are allowed to bring in food, store it in the kitchen refrigerator, warm it in the microwave, and eat it in the dining room, but no eating is allowed in the rooms. Guests can also use the washer/dryer to wash travel-weary clothing and iron out the wrinkles with the hotel iron. WiFi hookup in the lobby is free during the low season from November through February.

To his credit, long-term owner Paul Keniger has provided guests with a wealth of information on Paris, including a large detailed map of the *quartier* showing the métro stops, banks, pharmacies, money-changing offices, bakeries, and tourist sites. The management also clearly states the rules of the hotel, and guests are expected to abide by them or move out. They are listed in plain sight at the check-in desk, so no one can claim "I didn't know" not to put suitcases on the bed or to slam doors; not to eat or leave empty bottles or cans in the room; not to take a shower before 7 A.M. or after 10:45 P.M.; and never to go barefoot in public areas or on the stairs. And by all means, turn off the light when leaving. Between March and September, reservations are taken for a minimum of two nights.

TEL 01-43-54-63-81 **FAX** 01-43-25-16-69 **EMAIL** reserv-marignan@wanadoo.fr
  INTERNET www.hotel-marignan.com
FACILITIES & SERVICES Dining area, direct-dial phones, no elevator (6 floors), fans on request, free laundry and ironing area, French TV on request, hair dryer in some rooms and on request, office safe (no charge), WiFi in lobby
RATES Single 47–70€, double 55–85€, triple 80–110€, quad 90–125€, 5 people 110–155€; showers free; *taxe de séjour* included
  CREDIT CARDS MC, V
BREAKFAST Included, cannot be deducted

HÔTEL PARC SAINT-SÉVERIN ★★★ (8)
22, rue de la Parcheminerie, 75005
Métro: Cluny–La Sorbonne, St-Michel; RER St-Michel–Notre Dame
27 rooms, all with shower, bath, and toilet

Dyed-in-the-wool aficionados of life around St-Michel, who also like elegantly understated surroundings, will love this hotel. The owners are to be applauded for creating an alluring, modern establishment that is serene, serious, and pleasing to the eye. For someone very, very special, reserve No. 70, the private penthouse suite with its own elevator entrance. The wraparound terrace provides unequaled views of Notre Dame, St-Séverin Church (one of the most popular in Paris for weddings), the Panthéon, Collège de France, Tour Montparnasse, and in the distance, the Eiffel Tower and Sacré Coeur on Montmartre. The interior of this dream suite glows with a blend of antiques and contemporary furnishings. If No. 70 is booked, ask for No. 61, a corner room with a terrace and view of the Eiffel Tower, Cluny Gardens, St-Séverin cloister and church, and a peek of Notre Dame. The other rooms in the hotel display the same standards of excellence, and many have balconies and impressive views. The management and staff are exceptional in their attention and service for all of their guests. For those who want up-to-the-minute convenience and luxury in the heart of old Paris, the Parc Saint-Séverin is a favorite choice of many discriminating *Great Sleeps Paris* readers.

For other hotels within the Esprit de France hotel group, see Hôtel Brighton (page 71), Hôtel de la Place du Louvre (page 73), Hôtel Mansart (page 77), Hôtel d'Orsay (page 179), Hôtel des Saints-Pères (page 177), and Hôtel l'Aiglon (page 235).

TEL 01-43-54-32-17 **FAX** 01-43-54-70-71 **EMAIL** hpss@espritfrance.com
INTERNET www.esprit-de-france.com
FACILITIES & SERVICES Air-conditioning, direct-dial phone, elevator, hair dryer, laundry service, minibar, TV with international reception, room safe (no charge), WiFi
RATES Single 110–145€, double 145–150€, terrace rooms 200–305€; children under 12 free; *taxe de séjour* included **CREDIT CARDS** AE, DC, MC, V
BREAKFAST Buffet in dining room or Continental in room 11€ per person

HÔTEL RÉSIDENCE HENRI IV ★★★ (21)
50, rue des Bernardins, next to Square Paul Langevin, 75005
Métro: Maubert-Mutualité, Cardinal Lemoine
13 rooms, all with shower or bath and toilet and fully fitted kitchenette

Over twenty years ago, when I began writing my Paris hotel guide, this hotel had another name and an image of faded respectability. Several years ago it was taken over by Corinne Brethous-Moncelli, who owns other recommended hotels in the fifth arrondissement. I have found that whatever Mme. Moncelli touches is transformed with style and distinction, and this property is no exception. Quietly situated opposite the leafy Square Paul Langevin, at the end of rue des Bernardins, the hotel offers thirteen spacious rooms, each with the added plus of fully fitted kitchenettes, as well as all the hotel services and facilities that a guest could want. I think the best buys are the beautiful two-room suites because they offer separate sitting areas, marble fireplaces, and just enough extra space to make a long stay very comfortable. Number 22 has a magnificent gold-framed mirror over its fireplace. Hand-painted moldings and the original ceiling are carried through to the bedroom, which has a large armoire and a corner fireplace to add to its charm. Rooms 50 and 52 can be joined to accommodate a family. Number 1 on the ground floor is done in soft gray and cream and has a skylight in the bathroom. It faces the street and has no fireplace, but it is large enough for three. The hotel is peaceful and calm, yet it is minutes away from almost everything on a visitor's A-list of things to see and do around the *quartier* of St-Michel.

Also under the same ownership are Hôtel des Grands Hommes (page 117), Hôtel du Panthéon (page 120), Hôtel de la Sorbonne (page 114), and Jardin de l'Odéon Hôtel (page 163).

TEL 01-44-41-31-81 **FAX** 01-46-33-93-22 **EMAIL** reservation@
  residencehenri4.com **INTERNET** www.residencehenri4.com
FACILITIES & SERVICES Direct-dial phone, elevator (but not to the lower
  ground-floor breakfast room), fans on request, hair dryer, fitted
  kitchenettes, TV with international reception, room safe (no charge),
  WiFi in lobby and some rooms
RATES 1–2 persons standard 135€, larger rooms for 1–4 persons 165–310€;
  taxe de séjour included **CREDIT CARDS** AE, DC, MC, V
BREAKFAST Continental 10€ per person

HÔTEL RÉSIDENCE MONGE ★★ (31)
55, rue Monge, 75005
Métro: Place Monge, Cardinal Lemoine
36 rooms, all with bath or shower and toilet

It isn't posh by any means, just a modest, family Great Sleep run by a delightful manager, Mme. Julie Chatillon. The exceptionally clean, well-priced rooms are decorated in rose, blue, peach, pale green, or yellow. All are absolutely spotless and in perfect order, thanks to the three housekeepers who have worked here for more than twenty years. Number 31 is one of the best in the house. This quiet room is done in hues of salmon and blue with two windows overlooking a playground (which was once a Roman amphitheater) and a bathroom with both a tub and shower. Number 32 is also a nice double with good leg room and a large, light bathroom. Three can fit comfortably in No. 22, which has the bonus of a balcony. I can't say much for No. 23, a single on the front where it is a tight squeeze to sit at the desk (which is almost covered by the TV anyway), and the closet door will never open completely. You can expect some noise in Rooms 12 and 15 because they face the street. Imitation flowers and plants abound, especially in the breakfast room, which is overflowing with many bright varieties sitting in floral trimmed pots. A Chinese glass cabinet displays a collection of antique cars and hand-painted ducks.

TEL 01-43-26-87-90 **FAX** 01-43-54-47-25 **EMAIL** hotel-monge@wanadoo.fr
  INTERNET www.hotelmonge.com
FACILITIES & SERVICES Air-conditioning, direct-dial phone, elevator, hair dryer,
  minibar, TV with international reception, office safe (no charge)
RATES Single 68–84€, double 78–130€, triple 120–150€; *taxe de séjour* 1€
  per person, per day **CREDIT CARDS** MC, V
BREAKFAST Continental in breakfast room 6.50€ per person

HÔTEL SAINT-JACQUES ★★ (20)
35, rue des Écoles, 75005
Métro: Maubert-Mutualite, Cluny–La Sorbonne; RER St-Michel–Notre-Dame

38 rooms, 34 with shower or bath and toilet

Rooms with half as much appeal often cost twice as much as those at this outstanding two-star choice near the Sorbonne. Film buffs may recognize the facade and the stairway, which were used in the Audrey Hepburn and Cary Grant classic, *Charade*. From the doorstep you can easily walk to Notre Dame, the Panthéon, the Louvre, the islands, and all the interesting streets that make up this part of the Latin Quarter. Concern for artistic details, first-rate services, a friendly welcome from head receptionist Brijitte, and loads of amenities underscore the fact that affordable does not need to mean lacking in style or substance. The pretty frescoes in the sitting room (of a Victorian trio along the Seine) and in the streetside breakfast room (of Notre Dame) were done by Pierre Amblard, a painter who left his job as an English teacher to follow his passion for art. Downstairs, the breakfast room displays an old gramaphone, an antique gold National Cash register, a player piano, and a collection of old glass and spritz bottles gathered from visits to the Parisian *puces* (flea markets).

The thirty-eight reasonably priced rooms are an easy mixture of modern comforts, sculptured moldings, coordinated decor, and views of Notre Dame and the Panthéon. Everyone likes the tissue-lined No. 5, which has an original 1870 ceiling and two windows draped in fabrics that match the bed. The bathroom has a large tub and a shower guard. From the corner balcony in No. 8, you have a view of Notre Dame on the right and the Panthéon on the left. The bathroom has an enclosed stall shower and painted tile detailing around the mirror. In No. 28, guests who don't mind climbing a few stairs are rewarded with another balcony and a nice bathroom. Also on the sixth floor is No. 31, a cheaper double with a partial view of Notre Dame. Singles can reserve one of the three new rooms on the ground and first floor that were created out of an old Chinese restaurant next door. Guests staying longer than a week can request their own private fax and phone lines.

Also under the same management is the Hôtel Riviera (see page 269).

TEL 01-44-07-45-45 **FAX** 01-43-25-65-50 **EMAIL** hotelsaintjacques@wanadoo.fr
    INTERNET www.paris-hotel-saintjacques.com

FACILITIES & SERVICES Bar, direct-dial phone, elevator (to most floors), fans on request, hair dryer, magnifying mirrors in largest rooms, TV with international reception, room safe (no charge), 3 nonsmoking rooms, free WiFi in lobby

RATES Single 55€ (without bath), 84€ (with bath), double 95–104€, triple 152€; free hall showers; *taxe de séjour* included **CREDIT CARDS** AE, DC, MC, V

BREAKFAST Buffet 10€, Continental 8.50€ per person

LES DEGRÉS DE NOTRE-DAME HÔTEL (NO STARS, 10)
10, rue des Grands Degrés, 75005
Métro: Maubert-Mutualité; RER St-Michel–Notre-Dame
10 rooms, all with shower or bath and toilet

It takes a youthful mind-set and an agile body to stay at this hotel, which blatantly ignores trends and creates its own individual style. For starters, the ten rooms are located on five floors reached by a steep winding staircase hardly one person wide. Once you have schlepped your luggage to your room, you won't have to worry about where to put it all—the rooms are large and there is plenty of closet and drawer space. The colors are coordinated, the artwork probably not to everyone's taste, and the furnishings have that certain flea market flair. The towels in the bathroom are from another hotel; when I asked why, I was told, "They were cheap."

Number 36 (a three-flight workout) has a wood floor, dark furnishings, and a long bathroom with a tub, freestanding sink, and toilet behind a pocket door. In No. 24, a huge double up two flights, you can enjoy the neighborhood view from the three double windows and admire the nude painting over the bed. A painting of a woman reading a newspaper (which hides all but her shapely legs under her skirt and ruffly petticoat) is the focal point in No. 48. Red silk curtains frame the three windows. From the heavily beamed No. 47, you can see the tower of Notre Dame and bathe in the pink and green mosaic–tiled bathroom, which has the latest in double sinks and chrome trim. If your legs can make it to the top floor, you will sleep in a big room with a brass and chrystal chandelier, mirrored bed backdrop, and walls faux finished in pink, gray, and blue. The bathroom has a pair of six-foot nudes over the bathtub.

TEL 01-55-42-88-88 **FAX** 01-40-46-95-34 **EMAIL** contact@lesdegreshotel.com
 INTERNET www.lesdegreshotel.com
FACILITIES & SERVICES Bar, direct-dial phone with private number, no elevator
 (5 floors), hair dryer, restaurant, French TV, room safe (no charge)
RATES Hotel 1–2 persons 110–160€; studio apartments 160€; *taxe de séjour*
 included **CREDIT CARDS** MC, V
BREAKFAST Continental with fresh orange juice included

LES RIVES DE NOTRE DAME ★★★★ ($, 1)
15, quai St-Michel, 75005
Métro: St-Michel; RER St-Michel–Notre Dame
10 rooms, all with shower, bath, and toilet

If a room facing the Seine and Notre Dame is your idea of a Paris address, step right this way. However, be forewarned: what you gain in the dynamic location, you will sacrifice in peace and quiet, as this is one of the top must-see areas for every camera-toting visitor to the City of Light. Oozing charm from every pitched beam, bright print, and colorful floral arrangement, the ten delightful rooms transport guests to a small village in Provence or Tuscany. Everything is well done and well considered. Characteristic wrought-iron beds blend well with antique accent pieces to give each room its own personality.

Mix-and-match fabrics further set the country-style mood. The top-floor suite under the pitched mansard roof is a knockout in red. In addition to a king-size bed, there is a sofabed, round table and chairs, and plenty of room for a family of four to live in comfort. The marble bathrooms have peignoirs and slippers in addition to nice toiletries and magnifying mirrors. Morning croissants and coffee are served in a stone-walled breakfast room on tables set with linens and Villeroy and Boch fruit-patterned china. Excellent promotional rates on the hotel Website keep this Great Sleep in Paris fully booked year round.

TEL 01-43-54-81-16 **FAX** 01-43-26-27-09 **EMAIL** hotel@rivesdenotredame.com
   INTERNET www.rivesdenotredame.com
FACILITIES & SERVICES Air-conditioning, direct-dial phone, elevator, hair dryer, minibar, laundry service, TV with international reception, room safe (no charge), WiFi in rooms
RATES 1–2 persons: standard room 183–243€, superior room 237–289€, suite 400–550€; *taxe de séjour* 1.50€ per person, per day **CREDIT CARDS** AE, DC, MC, V
BREAKFAST Buffet 14€, Continental in room 11€, per person

MINERVE HÔTEL ★★★ (25)
13, rue des Écoles, 75005
Métro: Cardinal Lemoine, Maubert-Mutualité
54 rooms, all with shower or bath and toilet

Eric Gaucheron had two important life-changing events in 1999: his wife, Sylvie, bore him a son, and he bought the fifty-four-room Minerve Hôtel, next door to the Familia Hôtel, which he and his family have owned for many years (see page 111). Despite the fact that the Minerve occupies a noble 1850 building, before Eric renovated it completely, the hotel was, in a word, terrible. No more! Thank goodness energy, imagination, and enthusiasm are three attributes Eric has in spades. Twenty-four workmen toiled relentlessly for months to meet his exacting standards, and a phoenix rose from the ashes.

Everything continues to be of high quality: the mattresses; the attractive, custom-made antique-style furnishings; the coordinated fabrics; and of course, the marble-tile bathrooms with monogrammed towels. Allergy sufferers can reserve a room with either a wood or ceramic tiled floor. In addition to all the usual comforts, such as air-conditioning, international television reception, and triple-glazed windows to buffer the noise, all rooms have WiFi, four have cathedral ceilings, five have hand-painted ceilings, two have interior patios, ten have balconies, and many have hand-painted frescoes of French monuments. It is hard to pick a favorite, but I do like No. 607. The wall behind the bed was an old chimney, and from the balcony you have a view of Notre Dame and a twelfth-century abbey. Another favorite is No. 403, with a fresco of Monet's gardens at Giverney. Room 507 has two windows looking onto a balcony and a large bathroom with a tub. If you need absolute quiet, No. 608, with hand-painted scenes from the Greek Parthenon, double closets, and good lighting, is on the back and can sleep three. Both of the two inside patio rooms (Nos. 102 and 103) are also quiet.

A mural montage of Paris greets guests as they enter the hotel. Original 150-year-old tapestries hang on the exposed stone walls in the lobby and in the downstairs breakfast room. The appealing lobby has burnt orange and gold armchairs and settees arranged in groups for twos and threes. Toward the back is a glass-enclosed atrium with a fountain and bamboo trees. Along one wall is an antique bookcase holding some of Eric's antique book collection and a lovely old clock. Recent additions include two conference rooms, which seat thirty but can hold fifty for small weddings or private receptions. It all adds up to an impressive three-star hotel with great amenities and excellent prices.

TEL 01-43-26-26-04, 01-43-26-81-89 **FAX** 01-44-07-01-96
   EMAIL minerve@hotellerie.net **INTERNET** www.parishotelminerve.com
FACILITIES & SERVICES Air-conditioning, conference rooms (2), direct-dial phone, elevator, hair dryer, minibar, private parking, TV with international reception, room safe (no charge), WiFi throughout (free in the lobby)
RATES Single 88–134€, double 100–134€, triple 155€; parking 20€ for 24 hours; *taxe de séjour* included **CREDIT CARDS** MC, V
BREAKFAST Continental in room or buffet 8€ per person

PORT-ROYAL HÔTEL ★ (¢, 43)
8, boulevard de Port Royal, 75005
Métro: Gobelins
48 rooms, 20 with shower or bath and toilet

If you are looking for maximum value without sacrificing quality in either surroundings or service, you will find the Port-Royal Hôtel impossible to beat. In fact, it is so far ahead of most other one-star hotels in Paris (and many two- and three-star hotels for that matter) that there simply is no contest. I will admit that I had my doubts at first, as I trudged on and on down the long boulevard de Port Royal in a driving rainstorm looking for the hotel. Once inside, however, I found it nothing short of amazing. It is obvious that Claudine and Thierry Giraud are paying close attention to every detail and carrying on the traditions set by their father, who owned the hotel for over seventy years. On top of being an absolute steal for the money, it is spotless and, thanks to Claudine, exceptionally well decorated. The usual one-star dime-store taste—dusty plastic floral arrangements, mismatched colors, and exhausted, sagging furniture—is nowhere in sight. Instead, everything is in perfect order, from her magnificent collection of orchids and other blooms in the downstairs areas to the blue carpeted hallways with security and fire doors, to the well-coordinated rooms, all with attractive fabrics, touches of faux finishing, wicker and wrought-iron furnishings, and ceiling fans. Those on the front have double-paned windows that allow for a peaceful night's sleep. Many have beautiful new bathrooms, especially No. 20, a double with space, light, and a street view. I also like No. 11, with floral inserts on the tile walls wrapping around the deep tub. Even the showers have doors, a rare find in Paris and almost a curiosity in one-star hotels. Those selecting the smallest rooms need not feel deprived; these have many of the same nice touches of their more expensive neighbors, including a piece of candy on the pillow at night.

The facade has been repainted, enhancing the Art Deco glass gracefully curving over the front door. The inviting street-side sitting room, with its comfortable chairs and beautiful live green and flowering plants, belies the hotel's budget category. So does the breakfast room, overlooking a neatly manicured interior garden. Real flowers on the tables, caned chairs with upholstered seats, and an interesting collection of the family's antique woodworking tools add to the appeal.

The hotel is easily accessible to St-Michel, the Musée d'Orsay, the Louvre, and the Champs-Élysées by bus. It connects to Orly by direct bus from the métro stop. Close by is the Italie 2 shopping complex with 150 boutiques and a branch of Au Printemps department store, the famous rue Mouffetard with its open-air market, the Gobelins tapestry workshops, and the Jardin des Plantes. Also close are cinemas—including the Grand Ecran, which boasts the largest screen in Europe—and a selection of restaurants and cafés (see *Great Eats Paris*). Free street parking is available Monday to Friday 7 P.M. to 9 A.M. and all day Saturday, Sunday, holidays, and in August; otherwise, nearby underground parking costs around 20€ per day. All in all, it adds up to one of the best Great Sleeps for the money in Paris.

NOTE: Reservations are accepted by phone 7 A.M. to 7 P.M. only.

TEL 01-43-31-70-06 **FAX** 01-43-31-33-67 **EMAIL** portroyalhotel@wanadoo.fr
   INTERNET www.portroyalhotel.fr
FACILITIES & SERVICES Direct-dial phone, elevator, fans on 6th floor, hair dryer
   and iron available, nearby parking, French TV (in sitting room), office safe
   (no charge)
RATES Single 39€ (sink only), 51€ (with bath); double 51€ (sink only),
   77€ (with bath); deluxe 82–87€; showers in hall 2.50€; *taxe de séjour*
   included **CREDIT CARDS** None, cash only
BREAKFAST Continental 6€ per person

SELECT HÔTEL ★★★ (22)
1, place de la Sorbonne, 75005
Métro: Cluny–La Sorbonne; RER Luxembourg
68 rooms, all with shower or bath and toilet

In 1937, Eric Sevareid paid 50¢ a night at the Select. Things have changed . . . considerably.

The Select has one of the most unusual interior garden courts in Paris: it's a replica of a desert scene with assorted cacti and succulants, which would seem more at home in arid Arizona than in the middle of the Latin Quarter of Paris. At the entrance to the hotel, what appears to be a glowing rock fireplace in winter becomes a summertime aquarium filled with tropical fish. The lobby and reception areas are studies in ultramodern design, with chrome and leather furniture. This sleek approach is carried into the intimate bar, breakfast room, and seating alcoves tucked around the skylighted desert scene. There is even a separate television room with a large-screen plasma TV enticing sports fans to watch the current game. Hallways in speckled cement or cocoa-colored plastic showcase the work of Hyppolite Romain, who was commissioned specially to do all of the paintings.

Most of the rooms have as much modernistic appeal as the public areas, especially the renovated sites overlooking the interior desert, the place de la Sorbonne in front, or the facade of the Sorbonne. Some of those on the backside and in the annex have all the perks but are dark, viewless, and done in some hideous wallpapers and colors. An exception (well, maybe . . .) is No. 32. It has an interior view, but the area is filled with green plants to soften the outlook. The room itself feels like an exhibit space at the Centre Georges Pompidou. Curved metal doors halfway shield the room from the bathtub and stainless-steel sink with a long, narrow mirror. The toilet is enclosed, but there is no privacy for bathing or brushing your teeth. Other than the bed and a metal chair with a leather seat cushion, everything is built-in. The only color comes from the light gray bedspread with a pear, eggplant, and squash pattern. *Chaque à son gout!* A better backside room is No. 77, a tiny gray-green double with floating sinks in a new bathroom. Avoid No. 41, a duplex, due to the treacherous spiral staircase descending to the cavelike downstairs bedroom.

Two of the nicest rooms are Nos. 33 and 53, which display the original stone wall of the hotel and centuries-old oak beams. Two large floor-to-ceiling windows open onto the place de la Sorbonne below. Comfortable armchairs, good reading lights, a large working desk, hidden storage space, and a split bathroom make these favorites for longer stays. Number 29 is a roomy triple with beams and recessed lighting. It features a double closet in the entry, a stone wall behind the bed, a comfortable chair, double sinks in a marble bathroom, and a side view of the Sorbonne. Rooms 23 and 25 facing the place de la Sorbonne also have the modern look; I like the work and luggage space these rooms offer. An ideal Latin Quarter location, lower off-season rates, three-star creature comforts, and the friendly reception staff (headed by Jeanine for more than thirty years and by Isabelle for nine) make the Select Hôtel a front-runner in the *quartier*. Unfortunately, it no longer costs 50¢ a night.

TEL 01-46-34-14-80 **FAX** 01-46-34-51-79 **EMAIL** info@selecthotel.fr
   INTERNET www.selecthotel.fr
FACILITIES & SERVICES Air-conditioning, bar, direct-dial phone, elevator, hair dryer, porter, TV with international reception, room safe (no charge), WiFi
RATES 1–2 persons: standard 159€, superior 185–195€, executive or triple 190–220€, duplex 245€; extra bed 30% of room rate; *taxe de séjour* 1€ per person, per day **CREDIT CARDS** AE, DC, MC, V
BREAKFAST Buffet 6€ per person

Sixth Arrondissement

Literary and artistic Paris is the heart of the sixth, which is a continuation of the Latin Quarter and one of the most stimulating parts of the city. Intellectual, elegant, and very appealing, it has tiny side streets, old buildings, antique shops, designer boutiques, a thriving café life, and more atmosphere block for block than anyone could ever soak up. The square by the Église St-Germain-des-Prés, the oldest Roman abbey church in Paris, is the main focus of the district. Les Deux Magots and Café de Flore, two of the most celebrated cafés in Paris, were the hangouts of Hemingway, Sartre, Simone de Beauvoir, and James Joyce.

LEFT BANK
École des Beaux-Arts
excellent shopping
Jardin and Palais du
    Luxembourg
Odéon National Theater
St-Germain-des-Prés Church
St-Sulpice Church

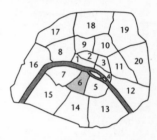

Today they are jammed with Parisians and tourists alike engaged in some of the best people-watching in the universe. Many of the major fashion designers have opened boutiques here, making the area a luxury shopping destination for world-class fashionistas. The École Nationale Supérieure des Beaux-Arts, the city's famous fine-arts school, is in a former convent that is open to the public for exhibitions. The Jardin du Luxembourg, one of Paris's most loved parks, draws more than three million joggers and walkers per year. The city employs seventy-two gardeners and spends eleven million euros per year to maintain it. Large photo exhibitions often line the metal grillwork along the rue de Vaugirard side of the park. At one end of the gardens is the Italianate Palais du Luxembourg, which was built for Marie de Médici, widow of Henri IV, and is now occupied by the French Senate.

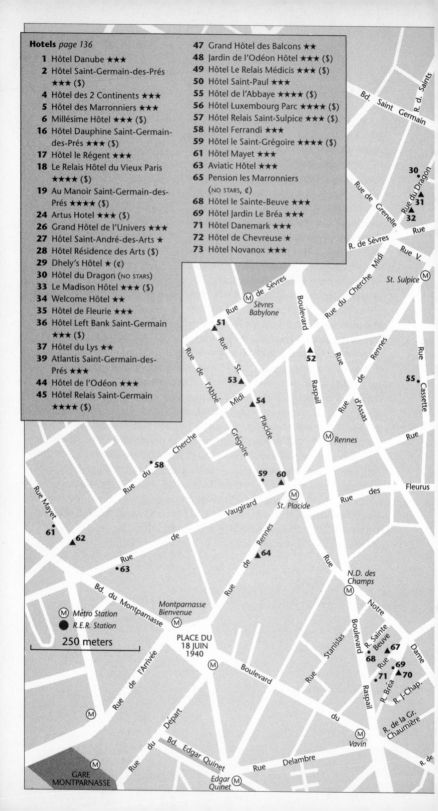

Ⓜ *Metro Station*
● *R.E.R. Station*

250 meters

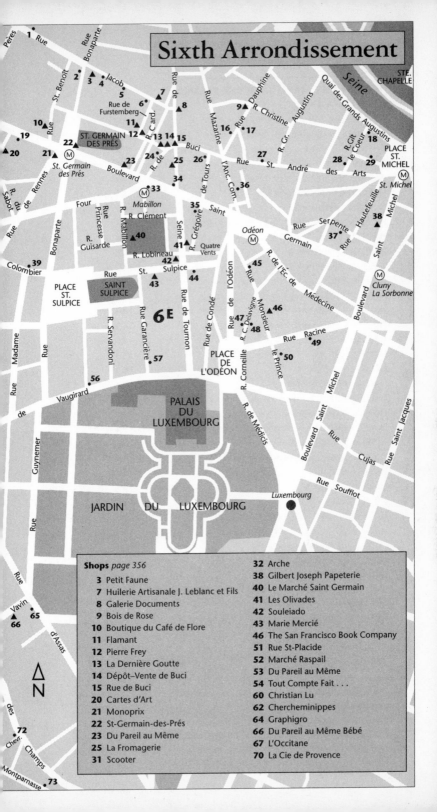

Sixth Arrondissement

Shops *page 356*

- 3 Petit Faune
- 7 Huilerie Artisanale J. Leblanc et Fils
- 8 Galerie Documents
- 9 Bois de Rose
- 10 Boutique du Café de Flore
- 11 Flamant
- 12 Pierre Frey
- 13 La Dernière Goutte
- 14 Dépôt–Vente de Buci
- 15 Rue de Buci
- 20 Cartes d'Art
- 21 Monoprix
- 22 St-Germain-des-Prés
- 23 Du Pareil au Même
- 25 La Fromagerie
- 31 Scooter
- 32 Arche
- 38 Gilbert Joseph Papeterie
- 40 Le Marché Saint Germain
- 41 Les Olivades
- 42 Souleiado
- 43 Marie Mercié
- 46 The San Francisco Book Company
- 51 Rue St-Placide
- 52 Marché Raspail
- 53 Du Pareil au Même
- 54 Tout Compte Fait . . .
- 60 Christian Lu
- 62 Chercheminippes
- 64 Graphigro
- 66 Du Pareil au Même Bébé
- 67 L'Occitane
- 70 La Cie de Provence

HOTELS IN THE SIXTH ARRONDISSEMENT

OTHER OPTIONS
Residence Hotels

($) indicates a Big Splurge; (¢) indicates a Cheap Sleep

ARTUS HÔTEL ★★★ ($, 24)
34, rue de Buci, 75006
Métro: Mabillon
27 rooms, all with shower or bath and toilet

Under the direction of architect Pierre Seignol, the owners of the Artus Hôtel have aggressively combined an imaginitive, ultra-modern interior with an old-period French building, and the results are nothing short of spectacular. The entrance of the hotel announces immediately that this is a place where creativity and pure whimsy have been raised to new levels. This space is divided into two sections: one with five linen-covered chairs on a raspberry-colored rug and the other with a brown nubuck sectional sofa and a Spanish olive wood tree trunk that resembles a woman's silhouette. A soft green and vibrant red glass-topped reception desk ties it together. On the wall leading downstairs to the lipstick red breakfast room is the latest in hotel art: a computer blow-up, on plasticized fabric, of a famous French painting—in this case of two Delacroix paintings. The dining room is lit by two angled windows giving diners a good view of passersby; inside, colored halogen lights hang over chrome and melmac–topped tables, and the American-style breakfast includes bacon and eggs. Presiding over this is an antique doll in a plexiglass case. To the back of the dining room is a mini-gym where guests are invited to relax in the sauna or to work off those extra calories on the exercise bicycle or step machine.

The two buildings of the hotel consist of twenty-five rooms, one junior suite, and one duplex room; all are simple yet extremely well planned. The clean lines of the gray carpeted, whitewashed hallways merge well with the sleek rooms and Philippe Starck–designed bathrooms. All rooms have contemporary color palates that are offset by white duvets and a multicolored linen and cotton coverlet placed at an angle on top. Every room has an original piece of art mounted on the wall in a see-through box: perhaps an eighteenth-century Romanian angel, a richly dressed Mandarin figure, a piece of sculpture, or unusual clothing. The furniture is black; the floors covered in short-shag carpeting or dark wood; the leather upholstery is in shades of aubergine and brown; and the result is terrific. The marble bathrooms with cascading Murano crystal water spouts are fabulous. They are not shut off behind doors, but are an integral part of the room, divided by a partition that may double as closet space or a console for the flat-screen television. Those in the junior suite and the duplex feature a double wide Jacuzzi and a glass-enclosed shower; the suite also has an extension of the private balcony with a St-Germain-des-Prés roofline view.

Also under the same ownership are Hôtel Bourgogne & Montana (see page 174), Le Madison Hotel (see page 164), and Terrass Hôtel (see page 278).

TEL 01-43-29-07-20 **FAX** 01-43-29-67-44 **EMAIL** info@artushotel.com
   INTERNET www.artushotel.com
FACILITIES & SERVICES Air-conditioning, bar, direct-dial phone, elevator, hair
   dryer, laundry service, minibar, robes for suite & duplex, room service,

flat-screen TV with international reception, room safe (no charge),
5 nonsmoking rooms, WiFi
RATES 1–2 persons: standard 215€; superior, duplex, and junior suite 330€;
taxe de séjour included; pets 15€ **CREDIT CARDS** AE, DC, MC, V
BREAKFAST American buffet 15€ per person

ATLANTIS SAINT-GERMAIN-DES-PRÉS ★★★ (39)
4, rue Vieux Colombier, 75006
Métro: St-Sulpice, St-Germain-des-Prés
27 rooms, all with shower or bath and toilet

Located opposite St-Sulpice Church, this hotel is in the thick of
things in this corner of the St-Germain-des-Prés *quartier*. Within an
easy five-to-ten-minute walk, you can be sipping a *café* at either Les
Deux Magots or Café de Flore on the boulevard St-Germain, shopping
at Bon Marché department store, browsing along the narrow streets
lined with designer boutiques, or jogging off that last pastry in the
Jardin du Luxembourg. The clean and efficient air-conditioned rooms
are maintained by a staff of housekeepers who take their job seriously.
Reaching them, however, means getting into an unbelievably small
elevator, even for one. Furnishings are an interesting fusion of Art Deco
and traditional French with brass beds, comfortable armchairs, good
wardrobe space, nicely coordinated fabrics, and duvets on all the beds.
The rooms ending in the number one or on the back are the largest, and
a few have balconies. The tiled bathrooms are modern and functional.
The downstairs sitting room with assorted artwork adds another pleasant dimension to the hotel, as does the skylighted breakfast room with
a grandfather clock in one corner. The desk staff is always helpful.

TEL 01-45-48-31-81 **FAX** 01-45-48-35-16 **EMAIL** paris@hotelatlantis.com
   INTERNET www.hotelatlantis.com
FACILITIES & SERVICES Air-conditioning, direct-dial phone, elevator, hair
   dryer, laundry service, minibar, TV with international reception, room safe
   (no charge), WiFi in lobby
RATES 1–2 persons 125–185€; extra bed 20€; ask about promotional rates;
   taxe de séjour included **CREDIT CARDS** AE, DC, MC, V
BREAKFAST Continental 11€ per person

AU MANOIR SAINT-GERMAIN-DES-PRÉS ★★★★ ($, 19)
153, boulevard St-Germain 75006
Métro: St-Germain-des-Prés
32 rooms, all with shower or bath and toilet

For a dynamic St-Germain-des-Prés address in the very heart of the
famous *quartier*, reserve a room in this gracious hotel. Over the years,
it has retained its dignified demeanor, displaying all the trappings of
a grand hotel with none of the stuffiness. The downstairs boasts one
of the prettiest series of garden-themed sitting and dining areas of any
Left Bank hotel. In the breakfast room, the garden motif is carried
out on green faux-finished wood and matching hobnail upholstery
on the chairs and banquettes. Eight garden frescoes, a basket of dried
fruits and leaves on each table, and a flowered carpet complete the
attractive scene. The bar has groupings of cushioned wicker chairs

and an old-fashioned sedan chair in one corner. Next to it on the left, a trompe l'oeil painting of a cat snoozing on a chair could convince you to try to touch its fur. In the sky-lighted conservatory, a trio of Majolica plates hang over the sofa, and an old tapestry trunk with a collection of men's hats reminds us of turn-of-the-century clothing formalities. Jardinières hold green and blooming plants, and two glass cases display a beautiful collection of antique floral plates

The coordinated rooms are generously proportioned; have twin, queen-, or king-size beds; and are furnished with all the comforts you would expect, including a Jacuzzi in every bathroom. Windows are double-glazed and the rooms are air-conditioned. If you need guaranteed quiet, request a room on the courtyard, but the view will not be interesting.

Also under the same ownership are the Hôtel Left Bank Saint-Germain (see page 152) and Best Western Premier Horset Opéra (see page 81).

TEL 01-42-22-21-65; toll-free in U.S. and Canada 800-528-1234 (Best Western) **FAX** 01-45-48-22-25 **EMAIL** msg@paris-hotels-charm.com **INTERNET** www.paris-hotels-charm.com

FACILITIES & SERVICES Air-conditioning, bar, direct-dial phone, elevator, hair dryer, Jacuzzis, laundry service, TV with international reception, room safe (no charge), WiFi

RATES Single 180€, double 180–260€; extra bed 35€; *taxe de séjour* 1.50€ per person, per day **CREDIT CARDS** AE, DC, MC, V

BREAKFAST Buffet or in-room Continental included

AVIATIC HÔTEL ★★★ (63)
105, rue de Vaugirard, 75006
Métro: Falguière, St-Placide, Montparnasse-Bienvenüe

43 rooms, all with shower or bath and toilet

Part of the hotel dates from the seventeenth century when the Marquise de Maintenon lived here and raised the children of Madame de Montespan and Louis XIV. The hotel is named after the World War I French aviators based at the Issy-les-Moulineaux airfield, who lived here to be closer to their hangars and, when not on duty, Parisian life. Today, Art Deco glass and a black wrought-iron awning over the door—flanked by matching lamps—set the welcoming stage for this businesslike hotel. The lobby has faux-marble columns and small groupings of velvet chairs and antique marble chests topped with bouquets of fresh flowers. To one side is the breakfast room, papered with vintage Parisian art posters.

A wide, winding stairway with overhead skylights leads guests up to forest green carpeted hallways and the forty-three rooms in two buildings. There is more than a touch of class in these well-thought-out chambers, which all have built-in luggage racks, good space to spread out and work, armchair seating, ample closets, soundproofing, and telephones in the bathrooms. Newer rooms come with hardwood floors and duvets on the bed. The rooms in the front building are bright and airy, with pretty views of the surrounding Montparnasse neighborhood. Those in the back are sunny, but they don't have much of a view.

TEL 01-53-63-25-50 **FAX** 01-53-63-25-55 **EMAIL** welcome@aviatic.fr
  INTERNET www.aviatic.fr
FACILITIES & SERVICES Air-conditioning, direct-dial phone, elevator, hair dryer, laundry service, minibar, robes in some rooms, parking, TV with international reception, room safe (no charge)
RATES 1–2 persons: traditional 140–170€, superior 164–199€, millennium 175–210€, suites 295–318€; extra bed 25€; children under 12 free; parking 25€ for 24 hours; *taxe de séjour* included
  CREDIT CARDS AE, DC, MC, V
BREAKFAST Buffet or in-room Continental 13€ per person

DHELY'S HÔTEL ★ (¢, 29)
22, rue de l'Hirondelle, off place St-Michel, 75006
Métro: St-Michel; RER St-Michel–Notre Dame
21 rooms, none with toilet or bathtub, 10 with shower

If you would rather splurge on dinner or a new outfit than on a night's sleep, this budget hotel, steps from the Seine and place St-Michel, is the place. The larger rooms have carpeting; the smaller ones have linoleum floors. Of course, the higher you climb, the lower the price and the better the view. Don't believe me? Book No. 1, a single that opens from the stairs and has a high window you can't see out of unless you stand on a chair, and when you do … all you see is a wall. There is nothing wrong with No. 3 that a few extra watts and new wall coverings wouldn't cure; this beamed room has a mahogany-like double bed facing a quiet street. There is a shower and sink in the room (and as with all the rooms, the toilet is down the hall). While the hotel is basic, it does have some redeeming architectural details, such as open beams, exposed stone walls, and the original sixteenth-century tiled entryway and classified historical stairway. In its most infamous moment, it was the home of Anne de Pisseleu, the favorite mistress of François Premier, king of France from 1515 to 1547. For the last twenty-eight years, the hotel has been owned by Mme. Kenniche.

TEL 01-43-26-58-25 **FAX** 01-43-26-51-06 **EMAIL** delhys@wanadoo.fr
FACILITIES & SERVICES Direct-dial phone, no elevator (5 floors), TV with international reception
RATES Single 44–74€, double 60–84€, triple 98–104€ ; shower 4€; *taxe de séjour* included **CREDIT CARDS** MC, V
BREAKFAST Continental included

GRAND HÔTEL DE L'UNIVERS ★★★ (26)
6, rue Grégoire-de-Tours, 75006
Métro: Odéon, Mabillon
34 rooms, all with shower or bath and toilet

If you like tapestries, brocades, oriental rugs, thick beams, stone walls, and rich, heavy fabrics offset by bowers of real blooming plants, check into this quiet hotel on a pedestrian street just off the boulevard

St-Germain-des-Prés. The hotel is owned by the same family who runs Hôtel Saint-Germain-des-Prés (page 161) and the Hôtel Duc de Saint-Simon (page 179), two longtime favorites with *Great Sleeps Paris* readers. It also has the same style of decorating, including masses of fabulous blooming plants and flowers. When I asked how the hotels maintained their flowers, I was told the manager goes weekly to Rungis, the famous wholesale food and flower market outside of Paris. No wonder these floral displays are always at their peak of perfection.

Each floor has a different color theme, and the doors to all the bedrooms have been hand-painted by an artist from the École des Beaux Arts. No two rooms are exactly alike, but all are well done in terms of colors and design. The marble bathrooms have nice sink space and good lighting. Three rooms on the sixth floor have views of the top of Notre Dame. Room 65, a double superior in rose with two windows, has a mezzanine area with a desk and a comfortable chair. Room 62 brings spring to life at any time of year with its cheerful tulip print fabrics. Number 36 is a double with good closet and luggage space, but the bathroom is smaller and the three windows face a wall. The rooms on the fourth floor and part of the fifth are reserved exclusively for nonsmoking guests.

TEL 01-43-29-37-00, toll-free in the U.S. 800-528-1234 (Best Western)
FAX 01-40-51-06-45 **EMAIL** grandhotelunivers@wanadoo.fr
INTERNET www.hotel-paris-univers.com
FACILITIES & SERVICES Air-conditioning, bar, direct-dial phone, elevator, hair dryer, laundry service, minibar, robes in superior rooms, trouser press in some rooms, TV with international reception, room safe (no charge), 4th floor and part of 5th floor entirely nonsmoking, free WiFi (Internet in lobby)
RATES Single 130–170€, standard double 150–185€, deluxe double 200–215€; *taxe de séjour* included **CREDIT CARDS** AE, DC, MC, V
BREAKFAST American hot buffet 10€ per person

GRAND HÔTEL DES BALCONS ★★ (47)
3, rue Casimir-Delavigne, 75006
Métro: Odéon, Cluny–La Sorbonne
50 rooms, all with shower or bath and toilet

The Grand Hôtel des Balcons is one of the most dignified, inexpensive hotel choices in this part of the Left Bank, and it's a perennial favorite with older, cost-conscious budgeteers who have found that it is a much better value than the other three-star hotels on the same block.

The impressive lobby is a masterpiece of Art Nouveau design, with glorious stained-glass windows and masterfully turned wood. There are always beautiful fresh flower displays, arranged by the owner's wife, who is a recognized international ikebana expert. On the reception desk is a tin of cookies, which you are invited to enjoy along with afternoon tea. Uniformed maids are relentless in keeping everything dust-free. To management's credit, rooms have been redecorated with nice wallpaper and new bedspreads. Each has a desk, at least one chair, and good reading lights. Many have double windows. Those ending in the number one are on a corner and have balconies. Almost all rooms have that one hard-to-find luxury in Paris . . . space. For these, request one of the eight that are similar to No. 204. Vintage baths tend to be small but are spotless. The location is tops, close to lots of budget restaurants (see *Great Eats Paris*) and near place de l'Odéon, boulevard St-Michel, St-Germain-des-Prés, and the Jardin du Luxembourg.

TEL 01-46-34-78-50 **FAX** 01-46-34-06-27 **EMAIL** resa@balcons.com; hotelbalcons@aol.com **INTERNET** www.balcons.com

FACILITIES & SERVICES Direct-dial phone, elevator, hair dryer, TV with international reception, office safe (no charge), WiFi

RATES Single 85–100€, double 100–150€, triple 185€; *taxe de séjour* included **CREDIT CARDS** AE, DC, MC, V

BREAKFAST Buffet or Continental 10€ per person

HÔTEL DANEMARK ★★★ (71)
21, rue Vavin, 75006
Métro: Vavin, Notre-Dame-des-Champs
15 rooms, all with shower, bath, and toilet

For Jean Nurit, nothing seems to be too much trouble when it comes to improving his hotel and thus pleasing his guests. He has a special fondness for Americans, many of whom have been repeat guests for years—even before the hotel became what it is today. M. Nurit is very proud of this fifteen-room hotel in Montparnasse, and he should be. It is an imaginative lesson in how to take an old student-style hotel and turn it into an eye-catching spot.

Cool blues and grays dominate the downstairs color scheme, with artist-inspired furnishings that look like exhibits from New York's Museum of Modern Art. The walls are dotted with a collection of dramatic posters of Parisian landmarks and famous race cars, along with bold paintings done by an architect friend of the family. Each floor has just three rooms, which are brightly done in modern furnishings and vibrant color concepts of either lime green and sky blue, hot orange and yellow, pink and purple, or yellow, red, and green. Thanks to the head housekeeper, who has been on duty for almost twenty years, they are spotless. While compact, they contain everything necessary for a comfortable stay. All rooms have their own Italian marble bathroom with heated towel racks, magnifying mirrors, good makeup lighting, and Annick Goutal troiletries; one has a Jacuzzi. The rooms from the third floor up have no interior views, and those on the top floor are under sloping, beamed ceilings with skylights. Rooms on the front face a pretty, white-brick apartment building with terrace gardens that was built by Henri Sauvage in 1912. The building was used as the set where Marlon Brando "died" on the balcony in the film classic *Last Tango in Paris.*

TEL 01-43-26-93-78 **FAX** 01-46-34-66-06 **EMAIL** paris@hoteldanemark.com **INTERNET** www.hoteldanemark.com

FACILITIES & SERVICES Air-conditioning, direct-dial phone, hair dryer, elevator, one Jacuzzi, minibar, TV with international reception, office safe (no charge), WiFi
RATES 1–2 persons 136–156€; *taxe de séjour* 1€ per person, per day
CREDIT CARDS AE, DC, MC, V
BREAKFAST Continental 11€ per person

HÔTEL DANUBE ★★★ (1)
58, rue Jacob, at the corner of rue des Saints-Pères, 75006
Métro: St-Germain-des-Prés
40 rooms, all with shower or bath and toilet

The two buildings that make up this hotel have had an interesting vantage on history. The American Treaty of Independence from Britain was signed next door on September 3, 1783. David Hartley represented the King of England and Benjamin Franklin, John Jay, and John Adams were the American representatives. During World War II, from September 1939 to June 1940, it was the home of General Sikorsky, head of the Polish government in exile in France. Today it is the Hôtel Danube, a St-Germain charmer with forty rooms offering good value for the price. The hotel is very well managed by Séverin Ferrand, and the desk staff is the friendliest and most accommodating in the neighborhood. The entry has red floral wallpaper and a multicolored tile floor. To one side is an inviting sitting room with a fireplace flanked by two cane wingback chairs. Just beyond an interior courtyard is a breakfast room with a collection of blue-and-white Asian porcelain on display.

The buildings are joined by an attractivly landscaped terrace. The large bedrooms are individually decorated with a mixture of styles that range from colonial Chinese and Indian to mid-Victorian and tropical. Most bathrooms are in marble. A floral theme prevails in No. 41, which is furnished with an antique sleigh bed and a matching marble-top side chest. The same type of furniture is in No. 16, a twin with double windows on the front. Single travelers will be comfortable in No. 21, which has an Egyptian theme carried out on the draperies and a new bathroom. In No. 35, guests can spread out in a two-room suite that faces a pink-and-white wall with wisps of tree branches cleverly painted on it. Number 41, a two-room apartment in pink and blue, is another large choice. It has an antique double bed in one room and two regular doubles in the second. The new marble tile bathroom has a tub with a handheld shower over it and sink space for toiletries. One of the best value rooms, for price and size, is No. 51, a top-floor standard room for one or two people. It is a big room with seventies-style stucco walls, a walk-in closet, and a big round table with two captain's chairs. There are five rooms similar to No. 6, which has a table flanked by two armchairs, a marble-top dresser, lighted closets, an older style bath, and a good working desk.

TEL 01-42-60-94-07 (reservations), 01-42-60-34-70 **FAX** 01-42-60-81-18
EMAIL info@hoteldanube.fr **INTERNET** www.hoteldanube.fr

FACILITIES & SERVICES Direct-dial phones, elevator (to most floors), fans, hair dryer, laundry service, TV with international reception, room safe (no charge)

RATES 1–2 persons: standard room 120–130€, superior room 154–170€; apartment (2–4 persons) 230€; extra bed 40€; *taxe de séjour* 1€ per person, per day **CREDIT CARDS** AE, DC, MC, V

BREAKFAST Continental 10€ per person

HÔTEL DAUPHINE SAINT-GERMAIN-DES-PRÉS ★★★ ($, 16)
36, rue Dauphine, 75006
Métro: Odéon

30 rooms, all with shower or bath and toilet

In the early days, the first and second floors of Parisian town homes were for the nobility, the higher floors for the servants. This explains the larger rooms and higher, beamed ceilings you encounter in this seventeenth-century building, which has been skillfully run by the Janvier family since 1984. Unfortunately, the rooms on the back (except on the top floor) and those ending in the number 4 face a boring back view, but they are larger, very quiet, and certainly have the same high decorating standards and amenities found in the rest of the hotel. Otherwise, there is plenty to choose from, including Nos. 55, 56, 65, and 66, which are exclusively reserved for nonsmoking guests. Number 61 is an orange, sloped-roof suite that can accommodate up to four. I like the four-poster bed, polished wooden floors, and antique desk and chairs covered in red and gold needlework. The mansard windows let in plenty of light and have a view of Notre Dame Cathedral and the dome of the Panthéon. Room 68 is frankly feminine, with its pink-and-white candy-striped walls blending perfectly with florals and checks. It has good light, a rooftop view, and the same excellent granite and marble bathroom features as elsewhere, plus heated towel racks, monogrammed towels, a drying line, large mirror, and a basket of quality toiletries.

A special feature of your morning routine here is the large breakfast buffet, which includes pastries and croissants baked in the hotel kitchen, fresh fruit, and cereals, as well as such extras as yogurt, ham, sausage, cheese, and mushrooms.

TEL 01-43-26-74-34, toll-free in U.S. 800-44-UTELL **FAX** 01-43-26-49-09
EMAIL hotel@dauphine-st-germain.com **INTERNET** www.dauphine-st-germain.com

FACILITIES & SERVICES Air-conditioning, bar (24-hour service), direct-dial phone with fax, elevator, hair dryer, laundry service, minibar, TV with international reception, room service for light snacks, room safe (no charge), several nonsmoking rooms, free WiFi

RATES 1–2 persons: standard 198€, superior 228€; suite: 1–2 persons 250€, 3–4 persons 292€; extra bed 56€; *taxe de séjour* included
CREDIT CARDS AE, DC, MC, V

BREAKFAST Buffet 15€ per person

HÔTEL DE CHEVREUSE ★ (72)
3, rue de Chevreuse, at rue Notre-Dame-des-Champs, 75006
Métro: Vavin
23 rooms, 16 with shower or bath and toilet

Nothing resembles a one-star at the Chevreuse but the prices. A hotel of some sort has been here for fifty years, but it took a new owner with some imagination to turn it into an eye-catching spot where no one need feel they are scrimping in order to stay within budget. The minute you walk into the reception and lobby, which shows off the owner's penchant for collecting, you get the feeling everything is well done, and it is. The room is divided by a bookcase holding vintage flower vases and an old photo of the hotel. Nearby is a 1920s clock, a trombone made into a floor lamp, assorted 1950 car models, and an old hat and umbrella rack next to a church pew. The sofa and chairs are covered in contemporary combinations of blue, white, and yellow. A small breakfast room with four tables and light metal and wood chairs is to one side.

Rooms are simple compositions with open closets, metal chairs, and built-ins. Since in-room showers resemble phone booths, and the shared hall showers are clean, acceptable, and free, you are actually better off and money ahead booking a showerless room. If you are on the fifth floor, you can keep fit because there is no elevator in the building.

TEL 01-43-20-93-16 **FAX** 01-43-21-43-72

FACILITIES & SERVICES Direct-dial phone, French TV, no elevator (5 floors), office safe (no charge), entirely nonsmoking hotel

RATES Single 43€, 1–2 persons 68€, 1–3 persons (largest room) 95€; free hall showers; *taxe de séjour* 0.50€ per person, per day **CREDIT CARDS** MC, V

BREAKFAST Continental 7€ per person

HÔTEL DE FLEURIE ★★★ (35)
32–34, rue Grégoire-de-Tours, 75006
Métro: Saint-Germain-des-Prés, Odéon
29 rooms, all with shower or bath and toilet

If you enjoy the colorful, round-the-clock atmosphere of St-Germain-des-Prés, then the dynamic Hôtel de Fleurie is for you. This exceptional hotel is owned and managed by the Marolleau family, who for two generations owned Brasserie Balzar (see *Great Eats Paris*). When they sold the brasserie, they bought this down-and-out hotel, and with a year of hard work, they completely transformed it into a delightful three-star that has become a hands-down favorite with readers of *Great Sleeps Paris*. As owner Arnaud Marolleau says, "Everything is possible with us. We don't sell just a room. We sell service and the quality of the stay."

The facade of the hotel has been restored to its former glory and is embellished with statues that are lighted at night. The lobby and sitting rooms are models of gracious comfort and charm, and on winter afternoons, tea and coffee are served. A spiral staircase leads from the reception desk down to a stone-walled *cave*, where a full buffet is served at tables covered with Provençal prints. Continental breakfasts, which include fresh orange juice, pound cake, and cheese in addition to the usual croissants and fresh bread, are served only in the rooms.

Almost all of the rooms have modern marble bathrooms and a good layout. Several connect to make nice family options. Room 60, on the top floor (with no elevator access), overlooks a beautiful mosaic-tiled building across the street. Other deluxe choices include Nos. 11, 14, 24, and 34. Nos. 14 and 24 have newer bathrooms and *toile de Jouy* wall covering in red and white. Closet and living space is excellent, and there's plenty of light from the two windows. Room 54, a standard double, has a writing table, white cane headboard, lighted mirrored closet in the entry, and heated towel racks in the bathroom. Number 50, with a double bed, has a small window with a view and a pink marble bathroom; it would be nice for a single visitor. So is No. 60, a small double sold as a single; its green-and-white-tiled bathroom has a shower and sky light.

TEL 01-53-73-70-00 **FAX** 01-53-73-70-20 **EMAIL** bonjour@hotel-de-fleurie.fr
   INTERNET www.hoteldefleurie.com
FACILITIES & SERVICES Air-conditioning, bar, direct-dial phone, elevator
   (to 5 floors, walk to 6th), hair dryer, laundry service, minibar, TV with
   international reception, robes, slippers, tea and coffee makers in deluxe
   rooms, room safe (no charge), free WiFi
RATES Single 135–150€, standard double 170–190€, deluxe room 245–270€,
   family rooms (up to 4 persons) 300–335€; children under 12 free; *taxe de
   séjour* included **CREDIT CARDS** AE, DC, MC, V
BREAKFAST Buffet downstairs or in-room Continental 12€ per person, 6€ for
   children under 12

HÔTEL DE L'ABBAYE ★★★★ ($, 55)
10, rue Cassette, 75006
Métro: St-Sulpice
44 rooms, all with shower or bath and toilet

In the sixteenth and seventeenth centuries, the Abbaye Saint-Germain was a Catholic convent. Today it is a very special four-star hotel for those who love its quiet location near St-Sulpice, its discreet staff (many of whom have been here for a quarter century), and its commendable service. The entrance is off the street through fifteen-foot-high green doors that open onto a cobblestone courtyard, where the nuns once gathered before going to chapel for daily prayers. The central reception room is handsomely furnished with magnificent antiques and comfortable sofas centered around a marble fireplace. Behind this are an exquisite salon with intimate seating, a wood-burning fireplace, a profusion of flowers, and a nice bar with big wicker armchairs. The addition of a glassed-in winter and summer garden, where breakfast can be served, enhances the hotel's charm and desirability.

Returnees vie for the top-floor terrace suites, with their arched ceilings, fireplaces, and rooftop views, or the two ground-floor rooms with private gardens. Number 303 is a two-level suite with a downstairs sitting room that boasts a fireplace, sofa, two chairs, lots of closets, and two big windows. Also on this level is a huge marble bathroom with six feet of sink space, a separate toilet, an enclosed glass shower, and a deep tub. Upstairs, the twin or king bedroom opens onto its own terrace. In addition, there are more lighted closets and a small half bathroom. One favorite is No. 34, a large twin done in florals. I like the granite bathroom with six shelves, a separate shower, and deep tub. Another is No. 32, a nicely appointed, light room with a view over the trees and a sunken bathtub that is just right for one. Many request No. 3, a large ground-floor choice with a private conservatory garden and white marble bathroom. For those who shun traditional and embrace cutting-edge minimalism, the three suite-salons might be appealing. These new rooms combine masculine, monochromatic colors of linens and leathers, lots of glass and chrome, and stunning bathrooms behind glass doors.

Because l'Abbaye is such a unique and outstanding choice, it is higher in price, and it is included for those with flexible budgets who are looking for a memorably romantic Parisian address.

TEL 01-45-44-38-11 **FAX** 01-45-48-07-86 **EMAIL** hotel.abbaye@wanadoo.fr
   INTERNET www.hotel-abbaye.com
FACILITIES & SERVICES Air-conditioning, bar, direct-dial phone, elevator, hair
   dryer, porter, trouser press in suites, TV with international reception, room
   service for light snacks, room safe (no charge), WiFi
RATES 1–2 persons: standard 214€, *grande* 319€, suite-salon 400€, suite-
   duplex 458€; *taxe de séjour* included **CREDIT CARDS** AE, MC, V
BREAKFAST Continental included, cannot be deducted

HÔTEL DE L'ODÉON ★★★ (44)
13, rue St-Sulpice, 75006
Métro: Odéon
29 rooms, all with shower or bath and toilet

Hôtel de l'Odéon has become a popular Paris destination for travelers who want luxury and impeccable service in a distinguished hotel that is still small enough to maintain a personal touch. The staff is exceptional; the prices are excellent, especially in low season; and the location is top drawer.

The interior is in the style of a seventeenth-century inn, beautifully blending antique charm and atmosphere with all the modern conveniences one expects in a top three-star hotel. In the charm department, the Odéon has it all: high beamed ceilings, original stone walls, stunning furniture, massive tapestries, intricately scrolled brass-and-metal beds with hand-crocheted coverlets, blooming flower boxes under the windows, lovely oil and watercolor paintings throughout, and a manicured atrium garden off to one side of the skylighted breakfast area. On the convenience side, the marble baths are large and the bedside lighting is good. Double-paned windows keep street noise to a minimum, air-conditioning allows warm-weather comfort, and the closets are large enough for more than the contents of an overnight bag. WiFi in the rooms and lobby allow guests to be connected 24/7.

TEL 01-43-25-70-11 **FAX** 01-43-29-97-34 **EMAIL** hotelodeon@wanadoo.fr
   INTERNET www.paris-hotel-odeon.com
FACILITIES & SERVICES Air-conditioning, direct-dial phone, elevator (to most
   floors), hair dryer, Internet in lobby, laundry service, TV with international
   reception, room safe (no charge), WiFi
RATES 1–2 persons: standard 175€, superior 225€, 2–3 persons: deluxe 250€,
   family room 275€; *taxe de séjour* 1€ per person, per day
   CREDIT CARDS AE, DC, MC, V
BREAKFAST Continental 12€ per person

HÔTEL DES 2 CONTINENTS ★★★ (4)
25, rue Jacob, 75006
Métro: St-Germain-des-Prés, Mabillon
41 rooms, all with shower or bath and toilet

The hotel is owned and operated by two sisters and two brothers who work with their parents to run five hotels in Paris (three of which are included in *Great Sleeps Paris*) and one in Versailles. What started out as a second career for the father (who was a cinematographer) and his wife (who owned a paper factory in the Loire Valley) has now become a full-time occupation for them all.

The hotel name honors the 1783 American Treaty of Independence that was signed with Great Britain down the street in a building that is now the Hôtel d'Angleterre. The mural in the lobby/dining area is of New York at the time of the treaty signing. Today, the family-owned hotel consists of three buildings, two of which are mostly accessible by elevator. If you are willing to climb a few stairs, the rooms in back, which are every bit as nice as those in the elevator-serviced buildings, will save you an average of 15€ per day. The forty-one rooms have the usual St-Germain-des-Prés look: Toile de Jouy fabric-covered walls, requisite beams, swagged draperies, multiple tassles, brass wall sconces, rustic furnishings mixed with wrought-iron, and marble baths. No matter which building you sleep in, prices are reasonable for the area.

Also under the same family ownership are Hôtel des Marronniers (see page 149) and Welcome Hôtel (see page 168).

TEL 01-43-26-72-46 **FAX** 01-43-25-67-80 **EMAIL** Continents.hotel@
   wanadoo.com **INTERNET** www.continents-paris-hotel.com
FACILITIES & SERVICES Air-conditioning in half the rooms, direct-dial phone,
   elevator in two buildings, no elevator in third building (3 floors), hair
   dryer, office safe (no charge), TV with international reception, WiFi in
   lobby
RATES Single 138€, double 147–160€, triple 195€; *taxe de séjour* included
   CREDIT CARDS MC, V
BREAKFAST Continental downstairs 10€, in room 11€, per person

HÔTEL DES MARRONNIERS ★★★ (5)
21, rue Jacob, 75006
Métro: St-Germain-des-Prés, Mabillon
37 rooms, all with shower or bath and toilet

The Hôtel des Marronniers is seductively tucked away in a lush garden just steps away from all the hustle and bustle of this popular Parisian *quartier*. The essentially *intime* rooms are heavily decorated with a mix of coordinated colors and fabrics with linen wall coverings and ship-shape marble bathrooms. Those facing the garden with its beautiful chestnut (*marronnier*) tree are naturally in great demand. Other views include the church of Saint Sulpice and La Tour Montparnasse. Of course it is quiet: all you hear are the bells from the St-Germain-des-Prés church, one of the oldest in Paris. Breakfast is served in a wonderful glass-enclosed dining room facing the garden, which is where the old-fashioned white metal tables and chairs are placed in warm weather. There is also a large stone cave dining and lounge area, but who wants to trade a garden setting for one underground?

Also under the same family ownership are Hôtel des 2 Continents (see page 148) and Welcome Hôtel (page 168).

TEL 01-43-25-30-60 **FAX** 01-40-46-83-56 **EMAIL** Hotel-des-marronniers@ wanadoo.fr **INTERNET** www.paris-hotel-marronniers.com

FACILITIES & SERVICES Air-conditioning, direct-dial phone, elevator, hair dryer, room safe (no charge), TV with international reception

RATES Single 110€, 1–2 people 153–173€, triple 208€, quad 248€; *taxe de séjour* included **CREDIT CARDS** MC, V

BREAKFAST Continental downstairs 10€, in room 11€, per person

HÔTEL DU DRAGON (NO STARS, 30)
36, rue du Dragon, 75006
Métro: St-Sulpice, St-Germain-des-Prés, Sèvres-Babylone
29 rooms, all with shower and toilet

Talk about a Great Sleep in Paris!

Despite its no-star status, the Hôtel du Dragon is one of the last outposts for decent budget anchorage in the heart of the Left Bank. Sprinkled throughout the public rooms and in some of the guest rooms are furnishings that belonged to the owner's grandparents when they started the hotel a century ago. The spotless rooms are bedecked in flowered or striped wallpaper and coordinating fabrics that look more up to date than some three-star hotels I could name. Rooms have space, beams, decent closets, adequate lights, and new bathrooms. Of course, there is no elevator, and for air-conditioning you must open the window. However, you do get orange juice with your morning baguette and jam; a television tuned to French, German, or CNBC in your room; and a warm welcome from the Rabier-Roy family, who are the fifth-generation owners of the hotel.

The bottom line for prudent sleepers in Paris: You get a great sleep for your money, and today, that is not always easy to find.

TEL 01-45-48-51-05 **FAX** 01-42-22-51-62 **EMAIL** Hotel.Du.Dragon@wanadoo.fr
INTERNET www.hoteldudragon.com
FACILITIES & SERVICES Direct-dial phone, no elevator (5 floors), hair dryer, TV, office safe (no charge)
RATES Single 79–89€, double 99–109€; extra bed 30% of room rate; *taxe de séjour* included **CREDIT CARDS** AE, MC, V
BREAKFAST Continental 8€ downstairs, 9€ in room, per person

HÔTEL DU LYS ★★ (37)
23, rue Serpente, 75006
Métro: Odéon, Cluny–La Sorbonne
22 rooms, all with shower or bath and toilet

The location is dynamite, the prices are still in line, and if you hit the right room, your stay should be very nice. The hotel is owned by Marie-Hélène Decharne, who took it over when her father retired after fifty years. She continues to make welcome improvements, and the result is a small hotel with more charm and romantic appeal than many in the area charging twice as much.

The rooms are done in a cozy French style with beams, a stone wall here, an antique there, and matching bedspreads and curtains. If you are reserving by telephone, please bear in mind that Mme. Decharne is usually at the hotel only on weekday mornings from 9 A.M. to noon. When reserving, I would request No. 14, a redone double room in red with rose print wallpaper and brass bedside lights. The bright blue bathroom has a new sink and an enclosed shower. In No. 12, sweetly turned out for one in blue and white, the headboard for the bed is an old antique door. The bathroom has ample counter space, but I don't like the TV pitched high on the ceiling. Number 9, which has a nice, bright bathroom, also features an old door as a headboard.

TEL 01-43-26-97-57 **FAX** 01-44-07-34-90 **EMAIL** hoteldulys@wanadoo.fr
INTERNET www.hoteldulys.com
FACILITIES & SERVICES Direct-dial phone, no elevator (4 floors), hair dryer, TV with international reception, room safe (no charge)
RATES 1–2 persons: small room 100€, large room 120€, triple 140€; *taxe de séjour* included **CREDIT CARDS** MC, V
BREAKFAST Continental included, cannot be deducted

HÔTEL FERRANDI ★★★ (58)
92, rue du Cherche-Midi, 75006
Métro: Vaneau, Falguière
42 rooms, all with shower or bath and toilet

Thoroughly dignified in every way, the hotel is successful in combining old-world style with modern comforts and expectations. Over time, it has developed a loyal clientele who overlook the graceful aging of some rooms and the definitely dated bathrooms in others. The downstairs sitting area is defined by an ornate marble fireplace and a crystal chandelier. Loads of comfortable chairs, fresh flowers, attractive art, and daily newspapers in French and English create a pleasing place to relax. Stained-glass windows add color to the front hall. The interior hallways, lined with ochre fabric to keep noise to a minimum, are gracefully joined by a winding staircase painted in a mustard-toned, faux-marble finish.

The rooms, all of which face the front, are furnished with period antiques and are done in soft shades of blues, browns, and pinks. Most have extra closet and luggage space and are just the ticket for those of us who do not travel lightly. For longer stays, I like Room 50, a ground-floor, two-room apartment with a roomy pink marble bathroom, or No. 43, with a four-poster bed, ornamental ceiling, plenty of drawer and closet space, good light, and inviting armchairs. Other favorites are No. 23, with a blue-and-white half-canopy bed, marble fireplace, and massive armoire; and No. 46, a deluxe twin or king in blue with a pink marble bathroom. Number 27, with a brass bed, double closet, and single chair, is the least expensive room; it's perfect for one. I would avoid No. 22 because of its old-style tiled bathroom, No. 26 because a futon is the third bed, and No. 29, which is noisy and too dark. Motorists will appreciate the hotel garage, and shoppers will love the many shopping opportunities within easy reach.

TEL 01-42-22-97-40 **FAX** 01-45-44-89-97 **EMAIL** hotel.ferrandi@wanadoo.fr

FACILITIES & SERVICES Air-conditioning, bar, direct-dial phone, elevator, hair dryer, laundry service, some minibars, private parking (must reserve ahead), office safe (no charge), TV with international reception and pay-per-view, WiFi

RATES 1–2 persons: standard 105–155€, superior 140–190€, deluxe 160–230€, suite for 2 persons 190–265€; private parking 25€ per day; *taxe de séjour* 1€ per person, per day **CREDIT CARDS** AE, DC, MC, V

BREAKFAST Continental downstairs, or in room, 11€ per person

HÔTEL JARDIN LE BRÉA ★★★ (69)
14, rue Bréa, 75006
Métro: Vavin, Notre-Dame-des-Champs
23 rooms, all with shower or bath and toilet

The floral theme of this attractive Montparnasse hotel starts the minute you enter the street-side sitting room, which has a framed art collage of rose petals and a big bouquet of silk red poppies in the window. Further charm is added by a marble-framed black-metal fireplace and a terra-cotta-tiled honor bar facing a winter garden. The small, compact rooms have all been done in yellow and Provençal red, and they reflect good taste and three-star comforts. Two rooms (Nos. 7 and 8) open onto the garden. Number 7 is a small yellow double with a stall shower; No. 8, a king, has slightly more space, but for some the twelve steps down a narrow spiral stairway to reach the bathroom would not be appealing. Room 11, a twin on the courtyard, has a large bathroom with good lighting. Number 14, a standard double on the street, has the advantage of a bathtub and more luggage space, as does No. 4, a superior with a king bed, two windows, and a large white tile bathroom. A buffet breakfast is laid out in a stone-walled room with wicker chairs and yellow-clad tables set with a bouquet of silk flowers.

NOTE: There are two parts to the hotel: the front consists of four floors accessible by an elevator, and the back has three floors (including some superior rooms) and no elevator.

TEL 01-43-25-44-41 **FAX** 01-44-07-19-25 **EMAIL** brea.hotel@wanadoo.fr
   INTERNET www.jardinlebrea-paris-hotel.com
FACILITIES & SERVICES Air-conditioning, bar, direct-dial phone, elevator to
   most rooms, hair dryer, laundry service, TV with international reception,
   room safe (no charge), WiFi
RATES Standard single 130€, double 150€, triple 170€; superior single/double
   170€; extra bed 25€; *taxe de séjour* 1€ per person, per day
   CREDIT CARDS AE, DC, MC, V
BREAKFAST Buffet 12€ or in-room Continental 14€, per person

HÔTEL LEFT BANK SAINT-GERMAIN ★★★ ($, 36)
9, rue de l'Ancienne Comédie, 75006
Métro: Odéon
31 rooms, all with shower or bath and toilet

It is hard to imagine a small hotel in Paris more appealing than this one, which is, quite frankly, just the sort of hotel that makes you fall in love with Paris in the first place. Located in the ever-popular St-Germain *quartier* and convenient to everything, it is run by Claude Teil and his family, who also operate several other outstanding hotels in Paris. The appeal of this hotel starts from the entrance where guests always stop to admire an adorable antique baby carriage filled with authentically dressed vintage dolls, and it continues to the large top-floor suite with dormer window views onto Notre Dame, Ste-Chapelle, and Centre Georges Pompidou. Adding to the overall allure, there are fresh flowers everywhere, museum-quality Aubusson tapestries, polished antiques mixed with special handmade furnishings from Perigord, excellent eighteenth-century reproductions, open oak beams, stone walls, and a very helpful, English-speaking staff.

The standard-size rooms are done in rich paisley prints with built-in minibars and room safes. The bathrooms are excellent and the court-yard views pleasant. The connecting rooms (housing up to four) are comfortable choices because they have desk space, larger baths, and out-of-sight storage space. Number 502, with a view of Notre Dame, is a cozy choice for one or two people, especially on a cold winter evening in Paris. The walls are covered in rose Toile de Jouy that blends with the floral quilted bedspread and the red and white curtains. In Suite 604, one window on the pitched roof has a tip-toe view of the Eiffel Tower, and at the other end of the room, the view is of Notre Dame, Centre Georges Pompidou, and Ste-Chapelle. The huge room sleeps up to five and has a red-velvet settee, two desks, a dressing table, and a nice bathroom.

Also under the same ownership are Au Manoir Saint-Germain-des-Prés (see page 138) and the Best Western Premier Horset Opéra (see page 81).

TEL 01-43-54-01-70; toll-free in U.S. and Canada 800-528-1234 (Best Western) **FAX** 01-43-26-17-14 **EMAIL** lb@paris-hotels-charm.com
   INTERNET www.paris-hotels-charm.com
FACILITIES & SERVICES Air-conditioning, direct-dial phone, elevator, hair dryer, Internet in lobby, laundry service, minibar, nonallergic pillows on request, tea & coffee maker, TV with international reception, room safe (no charge), first floor all nonsmoking, WiFi
RATES Single 175–220€, double 195–238€, triple 220–265€, quad 246– 290€, suite 317–355€; *taxe de séjour* 1€ per person, per day
   CREDIT CARDS AE, DC, MC, V
BREAKFAST Buffet or Continental included

HÔTEL LE RÉGENT ★★★ (17)
61, rue Dauphine, 75006
Métro: Odéon
25 rooms, all with shower or bath and toilet

For Parisian atmosphere in a setting of nonstop activity, it is hard to top the Régent, which offers guests traditional charm in a renovated eighteenth-century building. Fresh flowers and green plants add soft touches to the stone entry and reception areas, which are decorated with antiques and tapestry-covered chairs. A selection of Les Deux Magots teas, jams, champagne, and dishes is for sale in a display case . . . and why not? Both the famous café and this hotel are under the same ownership. If mobility is an issue, note that the elevator does not descend to the stone-walled dining room on the lower ground floor.

All the rooms are well maintained and have the creature comforts most deem necessary, with the added bonus of terry robes (on request) and trouser presses in the deluxe rooms. The bathrooms are modern, but the real showstoppers are in the rooms on the highest floors. For one of the prettiest pink-tile bathrooms in Paris, request Room 52. Number 41, a large twin with three windows, also has an outstanding spacious bathroom with monogrammed towels, a lighted magnifying mirror, and a deep glass-enclosed tub and shower. Room 11 on the first floor is just like it, but in shades and patterns of orange; however, because it faces front, guests should expect some street noise. Room 53 is a wood-paneled twin with a view to the top of Notre Dame. If I had to pick a favorite room, I would select No. 62, nestled under the eaves on the sixth floor. From the room, you can see Notre Dame Cathedral. Sitting on the balcony, you look over the rooftops to La Tour Montparnasse. I would recommend avoiding Nos. 14 and 15, which have inside views and provide no place to put luggage or sit down comfortably. The staff is very pleasant, but note that they are unable to promise specific rooms, though they will do their best to accommodate requests.

TEL 01-46-34-59-80 **FAX** 01-40-51-05-07 **EMAIL** hotel.leregent@wanadoo.fr
   INTERNET www.regent-paris-hotel.com
FACILITIES & SERVICES Air-conditioning, direct-dial phone, elevator, hair dryer, laundry service, minibar, robes upon request, trouser press and magnifying mirrors in some rooms, TV with international reception, room safe (no charge), WiFi

RATES 1–2 persons, standard 158€, deluxe 220€, deluxe superior 236€; *taxe de séjour* included **CREDIT CARDS** AE, DC, MC, V
BREAKFAST Continental 14€ per person

HÔTEL LE RELAIS MÉDICIS ★★★ ($, 49)
23, rue Racine, 75006
Métro: Odéon, Cluny–La Sorbonne
16 rooms, all with shower or bath and toilet

The jury is still out on whether heaven is as divine as a stay at Le Relais Médicis. I will admit it was love at first sight the minute I walked into this picture-perfect dream hotel, where something artistic and imaginative catches your eye at every turn—it might be a humorous bench with black bears carved on each end, or the marble fireplace with Majolica spice jars displayed on top. The total look of the hotel is characteristically French, with the mix of patterns, shapes, sizes, and colors all adding up to a stunning visual effect. In the lush salon, lovely oil paintings are set off by vibrant fuchsia fabric-covered walls and antique birdcages, which add a light touch. Garden paintings define the springtime feel of the breakfast room, where even the lights reflect the floral theme. Vintage black-and-white photos displayed throughout the halls of the hotel add notes of interest.

Two lifts take guests to the sixteen floral-themed bedrooms, all of which I could live in happily for a long Parisian stay. For instance, in No. 22 you are surrounded by soft greens and corals, with floral dust ruffles complementing the cotton bedspreads. An enviable display of turn-of-the-century colored prints of young women and children are offset by a solo modern painting. The marble bath has reproduction antique chrome fittings, and the mirrored wardrobe is large enough to hold everything you brought with you and also plan to buy in Paris. Room 36, a deluxe double with twin beds, has a sofa and a comfortable chair, windows overlooking both the garden and street, and an interesting painting of a bridge scene, divided into four panels. A huge double bookcase occupies one wall, and a four-drawer marble dresser another. If you occupy the quiet and secluded double-bedded No. 39, you will have a few steps to climb. The color scheme of the deluxe room is a soft orange sorbet, and the view is of the buildings across the way. Feminine No. 26, which is similar to No. 36, is a cheerful, large, beamed room with twin beds or a king, three windows, and an adorable old desk. Colors and fabrics are coordinated in blue and yellow; decorative accents include a gold clock and an assortment of old tins. Room 24 is a smaller standard double with a marble-top dresser. The mirrored wall gives the illusion of more space in this room, which is still big enough to accommodate a round table and two chairs, the perfect place to enjoy a Continental breakfast.

TEL 01-43-26-00-60 **FAX** 01-40-46-83-39 **EMAIL** reservation@ relaismedicis.com **INTERNET** www.relaismedicis.com
FACILITIES & SERVICES Air-conditioning, bar, direct-dial phone, elevator, hair dryer, laundry service, magnifying mirrors in most rooms, minibar,

robes in all rooms, porter, TV with international reception, room safe (no charge), in-room high-speed Internet

RATES Garden rooms: single 168€, double 198€, double deluxe 228€; street rooms: double 198€, double superior 228€, double deluxe 245€; *taxe de séjour* included **CREDIT CARDS** AE, DC, MC, V

BREAKFAST Continental included

HÔTEL LE SAINTE-BEUVE ★★★ (68)
9, rue Sainte-Beuve, 75006
Métro: Vavin, Notre-Dame-des-Champs
22 rooms, all with shower, bath, and toilet

Nicely positioned between the Jardin du Luxembourg and the boulevard Montparnasse, the Hôtel le Sainte-Beuve makes my short list of top upmarket hotel choices in this corner of Paris. The hotel and the street were named for Charles Sainte-Beuve, a nineteenth-century poet and famous literary critic who was a contemporary of Victor Hugo. As the story goes, he went to a dinner party and left with Victor Hugo's wife.

The hotel was artfully designed by decorator David Hicks, who boldly combines fabric patterns and furnishings in a harmony of colors. The result is an atmosphere that is rich in a contemporary French way, with many touches that give it a feeling of easy-going elegance. In the comfortable lounge are two oversized sofas and armchairs grouped around a lovely wood-burning fireplace. The owner's collection of drawings depicting M. Sainte-Bueve add just the right finishing touch.

Gray tweed hallways lined with antique Parisian prints lead to the bedrooms, all of which display a sense of style and grace. In No. 18, the modern poppy-red and beige colors set off the antique mirrored vanity dressing table and marble-top bedside chests. The easy-to-live-in room has good closet space and a bathroom with two windows. Number 12, a standard room on the back with a city view, can connect with No. 11 to form a family suite. The same layout exists for superior rooms 16 and 17. For the largest room, reserve La Chambre "Sainte-Beuve," a huge two-room suite with sisal floor covering topped with a leopard print rug. Two oversized twin beds covered in white linens blend with the soft beige tones, leather-top writing desk, and an interesting collection of oriental pots displayed in niches along a four-tiered glass wall. The closet and storage space never ends; in addition to a six-drawer walnut dresser, you have shelves in the bathroom and more in the room itself. Breads and pastries from the famous Gérard Mulot Pâtisserie are served for breakfast.

TEL 01-45-48-20-07 **FAX** 01-45-48-67-52 **EMAIL** saintebeuve@wanadoo.fr
INTERNET www.parishotelcharme.com

FACILITIES & SERVICES Air-conditioning, bar, direct-dial phone, elevator, hair dryer, laundry service, minibar, bathrobes and slippers, room service, TV with international reception, video on request, room safe (no charge), WiFi

RATES 1–2 persons: standard 135€, classic 178€, superior 188€, deluxe 240€, La Chambre "Sainte-Beuve" 280€, connecting rooms 338€; *taxe de séjour* included **CREDIT CARDS** AE, DC, MC, V

BREAKFAST Continental 14.50€ per person

HÔTEL LE SAINT-GRÉGOIRE ★★★★ ($, 59)
43, rue de l'Abbé Grégoire, 75006
Métro: St-Placide
20 rooms, all with shower or bath and toilet

Everyone raves about it because on all counts the Hôtel le Saint-Grégoire is a stunning hotel. I will warn you: After one or two nights at this hotel, you will face a dilemma—you will wish you never had to leave Paris. It is, admittedly, on the high side in peak season, but I can assure you it is one of the most popular Big Splurges in the book because so many readers believe it is worth the extra money, not only for the comfort and surroundings, but for the welcome and assistance extended by the staff, skillfully headed by M. François de Béné.

The color scheme is purple, yellow, orange, red, and beige . . . and it works. Decorator David Hicks has created an elegantly intimate atmosphere in this twenty-room hotel by mixing period antiques with handsome modern pieces and sprinkling interesting fabrics, patterned throw rugs, and rich silks throughout a garden setting. As a result, the hotel conveys a feeling of well-being, from the fireplace in the rose-filled lobby to the linen-covered tables in the *cave* dining room, where freshly squeezed orange juice and yogurt are served with the Continental breakfast.

Please forward all mail to me care of Room 100, a bright yellow, ground-floor double opening onto a small garden. It has a marble-top coffee table, a bureau large enough to hold the contents of my suitcase, and two comfortable chairs for lazy late-night reading. The bath has heated towel racks, Roger & Gallet toiletries, and enough towels to last (almost) forever. If this room is not available, I would be supremely happy in either No. 102, a junior suite, also on a garden—which has its own entryway leading to a large room with a sofa, two easy chairs, and a table at one end—or No. 16, a large room with a terrace on the back of the hotel. Room 20 is a spacious, pink, superior double; I like its antique drop leaf table with two white slip-covered highback chairs and its four-drawer chest. Families can request that Rooms 24 and 26 be combined. Number 24 is a small, peach-colored room with a wall hat rack; No. 26 is a larger double with a nice writing table, armoire, and black marble-top dresser, and it has a light bath with a separate enclosed toilet.

Also under the same ownership is the Hôtel Le Lavoisier (see page 201).

TEL 01-45-48-23-23 **FAX** 01-45-48-33-95 **EMAIL** hotel@saintgregoire.com
   INTERNET www.hotelsaintgregoire.com
FACILITIES & SERVICES Air-conditioning, bar, direct-dial phone, elevator, hair dryer, laundry service, minibar on request, TV with international reception, office safe (no charge), WiFi in lobby
RATES 1–2 persons: standard 195€, superior 245€, suite and rooms with private terrace 245–275€; dog 14€; *taxe de séjour* included
   CREDIT CARDS AE, DC, MC, V
BREAKFAST Continental 14€ per person

HÔTEL LUXEMBOURG PARC ★★★★ ($, 56)
42, rue de Vaugirard, 75006
Métro: St-Germain-des-Prés; RER Luxembourg
23 rooms, all with shower, bath, and toilet

Welcome to the Hôtel Luxembourg Parc, an elegant hotel across from the famous Luxembourg Gardens and within easy strolling distance to everything in and around St-Germain-des-Prés. A glass elevator takes guests to the rooms, which raise the standards for refined comforts and modern conveniences. Upon arrival in their rooms, guests receive a ceramic French bulldog named Mr. Pipin. The real Mr. Pipin is the owner's dog and the mascot of the hotel. The individually decorated rooms reflect either the style of Louis XV, Louis XVI, or Napoléon III. In addition to magnificent furnishings and lush fabrics, they offer parquet floors accented with oriental carpets, fluffy duvets, and the latest in marble bathrooms. Staying connected with the world is easy either via WiFi or international news programs on the flat-screen television. If you don't have your laptop with you, there is a guest computer in the library downstairs. While every room has something special to recommend it, the top choice has to be No. 51, a Louis XV two-room suite lighted by crystal chandeliers. This suite has an entire wall devoted to closet and cupboard space and a large flat-screen television encased in a gold-leaf frame (with DVD, video, and stereo surround sound). The spa-like bathroom offers a choice of where to bathe: in a double-size kidney-shaped tub or in the walk-in shower with massage jets. For something slightly less lavish, request two adjoining rooms, or No. 31: it's the largest double and very quiet because it opens onto an inner courtyard.

In the morning, a hot and cold buffet—which includes bacon and eggs along with pastries, cold meats, cheese, fruit, yogurt, and cereal—is served in a sunny breakfast room with wraparound windows overlooking the Luxembourg Gardens across the street.

TEL 01-53-10-36-50 **FAX** 01-53-10-36-59 **EMAIL** booking@hotelluxparc.com
  INTERNET www.hotelluxparc.com
FACILITIES & SERVICES Air-conditioning, bar, conference room, direct-dial phone, elevator, hair dryer, laundry service, minibar, robes, porter, room safe (no charge), room service, TV with international reception, WiFi and Internet connections
RATES 1–2 people: standard double 290–330€, double with terrace 355€, suite and deluxe 550€; *taxe de séjour* included **CREDIT CARDS** AE, DC, MC, V
BREAKFAST Buffet 17€ per person

HÔTEL MAYET ★★★ (61)
3, rue Mayet, 75006
Métro: Duroc, Falguière
23 rooms, all with shower or bath and toilet

The entrance of this hotel announces immediately that here creativity and pure whimsy are cleverly mixed within the framework of a century-old Parisian building. Two sitting rooms face the street, but privacy is assured by the white venetian blinds shielding the old-fashioned windows. In the first, graffiti-style paintings along one wall form the colorful background for the two plain-Jane, beige linen-covered sofas and a large coffee table, which is scattered with international periodicals. In the other, another pair of beige linen sofas along with two brown leather armchairs blend well with black-and-white photos framed in vibrant pink, yellow, and green. Behind the reception desk is a four-by-four-foot clock, and on the floor is a Scotty dog who serves as a shoe polisher. Guests using the downstairs computer station sit perched on a high metal bar chair. In the breakfast room, everyone sits at a long, communal table covered in primary colors that match the china. Guests can easily tell which downstairs bathroom they should use by the dancing stick figure of a boy or a girl painted on each door.

The industrially chic rooms are identical: they have been planned with a place for everything, and everything is precisely in its place. The doors to the rooms are red; inside the furniture is gray, as are the ceiling fans. The walls are gray and red, and the lampshades white. There is a red stool, but no chair. A large wall clock assures on-time departure and arrival for whatever you are doing in Paris. Crisp white duvets and large square pillows dress the beds. Hanging above is a shelf with four charcoal gray boxes. Nice wooden hangers are in the minimal closets. The modern bathrooms have good light, while rooms on the fifth floor have tiny balconies.

NOTE: The hotel is closed in August and the week between Christmas and New Year's.

TEL 01-47-83-21-35 **FAX** 01-40-65-95-78 **EMAIL** hotel@mayet.com
   INTERNET www.mayet.com
FACILITIES & SERVICES Air-conditioning, direct-dial phone, elevator, fans, hair
   dryer, office safe, no charge, TV with international reception, free WiFi
RATES Single 100€, 1–2 persons 120–140€, triple 160€; *taxe de séjour*
   included **CREDIT CARDS** AE, DC, MC, V
BREAKFAST Continental included

HÔTEL NOVANOX ★★★ (73)
155, boulevard du Montparnasse, 75006
Métro: Vavin, Raspail; RER Port Royal
27 rooms, all with shower or bath and toilet

From the outside it doesn't inspire. But inside, the future beckons at the Novanox, an impressive example of what a sense of style and imagination—with a little money thrown in—can do. Hats off to owner Bertrand Plasmans, who, a decade ago, gambled everything and took an old hotel and fashioned a modern re-creation with the latest designs and contemporary craftsmanship. The yellow-and-blue lobby, with dangling mobile lights, reminds me of a playful fairyland—everywhere you look the faces of Greek gods and goddesses are softly painted on the walls and depicted on the upholstered chairs and couches. At one end of the lobby is a breakfast area overlooking an enclosed, plant-rimmed sidewalk terrace. Dainty croissants and buttery brioches fill the breakfast baskets and are accompanied by an assortment of jams and a pot of sweet butter. A portion of cheese and fresh fruit round out the meal.

The rooms along the front have a chocolate-brown color scheme, with contemporary furniture specially built to fit the design of each room, and sparkling white-tile baths. The quiet rooms on the back are larger. Ten new bathrooms have granite floors, white stone tiles, recessed lighting, and toiletries from Roger and Gallet.

M. Plasman also owns the Hôtel Saint-Thomas-d'Aquin, a two-star in the seventh arrondissement (see page 188). His latest acquisition is Hôtel Saint Vincent, next door at 5, rue du Pré Aux Clercs. Unfortunately, the renovations for the Hôtel Saint Vincent were not completed when *Great Sleeps Paris* went to press, but knowing M. Plasmans innate sense of style, it too will be *magnifique*.

TEL 01-46-33-63-60 **FAX** 01-43-26-61-72 **EMAIL** hotel-novanox@wanadoo.fr
  INTERNET www.hotel-novanox.com
FACILITIES & SERVICES Bar, direct-dial phone, elevator, hair dryer, laundry
  service, minibar, TV with international reception, room safe (no charge),
  free WiFi
RATES Single 120€, double 140€; extra bed 28€; *taxe de séjour* included
  CREDIT CARDS AE, DC, MC, V
BREAKFAST Continental 9€ per person

HÔTEL RELAIS SAINT-GERMAIN ★★★★ ($, 45)
9, carrefour de l'Odéon, 75006
Métro: Odéon
22 rooms, all with toilet, shower, and bath

It would be hard to imagine a hotel with more charm and beauty than this Left Bank property, which is owned by well-known chef Yves Camdeborde and his wife, Claudine, who say, "The Relais Saint-Germain invites you to take a journey through time, history, art and culture." The hotel's rich green enamel entrance is guarded by two ceramic dogs, and the stunning interiors showcase the couple's eclectic art collection. Pieces are displayed with a sense of amusement and contemporary dash, giving you the feeling you are in the home of world collectors.

The richly appointed rooms, named after famous French writers, promise heavily beamed ceilings, designer fabrics in brocade and silk, and always bouquets of fresh flowers. The Diderot Room is a wonderful single or romantic double where the wall of mirrors behind the bed and on the closet doors reflect the wild red-and-blue floral theme of the curtains and upholstery. The Montesquieu Room is a dramatic junior suite featuring leopard skin–covered chairs, foot stools, and cushions. The windows are swagged in green damask-style tiebacks, and two prints of tropical birds add a note of brilliant color. Prints of American Indian chiefs set the theme of the Balzac Room, which also has its own balcony. More prints of a porcupine, camel, and gazelle, plus a three-by-three-foot painting of a tiger, add a touch of nature to the mix.

Breakfast is served in the rooms or next door in Camdeborde's popular brasserie, Le Comptoir. Just how popular is this brasserie? So much so that reservations for his Monday through Friday dinner-only tasting menu must be made months in advance. The brasserie operates with a traditional menu during the day and on the weekends, and reservations are not accepted at these times.

TEL 01-44-27-07-97 **FAX** 01-46-33-45-30 **EMAIL** hotelrsg@wanadoo.fr
INTERNET www.hotelrsg.com
FACILITIES & SERVICES Air-conditioning, bar, direct-dial phone, elevator to most rooms, hair dryer, laundry services, minibar, robes, room safe (no charge), room service, TV with international reception, free WiFi
RATES Standard single 210€, double 275–300€, deluxe 360€, junior suite 380€, suite with terrace 420€; *taxe de séjour* included **CREDIT CARDS** AE, DC, MC, V
BREAKFAST Continental in room or brasserie included

HÔTEL RELAIS SAINT-SULPICE ★★★ ($, 57)
3, rue Garancière, 75006
Métro: Mabillon, Odéon
26 rooms, all with shower, bath, and toilet

An inspired use of pattern and colonial African design characterizes the public areas of this attractive choice, which is close to designer boutique shopping and promenades through the Jardin du Luxembourg. The intimate sitting room, housing a small honor bar, is enhanced by an unusual collection of colorful beetles mounted under glass and a dhurrie rug tossed onto the plank floor. The large skylighted breakfast room has a contemporary tapestry of the Jardin du Luxembourg and hand-painted floor tiles from Provence set into an oak floor. In keeping with the theme of the hotel, the tables and chairs are crafted from twisted bamboo and wood, and a pretty garden bench is covered with African prints. To one side is the entrance to the complimentary guest sauna. The twenty-six livable rooms are done in shades of cream, biscuit, toffee, and soft green; wrought-iron bed frames and cushioned cane chairs may be complemented by a table from the 1930s or a vintage chest. Most rooms face the street and have a view of St. Sulpice Church; a few overlook a quiet central courtyard. The bathrooms have a bathtub and shower combination and are brightened by a colorful lizard design set into the tiles.

Also under the same ownership is Hôtel Relais Monceau (see page 204).

TEL 01-46-33-99-00 **FAX** 01-46-33-00-10 **EMAIL** relaisstsulpice@wanadoo.fr
INTERNET www.relais-saint-sulpice.com
FACILITIES & SERVICES Air-conditioning, honor bar, conference room, direct-dial phone, elevator, hair dryer, laundry service, minibar, free sauna, TV with international reception, room safe (no charge), WiFi
RATES 1–2 persons: standard room 175€, moderate room 180€, superior room 195€, deluxe room 210€, triple 245€; *taxe de séjour* included
CREDIT CARDS AE, DC, MC, V
BREAKFAST Buffet 12€ per person

HÔTEL SAINT-ANDRÉ-DES-ARTS ★ (27)
66, rue St-André-des-Arts, 75006
Métro: Odéon, St-Michel
32 rooms, all with shower or bath and toilet

The Saint-André-des-Arts continues to improve—well, sort of. Some of the airless, trainlike bathrooms with hot-red toilet seats are still in use, but various other rooms continue to get quickie facelifts (that is, a coat of paint has been slapped on). Then there are the things that will never change. For instance, No. 9, a too-tight triple, will never escape the ghastly view of pigeon droppings as you exit the room. The carved misericord, which priests used to sit on and lean against during long masses, still graces the entry, along with a row of raffia stools under the window, an exhausted black leather sofa, and two folding tables—one of which holds a TV with a stack of CDs on top and another holds the CD player. Most importantly, the friendly manager still stands behind his ruling philosophy, "We are a hotel without extras, including the charges." For instance, the Continental breakfast is complimentary, but he says, "If you want it served in your room, you take it there."

The location is strategic, the prices low, and the unconventional crowd of fashion groupies, hip musicians, budding actors, and starving backpackers is party-loving and carefree. For some people, the rooms are so small that cabin fever quickly sets in. Others may object to the unpleasant symphony of noises drifting through the walls at all hours or to the low-watt lights dangling from the ceilings. Nonsmokers won't appreciate that housekeepers are allowed to smoke on the job. But none of that matters to the devoted regulars, for whom this wrinkled hotel still has a tattered charm they love to romanticize and an attitude by management they eagerly applaud.

TEL 01-43-26-96-16 **FAX** 01-43-29-73-34 **EMAIL** hsaintand@wanadoo.fr
FACILITIES & SERVICES Direct-dial phone, no elevator (4 floors), fans on request, hair dryer, TV at reception, office safe (no charge)
RATES Single 68€, double 87–92€, triple 110€, quad 121€; *taxe de séjour* included **CREDIT CARDS** MC, V
BREAKFAST Continental included

HÔTEL SAINT-GERMAIN-DES-PRÉS ★★★ ($, 2)
36, rue Bonaparte, 75006
Métro: St-Germain-des-Prés
30 rooms, all with shower or bath and toilet

The hotel brochure states: "At the end of your visit, you are already longing to come back to this magical place." How true it is—the Saint-Germain-des-Prés is just the kind of small hotel everyone hopes to find, and return to, in Paris. Superbly located in the very *coeur* of St-Germain, only a few minutes from two of the city's most famous cafés—Les Deux Magots and Café Flore—it has a long history of famous guests. It began in 1778 as a Masonic lodge to which Voltaire, Benjamin Franklin, and U.S. Navy captain John Paul Jones belonged. After it became a hotel, it housed philosopher Auguste Comte, American playwright Elmer Rice, and authors Henry Miller and Janet Flanner. Ms. Flanner lived here for years and wrote her "Letters from Paris" column for the *New Yorker* from her top-floor suite.

The hotel is known for its lovely displays of fresh flowers, which are massed everywhere, from the entryway with its Venetian glass chandelier and hand-painted celestial ceiling to the antique- and tapestry-filled salon and breakfast room overlooking a walled garden filled with blooming hydrangeas and azaleas. Each floor has a different theme for the art work in the hallways: dancers, theater, La Belle Epoque, and musicians. The well-lit individualized rooms have hand-painted doors and brass or canopy beds, and they are done in dark woods and fabric-covered walls. The quiet suites face the courtyard. With their separate sitting rooms, they are captivating, especially No. 26, which has oriental rugs tossed on polished inlaid wooden floors, a canopy bed, leaded-glass windows, flower boxes, and a marble bath with Art Nouveau lights and fixtures. Space is well used in No. 25, a double on the back where built-in closets frame the bed; a small desk, chair, and luggage bench offer comfort. Air-conditioning in all the rooms is an added bonus on hot days in this noisy part of Paris. Finally, the hotel's deserved popularity today is due in no small measure to the thoughtfulness of its staff members, who go to great lengths to cater to the needs of their guests.

Under the same ownership are Grand Hôtel de l'Univers (see page 140) and Hôtel Duc de Saint-Simon (see page 179).

TEL 01-43-26-00-19 **FAX** 01-40-46-83-63 **EMAIL** hotel-saint-germain-des-pres@ wanadoo.fr **INTERNET** www.hotel-paris-saint-germain.com

FACILITIES & SERVICES Air-conditioning, bar, direct-dial phone, elevator, hair dryer, laundry service, minibar, robes, slippers and trouserpress in suites and deluxe rooms, room service for light meals, TV with international reception, room safe (no charge), free WiFi

RATES 1–2 persons 170–205€, deluxe 265€, suite 325€; *taxe de séjour* included
   CREDIT CARDS AE, MC, V
BREAKFAST Continental included

HÔTEL SAINT-PAUL ★★★ (50)
43, rue Monsieur-le-Prince, 75006
Métro: Odéon, Cluny–La Sorbonne
31 rooms, all with shower or bath and toilet

In the seventeenth century, this building served as a hostel for Franciscan monks. During World War II, the breakfast room served as a shelter during air raids. In the early 1960s, the hotel was full of American students studying at the Sorbonne. For the past forty-five years, it has been a hotel owned by the Hawkins family and is now competently run by their daughter, Marianne, and her husband, Daniel, who are ably assisted by an accommodating staff and the black-and-white house cat, Spoutnick. The family's collection of antiques, oriental rugs, and watercolor paintings has been used in the hotel with elegant results. The seasonal fresh flower bouquets that grace the public areas are grown and arranged by one of the housekeepers, who has been with the hotel for over two decades.

Custom-made curtains, fabric-covered walls, and interesting brass and four-poster beds combine with modern baths to create the pleasing rooms. Number 31, a single overlooking the garden, has too many strong colors and clashing fabrics for my taste. However, I do like the antique tapestry hanging behind the four-poster metal bed in No. 13, as well as the four-poster bed with a tapestry-covered headboard and matching canopy in No. 14. Twin sleigh beds and plenty of sunshine add to the enjoyment of Room 43, located on the front of the hotel. The "Starlight Room" on the ground floor is named for the multitude of starry fairy lights over the bed. The spa-inspired bathroom has the only Jacuzzi in the hotel. In No. 35, the fresco of bookshelves holds a painting of Spoutnick; the room is on the street and has a very nice bathroom. Many like No. 51, situated under the eaves; it has a cozy bedroom with a small sitting room and a bird's-eye view of École de Médecine. For those wanting more space, a good choice is No. 2, a duplex with twin beds downstairs and a circular stairway leading to a second bedroom with a double bed and bath.

TEL 01-43-26-98-64 **FAX** 01-46-34-58-60 **EMAIL** hotel.saint.paul@wanadoo.fr
   INTERNET www.hotelsaintpaulparis.com
FACILITIES & SERVICES Air-conditioning in 8 rooms, direct-dial phone, elevator, hair dryer, laundry service, minibar, TV with international reception, room safe (no charge), 8 nonsmoking rooms, WiFi
RATES Single 120–126€, double 136–168€, suite for 1–4 persons 206–238€; *taxe de séjour* included **CREDIT CARDS** AE, DC, MC, V
BREAKFAST Buffet 12€ per person

JARDIN DE L'ODÉON HÔTEL ★★★ ($, 48)
7, rue Casimir-Delavigne, 75006
Métro: Odéon; RER Luxembourg
41 rooms, all with shower or bath and toilet

Four massive Egyption sphynx bought from the Musée du Louvre guard the entrance and set the ochre and sand tones used in the lobby of this popular three-star hotel near the Luxembourg Gardens. Hand-painted reproductions of Botero and Klimt paintings hang throughout and add just the right note of contemporary panache and color. A glass-enclosed winter garden opens up to a larger outdoor sitting space that is perfect for a summer breakfast or cool afternoon drink. This sense of restrained elegance is carried out in all the rooms, many of which have private terraces or balconies, and of course all the perks discerning travelers rely upon. One of my favorite rooms is No. 12, which opens onto its own twenty-five-square-meter terrace fitted with a black metal table and chairs. Inside, the blue-and-gold room has space and a nicely tiled bathroom. Other top choices include No. 18, done in blue-and-white stripes and featuring a divided bathroom and toilet; No. 26, which daringly combines red and dark purple colors;

and ground-floor Rooms 1 and 2, thanks to their lattice-enclosed patios and deep bathtubs.

Also under the same ownership are Hôtel du Panthéon (see page 120), Hôtel des Grands Hommes (see page 117), Hôtel Résidence Henri IV (see page 125), and Hôtel de la Sorbonne (see page 114).

TEL 01-53-10-28-50 **FAX** 01-43-25-28-12 **EMAIL** reservation@hotel
  jardinodeonparis.com **INTERNET** www.hoteljardinodeonparis.com
FACILITIES & SERVICES Air-conditioning, direct-dial phone, elevator,
  hair dryer, laundry service, minibar, room safe (no charge), TV with
  international reception, WiFi in lobby
RATES 1–2 people classical room 195€, superior 240€, deluxe 300€; *taxe de
  séjour* included **CREDIT CARDS** AE, MC, V
BREAKFAST Buffet downstairs or in-room Continental 12€ per person

LE MADISON HÔTEL ★★★ ($, 33)
143, boulevard St-Germain 75006
Métro: Mabillon, St-Germain-des-Prés
54 rooms, all with shower, bath, and toilet

Le Madison Hôtel evokes the charm of a bygone era, when families packed trunks, set sail across the Atlantic, and spent months doing *Le Grand Tour* of Europe. Built in 1924, the hotel has played host to some famous guests. Nobel Prize–winner Albert Camus wrote *l'Étranger* while living here, and Hemingway was a regular at the bar, as was Juliette Greco, who was known as "the queen of St-Germain" in the fifties. André Malraux had his mistress ensconced here, and today, singer Carol King calls it her Paris home.

The beautiful reception and sitting areas are done in classic French style, with tapestries, rich velvet upholstery, oriental rugs, dramatic window treatments, and graceful antiques. Personal touches make guests feel at home: a picture of the owner's mother set over the wood-burning fireplace, bouquets of flowers scattered about, books and magazines to thumb through.

The rooms blend modern amenities and comforts with conventional fabrics and furnishings, accented by some unusual touches. For instance, each floor has a different painting on the door to the elevator. The bathroom in No. 27 is done entirely in lipstick red, right down to the tiles and towel racks. Color was also not lost on No. 28, which positively glows in shades of fiery orange. Aside from needing dark glasses to stay in this room, it has a dismal view, as do all rooms on the back side of the hotel. No one could fault No. 71, a charming single in green and turquoise with a view of St. Sulpice. In addition to excellent luggage space, a decent desk, and a mirrored closet, it has a pink-tile bathroom with a good shower and marble sink. Room 23, which can sleep two or three, has an amusing collection of antique golf prints. From No. 74, a yellow-and-green double, you have a sweeping view encompassing Montmartre and St-Germain-des-Prés Church. The bed is king-size, the bathroom marble, and the space excellent. Room 86, lavishly done in lavender and tawny gold, has the same view.

In No. 87, a suite, you get only a peek at St-Germain-des-Prés Church but enough space to swing three cats and entertain two dozen of your closest friends. The sitting room is pleasingly decorated in blue and green with coordinating tartan curtains pulled back to let in plenty of light. It is furnished with a green leather sofa, two comfortable armchairs, and a desk large enough to plug in your laptop and actually get some work done. The twin bedroom has more closet and luggage space than you will ever need and a well-lit bathroom with a separate stall shower and double sinks.

Three other outstanding hotels are under the same family ownership: Artus Hôtel (page 137), Hôtel Bourgogne & Montana (page 174), and Terrass Hôtel (page 278).

TEL 01-40-51-60-00 **FAX** 01-40-51-60-01 **EMAIL** res@hotel-madison.com
   INTERNET www.hotel-madison.com
FACILITIES & SERVICES Air-conditioning, bar, direct-dial phone, hair dryer,
   elevator, laundry service, minibar, robes in deluxe rooms and suites, TV
   with international reception, room safe (no charge), WiFi
RATES Single 160–200€, double 220–280€, executive 325€, suite/apt 400€;
   extra bed 65€; off-season rates Jan–Feb, Aug; *taxe de séjour* included
   CREDIT CARDS AE, DC, MC, V
BREAKFAST Buffet or in-room Continental included

LE RELAIS HÔTEL DU VIEUX PARIS ★★★★ ($, 18)
9, rue Gît-le-Coeur, 75006
Métro: Odéon; RER St-Michel–Notre-Dame
19 rooms, all with shower, bath, and toilet

Romance and nostalgia in a picture-perfect setting sum up Le Relais Hôtel du Vieux Paris. The building dates from the late 1400s, as do most of the others on this narrow lane just off the Seine. As King Henri IV passed by the street, he said, *"Gist mon coeur"* (Here lies my heart), because this was where his favorite mistress lived—thus, the name of the street and the spirit that still pervades it.

In its heyday in the 1950s and early 1960s, the hotel had no proper name, just a street number. It was the haunt of the movers and shakers of the Beat Generation: Allen Ginsberg, Harold Norse, William S. Burroughs, Harold Chapman, Thelma Shumsky, and many others. Guests painted, wrote, talked, and planned, and the inflexible Mme. Rachou presided over it all while standing on a box behind the little zinc bar. There were no carpets, no telephones, and the nineteenth-century electrical system was hit-or-miss. Toilet facilities consisted of a hole in the floor on each stair landing. In the mid-1960s, Mme. Rachou suddenly sold the hotel. The new owners named it, carpeted and painted the rooms, added phones, and, of all things, even installed private bathrooms in some rooms. Canvases, manuscripts, and sketches that may have been worth millions of dollars were burned in the battle to disinfect the hotel.

Currently under its third owner, Mme. Claude Odillard, the hotel has been completely redone and today bears no resemblance to its previous life. The guests are chic and well traveled, and few are aware of the hotel's history—all that remains are photos of some of its earlier guests. Placed throughout the public areas of the hotel are pieces from Mme. Odillard's own collection of antiques. The fourteen individually decorated rooms and five suites, which are coordinated in Pierre Frey fabrics and top-of-the-line furnishings, all have something special to offer. In No. 28, a blue floral double or twin, there is a massage shower; in No. 27, an executive double overlooking the street, there is a small sitting area. Number 35 is a feminine suite with red and white Toile de Jouy fabric, original beams, a Jacuzzi bathtub, and a desk by the window. Number 25, another two-room suite in blue and white, has its original beamed ceiling, a separate sitting area, a Jacuzzi, and a quiet vantage point. It is not surprising that the top-floor suite is always in demand: in addition to the king-size bedroom, sitting area, and marble bathroom on the first level, there is a mezzanine bedroom with a skylight that children adore.

Of further interest to many guests, the entire hotel is nonsmoking. A private limousine is available for airport pickup and departures, or day trips outside of Paris. Guests are urged to buy their tickets for the Louvre and Musée d'Orsay at the hotel reception, which means you do not have to waste time standing in long entrance lines. Honeymooners are toasted with a bottle of chilled champagne and a bouquet of fresh flowers, and everyone is personally welcomed and made to feel at home in this very lovely hotel with an amazing history.

TEL 01-44-32-15-90 **FAX** 01-43-26-00-15 **EMAIL** reservations@vieuxparis.com
    INTERNET www.vieuxparis.com or www.paris-hotel-vieuxparis.com
FACILITIES & SERVICES Air-conditioning, direct-dial phone, elevator, hair dryer, laundry service, minibar, TV with international reception, robes and Jacuzzis in suites, room safe (no charge), hotel entirely nonsmoking, WiFi
RATES 1–2 persons: deluxe 200–240€, executive 252–280€, suite 307–350€, duplex 337–350€; children under 12 free; *taxe de séjour* included
CREDIT CARDS AE, DC, MC, V
BREAKFAST Continental 13€ per person

MILLÉSIME HÔTEL ★★★ ($, 6)
15, rue Jacob, 75006
Métro: St-Germain-des-Prés
22 rooms, all with shower, bath, and toilet

If art is one of the cornerstones of your Parisian trip, the Millésime is a perfect launching pad for walks to the Louvre, Musée d'Orsay, or the Cluny. Also within easy reach are dozens of private art galleries and dealers in the neighborhood. For trips farther afield, a quick métro or bus ride takes you to the Rodin, Centre Georges Pompidou, or Picasso. This top-drawer location is also a heavenly address for dedicated shop hounds and those who want to adopt the café life.

The hotel is built around a pretty Provençal-style courtyard with trailing greenery and flowers. The interior is done in the warm countryside colors of this popular region: sunny yellow, earthy adobe, azure blue. Most of the rooms have pleasing neighborhood views. They are simply fitted with creature comforts and white-tile bathrooms, which admittedly are nothing other than small in the standard rooms. The largest is No. 50, the Millésime Room, with a sloping ceiling and cross support beams framing the window. Room 51, a one-flight walk up, is the only single on the fifth floor. It is designed to combine with No. 50, which has a larger bathroom, more sitting and work space, and a romantic view of the St-Germain-des-Prés Church. Breakfast is served in an arched stone cellar, where bright orange chairs are placed around white linen–covered tables.

TEL 01-44-07-97-97 **FAX** 01-46-34-55-97 **EMAIL** reservation@
  millesimehotel.com **INTERNET** www.millesimehotel.com
FACILITIES & SERVICES Air-conditioning, direct-dial phone, elevator (to most
  floors), hair dryer, laundry service, room service for light snacks, TV with
  international reception, room safe (no charge), WiFi
RATES 1–2 persons 185€, Millésime Room 220€; extra bed 45€; special 8%
  discount for *Great Sleeps Paris* readers; *taxe de séjour* included
  CREDIT CARDS AE, DC, MC, V
BREAKFAST Buffet 15€, Continental 12€, per person

PENSION LES MARRONNIERS (NO STARS, ¢, 65)
78, rue d'Assas (first floor on left, stairway A), 75006
Métro: Vavin, Notre-Dame-des-Champs
12 rooms, 2 with shower and toilet

The days of family-run pensions in France, and especially in Paris, are numbered, according to a documentary on the subject filmed here. This *incroyable* Cheap Sleep, across the street from one of the entrances to the Jardin du Luxembourg, is presided over by Marie Poirier, whose family members have been here since the turn of the century. At the Pension les Marronniers, the philanthropically low prices include not only a Continental breakfast Monday through Saturday, but a three-course dinner with cheese Monday through Friday. On the weekends, a cold tray is available. With advance notice, special dietary needs can be catered to. Students, Frenchmen from the provinces doing a work-study program, and smart budgeteers fill this first-floor walkup, which has the Laura Ashley decorating seal of approval in the dining and living rooms. Lennie, a gray-and-white sheepdog, is in charge of providing a friendly welcome. The bedrooms might seem primitive to many, but all are cleaned on a regular basis, and the linens changed weekly. Amenities run the gamut from no facilities to private shower and toilet plus telephone, minibar, and French TV. Reservations are absolutely essential months in advance, and guests who stay for a long time are preferred. Meals are part of the program and cannot be deducted for any reason.

TEL 01-43-26-37-71 **FAX** 01-43-26-07-72 **EMAIL** o_marro@club-Internet.fr
  INTERNET www.pension-marronniers.com
FACILITIES & SERVICES Direct-dial phones in rooms with toilets, no elevator
  (2 floors), minibar in some rooms, TV in lounge and some rooms, office
  safe (no charge), coin washer and dryer

RATES Single 27–62€, double 68–83€; special rates for long stays (20% discount for one month or longer); *taxe de séjour* 0.15€ per person, per day
 CREDIT CARDS None, cash only
BREAKFAST Included Mon–Sat; dinner included from Mon–Fri (Sat–Sun cold tray)

WELCOME HÔTEL ★★ (34)
66, rue de Seine, at boulevard St-Germain, 75006
Métro: Odéon, Mabillion, St-Germain-des-Prés
30 rooms, all with shower or bath and toilet

Unpretentious, clean rooms with well-worn furniture in a fun-filled location are combined with moderate prices to make a stay here more than welcome. Composed of thirty rooms on six floors, this spot is on the corner of rue de Seine and boulevard St-Germain. Because many of the rooms are on the small side, as are the closets, it is an especially suitable stopover for singles. Those wanting more spacious accommodations should ask for a corner room with a view (Nos. 21, 51, or 53). The best is No. 53, done up in pink. The plus here is the large bath (for this hotel) with a tub and shower nozzle. Other popular picks are No. 54, the best single because it has a writing table and a view, and No. 62, an attic nest with beams and a peaked ceiling. The worst is No. 64, with an open closet, a bathroom with no shelf space, and windows too high to see out. Despite double windows, quiet is not the rule here. For the least noisy bunks, request rooms that face rue de Seine (Nos. 21 or 51), not boulevard St-Germain. Top-floor rooms can get hot and stuffy in warm weather, but they are very desirable otherwise.

Also under the same family ownership are Hôtel des 2 Continents (see page 148) and Hôtel des Marronniers (see page 149).

TEL 01-46-34-24-80 **FAX** 01-40-46-81-59 **EMAIL** welcome-hotel@wanadoo.fr
 INTERNET www.welcomehotel-paris.com
FACILITIES & SERVICES Direct-dial phone, hair dryer, elevator, TV with international reception, office safe (no charge)
RATES Single 75–96€, double 96–106€, triple 125€; *taxe de séjour* included
 CREDIT CARDS MC, V
BREAKFAST Continental 9€ per person

Seventh Arrondissement

Known affectionately as "Seventh Heaven," this quiet, luxurious residential area is full of stately mansions built before the Revolution and now occupied by diplomats, government workers, well-to-do Parisians, and expatriates. The Champ-de-Mars served as the parade ground for the École Militaire and is the backyard of the Eiffel Tower. Also on the Champ-de-Mars is one of Paris's newest and most moving monuments: the Mur Pour la Paix (The Wall of Peace), based on the Wailing Wall in Jerusalem. It was built in 2000 to honor the hopes of peace in the new millennium. One part holds computer banks where people can write their own messages for peace here or on the Website (www.murpourlapaix.com).

LEFT BANK
Assemblée Nationale
Champ-de-Mars
École Militaire
Les Egouts de Paris
Eiffel Tower
Les Invalides
Musée d'Orsay
Musée Rodin
UNESCO

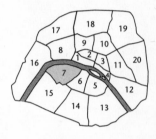

Built as a military hospital and still used for this purpose, Les Invalides is the home of four world-famous military museums and is the final resting place of Napoléon Bonaparte. To the west of Les Invalides is the École Militaire, a military academy built by Louis XV; Napoléon trained there. If you are interested in experiencing the sewers of Paris *(Les Egouts de Paris),* which date from the Second Empire and were designed by Baron Haussmann, the museum at the Pont de l'Alma (opposite 93, quai d'Orsay) runs guided tours. Tours of the Assemblée Nationale (the lower house of French parliament) are held on Saturdays when the chamber is not in session. Not to be missed are two museums: the Musée d'Orsay, originally a train station and now a repository of masterpieces of the Impressionists, and the lovely statues in the Musée Rodin. For premier antique shopping, stroll along the quai Voltaire and rue du Bac. Finally, there is the Eiffel Tower, which is best viewed across the river from Trocadéro. The 986-foot tower hosts six million visitors per year.

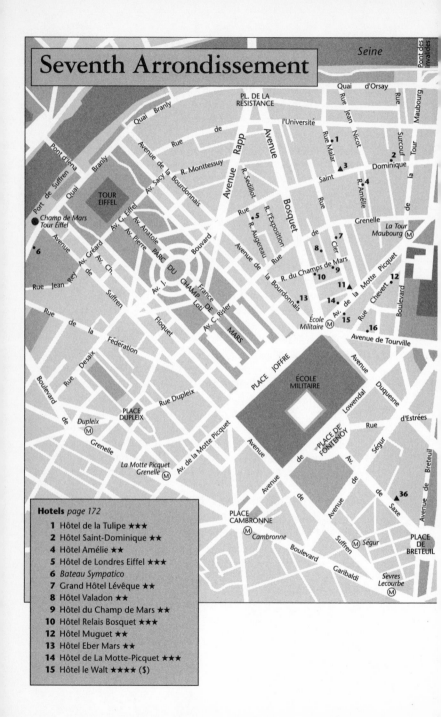

Seventh Arrondissement

Seine

Pont des invalides

Quai d'Orsay

PL. DE LA RÉSISTANCE

l'Université

Quai Branly

Rue de

Avenue de la Bourdonnais

Avenue Rapp

Avenue Bosquet

Rue Jean Nicot

Rue Malar

1

2

Surcouf

Av. de la Tour Maubourg

Rue de

R. Monttessuy

Av. Sacy

Av. G. Eiffel

Avenue

Saint Dominique

▲**3**

R. Sédillot

R. l'Exposition

R. Augereau

R. Amélie

4

Pont d'Iéna

Branly

Quai

Pont de Suffren

TOUR EIFFEL

Champ de Mars Tour Eiffel

6

Avenue

Av. Ch. Av. G. Eiffel

Av. Anatole

PARC DU CHAMP DE MARS

Av. Pierre

Bouvard

France

Av. J.

Av. Lou

Av. C. Risler

Rue Jean Rey

Av. Gréard

Rue de Suffren

Rue de la Fédération

Rue Desaix

Boulevard de Grenelle

Floquet

Rue

Grenelle

La Tour Maubourg Ⓜ

5

de

Rue du Champs de Mars

7

8

Cler

9

10

11▲

12

13

14

Av. de la Motte Picquet

Rue Chevert

Boulevard

15

16

École Militaire Ⓜ

Avenue de Tourville

de

Avenue de la Bourdonnais

PLACE JOFFRE

ÉCOLE MILITAIRE

Avenue

Lowendal

Duquesne

Rue Duplex

Rue Dupleix

PLACE DUPLEIX

Dupleix Ⓜ

Grenelle

La Motte Picquet Grenelle Ⓜ

Av. de la Motte Picquet

Avenue

de

PLACE DE FONTENOY

Rue de Ségur

d'Estrées

Avenue de Breteuil

Avenue

de

Av. de Saxe

▲**36**

PLACE DE BRETEUIL

PLACE CAMBRONNE

Cambronne Ⓜ

Suffren Ⓜ Ségur

Boulevard Garibaldi

Sèvres Lecourbe Ⓜ

Hotels *page 172*

1 Hôtel de la Tulipe ★★★
2 Hôtel Saint-Dominique ★★
4 Hôtel Amélie ★★
5 Hôtel de Londres Eiffel ★★★
6 *Bateau Sympatico*
7 Grand Hôtel Lévêque ★★
8 Hôtel Valadon ★★
9 Hôtel du Champ de Mars ★★
10 Hôtel Relais Bosquet ★★★
12 Hôtel Muguet ★★
13 Hôtel Eber Mars ★★
14 Hôtel de La Motte-Picquet ★★★
15 Hôtel le Walt ★★★★ ($)

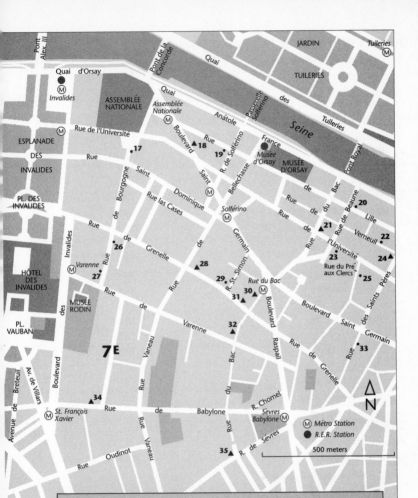

HOTELS IN THE SEVENTH ARRONDISSEMENT

OTHER OPTIONS
Boat on the Seine

($) indicates a Big Splurge

GRAND HÔTEL LÉVÊQUE ★★ (7)
29, rue Cler, 75007
Métro: École Militaire, Latour-Maubourg
50 rooms, all with toilet and shower (no bathtubs)

Committed pennywise sleepers who like the seventh arrondissement love the Lévêque. Set among the colorful food shops that line the rue Cler, it is close to all the things that one often forgets are so important on a trip: banks, a post office, good transportation, do-it-yourself laundries, cleaners, well-priced shops, cafés for a midmorning cup of hot chocolate, a street *marché,* and several exceptional cheese shops and *charcuteries* for inspired picnics.

The hotel has benefited from yearly improvements and now boasts a glass elevator and spiffy, no-nonsense, style-free rooms. Closets and shelves are spacious enough, but drawer space is limited. The best rooms face the front. Three on the fifth floor have balconies where you can observe the wonderful street scene below. In Nos. 51 and 52, you can lie in bed and see the Eiffel Tower. The hotel is always busy, and I predict it will be even more in demand thanks to the many improvements. If you are interested in staying here, book ahead at least one month and more during peak periods.

TEL 01-47-05-49-15 **FAX** 01-45-50-49-36 **EMAIL** info@hotel-leveque.com
   INTERNET www.hotel-leveque.com
FACILITIES & SERVICES Air-conditioning, direct-dial phone with private
   number, elevator, fans, hair dryer in most rooms, Internet in lobby, TV
   with international reception, room safe (5€ per stay)
RATES Single 60€, double 90–115€, triple 130€; *taxe de séjour* 0.78€ per
   person, per day **CREDIT CARDS** AE, MC, V
BREAKFAST Continental 9€ per person

HÔTEL AMÉLIE ★★ (4)
5, rue Amélie, 75007
Métro: Latour-Maubourg; RER Invalides
16 rooms, all with shower or bath and toilet

Quelle surprise! The plain and simple Hôtel Amélie has been fluffed and dusted, becoming a solid budget bet in the tony seventh arrondissement. New tile baths have been added to many rooms, which are fitted with easy-care furniture that has that "could be anywhere" look. The rooms in back may overlook a wall, but at least the wall is softened by green trellises. The red enamel stair rails on the fifty-two steps to the top floor match the red on the room doors and the flowering geraniums blooming in the window boxes. Okay, so some of the small closets have hangers facing out, drawer space is not a consideration, and neither is high-speed Internet. However, you can check into one of the nonsmoking rooms and enjoy staying in an interesting, upscale part of Paris.

TEL 01-45-51-74-75 **FAX** 01-45-56-93-55 **EMAIL** hotelamelie@wanadoo.fr
   INTERNET www.hotelamelie.fr
FACILITIES & SERVICES Direct-dial phone, no elevator (4 floors), hair dryer,
   minibar, office safe (no charge), TV with international reception,
   2 nonsmoking rooms
RATES Single 85€, double 95–105€; extra bed 20€; *taxe de séjour* included
   CREDIT CARDS AE, MC, V
BREAKFAST Continental 7€ per person

HÔTEL BERSOLY'S SAINT-GERMAIN ★★★ (20)
28, rue de Lille, 75007
Métro: Rue du Bac, St-Germain-des-Prés
16 rooms, all with shower or bath and toilet

Bersoly's Saint-Germain continues to be a very good value three-star, which has been owned since the mid-1980s by Mme. Carbonnaux. The old stone walls and floors in the lobby are clean and polished, and the flowery downstairs breakfast room is set with Villeroy and Boch china. Then there is the location: only minutes away from the Musée d'Orsay, the Louvre, serious shopping, and equally serious restaurants (see *Great Eats Paris*).

Every air-conditioned bedroom has been named for a famous French artist. In each case, a reproduction of one of the artist's paintings hangs in the room, and the mood and color scheme of the room are taken from the painting. If you like bold reds and black, request the ground-floor Picasso Room, with its entrance off the atrium. This is also the room you will get if you bring your pet to the hotel. If you prefer pastels, the Seurat or Sisley Rooms are the ones to ask for. The twin- or king-bed Gauguin Room can be joined with the Turner to form a family suite. The Cezanne has a beamed ceiling and two red leather armchairs. You will find almost the same in the fifth-floor Pissaro, done in blue and white fabric on the walls and curtains and cross beams in the bathroom.

TEL 01-01-42-60-73-79 **FAX** 01-49-27-05-55 **EMAIL** hotelbersolys@wanadoo.fr
   INTERNET www.bersolyshotel.com
FACILITIES & SERVICES Air-conditioning, bar, direct-dial phone, electric tea
   kettle, fans, elevator (to most floors), hair dryer, laundry service, private
   parking, room service, TV with international reception, room safe (no
   charge), WiFi in lobby and most rooms
RATES Single 100–120€, double 125–145€; dog 10€ per day; parking 30€
   per 24-hours; *taxe de séjour* included **CREDIT CARDS** AE, DC, MC, V
BREAKFAST Continental 10€ per person

HÔTEL BOURGOGNE & MONTANA ★★★★ ($, 17)
3, rue de Bourgogne, 75007
Métro: Assemblée-Nationale; RER Invalides
32 rooms, all with shower or bath and toilet

The formal Bourgogne & Montana, facing the Palais Bourbon, is located in a posh diplomatic neighborhood between Les Invalides and St-Germain. Famous neighbors include Lionel Jospin and fashion designer Karl Lagerfeld. Across the street is one of the best *pâtisseries* in the *quartier,* and next door, the boutique Loulou de la Falaise sells her fantasy collection of clothing, jewelry, and purses at equally fanciful prices. Combining a taste for tradition with a dignified clientele, the hotel is both regal and efficient, with large reception rooms and a historically classified 1924 elevator with lovely old ironwork and an open front that enables you to see the floors as you ascend.

No two rooms are the same, and many are in odd shapes, which not only adds interest but extra space. If cost is not too much of a factor, book a room on the fifth or sixth floor. I always hope for No. 67, a junior suite with wonderful views of place de la Concorde, the Madeleine Church, the Assemblée Nationale, and the roof of the Grand Palais. When the buildings are illuminated at night, it is pure fairyland. Done in blue and yellow, this twin-bed room has antiques, a comfortable sofa, large television, built-in closet, luggage space, and a divided bathroom with two sinks. If this is not available, ask for No. 61 with a mansard roofline and a round bathtub. Room 54 has a courtyard view and a gleaming tile bathroom with excellent fittings. Room 12 forms the backdrop for a collection of drawings of members of the Chamber of Deputies. Room 10, a deluxe, has a king-size bed and faces the quiet street, but you may need blinders to bathe in the brilliant turquoise bathroom, which has double sinks. Special rates during the off-season make this excellent choice even more affordable for many.

Also under the same ownership are Artus Hôtel (see page 137), Le Madison Hôtel (see page 164), and Terrass Hôtel (see page 278).

TEL 01-45-51-20-22; toll-free from U.S. 800-44-UTELL **FAX** 01-45-56-11-98
  EMAIL bmontana@bourgogne-montana.com **INTERNET**
  www.bourgogne-montana.com
FACILITIES & SERVICES Air-conditioning, bar, direct-dial phone, elevator, hair
  dryer, laundry service, minibar, free parking on the square (if you are
  lucky), robes in deluxe rooms and suites, TV with international reception
  and pay-per-view, office safe (no charge), WiFi in lobby
RATES Single 155–250€, double 180–250€, suite 305–320€; extra bed 70€;
  dog 15€; *taxe de séjour* included **CREDIT CARDS** AE, DC, MC, V
BREAKFAST Buffet included

HÔTEL DE LA MOTTE-PICQUET ★★★ (14)
30, avenue de la Motte-Picquet, 75007
Métro: Ecole Militaire
18 rooms, all with shower or bath and toilet

Monochromatic modernists must look the other way on this one, but if you never met a bright color or tassle you didn't like . . . read on.

The kaleidoscope of vivid colors that pervades the hotel is daring to say the least. From the minute you enter the gilded, swagged, tassled, and velvet-clad lobby, you are bombarded with ruffles and flourishes peeking out from every gaudy corner. And it just doesn't stop: in the multicolored breakfast room, the trio of colored tables accents the red velvet banquette with an additional bouquet of five colored throw pillows. Even the china keeps pace in ruby, two shades of green, purple, and yellow.

The rooms, which have an excessive angel/floral theme, fortunately do not require blinders. Number 202, a miniature double in lavender and soothing soft green, has angels on the walls, over the bed, and in framed prints hanging on the walls. Next door in No. 203, you will be wrapped in burgandy and peach in a flower-infused room with a white iron and brass bed complete with more flowers etched on the posts. Angels appear in bas relief hangings in No. 206, a room with slightly more space to accommodate a half-canopy over the bed, three crystal wall lights, and a reproduction three-drawer chest.

Also under the same ownership (but not the same decor) is the Grand Hôtel de Champagne (see page 69).

TEL 01-47-05-09-57 **FAX** 01-47-05-74-36 **EMAIL** book@hotelmottepicquet
  paris.com **INTERNET** www.hoteldelamottepicquetparis.com
FACILITIES & SERVICES Air-conditioning in some rooms, direct-dial phone,
  elevator (not to breakfast room), hair dryer, laundry service, minibar, robes

in some rooms, office safe, room safe in some rooms (no charge), TV with international reception, WiFi
RATES Single 130€, double 150–175€, suite 235€; *taxe de séjour* 0.78€ per person, per day **CREDIT CARDS** AE, MC, V
BREAKFAST Buffet 10€ per person

HÔTEL DE LA TULIPE ★★★ (1)
33, rue Malar, 75007
Métro: Latour-Maubourg
22 rooms, all with shower or bath and toilet

For years this former convent was a tired and tattered penny-pincher's choice *sans charme*. Thanks to the efforts of Jean-Louis Fortuit, a French film actor turned hotelier, and his charming wife, Caroline, it is finally a very sweet and romantic choice. The twenty-two rooms are tightly snuggled around a tree-shaded garden patio. Bright prints in Provençal colors, grass cloth–covered walls, wrought-iron and wicker furniture, beams galore, ancient stone walls, and peaceful garden views work nicely together, creating the illusion that the small rooms are in a country cottage miles away from Paris. If romance is on your itinerary, book No. 25, which once served as the chapel and still has two of the original stone walls and three windows opening onto the patio. If it's space you need, reserve the two-room, two-bath suite, which can sleep five. Many request the ground-floor Room 27, which has either a king or twin beds, two rough stone walls, a handicapped shower, and an old-fashioned dressing table with mirror. From the hotel, you are in close range for shopping along rue St-Dominique, soaking up the market atmosphere along rue Cler, and trying many of the favored restaurants in *Great Eats Paris.* For tourist endeavors, the Eiffel Tower is within walking distance for most, and so is Invalides, the Seine, and the Musée d'Orsay.

TEL 01-45-51-67-21 **FAX** 01-47-53-96-37 **EMAIL** hoteldelatulipe@wanadoo.fr
   INTERNET www.hoteldelatulipe.com
FACILITIES & SERVICES Direct-dial phone, no elevator (2 floors), fans on request, hair dryer, minibar, parking (must be reserved), TV with international reception, room safe (no charge), WiFi
RATES Single 120€, double 160€, triple 170€, suite 270€; parking 25€ per 24 hours; *taxe de séjour* included **CREDIT CARDS** AE, MC, V
BREAKFAST Continental 10€ per person

HÔTEL DE LONDRES EIFFEL ★★★ (5)
1, rue Augereau, 75007
Métro: École Militaire
30 rooms, all with shower or bath and toilet

Beautifully decorated rooms, realistic prices, a very quiet location, and easy walking distance to the Eiffel Tower and Champ-de-Mars, UNESCO, shopping, and a good métro connection add up to make this a fine hotel selection. Making it even more attractive is the hardworking owner, Isabelle Prigent, who told me, "I put my heart in this hotel. I want it to be just like my house." Isabelle has indeed succeeded at creating a very welcoming hotel where her guests can relax and feel quite at home.

The well-thought-out bedrooms are named after Isabelle's favorite French poets, and they all display her good taste and attention to detail. The bathrooms are *au courant* with marble sinks and good lighting. I like her collection of whimsical prints of old-fashioned ladies *chaussures* (shoes), which hangs throughout the silvery-gold metallic striped hallways. Rooms 52, 54, 62, and 64 have Eiffel Tower views. Rooms 102 (for two) and 103 (a triple) are quiet ground-floor choices overlooking the garden. The six larger, nonsmoking rooms in the back building, called Pavillon des Poets, are also quiet, but there is no elevator for the two floors. Off the reception area is a sunny yellow breakfast room with chairs draped in ruby red fabric and anchored by a bow. A collection of antique wire baskets adds an interesting touch.

TEL 01-45-51-63-02 **FAX** 01-47-05-28-96 **EMAIL** info@londres-eiffel.com
   INTERNET www.londres-eiffel.com
FACILITIES & SERVICES Air-conditioning, direct-dial phone, elevator (to most
   floors), hair dryer, minibar, plasma TV with international reception,
   6 nonsmoking rooms, free WiFi
RATES Single 99–120€, double 110–175€, triple 165–195€; extra bed 20€;
   taxe de séjour included **CREDIT CARDS** AE, DC, MC, V
BREAKFAST Buffet 12€ per person

HÔTEL DES SAINTS-PÈRES ★★★ (33)
65, rue des Saints-Pères, 75007
Métro: St-Germain-des-Prés
39 rooms, all with shower or bath and toilet

The distinguished Hôtel des Saints-Pères occupies a perfect spot in the heart of St-Germain and has a notable history. The seventeenth-century building was built in 1658 by Alphonse Daniel Gittard, Louis XIV's architect and founder of the Academy of Architecture. His portrait hangs in full view behind the reception desk, so his presence remains. The hotel has been host to many famous guests, including Edna St. Vincent Millay, who lived here in 1921 when she was the foreign correspondent for *Vanity Fair*.

Over the years the hotel has maintained its classic character and charm in its rooms and suites, which look out on a lush garden where breakfast, afternoon tea, or cocktails are served. While all the accommodations are recommended, the *pièce de résistance* is definitely Room 100, the *Chambre á la Fresque*, with its seventeenth-century *École de Versailles* ceiling frescoe. Clearly, ingenuity was required to provide the room with private facilities, as the authorities rightfully refused to grant permission to install a wall, and thus disturb the famous frescoe. The unusual solution was to install an oval tub and a set of double sinks right in the room, backing the area with black mirrors and shielding it with a huge screen. The toilet is in its own compartment to one side.

Not everyone will be checking into the frescoed bedroom, but guests should be happy with any of the other very comfortable rooms. For

...ose who don't mind a few stairs, No. 405 qualifies as a Great Sleep: it's a beamed duplex in burgundy with two easy chairs, a nice desk with good light, and a garden view. The bathroom has a wonderful bathtub, three-way mirrors, and a separate toilet. Number 205 is a spacious suite with an enclosed shower and bathtub, and a choice of king or twin beds. For something more modest, request the garden-facing No. 404, decorated in soft blue and cream and featuring an antique desk.

The hotel is part of the outstanding Esprit de France group, which includes beautiful hotels throughout the country, including the following in Paris: Hôtel Brighton (see page 71), Hôtel Mansart (see page 77), Hôtel d'Orsay (see page 179), Hôtel Parc Saint-Séverin (see page 124), Hôtel de la Place du Louvre (see page 73), and Hôtel l'Aiglon (see page 235).

TEL 01-45-44-50-00 **FAX** 01-45-44-90-83 **EMAIL** hsp@espritfrance.com
   INTERNET www.esprit-de-france.com
FACILITIES & SERVICES Air-conditioning in most rooms, bar, direct-dial phone, elevator to most floors, hair dryer, laundry service, minibar, porter, room safe (no charge), TV with international reception, WiFi
RATES Single 115€, double 130–200€, suite 300€, *Chambre à la Fresque* 330€; *taxe de séjour* included **CREDIT CARDS** AE, MC, V
BREAKFAST Continental 12.50€ per person

HÔTEL DE VARENNE ★★★ (27)
44, rue de Bourgogne, 75007
Métro: Assemblée-Nationale, Varenne; RER Musée d'Orsay
24 rooms, all with shower or bath and toilet

Over the years, I've never given up hope that someone would pull this establishment out of the decorating doldrums and create a charming hotel. *Enfin!* It has been revived by Jean Marc Pommier, and it is now a delightful garden hotel in the heart of the cosmopolitan seventh. The revival is apparent in the attitude of his staff, who stand firmly behind the hotel motto: "Guest service is our top priority—nothing will be spared to make your stay as pleasant as possible."

The rooms, which have enough space for a luggage rack and comfortable armchair, have been refitted with Napoléonic-style furniture, and they have gold tissue–covered walls and blue or red upholstery and drapery fabrics. In Nos. 31 and 41, there is a peek of the Eiffel Tower. On the fourth floor, the rooms have mansard rooflines that slant down the middle of the room. While the largest rooms in the hotel, these probably would not suit someone who is tall. One of the nicest features of the hotel is the well-landscaped private garden. Tables and chairs are here for guest enjoyment, whether it be for a relaxing afternoon drink or an early breakfast on a warm morning. Now boasting a brand-new look and loaded with amenities, this small hotel offers good value for those seeking a moderately priced Great Sleep in a very desirable area.

TEL 01-45-51-45-55 **FAX** 01-45-51-86-63 **EMAIL** info@hoteldevarenne.com
   INTERNET www.hoteldevarenne.com

FACILITIES & SERVICES Air-conditioning, direct-dial phone, elevator, hair
   dryer, minibar, flat-screen TV with international reception, free DVD
   library, room safe (no charge), WiFi
RATES 1–2 persons 120–167€; extra bed 30€; *taxe de séjour* included
   CREDIT CARDS AE, MC, V
BREAKFAST Continental 10€ per person

HÔTEL D'ORSAY ★★★ (19)
93, rue de Lille, 75007
Métro: Assemblée-Nationale, Solférino; RER Musée d'Orsay
41 rooms, all with shower or bath and toilet

In its past life, the Hôtel d'Orsay was two hotels. Now the renovated, side-by-side eighteenth-century buildings are an exercise in
understated elegance and good taste. The sedate location is ideal for
walking either to the Louvre via the new Solferino footbridge over the
Seine or to the Musée d'Orsay just a few blocks away.

The warmly decorated rooms are rich with comforts. Several overlook a quiet garden and are light and cheerful. One of these, Room
10, is plain with fabric-covered headboards and matching curtains,
and because it is smaller, it would suit one guest very well. The
largest rooms have twin beds and bathtubs. I like the twin-bedded
No. 12 because it has extra space and a stylish floral color scheme
in blue and white. The top-floor junior suite requires climbing a
flight of stairs, but the skylighted room is worth the slight exertion
because it is ample enough to allow for two working desks, a chair,
a marble-topped dresser, and a great bathroom with double sinks, a
separate shower, and plenty of room to move. There is also the bonus
of a private balcony. A breakfast buffet is served beneath an opaque
glass ceiling in a stark setting highlighted by three framed splashes
of color on the walls.

Hotels under the same ownership and management include Hôtel
Brighton (see page 71), Hôtel Mansart (see page 77), Hôtel de la Place
du Louvre (see page 73), Hôtel Parc Saint-Séverin (see page 124), and
Hôtel Saints-Pères (see page 177).

TEL 01-47-05-85-54 **FAX** 01-45-55-51-16 **EMAIL** orsay@espritfrance.com
   INTERNET www.esprit-de-france.com
FACILITIES & SERVICES Air-conditioning, direct-dial phone, elevator (to
   most floors), hair dryer, laundry service, minibar, TV with international
   reception, room safe (no charge), WiFi
RATES Single 130–155€ , double 153–180€, suite 285–325€; *taxe de séjour*
   included **CREDIT CARDS** AE, DC, MC, V
BREAKFAST Small buffet 12€ per person

HÔTEL DUC DE SAINT-SIMON ★★★★ ($, 29)
14, rue de St-Simon, 75007
Métro: Rue du Bac
29 rooms and 4 suites, all with shower or bath and toilet

Everyone has his or her first hotel in Paris, and this was mine. Of
course, in those days it bore about as much resemblance to what it is
today as a simple one-star does to the Hôtel Ritz. And yet, over the

years, and through many changes, my enthusiasm for the hotel has not dimmed, and it still tops my short list of ideal small Parisian hotels.

I am drawn to the Duc de Saint-Simon, named for a famous eighteenth-century French writer, for many reasons—but particularly for its intimate romantic feeling, wonderful sense of privacy, overall beauty, and high degree of personalized service. Many of the individually decorated rooms, with exclusive fabrics designed specially for the hotel, have views of the green interior courtyard garden, while several larger rooms and suites open onto their own private terraces. Everything is beautifully coordinated: the monograms on the sheets and towels match the room color, as do the drinks tray and limoges china used for room service. When I first walked into No. 19, a large suite on the first floor, I thought, This is it—I am never leaving! The antique-filled sitting room has comfortable seating, a lovely writing desk, and good lighting. The quiet bedroom has its own television and a double bed where, in the morning, you are awakened by the birds singing outside your garden window. The older-style bathroom has all the nice extras: heated towel racks, a magnifying mirror, a tub with a water shield, and a telephone.

I like all the other rooms in this very special hotel, but another favorite has always been No. 11, which is decorated in rich fabrics with a corner sitting area and windows that open onto the gardens, seemingly bringing them inside. Another beautiful room is No. 37. It is a soft, feminine room with a floral theme carried out on the wallpaper, curtains, spread, and lamp shades. I also like the two-drawer antique dresser, framed embroideries, and the roomy bathroom with its inset sink, shelf space, and separate stall shower. Room 34 has a double bed framed by lighted closets and a view overlooking the terraces below. It is elegantly decorated with warm yellow and rose floral colors and furnished with a comfortable armchair, four-drawer marble dresser, and crystal chandelier.

Antique collectors will appreciate the hotel's handsome collection positioned throughout the hotel, from the beautiful grandfather clock in the lobby to the graceful marble-top dressers in the bedrooms. The downstairs seventeenth-century bar, in what was originally a coal and wine cellar, has pillowed niches and quiet corners just big enough for two to sip drinks and talk about life and love.

The prices for a stay here are high, no doubt about it. But for those seeking a quietly elegant, discreet stay in Paris, this should be the hotel of choice.

Other hotels under the same ownership are Hôtel Saint-Germain-des-Prés (see page 161) and Grand Hôtel de l'Univers (see page 140).

TEL 01-42-22-07-52 (reservations), 01-44-39-20-20 **FAX** 01-45-48-68-25
   EMAIL duc.de.saint.simon@wanadoo.fr **INTERNET** www.hotel
   ducdesaintsimon.com

FACILITIES & SERVICES Air-conditioning in some rooms, bar, direct-dial phone, elevator, hair dryer, laundry service, minibars in suites and some rooms, robes, room service for light snacks, TV with international reception, room safe (no charge), free WiFi
RATES 1–2 persons 220–280€, suite 350–375€; extra bed 30€; *taxe de séjour* included **CREDIT CARDS** AE, MC, V
BREAKFAST Continental 15€ per person

HÔTEL DU CHAMP DE MARS ★★ (9)
7, rue du Champ de Mars, 75007
Métro: École Militaire
25 rooms, all with shower or bath and toilet

Under the competent ownership of Françoise and Stéphane Gourdal, and their friendly springer spaniel Cannelle, the Hôtel du Champ de Mars is a prudent choice for guests who want to watch their budget but not feel deprived in the process.

The hotel's look reflects the time, talent, enthusiasm, and downright hard work of this delightful couple, who transformed it from stem to stern. The French way with color is often daring. Others might have stopped short of the mix of brightly hued fabrics, but Françoise had both the courage and good taste to pull it off. Her love of flowers is the underlying theme throughout. In the downstairs breakfast room, round tables draped in orange-and-yellow plaid hold bouquets of dried flowers. An old chest with a bowl of potpourri, framed fruit prints hanging on the stone walls, and soft background music create a relaxing place for morning coffee and croissants. The series of golf prints hanging by the elevator are a nod to her husband's enthusiasm for the game.

White doors with big brass doorknobs lead to the yellow-and-blue rooms, all of which are named after French flowers. Tournesol (No. 25) is a pretty yellow-and-blue double with three floral prints over the bed and two windows that let in light from the front of the hotel. Myosotis (No. 55), on the front, is a single with great allure thanks to its small entry, light blue interior, and glimpse of the Eiffel Tower. Mimosa (No. 54) is another pleasant single with a nice view onto the court and rooftops beyond. If it is twin beds you want, ask for Muguet (No. 24). You enter Lilas (No. 4) through a little garden; the striped wallpaper, curtains, bedspreads, and rug are color coordinated in yellow, blue, and white to create a very sweet setting.

Last, but certainly not least, guests will find excellent discount shopping, several banks, a main post office, the métro, a street *marché* on rue Cler, and lots of favorite *Great Eats Paris* restaurants all close at hand.

TEL 01-45-51-52-30 **FAX** 01-45-51-64-36 **EMAIL** reservation@hotelduchamp demars.com **INTERNET** www.hotelduchampdemars.com
FACILITIES & SERVICES Direct-dial phone, elevator, hair dryer, TV with international reception, room safe (no charge)
RATES Single 78–85€, double 84–88€, triple 105€; *taxe de séjour* included **CREDIT CARDS** MC, V
BREAKFAST Continental 7€ per person

HÔTEL DU PALAIS BOURBON ★★ (26)
49, rue de Bourgogne, 75007
Métro: Varenne
32 rooms, 29 with shower, bath, and toilet

The Palais Bourbon has long been a reliable staple for readers of *Great Sleeps Paris* who want a respectable budget hotel suitable for the entire family. The hotel is in a quiet residential area of Paris that is only a half block from the Musée Rodin, five minutes from Invalides, about ten minutes from the Musée d'Orsay, and just across the Seine from the Tuileries Gardens. The Claudon family has owned, managed, and lived in the hotel for more than fifty years, and they keep a steely eye out for anything, or anyone, out of line. Madame Claudon, who is a grandmother with more energy than most people half her age, told me, "I work all the time. I am of another time." It must agree with her, since she has a spring in her step and a twinkle in her eye that could not possibly go unnoticed.

The hotel may not be the snazziest place to sleep in the *quartier,* but it is one of the best budget values, not only in the seventh, but in the entire city. The rooms are very large by Parisian standards and extremely clean, thanks to vigilant housekeeping and an ongoing maintenance program. The lobby has been redone and the breakfast room expanded to the centuries-old *caves* in the basement. Continuing improvements include air-conditioning in all rooms, the addition of more tiled bathrooms (many with bidets), hardwood floors throughout, new beds, and LCD plasma televisions in the larger rooms. Popular rooms are No. 3, which can connect with the room next door if larger quarters are needed; No. 4, a quiet double; and No. 1, a twin, also on the back. Number 8 is a large, light twin room facing the street, and No. 24, a back double on the top floor, has a queen-size bed and beamed ceiling.

Because the hotel is so popular, reservations are essential as far in advance as possible. When booking, please be sure to inquire about the cancellation and change in departure date policies, which are stricter than most.

TEL 01-44-11-30-70 **FAX** 01-45-55-20-21 **EMAIL** htlbourbon@aol.com
   INTERNET www.hotel-palais-bourbon.com
FACILITIES & SERVICES Air-conditioning, direct-dial phone (on request, private numbers at no charge), elevator (to most floors), hair dryer, some magnifying mirrors, some minibars, plasma TV with international reception, room safe (no charge), WiFi
RATES Single 70–99€, double 125€, triple 145€, quad 165€; *taxe de séjour* included **CREDIT CARDS** MC, V
BREAKFAST Continental included, cannot be deducted

HÔTEL EBER MARS ★★ (13)
117, avenue de la Bourdonnais, 75007
Métro: École Militaire
24 rooms, all with shower or bath and toilet

For years this hotel was unfortunately owned and run by a sour-faced fellow and his equally dour wife, who ruled their hotel like potentates granting rooms only to a chosen few. Despite their unwavering rudeness, I was intrigued by their amazing collection of Art Deco furnishings. However, after years of snarling responses that left me literally standing on the street, I finally gave up on them and their property.

On a recent visit to Paris, I happened to walk by the hotel and saw a crew of plaster-covered workmen tearing apart the front of the building. Eureka! I was happy to learn the hotel had been sold, and I was especially delighted to know that it had been purchased by Jean-Marc Eber, who owns Hôtel Eber Monceau (see page 265), one of the nicest small boutique hotels in the seventeenth arrondissement. He certainly had his work cut out for him. This hotel required far more than a quick coat of paint, new carpeting, and a big vase of flowers on the receptionist's desk. Everything—from the front door handle to the stairs, electrical system, and, of course, beds—had to be either thrown out or redone. Amazingly enough, the bathrooms were not bad; though somewhat dated in terms of tile colors, they were in remarkably good condition and have the advantage of being spacious, so they remain. The rooms also have that hard-to-find-Paris commodity: space. All have been repapered, recarpeted, and refitted in a linear 1930s look using neutral colors.

The new thirties-style dining room features a long communal table where guests gather for their morning coffee and croissants. Black-and-white photos of French actors and actresses hanging on the light wood paneled walls keep film buffs busy trying to name them all. If you are wondering about the photo over the front desk, it is of Gustave Eiffel.

TEL 01-47-05-42-30 **FAX** 01-47-05-45-91 **EMAIL** reservation@
hotelebermars.com **INTERNET** www.hotelebermars.com
FACILITIES & SERVICES Bar, direct-dial phone, elevator, hair dryer, TV with
international reception, office safe (no charge), free WiFi in lobby
RATES Single 90€, double 105–124€, triple 155€; *taxe de séjour* included
CREDIT CARDS MC, V
BREAKFAST Continental 10€ per person, served all day

HÔTEL LENOX SAINT-GERMAIN ★★★ (23)
9, rue de l'Université, 75007
Métro: Rue du Bac; RER Musée d'Orsay
34 rooms, all with shower or bath and toilet

Featuring a beautiful Art Deco–style lobby and adjoining jazz bar, the Lenox appeals to a design-conscious crowd who appreciate the many boutiques and interesting art galleries in the quarter. The Lenox Club Bar pays homage to the jazz greats of the twentieth century with its life-size, wood marquetry inlays, collection of musical instruments, and large framed black-and-white photos and posters. Indian rosewood and leather armchairs may tempt you into a long stay, and that's possible, since the bar is open to the public and hotel guests from 4:30 P.M. to 1:30 A.M.

The lobby is well done in polished marble and wood with leather seating arrangements. Two large animal statues—an elephant and a panther—guard the room. An Egyptian fresco sets the tone for the downstairs breakfast room as well as the glass elevator. In a design departure from the rest of the hotel, the rooms are classically done in coordinating colors and fabrics, and they have aged well over time. Those on the fourth and fifth floors have small balconies. Bathrooms have good lighting and space. Number 51, the attic room, is a two-level affair with yellow faux-finished furniture and a mezzanine bathroom with a skylight. In the *au courant* noncolors of beige-on-beige, No. 54 is another two-level suite with the bedroom on one level and a sitting room and bath on the other.

TEL 01-42-96-10-95 **FAX** 01-42-61-52-83 **EMAIL** hotel@lenoxsaintgermain.com
   INTERNET www.lenoxsaintgermain.com
FACILITIES & SERVICES Air-conditioning, bar, direct-dial phone, elevator, hair dryer, laundry service, robes in rooms with bathtubs, TV with international reception, room safe (no charge), WiFi in lobby and some rooms
RATES 1–2 persons 130–170€, attic room 210€, duplex 280€; *taxe de séjour* 1€ per person, per day **CREDIT CARDS** AE, DC, MC, V
BREAKFAST Buffet 15€, in-room Continental 12€, per person

HÔTEL LE TOURVILLE ★★★★ ($, 16)
16, avenue de Tourville, 75007
Métro: École Militaire
30 rooms, all with shower, bath, and toilet

The Tourville has infused a breath of fresh air into this part of the conservatively staid seventh arrondissement, known best for its diplomatic missions and upper-bourgeois lifestyle, not for anything avant-garde. The creative interiors knowingly mix antiques, beautiful fabrics, original prints, and a collection of northern African tribal rugs, then add twenty-first-century comforts. Room 104, a junior suite, leads off the back of the hotel sitting room, but is separated from it by a clever little private sitting space that has two wicker chairs and a mahogany chest with the top drawer filled with pinecones. The attractive *cave* breakfast room has wicker seating around tables set with a silk flower and miniature pots of jams and jellies.

The other rooms are exceptional in every detail. The three junior suites have Jacuzzis, and all rooms have some antiques and nicely framed prints in a background of sand, rose, or golden yellow. The standard rooms face avenue de Tourville, but the windows have double glazing, which helps to buffer noise. Room 100 is one of these; it's nicely done with an antique chest in the entryway and a dhurrie rug beside the bed. The bathroom is distinguished by marble insets around the sink and bathtub. It is perfect for one, but could be a tight squeeze for two. Room 16, a superior that comfortably sleeps three or four, has two doors opening onto a terrace and a large marble bathroom. Occupying the entire top floor are two junior suites: No. 60, with an old-fashioned hat and umbrella stand and a super bathroom with a Jacuzzi tub and separate shower; and No. 62, with dormer windows and an antique washstand.

The staff is friendly, yet professionally efficient. A stay here in any room will certainly encourage you to settle right in, open a bottle of champagne, and rejoice in what Paris is all about.

TEL 01-47-05-62-62 **FAX** 01-47-05-43-90 **EMAIL** hotel@tourville.com
  INTERNET www.hoteltourville.com
FACILITIES & SERVICES Air-conditioning, bar, direct-dial phone, elevator, hair dryer, Jacuzzis in junior suites, laundry service, minibar, robes in suites with Jacuzzi, TV with international reception, office safe, room safe in suites (no charge), suites are nonsmoking, WiFi
RATES 1–2 persons: standard 175€, superior 225€, room with private terrace 255€, junior suite 315–335€; extra bed 25€; *taxe de séjour* included
  CREDIT CARDS AE, MC, V
BREAKFAST Continental 12€ per person

HÔTEL LE WALT ★★★★ ($, 15)
37, avenue de la Motte-Picquet, 75007
Métro: Ecole Militaire
25 rooms, all with shower or bath and toilet

The distinctly modern Le Walt is the brainchild of a group of Texas financiers who decided they wanted to set up camp in their own hotel when they came to Paris. In so doing, they found a rumpled hotel and refashioned it into twenty-five minimalistic rooms with size as the only difference between them. True, all the rooms are still basically small, but the amenities are prolific, including DVD and CD players, 24-hour food and drink room service, two telephones, and A+ marble bathrooms. In each room, a copy of a famous artist's painting serves as a backdrop behind the bed and dictates the color scheme used in the fabrics and wall treatments. The furniture was designed in France and custom made in Italy; the floors are hardwood. Sixth-floor rooms have an Eiffel Tower view, while others look onto the hotel's inside terrace.

TEL 01-45-51-55-83 **FAX** 01-47-05-77-59 **EMAIL** lewalt@inwoodhotel.com
  INTERNET www.lewaltparis.com
FACILITIES & SERVICES Air-conditioning, bar, direct-dial phones, elevator, hair dryer, laundry service, minibar, room safe (no charge), 24-hour room service, TV with international reception, DVD/CD player (movies no charge), 4 nonsmoking rooms, WiFi
RATES Classic single 250€, double 270€; superior single 270€, double 300€; deluxe single 300€, double 320€; *taxe de séjour* included
  CREDIT CARDS AE, DC, MC, V
BREAKFAST Continental 13€ per person

HÔTEL MUGUET ★★ (12)
11, rue Chevert, 75007
Métro: Latour-Maubourg, École Militaire
43 rooms, all with shower or bath and toilet

The Hôtel Muguet continues to be one of the smartest, most stylish two-star values in Paris. Savvy readers obviously agree: they come here in droves, making it necessary to reserve the view rooms or suite at least six months in advance. Staying here will make anyone feel like a privileged budget traveler, especially in the suite, with its lovely tiled bathroom. The recently renovated rooms are air-conditioned, which is a rare extra in a two-star, let me assure you. All are outfitted in quality furnishings and fabrics, and the headboards of the beds all have inlays of the muguet flower. Closet space is generous. The modern bathrooms are absolute knockouts with their black-and-white marble sinks, heated towel racks, magnifying mirrors, and large showers and tubs. From Nos. 61 and 62, on the sixth floor, you can see the Eiffel Tower. From No. 63, your vista is over Invalides. On the fifth floor, ask for No. 51, with a balcony and good Eiffel Tower view. The glass-roofed breakfast area leads to a lush winter garden that allows Mme. Pelettier to show off her talent with plants. Three doubles opening onto this garden terrace are small but cozy for a single traveler.

Thankfully, the parts of the hotel that give it a special character also remain. The black and gray-green marble facade is intact, and so is the lovely grandfather clock next to the reception desk. The attractive owners, the Pelettier family and their sweet fox terrier, Volgane, are always ready with their friendly smiles to make their guests feel very special and at home. In this effort, they are ably assisted by their outstanding receptionist, Jacqueline Bonnet. I think Mme. Pelettier's comment to me perfectly sums up the philosophy of the hotel: "Everything is done with the comfort of the client in mind." In that regard, the entire hotel is smoke-free.

The immediate neighborhood could hardly be dubbed "the miracle mile," but it is quiet both day and night. After a nice ten-minute stroll, you can be at Invalides viewing Napoléon's tomb or on a park bench at the Champ-de-Mars, admiring the Eiffel Tower while eating a gourmet picnic put together from the food shops that line rue St-Dominique and rue Cler. Good restaurants are within very easy walking distance (see *Great Eats Paris*).

TEL 01-47-05-05-93 **FAX** 01-45-50-25-37 **EMAIL** muguet@wanadoo.fr
   INTERNET www.hotelmuguet.com
FACILITIES & SERVICES Air-conditioning, direct-dial phone, elevator (to most floors), hair dryer, free high-speed Internet in rooms and lobby, magnifying mirrors, flat-screen TV with international reception, room safe (no charge), hotel entirely nonsmoking
RATES Single 100€, double 130€, triple 170€; rooms with views 175€; *taxe de séjour* included **CREDIT CARDS** MC, V
BREAKFAST Buffet 9.50€ per person

HÔTEL RELAIS BOSQUET ★★★ (10)
19, rue du Champ de Mars, 75007
Métro: École Militaire
40 rooms, all with shower or bath and toilet

The Relais Bosquet is an outstanding Great Sleep because it offers guests exceptional comfort, space, and peacefulness. Each of the forty rooms in the renovated hotel, which is built around a courtyard, has all the three-star perks and more: an iron and ironing board, electrically controlled shutters, tea and coffee makers, WiFi, and an assortment of current periodicals. Five have Eiffel Tower views, and five more take in the dome of Les Invalides. Several connect. If you are traveling with an infant, the hotel will provide a free baby bath, chair, food warmer, and bed. Secure private parking is available at a very modest rate. All rooms sport decor that is attractively uniform hotel-issue, with creamy wall coverings and nice-quality furnishings. Brass poles, artistically hung with soft pillows covered in the same material as the curtains, are mounted as headboards behind the beds. Baths have three-tiered rolling carts and nice towels.

Top room choices are No. 52, a large twin superior on the back with excellent space in both the room and the bathroom, which includes a stretch-out tub and shower; No. 54, which can serve as a small double or generous single; and No. 32, a big room for two with double sinks in the well-lit bathroom. The street is quiet, so consider No. 53 with two windows facing front as a good option. The hardworking owner, Philippe Hervois, is on site daily and pays careful attention to the needs of his guests. The upscale residential area of the seventh arrondissement is close to the Champ-de-Mars, Eiffel Tower, and Les Invalides. It also offers a number of *Great Eats Paris* dining choices and has easy access by métro or bus to the rest of Paris.

NOTE: The hotel offers special rates from November 15 to March 30 (except the week between Christmas and New Year's) and from July 15 to August 30.

TEL 01-47-05-25-45 **FAX** 01-45-55-08-24 **EMAIL** hotel@relaisbosquet.com
   INTERNET www.relaisbosquet.com
FACILITIES & SERVICES Air conditioning, free baby equipment, direct-dial phone, dogs accepted (no charge), electric fans, elevator, hair dryer, iron and ironing board, minibar, parking, tea and coffee maker, room safe (no charge), TV with international reception, free WiFi
RATES Single 140–160€, double 155–174€; extra bed 20€; parking 16€ per day; *taxe de séjour* included **CREDIT CARDS** AE, DC, MC, V
BREAKFAST Continental 11€ per person

HÔTEL SAINT-DOMINIQUE ★★ (2)
62, rue St-Dominique, 75007
Métro: Latour-Maubourg
34 rooms, all with shower or bath and toilet

In the 1700s, this building was home to Dominican nuns who prayed in a downstairs chapel. Today, it is a rustically quaint hotel on a busy shopping street. An English country theme begins in the beamed lobby and continues through the tight rooms, which are furnished in pine and wicker and have soft, billowing curtains dressing the windows. Generally matching spreads, coordinated wall coverings, and a pretty Provençal-style streetside breakfast room are other positive points. My favorite rooms are the two that open onto the terrace, where breakfast is served on warm spring and summer mornings. I also like No. 8, a twin on the back: although the floors slant a bit, the roomy bedroom and bathroom, with a rolling cart for toiletries, save the day. Forget No. 34, a dark double with a bathroom way past its due date, and No. 31, a depressing single. The rooms do not boast exciting views, not all have a chair (only a backless stool), the furniture needs a big shot of TLC, and the elevator does not service the back building or the fifth floor in the main building. While these may be deterrents for some, many guests overlook them in favor of a tranquil stay in a hotel with reasonable rates.

TEL 01-47-05-51-44 **FAX** 01-47-05-81-28
    EMAIL saint-dominique.reservations@wanadoo.fr
    INTERNET www.hotelstdominique.com
FACILITIES & SERVICES Direct-dial phone, elevator to most rooms, minibar, room safe (no charge), TV with international reception, WiFi
RATES Single 105€, double 125–135€, triple 155€; *taxe de séjour* included
    CREDIT CARDS AE, MC, V
BREAKFAST Continental 10€ per person

HÔTEL SAINT-THOMAS-D'AQUIN ★★ (25)
3, rue Pré-aux-Clercs, 75007
Métro: St-Germain-des-Prés
21 rooms, all with shower or bath and toilet

Talented hotelier Bertrand Plasmans, who owns the Hôtel Novanox (see page 158) and the Saint Vincent next door, has magnificently transformed this once dull two-star into a smartly designed example of urban chic in the heart of the Rive Gauche. The hotel's high standards appeal to those seeking a modern escape for less per night than the cost of a coin purse at many of the top designer boutiques in the neighborhood. The soft cream walls form the perfect backdrop for the interesting palette of chocolate and cocoa colors on the furnishings and fabrics. Not all is monochromatic . . . every so often there is an unexpected dash of muted color: such as a lavender easy chair in No. 518, the top-floor room with a mansard roof; Provençal red and gold offsetting the stylized black bed and tables in No. 102; and a green checked bedspread in No. 103. Room 206 has more light than most, plus a cushioned easy chair and a balcony. The best rooms face the quiet street. A few on the back overlook a nearby hotel's glass elevator, and you probably don't want one of these. Bathrooms are fitted with excellent toiletries and monogrammed towels. The very moderate rates for the top-drawer neighborhood have made the much-sought-after rooms hard to come by, unless you book far in advance. Bravo, M. Plasmans, on another great success!

NOTE: The Hôtel Saint Vincent, at 5, rue Pré-Aux-Clercs, was scheduled to open after this edition went to press. Given M. Plasmans' track record, I am quite sure it will be another *Great Sleep Paris.*

TEL 01-42-61-01-22 **FAX** 01-42-61-41-43 **EMAIL** hotelsaintthomasdaquin@
  wanadoo.fr **INTERNET** www.hotel-st-thomas-daquin.com
FACILITIES & SERVICES Direct-dial phones, elevator (to most floors), fans, hair
  dryer, TV with international reception, room safe (no charge), free WiFi
RATES 1–2 persons 120–130€; *taxe de séjour* included
  CREDIT CARDS AE, MC, V
BREAKFAST Continental 9€ per person

HÔTEL VALADON ★★ (8)
16, rue Valadon, off rue de Grenelle, 75007
Métro: École Militaire
12 rooms, all with shower (1 with bathtub) and toilet

Victor and Maria Orsenne spent one year and serious money trans-forming this dumpy one-star hotel with an uncertain pedigree into a perky budget choice with a neo-industrial look and feel. Inspired by the black, white, and gray colors of a favorite piece of fabric, the couple added carpets and furnishings, and to avoid an overdose of somber black and white, they infused splashes of red throughout. Each room is designed to comfortably sleep three on a twin and a queen-size bed. The floors are hardwood, the closets and shelves open, and the prints and photos on the wall remind guests they are in Paris. Six smoke-free rooms guarantee guests can breathe easily. A red stripe here, a red line there, add a bit of life to the gray-tile bathrooms. One of the nicest rooms is No. 2 on the back, provided going down stairs to the large, well-lit bathroom would not be a problem. The subterranean Nos. 1 and 2 might not appeal to claustrophobics. The only light is from a skylight and a tiny six-by-twelve-inch window over a built-in desk. To create more space, the rooms combine, but it's the bathroom that connects them.

Breakfast is served in a two-tone room with gray and red cush-ioned chairs around bare black tables. In keeping with the family atmosphere of the hotel, guests are invited to use a shared refrigerator in the breakfast room, borrow the hotel's dishes and cutlery, and enjoy light snacks here (but please, never in the rooms). The front desk reception policy is unique: the desk is covered from 7:30 A.M. to 1 P.M., and outside those hours, only by request. Guests are given keys and codes for access otherwise.

Many long-time readers of *Great Sleeps Paris* fondly recall pleasant stays at Hôtel Latour-Maubourg, which was also owned and run by the Orsennes and their dogs, Faust and Othello. Inevitably there are changes in life: Faust is no longer alive, and the Orsennes have sold the Hôtel Latour-Maubourg. Now, along with Othello, they concentrate on welcoming their guests at the Hôtel Valadon.

TEL 01-47-53-89-85 **FAX** 01-44-18-90-56 **EMAIL** info@hotelvaladon.com
  INTERNET www.hotelvaladon.com

FACILITIES & SERVICES Direct-dial phone, elevator (to most rooms), hair dryer,
TV with international reception, room safe (no charge), 6 nonsmoking
rooms, free WiFi
RATES Single 99€, double 115€, triple 140€, family room 100–160€; *taxe de
séjour* included **CREDIT CARDS** MC, V
BREAKFAST Continental included

HÔTEL VERNEUIL ★★★ (22)
8, rue de Verneuil, 75007
Métro: Rue du Bac; RER Musée d'Orsay
26 rooms, all with shower or bath and toilet

For museumgoers, the Hôtel Verneuil is ideally located within
walking distance to the Musée d'Orsay, the Louvre, and the Musée
Rodin. Antique lovers are also in heaven, as are browsers and
shoppers—the tantalizing stores, art galleries, and boutiques that
line this area could keep them busy for a week. The owner, Sylvie de
Latte, is continually full of ideas and plans for her small and charming hotel. In a seventeenth-century building that retains its original
cross beams and rough stone walls, it is a haven of peace and comfort
where I always feel as though I am a guest in a lovely French home.
Mme. de Latte is an art collector, and she has skillfully hung many of
her favorite pieces throughout the hotel. The black-and-white photos
are by her son, who lived in India. The vaulted stone-cellar breakfast
room is down a winding spiral staircase with no elevator access.

The rooms are all personalized with rich fabrics, solid furnishings,
and interesting photos and prints. Some have canopy beds, most have
wood-beam ceilings and ornate doors, and those ending in number
2 or 4 have wall murals of Parisian landmarks. Comfortable seating
and adequate closet space are not an issue. The room and marble
bathroom sizes vary. The biggest rooms are Nos. 402 and 502, and the
smallest room is No. 308. Number 302 is a romantic favorite, mixing
red, green, and white fabrics and beams in the bathroom. However,
whichever room you occupy, the charm and feeling of well-being in
this wonderful hotel never wavers.

Mme. de Latte also runs Hôtel Thérèse (see page 79).

TEL 01-42-60-82-14 **FAX** 01-42-61-40-38 **EMAIL** info@hotelverneuil.com
INTERNET www.hotelverneuil.com
FACILITIES & SERVICES Air-conditioning in some rooms, bar, direct-dial phone,
elevator (to most floors), fans, hair dryer, laundry service, minibar, robes
in deluxe rooms, TV with international reception, room safe (no charge),
WiFi
RATES Single 135€, double 160€, deluxe 210€; extra bed 25€; *taxe de séjour*
included **CREDIT CARDS** MC, V
BREAKFAST Continental 12€ per person

Eighth Arrondissement

The ten-lane Champs-Élysées, sweeping dramatically from the Arc de Triomphe to the place de la Concorde, is the most famous avenue and parade ground in the world, and it is definitely worth a serious look and stroll. But save the shopping, partying, and eating for less touristy areas. This is the traditional watering hole for show-biz celebrities, glamour girls on the way up or down, tourists in baseball caps, heavy-set men and their young companions, and anyone else who wants to hide behind dark glasses twenty-four hours a day. The flame on the tomb of the unknown soldier burns under the Arc de Triomphe, and the view from the top is inspiring. Twelve avenues radiate from the Arc de Triomphe, forming the world-famous, death-defying traffic circle known as l'Étoile.

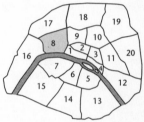

The place de la Concorde is the largest square in Paris. Two of its most famous occupants are the luxurious Hôtel de Crillon and the American Embassy. It is thrilling to stand on this strikingly beautiful square and be surrounded by some of the greatest landmarks in the world: the Tuileries Gardens, the Louvre, and the view up the Champs-Élysées to the Arc de Triomphe, across the Seine to the Palais Bourbon, and up the rue Royale to the Madeleine Church, built as a replica of a Greco-Roman temple by Napoléon I. In the evening, when it is all illuminated and the fountains are playing, it is a sight you will never forget.

Famous names in *haute couturière* are displayed in boutiques lining rue Faubourg St-Honoré and avenue Montaigne. World-class gourmet shopping surrounds the place de la Madeleine.

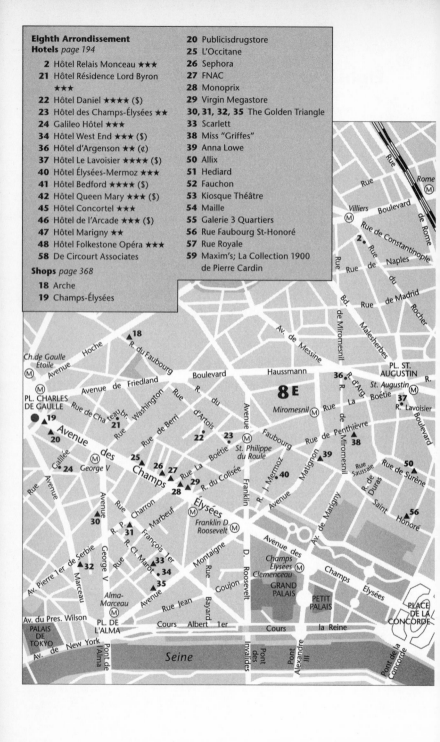

Eighth and Ninth Arrondissements

Ninth Arrondissement
Hotels *page 207*

1 Hôtel Rotary (NO STARS, ¢)
3 Woodstock Hostel
4 Perfect Hôtel ★ (¢)
5 Résidence Hôtel des Trois Poussins ★★★
6 Hôtel Lorette Opéra ★★★
7 Hôtel France Albion ★★
8 Hôtel Langlois ★★
10 Hôtel Saint-Louis Opéra ★★
16 Hôtel Chopin ★★

Shops *page 374*

9 Tout Compte Fait . . .
11 Printemps
12 Galeries Lafayette
13 À la Mère de Famille
14 Sulmaco
15 Passage Verdeau
17 Passage Jouffroy
43 Musée de la Parfumerie Fragonard
44 Louis Pion
49 Annexe des Créateurs

HOTELS IN THE EIGHTH ARRONDISSEMENT

OTHER OPTIONS
Apartment Rental Agencies

($) indicates a Big Splurge; (¢) indicates a Cheap Sleep

GALILEO HÔTEL ★★★ (24)
54, rue Galilée, 75008
Métro: George-V; RER Charles-de-Gaulle-Étoile
27 rooms, all with shower or bath and toilet

Contented guests with sophisticated, artistic temperaments continue to fill Roland and Elisabeth Buffat's popular hotels: two on the Île St-Louis—Hôtel de Lutèce (see page 99) and Hôtel des Deux-Îles (see page 101)—and their latest, Hôtel Henri IV (see page 122). Their fourth tempting option is the Galileo, a Right Bank hotel that re-creates an elegant French town home in an oasis of calm, only a few steps from the Champs-Élysées.

Like the flowers in the boutique lobby and garden, guests are beautifully arranged in the elegantly pristine rooms, all fashioned alike in comforting colors of beige, brown, and cocoa. Number 403, a double with two armchairs, a desk, and gray marble bath, has a Rear Window–type view onto the life within the nearby apartment building. Room 200, facing a walled garden, is the largest twin. On the ground floor, it has a small sitting area and a huge marble bathroom. I also like No. 203: its entryway leads to a quiet bedroom with a queen-size bed, small purple chair in a sitting corner, and a long workspace overlooking the garden. You'll hit the jackpot in space in either of two fifth-floor rooms (Nos. 501 and 502). In addition to being the biggest, their allure comes from their delightful glass-covered, screened verandas with wicker seating, which invite year-round usage. Butcher block tables adorn the below-ground, mirrored dining room, and green plants and posters of familiar Paris landmarks add interest.

TEL 01-47-20-66-06 **FAX** 01-47-20-67-17 **EMAIL** hotelgalileo@wanadoo.fr
   INTERNET www.galileo-paris-hotel.com
FACILITIES & SERVICES Air-conditioning, direct-dial phone, elevator, hair
   dryer, minibar, TV with international reception, room safe (no charge),
   WiFi
RATES Single 148€, double 170€; *taxe de séjour* 1€ per person, per day
   CREDIT CARDS AE, DC, MC, V
BREAKFAST Continental 12€ per person

HÔTEL BEDFORD ★★★★ ($, 41)
17, rue de l'Arcade, 75008
Métro: Madeleine, Havre-Caumartin
145 rooms, all with shower, bath, and toilet

Generally, the eighth arrondissement provides a stay on the dull side in terms of active day-to-day Parisian living. It is predominantly a business district that is busy during the day Monday to Friday, but in the evening and on weekends the sidewalks roll up and you have the streets to yourself. However, all is not lost when staying at the Bedford. Shop hounds will be happy bagging buys at Galeries Lafayette and Printemps, the two famous Parisian department stores less than a ten-minute walk away, and foodies will have a field day with all the nearby gourmet food emporiums surrounding place de la Madeleine. Guests are also within easy strolling distance to the Champs-Élysées, Tuileries Gardens, and the Seine.

The hotel provides unobtrusive and efficient service in a low-key, discreet atmosphere reminiscent of the 1940s. Rooms won't dazzle, but they will impress with their size and layout. Most come equipped with a desk, two comfortable chairs, luggage space, and large closets with shelves and enough hanging space. Bathrooms follow suit in size with plenty of monogrammed towels and deep tubs with either a shower overhead or separate stall. On each floor there is a two-room suite that is comfortable for a family stay. A bonus for many is the beautiful nineteenth-century dining room with its original painted-glass domed ceiling. In addition to breakfast, a formal lunch is served here, but in the evening, guests eat in a smaller grill room. Lower December and August rates are drawing cards for many.

Also under the same management and on the same street is Hôtel de l'Arcade (see page 198).

TEL 01-44-94-77-77 **FAX** 01-44-94-77-97 **EMAIL** reservations@
   hotel-bedford.com **INTERNET** www.hotel-bedford.com
FACILITIES & SERVICES Air-conditioning, bar, direct-dial phone, elevator,
   hair dryer, laundry service, minibar, restaurant, room service, TV with
   international reception, room safe (no charge), WiFi
RATES Single 164€, double 188–208€, superior 246€, apartment/suite 330€;
   extra bed 26€; lower rates in Aug and Dec; *taxe de séjour* included
   CREDIT CARDS AE, MC, V
BREAKFAST Buffet or Continental 17€ per person

HÔTEL CONCORTEL ★★★ (45)
19–21, rue Pasquier, 75008
Métro: Madeleine
46 rooms, all with shower or bath and toilet

For many years, the conveniences and comforts of the Concortel have appealed to those seeking a modestly priced midcity location to combine sight-seeing with business. In other words, they want a hotel whose price fits within their allotted per diem with a little left over for dinner or some other Parisian activity. The hotel consists of two blocks of rooms joined by a courtyard that is filled in the spring and summer with bright blooming plants. The color-coordinated bed chambers are hardly exciting, but they are well arranged and offer the space and perks that business travelers desire. Nothing much has changed in the past few years, except the addition of WiFi in the rooms, which is a distinct advantage to those who must stay constantly in touch.

TEL 01-42-65-45-44 **FAX** 01-42-65-18-33 **EMAIL** concortel@wanadoo.fr
   INTERNET www.hotelconcortel.com
FACILITIES & SERVICES Air-conditioning, bar, conference room, direct-dial
   phone, elevator (to most floors), hair dryer, laundry service, minibar,
   porter, private parking, radio, TV with international reception and pay-
   per-view, office or room safe (no charge), WiFi
RATES Standard single 125€, double 135€, superior double 155–185€, triple
   204€; private parking 25€ per day; *taxe de séjour* included
   CREDIT CARDS AE, DC, MC, V
BREAKFAST Continental 8€ per person

HÔTEL DANIEL ★★★★ ($, 22)
8, rue Frédéric Bastiat, 75008
Métro: St-Philippe-du Roule, George V
26 rooms with shower or bath and toilet

The Hôtel Daniel offers sophisticated travelers a haven from stress in a magnificent setting that blends East and West. In this special hotel, the riches from these two cultures balance and compliment each other in such a way that beauty and comfort are in perfect harmony. Using fine taste and spectacular works of art, the interior designer and hotel owners have taken inspiration from the eighteenth century, mixing oriental influences and images from the Silk Road with the traditional designs of the West. As a result, the cosmopolitan, romantic hotel is an oasis of calm that is not just a place to stay but an experience to be lived, inspiring dreams of faraway places.

Everything you see was especially created for or gathered by the owners on their world travels for the hotel. Daring combinations of rich silks, velvet brocades, and shimmering satins blend vibrantly to give the hotel its very personal look. The hand-painted Chinese wallpaper combines flowers, birds, and hunting scenes on a green background, while the sofas and armchairs were made in England. Tables on the ground floor were imported from Beirut, and the billowing curtains and bedspreads were handcrafted in Rheims. The

Baroque lounge has painted glass panels inlaid with feathers and gold dust, delicate fans hang on the walls, and a display cabinet holds a magnificent collection of fine glassware. Completing the room's exotic ambience are Kazakhstan carpets spread on the parquet floor, silver trays from Turkey, and panels of Chinese calligraphy. A banquette that equals the length of the bar is lighted from an overhead window and covered in a fabric printed with butterflies and leaves. Throughout the rest of the hotel, eighteenth-century paintings, blue-and-white Chinese porcelain, carved bronzes, and cloisonné vases are displayed.

Each bedroom is its own haven of elegance and charm, furnished with unique, inlaid mother-of-pearl boxes and dressers and night stands from Damascus. Eighteenth-century Toile de Jouy fabrics tell stories of elephant hunting trips, of Mongolian musicians strumming their lutes, or of a slender young lady being courted near a lake. The Italian marble or Moroccan ceramic tiled bathrooms offer handmade jasmine and olive oil soaps, shampoo and bath gel from Molton Brown in London, and bath salts from the Dead Sea. Several have windows covered in Russian linen curtains. Lighted closets have five types of hangers, white-lined and lace-lined shelves, and a basket with slippers, laundry bags, sewing kit, and a fragrant lavender sachet.

The hotel bar, restaurant, and café are open all day serving breakfast, coffee, tea, lunch, cocktails, and dinner. The highly regarded chef has created an international menu that attracts both guests and knowledgable residents. The bread is from Kayser, the pastries from Ladurée, the tea from Mariage Frères, the fresh fruit and produce from the Poncelet Marché . . . and the results are delicious.

The hotel is a member of the prestigious Relais & Chateaux group, which is known for its elegant surroundings and attitude as well as its uniformly excellent service. For many, the Hôtel Daniel is a truly special Big Splurge, one that lives up to all its promises and leaves a lasting impression.

TEL 01-42-56-17-00 **FAX** 01-42-56-17-01 **EMAIL** hoteldanielparis@ hoteldanielparis.com **INTERNET** www.hoteldanielparis.com

FACILITIES & SERVICES Air-conditioning, bar, bicycles available, cellular phones and personal computers on request, CDs and DVD players on request, 24-hour concierge service, direct-dial phone, elevator, hair dryer, laundry service, valet or private parking, robes and slippers, down or nonallergic pillows on request, restaurant (for breakfast, lunch, and dinner), room safe (no charge), 24-hour room service, secretarial services, complimentary shoe shine, plasma TV with international reception, nonsmoking rooms, wheelchair-accessible rooms, free WiFi

RATES Single classic 320€, double classic 380€, double deluxe 440€, junior suite 490€, "Daniel" Suite 690€; extra bed 75€; parking 25€ per 24 hours; *taxe de séjour* included; see Website for special offers and promotions **CREDIT CARDS** AE, DV, MC, V

BREAKFAST Continental 20€, American 28€, per person; children under 12 free

HÔTEL D'ARGENSON ★★ (¢, 36)
15, rue d'Argenson, at 111 boulevard Haussmann, 75008
Métro: Miromesnil
28 rooms, 26 with shower or bath and toilet

Veteran Paris visitors know that the business-centered eighth arrondissement is normally Big Splurge territory. Coming to the rescue is this twenty-eight-room, second-floor walkup, perched above Rene Saint-Ouen, a famous bakery in Paris. How famous? It was selected to provide all the baguettes to the Élysée Palace, and that is quite an honor. Those who are familiar with this part of Paris know that noise is part of the deal, and it won't escape you at this hotel. However, if cost is your guiding light, give this one consideration.

You first enter the small wood-paneled salon, which has two chairs. Martine, the owner's daughter, is usually behind the desk, along with her black-and-brown cocker spaniel, Flash. The fifties-style rooms that once varied from frankly fussy to downright tacky have been toned down to some extent, though they still say "budget!" In most rooms, at least the curtains and bedspreads match somewhat, and the wild wallpaper has been removed from the ceilings. I have trouble with the mustard yellow and beer brown tiles in the bathrooms, which definitely clash with the plaid towels. Rooms on the second and fifth floors have balconies; three others (Nos. 20, 30, and 40) face a blank wall. There are no twin-bed rooms, but an extra bed can be added at no additional cost. Martine's husband stays on top of maintenance, claiming to redo one room per year. In the end, the hotel is notable because it is cheap and clean, and the rooms are big enough to satisfy almost anyone.

TEL 01-42-65-16-87 **FAX** 01-47-42-02-06 **EMAIL** hoteldargenson@aol.com
   INTERNET www.hotel-argenson.com
FACILITIES & SERVICES Direct-dial phone, elevator (to most floors), fans, hair
   dryer at desk, French TV, room safe (no charge)
RATES Single 78–92€, double 83–97€, triple 114–121€; *taxe de séjour* included
   CREDIT CARDS MC, V
BREAKFAST Continental in room included

HÔTEL DE L'ARCADE ★★★ ($, 46)
9, rue de l'Arcade, 75008
Métro: Madeleine, Havre-Caumartin
41 rooms, all with shower, bath, and toilet

Good taste is everywhere evident at the Hôtel de l'Arcade, and no wonder when you learn it was decorated by Gerard Gallet, who also did the Orient Express. Everything about the hotel is exceptional, and something complimentary can be said about all the soundproofed rooms. The divided lobby, done in subtle celery green and beige, is softened further with fresh flowers and green plants. Wingback chairs, sofas, and a writing desk are complemented by a decorative stone fireplace. The crowning touch is a beautiful green wrought-iron chandelier with twelve candle lights entwined with white metal flowers. A banquette, the owner's collection of black-and-white etchings, and windows shaded by white linen café curtains set the stage for the street-side breakfast room.

All the soundproofed bedrooms have beige walls with wood built-ins, good closets, and appealing bathrooms with Sardinian tiles. They all face front, so there will be no depressing wall views, and the standard rooms connect. Two floors are exclusively nonsmoking. Room 602 is a good choice for two. The corner location with three large windows, two closets, armchair seating, and a lovely, light bathroom make it an inviting choice for a longer stay. Number 605 is one of four duplexes. It is a two-story suite with double televisions, three telephones (including one in the bathroom), and an upstairs bedroom with a small balcony and a skylight.

Breakfast has been served in a sunny dining room by the same lady for fifteen years. She has a remarkable memory about her guests, even remembering which morning newspaper they prefer. When guests return from an evening out, they find the evening housekeeper has changed the towels and turned down the beds. Lower summer and winter rates make this smart hotel an even more exceptional value.

Also under same management and on the same street is the Hôtel Bedford (see page 195).

TEL 01-53-30-60-00 **FAX** 01-40-07-03-07 **EMAIL** reservations@hotel-arcade.com **INTERNET** www.hotel-arcade.com

FACILITIES & SERVICES Air-conditioning, conference rooms, direct-dial phone, elevator, hair dryer, minibar, TV with international reception, room safe (no charge), 2 floors exclusively nonsmoking, WiFi

RATES Single 151–177€, double 193€, duplex or triple 235€; extra bed 118€ (free baby cot); *taxe de séjour* included **CREDIT CARDS** AE, MC, V

BREAKFAST Buffet or in-room Continental 12€ per person

HÔTEL DES CHAMPS-ÉLYSÉES ★★ (23)
2, rue d'Artois, 75008
Métro: St-Philippe-du-Roule
35 rooms, all with shower or bath and toilet

During World War II, this hotel housed Dutch and American soldiers. It now houses mostly business travelers who want an inexpensive and reliable nest near the Champs-Élysées and the Arc de Triomphe.

The thirty-five attractive rooms and modern baths have coordinated colors and good space usage, and most importantly, they provide many three-star amenities for two-star prices. Bathrooms are servicable. Adding to the hotel's popularity is the Art Deco sitting room with a multicolored mural and Erté-style lamp. Behind the inlaid wooden bar is a glass-roofed atrium with a small pool framed by Grecian columns and a wraparound mural of the Parc Monceau. In the sitting area, be sure to notice the nostalgic black-and-white photos of the owner of the hotel as a little girl, being held by her parents and grandparents.

TEL 01-43-59-11-42 **FAX** 01-45-61-00-61 **EMAIL** resa@champs
elysees-paris-hotel.com **INTERNET** www.champselysees-paris-hotel.com
FACILITIES & SERVICES Air-conditioning, direct-dial phone, elevator, hair
dryer, laundry service, minibar, TV with international reception, room safe
(no charge), WiFi
RATES Single 92–102€, double 100–115€, triple 135€; *taxe de séjour* included
CREDIT CARDS AE, DC, MC, V
BREAKFAST Continental 8€ per person

HÔTEL ÉLYSÉES-MERMOZ ★★★ (40)
30, rue Jean-Mermoz, 75008
Métro: St-Philippe-du-Roule, Miromesnil
27 rooms, all with shower or bath and toilet

What sets the Élysées-Mermoz apart from dozens of other three-
star hotels in the area, which is only a short walk from the Champs-
Élysées, place de la Concorde, and the Tuileries Gardens? Friendly,
personalized service, for one thing; competitive rates for another; and
rooms and suites done in Pierre Frey fabrics and quality furnishings.
The largest rooms face the street, which is quiet; smaller quarters and
the suites overlook an interior courtyard. The mirrored bathrooms
in all are modern, with heated towel racks, good sink space, and
separate glass-enclosed showers (in the suites). The breakfast room
has an Italian flair to it, thanks to its burnt umber colors and tile
floor. The inviting sitting room is casually outfitted with wicker and
bamboo seating under a skylight roof. You could hear a pin drop in
the evening and on the weekends, when workers in this nine-to-five
business area lock their offices and shop doors and go home.
NOTE: This is a nonsmoking hotel.

TEL 01-42-25-75-30 **FAX** 01-45-62-87-10 **EMAIL** hotel@emhotel.com
INTERNET www.hotel-elyseesmermoz.com
FACILITIES & SERVICES Air-conditioning, business center, conference room,
direct-dial phone, elevator, hair dryer, ADSL Internet connection, laundry
service, magnifying mirrors, minibar, TV with international reception,
room safe (no charge)
RATES Single 152–165€, double 165–189€, suite 247€; *taxe de séjour* included
CREDIT CARDS AE, DC, MC, V
BREAKFAST Buffet 11€, in-room Continental 9€, per person

HÔTEL FOLKESTONE OPÉRA ★★★ (48)
9, rue de Castellane, 75008
Métro: Madeleine, Havre-Caumartin
50 rooms, all with shower or bath and toilet

The Folkestone is part of the Best Western chain in Paris, and it's
definitely one of the better choices in an area where prices are usually over the top. A stay here puts you in the middle of the business,
high-fashion, and entertainment precinct of the city.

An interesting collection of framed French country homes line
the hallways leading to the contemporary bedrooms, which are decorated in peach, pale gray, and cream, with polished cotton fabrics
on the beds and covering the windows. With the exception of the

suites, most of the rooms do not have space as a virtue. The smallest doubles, at the back, have miniature bathrooms and no view. The bright rooms on the street offer more space and have double windowpanes to buffer noise. Exceptions on the front are Nos. 301 and 303, with so little extra space that you cannot open a suitcase unless it's on the bed, and once you do, there is only a tiny armoire to hold its contents. Deluxe Room 103 is much better. Here you have a sofa and comfortable chair, working desk, luggage and closet space, and a beamed bathroom with a recessed tub. Another option for more space is to reserve one of the connecting rooms. From the hotel door, it is less than a fifteen-minute walk to shopping along rue du Faubourg St-Honoré or at Galeries Lafayette and Printemps, place de la Madeleine, place de la Concorde, the Tuileries Gardens, and the Champs-Élysées.

TEL 01-42-65-73-09; toll-free in U.S. and Canada 800-528-1234 (Best Western) **FAX** 01-42-65-64-09 **EMAIL** hotel@bwfolkestoneopera.com **INTERNET** www.bwfolkestoneopera.com

FACILITIES & SERVICES Air-conditioning, bar, direct-dial phone, elevator, hair dryer, Internet in lobby, laundry service, minibar, TV with international reception, room safe (no charge), some nonsmoking rooms, WiFi

RATES Single 121–145€, double 130–165€, superior double & suite 170–245€; *taxe de séjour* included **CREDIT CARDS** AE, DC, MC, V

BREAKFAST Buffet or in-room Continental 11€, per person

HÔTEL LE LAVOISIER ★★★★ ($, 37)
21, rue Lavoisier, 75008
Métro: St-Augustin
30 rooms, all with shower, bath, and toilet

Michel Bouvier's latest hotel venture was a hit even before it opened. His other hotel on the Left Bank—Le Saint-Grégoire in the sixth (see page 156)—is always continuously booked by Paris insiders, and when word got out about Le Lavoisier, discreetly placed between the Saint-Augustin Church and the Faubourg Saint Honoré, the trendsetters lost no time in filling the rooms. The nineteenth-century town-house hotel creation was placed confidently in the skillful hands of Jean-Philippe Nuel, who mixed bold colors with a sprinkling of antiques for character and interest in a thoroughly contemporary setting. The Georgian lobby and adjoining library bar are done in blackened pearwood furnishings surrounded by clay-colored walls with rose and white accents. A painting of two girls with their doll and teddy bear adds a warm touch to the room. The daring use of flamenco red and adobe brown adds spice to the bare wood tables and black wicker chairs in the breakfast room. Each table has its own light, so guests can scan the local papers while enjoying their breakfast. The rainbow of colors continues in the cerise-pink linen-lined halls that are richly carpeted in deep eggplant and lighted by stylized oak leaf sconces. While the rooms do not have the same dramatic colors as the public areas of the hotel, they are beautifully done in uniform good taste using quality fabrics and furnishings. Soft gray wood accents compliment the yellow and rose fabrics, polished black wood furnishings, and crisp white bed linens. Wooden shutters are used instead of curtains to control the light. Some rooms have private terraces, the suites have Jacuzzis, and all rooms have WiFi. The youthful staff is enthusiastic and helpful.

TEL 01-53-30-06-06 **FAX** 01-53-30-23-00 **EMAIL** info@hotellavoisier.com
INTERNET www.hotellavoisier.com
FACILITIES & SERVICES Air-conditioning, bar, direct-dial phone, hair dryer, elevator, Jacuzzi in suites, laundry service, room service, TV with international reception, office safe (no charge), WiFi
RATES 1–2 persons: superior 200–230€, terrace room 245–261€, junior suite 290–305€, executive suite 385–401€; extra bed 16€; *taxe de séjour* included **CREDIT CARDS** AE, DC, MC, V
BREAKFAST Continental 14€ per person

HÔTEL MARIGNY ★★ (47)
11, rue de l'Arcade, 75008
Métro: Madeleine, Havre-Caumartin
32 rooms, 26 with shower or bath and toilet

Only a few hundred yards from the Madeleine Church and a bracing ten minutes from Gare St-Lazare and place de la Concorde is this reliable roost run for years by the Maugars family. The neighborhood is dull as dishwater after 7 P.M. and on weekends, but the prices are right and the métro is close. The spotless rooms are reached by the same antique birdcage elevator that Marcel Proust used when he lived and wrote in the hotel. Most of the rooms are sunny, several connect, and those on the sixth floor, which have double beds only, have balconies where you can step out and enjoy the view. The rooms that have been redone are preferable, especially No. 61, a double with a shower. The room is simply decorated in white textured wallpaper, with matching floral fabrics on both the bed and curtains. Another new room is No. 10, a cozy nest with blond wood furniture and a red leatherette accent wall. It has a shower and sink, but the toilet is outside in the hall. Number 112 is a beamed twin on the front with a built-in closet, 1950s leather-and-chrome chairs, and a smart new black mosaic–tile bathroom. When I asked about the framed artwork over the bed (which resembles a crumpled painting by a frustrated ten year old), M. Maugars sighed, "It was the interior designer's idea, and so are those in the salon." If you need more room and want everyone to be together, this room connects with the one next door, which has a double bed. Back rooms are equal in amenities and will be quiet, but you may find yourself in a room, such as No. 54, with a frosted window that affords absolutely no view.

TEL 01-42-66-42-71 **FAX** 01-47-42-06-76 **EMAIL** hotel-marigny@wanadoo.fr
INTERNET www.paris-hotel-marigny.com
FACILITIES & SERVICES Air-conditioning (for a surcharge), direct-dial phone, elevator, hair dryer in new rooms (otherwise on request), minibar, French TV, office safe (no charge), WiFi at reception

RATES Standard single 105–110€, double 110–115€, superior double 127€; air-conditioning 10€ for older room, 12€ for new room; *taxe de séjour* included **CREDIT CARDS** MC, V
BREAKFAST Continental 6€ per person

HÔTEL QUEEN MARY ★★★ ($, 42)
9, rue Greffulhe, 75008
Métro: Madeleine, Havre-Caumartin
36 rooms, all with shower or bath and toilet

Visitors to Paris who desire a distinguished hotel in the center of the city between the Opéra and the Madeleine Church will have a hard time doing better than the Queen Mary, where every effort is made to assure that guests feel right at home in a warm and welcoming atmosphere. Many thoughtful touches make the difference here: a decanter of sherry in each room, happy hour from 6 to 8 P.M. in the friendly blue-and-white bar off the entry, afternoon tea served in the salon, room service from nine international restaurants or light snacks prepared at the hotel, and drinks served in a tiny fountain garden when weather permits.

Beautiful ceiling details and thick moldings soften the rooms, which are uniformly done with English carpeting, rich fabrics, and built-in mahogany furniture. Enhancing the rooms are many luxury accessories, such as air-conditioning, double-glazed windows, twenty-channel TV plus pay-per-view channels, FM radio and alarm clock, two telephones, and beautiful bathrooms. Those on the second and fifth floors have balconies; superior rooms and suites face front. Anyone looking for extra-special accommodations will do well in the sunny, top-floor, beamed suite with its rooftop view, two televisions, private fax, and large gray-tile bathroom with its own window. A hot American breakfast that includes bacon, eggs, and cornflakes (along with your croissants, butter, and jam) is served on fruit-designed Limoges plates in a yellow-and-red basement dining room with murals of Tuscany. Shoppers take serious note: You are in ultra-chic Fashion Country here. The names Lanvin, Yves St-Laurent, Jean-Paul Gaultier, and many more grace boutiques no more than a ten- to fifteen-minute browse from the hotel door.

Also under the same owner and management is the Hôtel du Bois (see page 249).

TEL 01-42-66-40-50 **FAX** 01-42-66-94-92 **EMAIL** reservations@ hotelqueenmary.com **INTERNET** www.hotelqueenmary.com
FACILITIES & SERVICES Air-conditioning, bar, direct-dial phone, elevator, private fax in suites, hair dryer, Internet in lobby, laundry service, minibar, radio, room service, electric tea kettle (in suite), trouser press, TV with international reception and pay-per-view, room safe (2€ per day)
RATES Single 165€, single or double 189–219€, suite for 1–4 people 299€; extra bed 80€; *taxe de séjour* included **CREDIT CARDS** AE, DC, MC, V
BREAKFAST American buffet 19€ per person

HÔTEL RELAIS MONCEAU ★★★ (2)
85, rue du Rocher, 75008
Métro: Villiers
51 rooms, all with shower or bath and toilet

The recently refreshed Hôtel Relais Monceau appeals to visitors looking for something in a quiet residential area that's also an easy commute to Paris's must-see attractions. I like the red-trimmed doors that line the long halls; inside, the attractive red-and-taupe rooms display wood, wicker, and chrome furnishings without looking industrial and impersonal in the process. Twin-bedded nests face the street; doubles are on the quiet, viewless back. Most of the rooms are unchangeably small, but touches of ingenuity make them seem bigger. Closets are open with cubby holes for foldables and hanging space for coats. Some are cleverly hidden behind the beds. Flat televisions have replaced the chunky old models. Mirrors add dimension, and the simple furnishings are kept to the bare minimum. The chocolate brown bathrooms have dark wood floors, double sinks, and Life Saver–colored glass marble accent trim. A planned roof garden with a bracing sauna will eventually be further draws at this attractive hotel.

Also under the same ownership is the Hôtel Relais Saint-Sulpice (see page 160).

TEL 01-45-22-75-11 **FAX** 01-45-22-30-88 **EMAIL** relaismonceau@wanadoo.fr
   INTERNET www.relais-monceau.com
FACILITIES & SERVICES Air-conditioning, bar, business center, conference room,
   direct-dial phone, elevator, hair dryer, laundry service, minibar, room safe
   (no charge), sauna, TV with international reception, WiFi
RATES 1–2 people 170€; *taxe de séjour* included **CREDIT CARDS** AE, DC, MC, V
BREAKFAST Buffet or in-room Continental 11€, per person

HÔTEL RÉSIDENCE LORD BYRON ★★★ (21)
5, rue Chateaubriand, 75008
Métro: George-V; RER Charles-de-Gaulle-Étoile
31 rooms, all with shower or bath and toilet

The Résidence Lord Byron provides lodgings for half the price of many other hotels in this prestigious, expensive *quartier.* On a quiet, winding street still close to the bright lights and excitement of the Champs-Élysées, it is so peaceful that it's listed in the *European Guide to Silent Hotels.* Many of the larger-than-average deluxe rooms overlook a garden courtyard where morning coffee and afternoon tea are served in the summer. In the spring, the garden is resplendent with tulips, daffodils, and fragrant narcissus. Rooms on the fifth floor require climbing one flight of stairs, but the payoff is two-fold: they are cheaper and have a view of the Eiffel Tower. The hotel, formerly a *hôtel particulière* (privately owned town home), is furnished with a wide range of lovingly worn and near antiques, making no pretenses at modernization. However, it is decorated in pleasing colors and coordinated fabrics. The suites are always in demand: No. 7 is a blue, two-room suite with a tassle design on the heavy Besson draperies and an older bathroom; No. 2 has a king-size bed, double sinks in the bathroom, and two large closets. Number 17 is a cozy, yellow-and-green single under the eaves on the fifth floor, with good closet and desk space; its Eiffel Tower view never lets you forget exactly where you are lucky enough to be! If red is one of your colors, you will revel in No. 31, a garden-facing double with a ruby red color scheme making a sharp contrast to the stark white walls.

TEL 01-43-59-89-98 **FAX** 01-42-89-46-04 **EMAIL** lord.byron@escapade-paris.com **INTERNET** www.escapade-paris.com

FACILITIES & SERVICES Air-conditioning, direct-dial phone, elevator (to most floors), hair dryer, laundry service, minibar, small pets accepted, room service for light snacks, TV with international reception, room safe (no charge), 4 nonsmoking floors, WiFi

RATES Single 135–165€, double 165–185€, junior suite (2–4 people) 260–300€; extra bed 30€; no charge for small pet; *taxe de séjour* included

CREDIT CARDS AE, DC, MC, V

BREAKFAST Buffet or in-room Continental 14€, per person

HÔTEL WEST END ★★★ ($, 34)
7, rue Clément Marot, 75008
Métro: Alma-Marceau, Franklin-D-Roosevelt
49 rooms, all with shower, bath, and toilet

The glossy, eye-catching hotel brochure has not one word of text. It doesn't have to because the pictures speak for themselves. After one glance, you know immediately that this is an elegant hotel in a glamorous and luxurious part of Paris. What is so surprising is the price, which is vastly less than most of the neighborhood's other all-stars. The hotel is located just off the Champs-Élysées in the middle of couture heaven around fashionable avenue Montaigne. The intimate sitting area and bar are rich in the French way, furnished in a fine style that mixes patterns, stripes, and velvets, which ultimately come together in a charming way.

The rooms are comfortable and equally suited to a business stay or one decidedly romantic. Streamlined marble bathrooms are in various sizes. In several, the green marble sink stretches the width of the ten-by-eight-foot bathroom, which is larger than many Parisian hotel rooms. Rooms on the second and fifth floor have balconies facing either the street or an interior courtyard. If sheer luxury is on your agenda, reserve a junior suite, perhaps No. 100. In addition to a sitting room with two leather chairs, and a king-size bedroom with adjustable bedside lights, there is a walk-in closet and a wonderful bathroom with double sinks and separate shower and toilet units. The standard rooms are not as lavish, but you have all the amenities: tissue-covered walls that form neutral backdrops for the lush fabrics of the curtains and beds, adequate closet and luggage space, and always a desk should work demand your attention. Services are everything you would expect, from the helpful porter carrying your bags to the housekeeping staff who check your room twice a day and always turn down your bed at night.

TEL 01-47-20-30-78 **FAX** 01-47-20-34-42 **EMAIL** reservation@hotel-west-end.com **INTERNET** www.hotel-west-end.com

FACILITIES & SERVICES Air-conditioning, honesty bar, concierge, direct-dial phone, elevator, hair dryer, laundry service, luggage room, minibar, porter, room service for light meals, TV with international reception, DVD players on request, room safe (no charge), free WiFi

RATES 1–2 persons: standard 245€, superior 260€, executive 300€, deluxe 350€; junior suite, 1–3 persons 370€; extra bed 40€; children under 12 free; *taxe de séjour* included **CREDIT CARDS** AE, DC, MC, V

BREAKFAST Hot American buffet 20€, in-room Continental 15€, per person

Ninth Arrondissement

In the southern part of this arrondissement is the beautiful Second Empire Opéra National de Paris Garnier with its famous Chagall ceiling, along with many large banks and shopping at Galeries Lafayette and Printemps. At the northern end is the infamous Pigalle, a sleazy neighborhood lined with twenty-four-hour peep shows, bordellos, "ladies of the night"—anything, generally, that gravitates toward the seamier side of life. Avoid the métro stops Anvers, Pigalle, and Barbès-Rochechouart after dark.

RIGHT BANK
department stores (Printemps and Galeries Lafayette)
Opéra
Pigalle

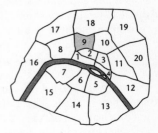

HOTELS IN THE NINTH ARRONDISSEMENT (see map page 192)

(¢) indicates a Cheap Sleep

HÔTEL CHOPIN ★★ (16)
10, boulevard Montmartre (46, passage Jouffroy), 75009
Métro: Richelieu-Drouot, Grands Boulevards
36 rooms, all with shower or bath and toilet

Parisians were mall shoppers long before Americans. At the turn of the century, Paris had enclosed, skylighted shopping walkways called *passages*. Today, these lovely covered areas house a variety of restaurants and shops selling everything from art and antiques to dubious-quality clothing. The Hôtel Chopin is a listed historic monument occupying a unique location at the end of the passage Jouffroy. This *passage* has some interesting boutiques, including one specializing in dollhouses and toys, another in secondhand books, and the Musée Grevin, Paris's version of a wax museum. The door to the hotel was opened the same year as the *passage* (1846), and it has never been locked. The hotel remains a favorite, with many repeat guests, thanks to the exceptionally warm, friendly welcome and care extended by Sandrine, the receptionist here for many years.

Given its longevity, be prepared for some things that may not be totally *au courant*. Fortunately, the hotel has been redone, and now the rooms have bathrooms. The vibrant salmon pink-and-green hallways display some pretty painted chests, screens, and chairs; the rooms, done up in hot pink and green, are all clean and quiet. The best rooms are on the top floors because they have skyline views and more natural light, but in No. 409, the tub is under a sloping eave, making upright showering a bit tricky for taller guests. Perhaps a better choice would be No. 406, where you have height in the bathroom, but no shower curtain.

Also under the same ownership is the Hôtel de la Bretonnerie (see page 98).

TEL 01-47-70-58-10 **FAX** 01-42-47-00-70 **INTERNET** www.hotelchopin.fr
FACILITIES & SERVICES Direct-dial phone, elevator (to most floors), electric fans, hair dryer available, French TV, room safe (no charge)
RATES Single 80€, double 92€, triple 110€; *taxe de séjour* included
   CREDIT CARDS AE, MC, V
BREAKFAST Continental (with fresh orange juice) 8€ per person

HÔTEL FRANCE ALBION ★★ (7)
11, rue Notre-Dame de Lorette, 75009
Métro: St-Georges
34 rooms, all with shower or bath and toilet

The two-star France Albion stands out as a modestly priced hotel that is loaded with many amenities missing from its high-flying three-star neighbors. Just what to expect? First, very competent service, but also robes in superior rooms and the suite; a cooked breakfast buffet complete with bacon and eggs, potatoes, cereals, meats and cheese; and champagne for honeymooners. Plus, you get the chance to occupy a suite for about the same price as a pair of designer running shoes. The rooms are basically the same: quilted blue bedcovers on double beds (only one room has twins), blond furniture, luggage and work space, showers in the single rooms, and shower/tub combos in the doubles. As usual, it is quieter in the courtside rooms, but the street is not a major crossroads or lined with all-night bars, so if you face front, you shouldn't spend the night lying awake counting the motor scooters and late-night revelers passing by.

TEL 01-45-26-00-81 **FAX** 01-53-21-05-33 **EMAIL** infos@
albion-paris-hotel.com **INTERNET** www.albion-paris-hotel.com
FACILITIES & SERVICES Air-conditioning, bar, conference room, direct-dial
phone, elevator, hair dryer, robes in superior rooms and suite, room safe
(no charge), TV with international direction, WiFi
RATES Single 85–105€, double 104–115€, suite 170€; extra bed 20€; *taxe de
séjour* included **CREDIT CARDS** AE, DC, MC, V
BREAKFAST Hot buffet 12€ per person

HÔTEL LANGLOIS ★★ (8)
63, rue Saint-Lazare, 75009
Métro: Trinité, St-Lazare
27 rooms, all with shower or bath and toilett

The hotel's building was constructed in 1870 and used as a bank until 1896, when it became a hotel and was owned by the same family for over eighty years. A change in ownership resulted in a massive renovation, which combined the charm of the Belle Epoque and Art Nouveau styles inherent in the building. All the bathrooms have been redone, the windows sound-proofed, and satellite television and minibars installed. The furnishings have been restored or replaced with something from either era, and all the paintings, sculptures, and other decorative objects are equally authentic.

The rooms on the first and second floors are done in the style of the 1930s and 1940s; those on the top floors reflect the Belle Epoque style of the early 1900s. Five uniformed maids toil relentlessly to keep them in pristine order at all times. For a real tour de force, reserve No. 11, with a massive bathroom and equally massive bedroom that has a wonderful blond laminated Art Deco wardrobe and its original ceramic-tile fireplace. Two wicker armchairs are positioned overlooking a small garden below. Room 15 has two fireplaces: one in the large bedroom and a marble one in the bathroom! Of course, neither one work, but they do add a certain panache. In No. 63, I like the arched sitting space with two soft armchairs padded in the same material as the headboard, the original tile fireplace, and the sky view over the back of the hotel. The only disappointment is No. 44, a suite with two lumpy futons, and no convenient place to plug in a laptop.

In 2001, the hotel was used as a setting in the remake of the Audrey Hepburn classic *Charade*. In the film, the hotel was named Langlois, and because the owners liked this name better than the actual one, "Hôtel des Croisés," they decided to change it. The hotel is a few minutes' walk from the St-Lazare station and a taxi ride away from the

Eurostar terminal at Gare du Nord. Also within walking distance is the Gustave Moreau Museum, Galeries Lafayette, and Printemps.

TEL 01-48-74-78-24 **FAX** 01-49-95-04-43 **EMAIL** info@hotel-langlois.com
   INTERNET www.hotel-langlois.com
FACILITIES & SERVICES Air-conditioning, direct-dial phone, elevator, hair dryer, TV with international reception, office safe (no charge), WiFi downstairs only
RATES Single 95–109€, double 109–130€, suite 170€; extra bed 20€; *taxe de séjour* 0.78€ per person, per day **CREDIT CARDS** AE, DC, MC, V
BREAKFAST Continental 8€ per person

HÔTEL LORETTE OPÉRA ★★★ (6)
36, rue Notre-Dame de Lorette, 75009
Métro: St-Georges
84 rooms, all with shower or bath and toilet

Located midway between the Opéra district and Montmartre, and within a ten-minute hike to the major department stores on boulevard Haussemann, the Best Western Lorette Opéra offers spacious, uncluttered rooms designed along clean, modern lines. Large stone walls and dividers create the stylized sitting room, part of which is furnished with cocoa suede wingchairs and setées, and in another, black armchairs enclose a table with a bouquet of stylized fresh flowers. The wide plank floor is embedded with a fairyland of tiny white lights. Other lighting treatments are just as dramatic, especially the lamp on the check-in desk, which is made of tufted white netting. The large breakfast room repeats the suede wingchair seating around some of the tables, while other blond wood tables utilize plastic armchairs.

Riding to your room is an eye-popping experience: the mirrored lift has metal hand and foot rails, hot yellow plastic walls, and a white ceiling strewn with bunches of red petals. Thankfully, the rooms are effortlessly cool. Stand tall in No. 603 and you will see the tip of the Eiffel Tower. This two-room suite, done in yellow, with mansard windows and a large bathroom, has burled blond built-ins, a carrot orange plastic chair, and a picture of a contented, haughty Weimaraner sitting on a velvet-covered wrought-iron bed. Room 404, a twin, has the same yellow colors as the suite, with light wood paneling behind the beds and framing the desk. Number 408 is a quiet standard double on the back with a good shower in the well-lit white-tile bathroom.

TEL 01-42-85-18-81; toll-free in U.S. 800-528-1234 (Best Western)
   FAX 01-42-81-32-19 **EMAIL** hotel.lorette@astotel.com
   INTERNET www.astotel.com
FACILITIES & SERVICES Air-conditioning, bar, direct-dial phone, elevator, hair dryer, laundry, room safe (no charge), TV with international reception, 3 nonsmoking floors, WiFi
RATES 1–2 persons: standard 121–195€, superior 260€; *taxe de séjour* 1€ per person, per day **CREDIT CARDS** AE, DC, MC, V
BREAKFAST Buffet 11€ per person

HÔTEL ROTARY (NO STARS, ¢, 1)
4, rue Vintimille, 75009
Métro: Blanche, Place Clichy
17 rooms, all with shower and sink, none with toilet

The Hôtel Rotary appeals to those whose aesthetic mind-set matches that of the hotel's interior design guru, whose ample use of *junque* has created a glowing bouquet of gloriously tacky enclaves. For instance, take No. 5, "The Chinese Room." It has a green velvet–draped, inlaid mother-of-pearl bed fit for a king—or queen, as the case may be. Two old tapestries hang on the wall, oriental rugs are tossed on the floor, a bentwood hat rack subs for the closet, and the bathroom is in black and gold mosaic tiles. There isn't much light to read by, but is anyone really going to read here? I don't think so, because when you turn off all the lights, the ceiling sparkles like a star-studded midnight sky. The only window is opaque, but no matter—the interior will keep you plenty preoccupied.

Room 8 is known as "The Grotto." Here you share the room with a statue of Aphrodite standing in a shallow bath backed by mirrors. A sea nymph motif encircles the room, which is dimly lit with glistening seashell lights. When you turn off the lights, Aphrodite continues to glow. Again the window in this room is opaque. Number 4 could be dubbed "The Red Room," thanks to its bright red ceiling and matching tiled bathroom with a hot-pink shower curtain. In the bedroom, the etching of a girl's face on the mirror was done by a friend of the hotel owner. If anyone staying here wants a "normal" room, perhaps No. 2 would qualify; its only claim to fame is its pink-bubble-gum-colored interior. By comparison, No. 3 is really boring, with its gun-metal gray floors and lavender walls. Amenities are few: no room phone, no elevator, and no cable television. WiFi? You must be joking! The hotel is not close to much on a tourist map, but the hotel itself may be attraction enough.

TEL 01-48-74-26-39 **FAX** 01-48-74-33-42 **EMAIL** hotel.rotary@wanadoo.fr
INTERNET www.hotel-rotary.fr
FACILITIES & SERVICES No elevator (6 floors), hair dryer on request, French TV, office safe (no charge), 3 rooms per floor share one toilet
RATES Single 44€, double 50€, theme rooms 63–70€; *taxe de séjour* included
CREDIT CARDS None, cash only
BREAKFAST Continental in room only (no croissants) 6€ per person

HÔTEL SAINT-LOUIS OPÉRA ★★ (10)
51, rue de la Victoire, 75009
Métro: Le Peletier, Notre-Dame de Lorette
17 rooms, all with shower or bath and toilet

Philippe le Guennec and Jean-Michel Tournu have a knack for turning faded hotels into smartly appealing two-star boutique lodgings everyone likes. They did this first with Hôtel Saint-Louis Marais (see page 104), and now have transformed this little nest, located within easy shopping distance to Galeries Lafayette and Printemps. A drawback for some might be the neighborhood, which is hardly in the fast track. Also, the backside rooms face a dismal, peeling wall and a filthy skylight, especially Nos. 10 and 11, and until the construction site is finished, avoid No. 35. However, the pretty rooms and soothing prices are enough for most to keep this little spot perking right along. The bedrooms evoke Provence with their polished terra-cotta stone floors, rosy red and orange colors, and wrought-iron furnishings. Bathrooms are uniformly modern. Each one has something of interest: a marble dresser, antique mirror, a colorful throw rug. Other attractions are the rooftop garden and the fact the hotel is completely nonsmoking.

The same owners run several short-term apartment rentals in the Marais (see page 294), as well as Hôtel Saint-Louis Marais (see page 104) and Hôtel Saint-Louis Bastille (see page 220).

TEL 01-48-74-71-13 **FAX** 01-44-53-98-80 **EMAIL** slopera@noos.fr
  INTERNET www.saintlouisopera.com
FACILITIES & SERVICES Direct-dial phones, elevator, hair dryer, room safe (no charge), TV with international reception, hotel entirely nonsmoking, WiFi
RATES Single 94€, standard double 110€, superior double 130€, triple 145€; *taxe de séjour* 0.78€ per person, per day **CREDIT CARDS** AE, DC, MC, V
BREAKFAST Continental 9€ per person

PERFECT HÔTEL ★ (¢, 4)
39, rue Rodier, 75009
Métro: Cadet, Anvers
42 rooms, 23 with shower and toilet

Finding budget accommodations in Paris is becoming more and more of an art. Sleeping cheap in the *centre ville* is nigh unto impossible, which forces the frugal to the fringes. The Perfect Hôtel is well named if your budget is on the ropes or you just want to cut corners. It's located in a tourist wilderness, so guests must be willing to master several routes of public transportation to get to the action.

The rooms are neat and clean, scrape- and tear-free, and without the usual one-star garish color mismatches that can cause five-star nightmares. The best bets are top-floor rooms, which have sky views and sunshine, or one with a balcony on the fifth floor. Since the public showers off the hall are free, you could opt for the cheapest rooms. The murals throughout the hotel and in some of the rooms were done by M. Mario, a friend of the owner. Breakfast is a breathtakingly low 3€ and is served in a plain room that has an interesting collection of old model sailing ships. Owners M. and Mme. Souer and their daughter are what the French call *sympa,* which means friendly and welcoming, and in any language, these attitudes are always appreciated.

TEL 01-42-81-18-86, 01-42-81-26-19 **FAX** 01-42-85-01-38
  EMAIL perfecthotel@hotmail.com
FACILITIES & SERVICES Elevator, luggage storage, French TV in lounge, office safe (no charge)
RATES Single 40–60€, double 50–60€; extra bed 15€; *taxe de séjour* included
  CREDIT CARDS MC, V
BREAKFAST Continental (no croissants) 3€ per person

Eleventh Arrondissement

The eleventh and twelfth arrondissements are known as *quartiers populaires* because they are traditional working-class neighborhoods. These are not hotbeds of tourist activity, but they do provide interesting glimpses of both the blue-collar Parisian way of life and the new-wave artists. More importantly, the area has some of the cheapest sleeps in Paris. Place de la Bastille joins the third, eleventh, and twelfth arrondissements and still serves as the rallying point for demonstrations, just as it did in the French Revolution. The column in the middle stands where the prison once was. The neighborhoods around the Bastille and the futuristic Opéra Bastille, which opened in 1989, are the city's bohemia, full of art galleries, lofts, cafés, nightclubs, and boutiques featuring the apparel craze of the moment. Humming night and day, this area is definitely one of the "in" places for anyone who likes to walk on the wild side and stroll on the cutting edge. On the weekends after midnight, it is only recommended for very hardcore night crawlers.

RIGHT BANK
Bastille
Opéra Bastille
place de la République

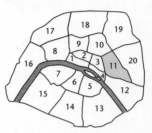

HOTELS IN THE ELEVENTH ARRONDISSEMENT

OTHER OPTIONS
Hostels

Residence Hotels

($) indicates a Big Splurge; (¢) indicates a Cheap Sleep

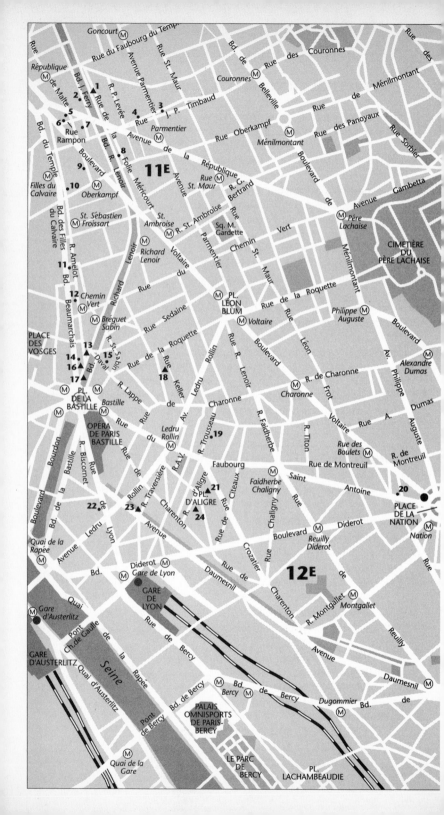

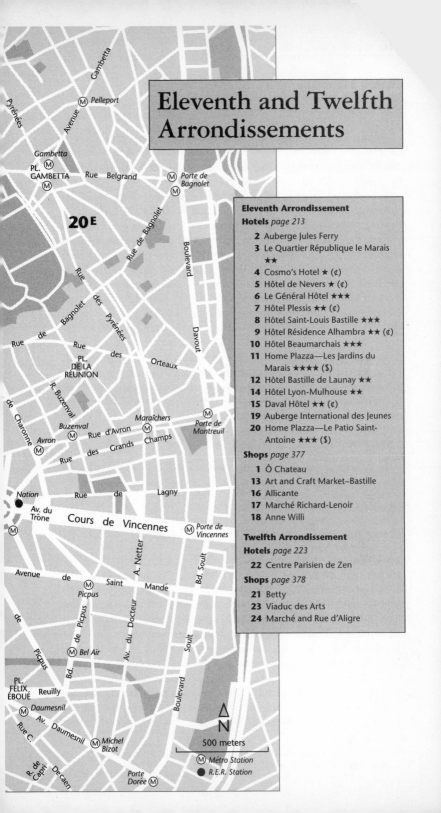

Eleventh and Twelfth Arrondissements

Eleventh Arrondissement

Hotels *page 213*

2 Auberge Jules Ferry
3 Le Quartier République le Marais ★★
4 Cosmo's Hotel ★ (¢)
5 Hôtel de Nevers ★ (¢)
6 Le Général Hôtel ★★★
7 Hôtel Plessis ★★ (¢)
8 Hôtel Saint-Louis Bastille ★★★
9 Hôtel Résidence Alhambra ★★ (¢)
10 Hôtel Beaumarchais ★★★
11 Home Plazza—Les Jardins du Marais ★★★★ ($)
12 Hôtel Bastille de Launay ★★
14 Hôtel Lyon-Mulhouse ★★
15 Daval Hôtel ★★ (¢)
19 Auberge International des Jeunes
20 Home Plazza—Le Patio Saint-Antoine ★★★ ($)

Shops *page 377*

1 Ô Chateau
13 Art and Craft Market–Bastille
16 Allicante
17 Marché Richard-Lenoir
18 Anne Willi

Twelfth Arrondissement

Hotels *page 223*

22 Centre Parisien de Zen

Shops *page 378*

21 Betty
23 Viaduc des Arts
24 Marché and Rue d'Aligre

HÔTEL ★ (¢, 4)
..., rue Jean-Pierre Timbaud, 75011
Métro: Parmentier, République
36 rooms, all with shower and toilet (no bathtubs)

Wanted: A neat, clean, safe, and comfortable temporary abode in the eleventh arrondissement. Found: Claire and Gerard Vedrines's spotless thirty-six-room super Cheap Sleep, which definitely delivers the goods.

I discovered Cosmo's Hôtel by mistake. I was walking by, disappointed that a two-star up the street had fallen by the Great Sleep wayside, when suddenly the modern lobby caught my eye. I went in and was warmly greeted by Mme. Vedrines, whose family has been here for four decades, and the house mascot, Bille, a friendly cat who holds court in the lobby. Though a simple place, I was quite taken with it: slat chairs in the sitting area are backed by a forest green wall and a bouquet of fresh (not fake) flowers. Downstairs, morning croissants and hot coffee, chocolate, or tea are served in side-by-side breakfast rooms. Even the smallest rooms have space and simple comforts. Some of the larger rooms have two windows and pleasing neighborhood views. Black-and-white Paris photos adorn the walls, bathrooms are as spotless as the rest of the hotel, the towels are good, and the showers have curtains. Bottom line: You can count on a very pleasant Great Sleep here without jeopardizing the budget or needing to don rubber gloves and spray disinfectant before you unpack.

TEL & FAX 01-43-57-25-88 **EMAIL** info@cosmos-hotel-paris.com
  INTERNET www.cosmos-hotel-paris.com
FACILITIES & SERVICES Direct-dial phone, elevator to most floors, hair dryer, French TV, room safe (no charge)
RATES Single 43€, double 56€, triple 63€, quad 68€; *taxe de séjour* included
  CREDIT CARDS AE, DC, MC, V
BREAKFAST Continental 6€ per person

DAVAL HÔTEL ★★ (¢, 15)
21, rue Daval, 75011
Métro: Bastille, Bréguet Sabin
23 rooms, all with shower or bath and toilet

Monsieur Gonod runs this Bastille budget hotel with good sense, good humor, and kindness. Valued mainly for its "in" location and conservative prices, the Daval Hôtel occupies a platinum position in the white-hot Bastille area, only a short promenade from the Opéra Bastille and all the cafés, boutiques, and galleries—as well as the weekend Bastille hotspots—that characterize this popular *quartier.* The blue rooms all have the same functional, easy-maintenance style: open closets, compact baths, built-in beds and side tables, quilted bed spreads, and industrial-strength carpeting. There are no twin beds, but all rooms are air-conditioned, which is an almost unheard-of luxury in this price range.

TEL 01-47-00-51-23 **FAX** 01-40-21-80-26 **EMAIL** hoteldaval@wanadoo.fr
  INTERNET www.hoteldaval.com

FACILITIES & SERVICES Air-conditioning, direct-dial phone, elevator, hair
   dryer, TV with international reception, room safe (no charge), WiFi
RATES Single 69€, double 73€, triple 86€, quad 100€; *taxe de séjour* included
   CREDIT CARDS AE, DC, MC, V
BREAKFAST Continental 9€ per person

HÔTEL BASTILLE DE LAUNAY ★★ (12)
42, rue Amelot, 75011
Métro: Chemin Vert, Bastille
36 rooms, all with shower or bath and toilet

   The Bastille de Launay is a great two-star value near the Marais
that won't set off firecrackers, but neither will its tariff burn a hole in
your pocket. The pale, uncluttered rooms are all just about the same:
small and uniformly furnished with a colorful blend of fabric prints
and stripes, easy-care furniture, a framed print on the wall, the TV
pitched in a high corner, and WiFi access. Basic baths have shower
guards on the tubs, but the rooms could use a wattage increase in
the lighting. The lobby has nice groupings of easy chairs, an attractive wall covering, and the usual green plants. Breakfast is served in
a stone cellar. That's it for this tastefully done, affordable pit stop on
the edge of a much more expensive area of the Marais.

TEL 01-47-00-88-11 **FAX** 01-42-33-95-64 **EMAIL** launay@
   paris-hotel-capital.com **INTERNET** www.paris-hotel-launay.com
FACILITIES & SERVICES Air-conditioning, direct-dial phone, elevator, hair
   dryer, minibar, TV with international reception, office safe (no charge),
   WiFi
RATES Single 73€; double 102–129€; dog 10€; *taxe de séjour* included
   CREDIT CARDS AE, DC, MC, V
BREAKFAST Buffet 9€ per person

HÔTEL BEAUMARCHAIS ★★★ (10)
3, rue Oberkampf, 75011
Métro: Filles-du-Calvaire, Oberkampf
31 rooms, all with shower or bath and toilet

   The popular Hôtel Beaumarchais merges high-style colors with
quality materials to produce quirky results. No one tried to camou-
flage the big metal heat exhaust pipe, which is in full view behind
the reception desk. But never mind—it takes a design page from the
Centre Georges Pompidou and fits right in. In the tiled lobby, the
seating space mixes orange, hot pink, and yellow barrel chairs with
gray metal tables. These colors are repeated on the bold, hand-painted
pottery used in the breakfast room, which overlooks an interior garden
with a central magnolia tree. If you like this pottery, which is called
"Creations Jos" (it's handmade by the hotel's owner, Jos Didier), the
pieces are for sale. Don't worry, they are also lead-free and dishwasher
safe. M. Didier likes to encourage his fellow local artists by holding
exhibits of their works, all of which are for sale at affordable prices.
   The vividly colored rooms are upbeat and cheerful, each with
Italian-designed lighting and a framed abstract art print on the
walls. In No. 56, a single with a shower, the view is of the dome of

the Cirque de l'Hiver (winter circus building). Room 23, a twin on the front, surrounds occupants in yellow: on the walls, the bedside tables, and the lampshades. Number 24 and 25 can connect, but the mix of magenta bedspread, turquoise headboard, and yellow walls and drapes might require dark glasses. The junior suites are good buys if more space is a priority but a bathtub is not . . . they only have showers. I like junior suite No. 11 with its sitting area overlooking the hotel courtyard. It has a nice blue sofa, a desk with a red Eames-style chair, natural light, and mirrored wardrobes.

TEL 01-53-36-86-86 **FAX** 01-43-38-32-86 **EMAIL** reservation@hotel beaumarchais.com **INTERNET** www.hotelbeaumarchais.com

FACILITIES & SERVICES Air-conditioning, bar, direct-dial phone, elevator (to most floors), hair dryer, TV with international reception, room safe (no charge), WiFi

RATES Single 75€, double 110€, triple 170€, junior suite 150€; *taxe de séjour* included **CREDIT CARDS** AE, MC, V

BREAKFAST Buffet or in-room Continental 10€ per person, served anytime

HÔTEL DE NEVERS ★ (¢, 5)
53, rue de Malte, at avenue de la République, 75011
Métro: Oberkampf, République
32 rooms, 24 with shower or bath and toilet

For cash-strapped globetrotters beholden to the bottom line, Paris hotel prices usually lead to one of two catastrophes: of budget or of well-being. Coming to the rescue is this great little Cheap Sleep near place de la République. For seventeen years, Alain and Sophie Bourderau and their cats—Misty, stretched out in reception, and Lea, a Scottish feline with attitude—have been dispensing their one-star, bright-colored, mixed-pattern, plebeian-furnished time-warped roosts to scores of happy visitors. You get a bed and not much more, and for bathless abodes, guests have one toilet per floor, and only one shower on the third. However, all complaints are quieted when you get your bill and realize that these are some of the lowest prices in Paris.

TEL 01-47-00-56-18 **FAX** 01-43-57-77-39 **EMAIL** reservation@hoteldenevers.com **INTERNET** www.hoteldenevers.com

FACILITIES & SERVICES Direct-dial phone, elevator (to most floors), hair dryer on request, free Internet in the lobby, free luggage storage, no TV, office safe (no charge)

RATES 1–2 persons 34–52€, triple 68–80€; showers 5€; *taxe de séjour* 0.42€ per person, per day **CREDIT CARDS** MC, V

BREAKFAST Continental 5€ per person

HÔTEL LYON-MULHOUSE ★★ (14)
8, boulevard Beaumarchais, 75011
Métro: Bastille
40 rooms, all with shower or bath and toilet

The hotel, owned and run for many years by Nathalia and Jean-Louis Corruble, is named for the cities of Lyon and Mulhouse, two stops that stagecoaches made when leaving Paris from the Bastille. This has been a hotel since 1920, and when looking at the early photos, you will see that from the outside nothing has changed, except that the saplings out front are now mature trees whose branches reach the top floor. There is absolutely nothing fancy or pretentious about the plain rooms, but they are very good value, not only for their more than ample size but for their spare, coordinated looks, WiFi access, views, and bathrooms with elongated tubs. The only view rooms are singles, and they are Nos. 43, 44, and 46, three cozy top-floor nests under the eaves with vistas of the Eiffel Tower and Montparnasse, Invalides, and the Panthéon. I would avoid No. 45, which somehow got lost in sequential numbering and is on the ground floor. While it has space in the room and the bathroom, you also must put up with the continuous rumble of the métro, which runs from 6 A.M. to 1 A.M. Room 30, a quiet quad on the back, has a partial view of the Opéra Bastille, double sinks in the bathroom, and a separate toilet unit. Just once while you are here, take the stairs and notice the pictures hanging in the hallways, which feature famous Paris landmarks: the Bastille, Eiffel Tower, Lapin Agile in Montmartre, Les Deux Magots, the Louvre, and Les Halles.

TEL 01-47-00-91-50 **FAX** 01-47-00-06-31 **EMAIL** hotelyonmulhouse@ wanadoo.fr **INTERNET** www.1-hotel-paris.com

FACILITIES & SERVICES Air-conditioning, direct-dial phone, elevator, hair dryer, TV with international reception, office safe (1.60€ per day), WiFi

RATES Single 65–140€, double 78–140€, triple 120–140€, quad 140€; *taxe de séjour* included **CREDIT CARDS** AE, DC, MC, V

BREAKFAST Continental 6€ per person

HÔTEL PLESSIS ★★ (¢, 7)
25, rue du Grand Prieuré, near avenue de la République, 75011
Métro: Oberkampf, République
50 rooms, 38 with shower or bath and toilet

The hotel was built in 1925, and since 1953, it has been run by members of the Montrazat family, who take pride in their well-priced, clean, friendly accommodations that pennywise travelers from around the globe call home when in Paris. The safe neighborhood is hardly a tourist command post; rather, it's a place where you will see a mix of old ladies in fuzzy slippers tossing baguettes to the pigeons, children playing, and men gathered in cafés.

The six overstuffed Naugahyde armchairs in the faux wood–paneled lobby, which also fits in a cold drink machine and mezzanine bar with an upright piano, make clear that no one has ever called in a decorating team for advice. However, you are not sleeping here. Instead, your room will be a perfectly adequate, clean chamber where the colors go together, there is space for your luggage, a chair to sit on, and the shower has a curtain. Rooms on the fifth floor have balconies; those without toilets and showers definitely say budget. Two student-style rooms, Nos. 643 and 644, have views of the tip of the Eiffel Tower. There are good restaurants nearby and nightlife around the Bastille. The Marais is only two métro stops away, and you are a heartbeat from place de la République, where buses, métros, or taxis can take you wherever you want to be in the city.

TEL 01-47-00-13-38 **FAX** 01-43-57-97-87 **EMAIL** hotel.plessis@club-Internet.fr

FACILITIES & SERVICES Bar, direct-dial phone, elevator, fans, hair dryer, TV with international reception in rooms with bath, office safe (no charge), one sitting room for nonsmokers, WiFi

RATES Single 62–72€, double 67–75€; free shower, towel 1.50€; *taxe de séjour* included **CREDIT CARDS** AE, DC, MC, V

BREAKFAST Buffet or Continental 7€ per person

HÔTEL RÉSIDENCE ALHAMBRA ★★ (¢, 9)
11 bis and 13, rue de Malte, 75011
Métro: Oberkampf, Filles-du-Calvaire
58 rooms, all with shower or bath and toilet

Here is a textbook example of getting what you pay for. Out of the way? Yes, more than a New York minute to get to what's really happening. Close to the métro? Yes, five major lines serve place de la République. A good deal? Yes, a pleasant Parisian stopover that would cost much more in tonier parts of the city.

The hotel is better than the neighborhood suggests. Automatic doors lead from the street into the light wood–paneled lobby, which looks onto a country garden. Open closets, no drawers, a built-in desk, and one chair sum up the rooms. Plumbing is of recent vintage in the tiled bathrooms, which have either a stall shower or shower and tub combination. Thirty-three of the rooms overlook the hotel garden. If you are lucky and secure one of these prime spots in the spring, summer, or early fall, you will overlook rose bushes, seasonal flowers, and trees, all lovingly cared for by the owner's sister. Tables and chairs are set outside in the summer, making it an especially nice place to have your morning croissant and *café*.

TEL 01-47-00-35-52 **FAX** 01-43-57-98-75 **EMAIL** info@hotelalhambra.fr
INTERNET www.hotelalhambra.fr

FACILITIES & SERVICES Direct-dial phone, elevator, TV with international reception, office safe (no charge), WiFi in lobby

RATES Single 65€, double 72–76€, triple 88–109€, quad 122€; *taxe de séjour* 0.78€ per person, per day **CREDIT CARDS** AE, MC, V

BREAKFAST Continental 7€ per person

HÔTEL SAINT-LOUIS BASTILLE ★★★ (8)
114, boulevard Richard Lenoir, 75011
Métro: Oberkampf
27 rooms, all with shower or bath and toilet

The immediate neighborhood holds little to capture a tourist's attention, but on second glance, it may appeal to those who don't have to be in the thick of things. The location, in the up-and-coming Oberkampf *quartier,* is two métro stops from the historic Marais and place des Vosges. The place de la République with five métro lines, numerous buses, and taxi stands is less than a ten-minute walk from the hotel door. Also of interest is the very popular Marché Richard-

Lenoir, an enormous Thursday and Sunday morning open-air market selling everything from food and wine to jewelry and scarves.

The hotel was recently redone, combining marble, terra-cotta, limestone, slate, and wood paneling to create cozy country-style rooms. Contemporary fabrics and soft taupe and gray colors prevent them from feeling too closed in and heavy. The floors are stone, the baths marble with good space, and the closet space is admirable. I would avoid Room 303 and the five others like it because of the terrible views.

Also under the same ownership and management are Hôtel Saint-Louis Marais (see page 104), Hôtel Saint-Louis Opéra (see page 211), and Saint-Louis Marais Résidence, which are very nice short-term apartment rentals (see page 294).

TEL 01-43-38-29-29 **FAX** 01-43-38-03-18 **EMAIL** slbastille@noos.fr
   INTERNET www.saintlouisbastille.com
FACILITIES & SERVICES Direct-dial phone, elevator, hair dryer, TV with
   international reception, room safe (no charge), first floor is nonsmoking,
   WiFi
RATES Single 85€, standard double 105€, superior double 125€; extra bed
   25€; *taxe de séjour* 1€ per person, per day **CREDIT CARDS** AE, DC, MC, V
BREAKFAST Buffet or in-room Continental 10€ per person

LE GÉNÉRAL HÔTEL ★★★ (6)
5/7, rue Rampon, 75011
Métro: République
47 rooms, all with shower or bath and toilet

New hotels are opening in areas of Paris once considered way off limits for savvy visitors. Not anymore! Now the A-listers and fashionistas flock to these off-the-beaten-track hotel destinations because they can offer so much more in terms of space, services, and value. Need some "wow factor" in the eleventh? Designer Jean-Philippe Nuel has succeeded in designing Le Général Hôtel so that guests feel they are living in an eclectic glam-rock performance space. Let's start with what the hotel offers over and above a place to sleep. There is a fitness center with all the whistles and bells any workout demands. After pumping iron, take your choice between a sauna and shower or reserve a relaxing massage. To keep in touch, just show up at the business center. Hungry or thirsty any time of day or night—call room service, or stop by the bar, which is open until 2 A.M.

Upon arrival, don't look for the usual reception desk separating you from the staff. Here, reception consists of a computer terminal operated by a young crew wearing pink scarves or ties. The sitting area is done in dark chocolate with a soft yellow chair and another covered in a huge pink floral print; a glass coffee table displays a fresh spray of orchids. The buffet breakfast is served in a fifties-style room with square stools, white plastic bucket chairs, and an upholstered armchair.

Ready to go to your room? Each hallway surrounds you in purple carpeting and hot, hot pink enameled doors. Candies on your pillow? That's soooo five minutes ago! Here you will get a fresh green apple. Blond Ikea-style furnishings, black-and-white Paris photos, clear plastic chairs (amazingly comfortable), and *Rear Window*–type views define most bedchambers. In each state-of-the-art bathroom is a little rubber, squeaking duck for you to play with in the tub and then take home as the hotel's gift to you.

Of course, this hotel is not for everyone, but if it is for you, you will know immediately and book as far ahead as possible, because this is one cool hot-spot.

TEL 01-47-00-41-57 **FAX** 01-47-00-21-56 **EMAIL** info@legeneralhotel.com
   INTERNET www.legeneralhotel.com
FACILITIES & SERVICES Air conditioning, bar, business center, conference
   room, direct-dial phone, elevator, fitness center, hair dryer, laundry
   service, luggage room, masseuse, tea and coffee makers, sauna, TV with
   international reception and pay-per-view, room safe (no charge), 3 floors
   nonsmoking, WiFi
RATES Single standard 130–150€, double standard 160–190€, double superior
   190–220€, suite 1–4 persons 230–260€; *taxe de séjour* included
   CREDIT CARDS AE, DC, MC, V
BREAKFAST Buffet 12€ per person

LE QUARTIER RÉPUBLIQUE LE MARAIS ★★ (3)
39, rue Jean-Pierre Timbaud, 75011
Métro: Parmentier
41 rooms, all with shower or bath and toilet

The name suggests you are staying in, or at least near, the Marais. Not quite! In fact you are five métro stops plus a line change away. That is not to say the hotel has nothing to offer. On the contrary. Its out-of-the-way location puts guests in a working-class neighborhood where average Parisians live, work, go to school, shop, and sit in cafés and bars and play the game "Spot the American." They are usually quite easy to recognize; just look for jogging shoes (sometimes in white, *quelle horreur!*), baseball caps, digital cameras, and dangling bottles of water.

The hotel offers several nonsmoking floors, an exercise room and sauna, free WiFi access, and could-be-anywhere rooms, for one or two persons only, in neutral colors that won't jar the senses or send the budget into orbit. Really, it's not bad when you stop to think about it.

TEL 01-48-06-64-97 **FAX** 01-48-05-03-38 **EMAIL** info@lequartierhotelrm.com
   INTERNET www.lequartierhotelrm.com
FACILITIES & SERVICES Direct-dial phone, elevator, exercise room and sauna,
   hair dryer, tea & coffee makers, TV with international reception, office safe
   (no charge), several nonsmoking floors, free WiFi
RATES Single standard 92–100€, double standard 97–105€; *taxe de séjour*
   included **CREDIT CARDS** AE, DC, MC, V
BREAKFAST Buffet 8.50€ per person

Twelfth Arrondissement

The twelfth leads away from the place de la Bastille and the Colonne de Juillet, a monument to the Parisians killed in the revolutions of 1830 and 1846. One of the district's nicest attractions is the Viaduc des Arts. Once a railway viaduct, it now showcases craft and new-wave design boutiques on the street level, and a pleasant green space—called the Promenade Plantée—runs along the top. Farther east is the vast Bois de Vincennes (with a lake, Buddhist temple, flower gardens, and a racetrack) and the Musée d'Afrique et d'Océanie,

RIGHT BANK
Bercy Village
Bois de Vincennes
Musée d'Afrique et d'Océanie
Opéra Bastille
Viaduc des Arts

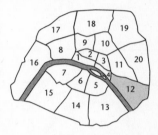

which has an outstanding collection of African tribal artifacts. The old brick wine warehouses at Bercy Village, across the river from the new Bibliothéque National, have been restored and developed into a pedestrian mall with shops, wine bars, cafés, and nightlife.

HOTELS IN THE TWELFTH ARRONDISSEMENT (see map page 214)

OTHER OPTIONS
Residence Hotels
Centre Parisien de Zen

305

Thirteenth Arrondissement

LEFT BANK

Bibliothèque Nationale de
    France–François Mitterand
Butte aux Cailles
Chinatown
Gobelins tapestry factory
    (Manufacture des
    Gobelins)

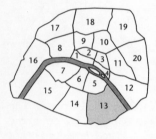

This large, working-class area is generally thought of as a tourist-free zone. It is the sort of place dedicated Parisian visitors see on their seventh or eighth trip, after they have done everything else they thought important. The area does hold some interesting surprises and should not be totally overlooked. There is the still-functioning Manufacture Nationale des Gobelins tapestry factory, which is open to the public. A stroll around the winding streets of the Butte aux Cailles district provides a delightful look at one of Paris's oldest yet least known and untouched parts, but one that is getting renewed attention from insiders who think the eleventh has become *passé*. The arrondissement also has a huge Asian population, which produces some of the best, and certainly the cheapest, Asian meals to be had in Paris; head for avenue de Choisy, the main street of Chinatown. The Bibliothèque Nationale de France–François Mitterand, designed to replace the Bibliothèque National, is a multi-million-euro project, covering 288,000 square meters along the Seine across from the Ministry of Finance. This enormous new library, built to resemble four open books, has incited as much controversy as the Opéra Bastille did (and still does).

HOTELS IN THE THIRTEENTH ARRONDISSEMENT

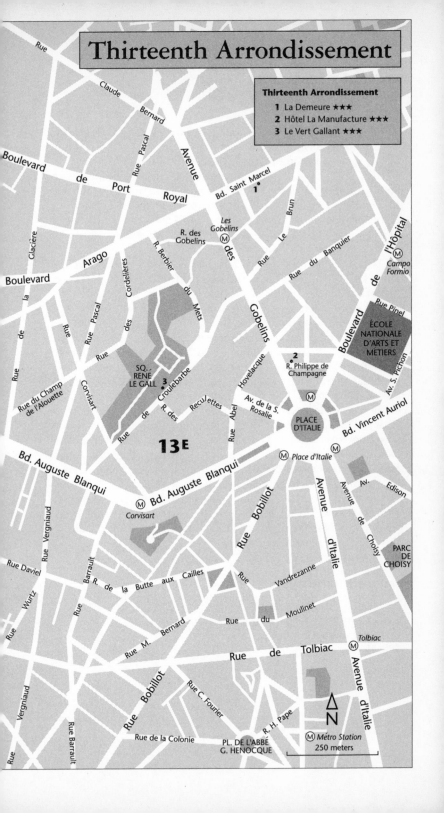

HÔTEL LA MANUFACTURE ★★★ (2)
8, rue Philippe de Champagne, 75013
Métro: Place d'Italie, Gobelins
57 rooms, all with shower or bath and toilet

Your quest stops here if you are looking for a stylish yet starkly designed hotel room in an area that's on the upswing with locals but largely ignored by most tourists. The hotel is just off the busy place d'Italie, which has a huge shopping mall and cinema multiplex. You are a ten-minute brisk walk from the colorful rue Mouffetard, fifteen to teeming Chinatown, and a mere two hundred meters from the Gobelins tapestry factory. The Butte aux Cailles, one of the city's oldest neighborhoods, still retains its village-like atmosphere and is another pleasant walk from the hotel.

The low-lying coral slipcovered sofas and stool modules in the lobby are eye-catching to say the least, and so are the high-backed red-and-white-checked banquettes and ocean-liner deck chairs in the dining room. Paolo Conté, a contemporary Left Bank painter, was commissioned to do the artwork, which is in direct contrast with the traditional fruit prints that line one wall. A stainless-steel, mirrored elevator takes guests to their rooms, which are on the cutting edge of modern, with simple lines, customized furniture, and crisp white bed coverings offset by red striped carpets. Two floors have balconies, and several rooms connect, but there are no suites. Some favorite rooms are on the seventh floor, especially No. 74, offering a view of the rooftops of Paris and the Eiffel Tower. Depending on the circumstances, the other view from this room could be considered infamous, since it is a direct look at the *quartier* city hall and police department. The bathroom is large enough for two pedestal sinks, a table, and a tub. In No. 72, you have a similar view of police doings in the neighborhood. All rooms on the seventh floor have tea- and coffee-making facilities, bathrobes, and scales. From No. 49, all you see is the courtyard from inside a very small room. Number 63 has a balcony, and the five framed damsels dictated the pink colors in the room.

TEL 01-45-35-45-25 **FAX** 01-45-35-45-40 **EMAIL** lamanufacture.paris@
   wanadoo.fr **INTERNET** www.hotel-la-manufacture.com
FACILITIES & SERVICES Air-conditioning, bar, direct-dial phone, elevator,
   hair dryer, laundry service, robes in some rooms, TV with international
   reception, office safe (4€ per day), 2 nonsmoking floors, WiFi
RATES Single 145€, double 145–255€; *taxe de séjour* included
   CREDIT CARDS AE, DC, MC, V
BREAKFAST Buffet 10€ per person

LA DEMEURE ★★★ (1)
51, boulevard Saint-Marcel, 75013
Métro: Gobelins, St-Marcel
43 rooms, all with shower or bath and toilet

La Demeure is a family-run hotel that prides itself on its personal atmosphere, yet offers its discerning guests all the advantages of a larger hotel. Before purchasing the hotel, the Cauët family looked at more than three hundred properties, then they spent six months conducting a total renovation. The result is a class act from top to bottom, down to the last designer detail. All the furniture has been custom made, including the Marly chairs and tables in the breakfast room, which are copies of those at the famous Café Marly facing the Louvre. Completing the look here is a collection of Italian art work that combines leaves, pods, and bamboo mounted on plastic backing. A fascinating collection of original photos taken between the two World Wars hangs throughout the rest of the hotel, including the dramatic sitting room done in fiery red.

The rooms are decorated in textured colors of blue, gray, beige, coral, and yellow; the higher the floor, the lighter the color. Ceilings are painted the same color as the walls, which mutes the reflection of light from passing traffic. The rooms on the fourth through the sixth floors have city-of-Paris views, including some with the Eiffel Tower or the Panthéon. Suites have sliding doors to separate the sleeping area from the living space. Bathrooms are generous in size, and many offer pulsating massage showers. Another major plus: The entire hotel is nonsmoking.

TEL 01-43-37-81-25 **FAX** 01-45-87-05-03 **EMAIL** la_demeure@netcourrier.com
  INTERNET www.hotel-paris-lademeure.com
FACILITIES & SERVICES Air-conditioning, baby cot, babysitting, bar, concierge services, direct-dial phone, elevator, hair dryer, free ADSL Internet, laundry service, minibar, private parking (17€ per 24 hours), room service, flat-screen TV with international reception and an English movie channel, room safe (no charge), entire hotel is nonsmoking
RATES 1–2 persons: superior 155€, deluxe 190€, triple 213€, suite 230–291€; *taxe de séjour* 1€ per person, per day **CREDIT CARDS** AE, DC, MC, V
BREAKFAST Buffet 13€ per person

LE VERT GALLANT ★★★ (3)
41–43, rue Croulebarbe, 75013
Métro: Place d'Italie, Gobelins
15 rooms and studios, all with shower or bath and toilet

Balzac said it well: "Paris is an ocean in itself. There is always some spot never seen before, some unknown cavern, flower, pearls, delight hitherto unknown."

A stay at the appealing Le Vert Gallant provides that wonderful feeling of discovery, of finding an unknown corner of Paris for your very own. Located in the Gobelins district, this hidden garden hotel is a charming oasis for those who know Paris well and are looking for something a bit beyond the usual hotel room—and who are willing to sacrifice a dead-center location to get it. Across the street from the hotel is the René Le Gall Square, a green park filled with the sound of children's voices, *mamans* pushing strollers, and elderly men and women out for a few minutes of gossip or a quiet moment to read the papers. For anything else, you will need the métro, which is a ten-minute walk. Next door to the hotel is its restaurant, l'Auberge Etchegorry, a Basque retreat that offers hotel guests special prices on prix-fixe meals. For more on this restaurant, see *Great Eats Paris*.

The hotel is made up of fifteen rooms, all of which have windows framing a garden courtyard, which has thirty-seven grapevines. Your morning wakeup call will be the songs of birds in the trees, not the usual rude Parisian awakening of grinding garbage trucks or furious horn-honking motorists. If you want to cook during your stay, reserve a studio on the ground floor. The rooms above also have kitchens, but because of fire regulations, no actual cooking is allowed on the higher floors. All rooms have an uncluttered, modern look. Colors are soft and pleasing, the accessories appropriate, and the fabrics well coordinated. Bathrooms are small but modern. Two affordable parking places must be reserved ahead. Maïté and Henri Laborde, your hosts here and at their restaurant, attend graciously to their guests, which further contributes to the overall feeling of well-being one has when staying at this special hotel. A warning is in order: Before arrival, have your affairs in order at home—you may never want to leave.

TEL 01-44-08-83-50 **FAX** 01-44-08-83-69

FACILITIES & SERVICES Direct-dial phone, no elevator (2 floors), hair dryer, some kitchenettes, minibar, parking (10€ per day), TV with international reception, room safe (no charge), all rooms nonsmoking, WiFi

RATES 1–2 persons 87–100€; extra bed 15€; *taxe de séjour* included

   CREDIT CARDS AE, MC, V

BREAKFAST Continental 7€ per person

Fourteenth Arrondissement

Montparnasse has become the victim of a tragically insensitive redevelopment policy exemplified by the Tour Montparnasse. During the 1920s and 1930s, the fourteenth was well known as the artistic headquarters of the modern art and literary worlds, where Picasso, Modigliani, Chagall, and Léger all had studios. Nostalgia buffs return today and head for the historic brasseries Le Dôme and La Coupole to rekindle memories of the famous patrons who ate and drank there, but

LEFT BANK
Catacombs
Montparnasse
Parc Montsouris

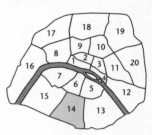

they find the spirit is just not the same. Spirits of a different sort can be found at place Denfert-Rochereau, where the Catacombs are located. These underground cemeteries, created in 1785 as a hygienic alternative to the above-ground ones, hold the bones of six million Parisians, and during World War II, they were used as a headquarters by the French resistance. The Mémorial du Maréchal Leclerc & Musée Jean Moulin are dedicated to the Resistance movement in France during World War II. Another final resting place is the Cimetière du Montparnasse, where many famous writers and artists lie, including Jean Paul Sartre and Simone de Beauvoir, Baudelaire, Maupassant, Samuel Beckett, and André Citroën. The Parc Montsouris, designed by Alphand during the time of Baron Haussmann, is one of the prettiest parks in Paris.

HOTELS IN THE FOURTEENTH ARRONDISSEMENT

Hôtel de Blois ★ (¢)	**232**
Hôtel Delambre ★★★	**232**
Hôtel de l'Espérance (NO STARS, ¢)	**233**
Hôtel des Bains ★	**234**
Hôtel l'Aiglon ★★★	**235**
Hôtel Lenox Montparnasse ★★★	**236**
Hôtel Montparnasse Daguerre ★★★	**237**

(¢) indicates a Cheap Sleep

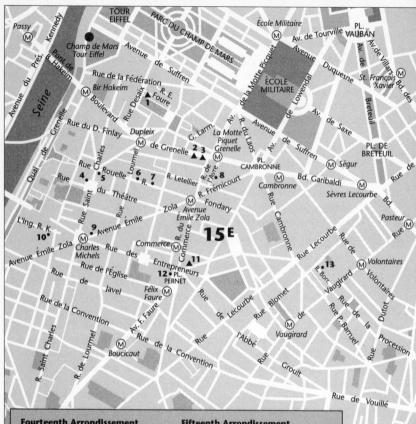

Fourteenth Arrondissement

Hotels *page 229*

16 Hôtel des Bains ★
17 Hôtel Delambre ★★★
18 Hôtel Lenox Montparnasse ★★★
19 Hôtel l'Aiglon ★★★
21 Hôtel Montparnasse Daguerre ★★★
23 Hôtel de l'Espérance (NO STARS, ¢)
26 Hôtel de Blois ★ (¢)

Shops *page 379*

14 Galeries Lafayette
14 Maine-Montparnasse
15 Art and Craft Market–Montparnasse
20 La Boutique de l'Artisanat Monastique
22 Divine
24 Rue Daguerre
25 Arche
27 Rue d'Alésia
28 Marché de Vanves

Fifteenth Arrondissement

Hotels *page 238*

4 Hôtel Beaugrenelle St-Charles ★★
5 Mercure Paris Saint Charles ★★
6 Au Pacific Hôtel ★★ (¢)
7 Family Hôtel Résidence
8 Hôtel de l'Avre ★★
9 Hôtel Alizé Grenelle Tour Eiffel ★★★
10 Practic Hôtel (NO STARS, ¢)
12 3 Ducks Hostel
13 Aloha Hostel

Shops *page 380*

1 Fat Tire Bike Tours
2 Marché Dupleix
3 Rue du Commerce
11 Mon Bon Chien

Fourteenth and Fifteenth Arrondissements

Rue de Babylone
Sèvres Babylone Ⓜ
Rue de Sèvres
Vaneau Ⓜ
Rue du Cherche Midi
Invalides
Rue de Vaugirard
St. Placide Ⓜ
Duroc Ⓜ
Rue de Rennes
Sèvres
Bd.
Falguière Ⓜ
Rue d'Assas
Rue de Vaugirard Ⓜ
PL.18 JUIN 1940
Montparnasse Bienvenüe Ⓜ
14 ▲
Av. du
Rue du
Montparnasse Ⓜ
Montparnasse
N. D. des Champs
Vavin Ⓜ
N. D. des Champs
Bd. Saint Michel
Rue Claude Bernard
Port Royal ●
15 ▲
R. Delambre •18
Raspail
Boulevard
Boulevard de Port Royal
Vaugirard
Bd.
du Maine
16 •
17
• E. Quinet
19 •
Camp. Pre.
20 ▲
Denfert Rochereau
Pasteur
Bd. de Maine
GARE MONTPARNASSE
Edgar Quinet Ⓜ
Edgar Quinet
Raspail
Raspail
Ave.
Rue du Fau. St. Jacques
Boulevard Arago
Gaîté Ⓜ
CIMETIÈRE DU MONTPARNASSE
PL. DE CATALOGNE
21 •
Rue
Daguerre
Denfert Rochereau
Denfert Rochereau Ⓜ
PL. D. ROCHEREAU
St. Jacques
Ⓜ
B. St. Jacques
Glacière Ⓜ
Pernety Ⓜ
R. Pernety
22 ▲
23 •
24 ▲
● Denfert Rochereau
Rue de
Rue R. Losserand
Gergovie
Avenue du Maine
R. M. Duvernet
Leclerc
Avenue René Coby
14 ᴱ
R. Brézin
Mouton Duvernet Ⓜ
Plantes
Général
Plaisance Ⓜ
Rue
d'Alésia
R. Moulin
•26
Vert
25 ▲
d'Alésia
Alésia Ⓜ
Raymond Losserand
Didot
27 ▲
PL. BASCH
Rue
d'Alésia
Rue des
Reille
Boulevard
Brune
Av. Jean Moulin
Avenue du
Rue de la Tombe Issoire
Avenue
PARC MONTSOURIS
Av. M. Sangnier
28 ▲
Av. G. Lafenestre
Av. M. d'Ocagne
Porte d'Orléans Ⓜ
PL. DU 25 AOÛT 1944
Boulevard
Jourdan
Porte de Châtillon
Ⓜ *Métro Station*
● *R.E.R. Station*
Porte d'Orléans
500 meters

◁ N

HÔTEL DE BLOIS ★ (¢, 26)
5, rue des Plantes, 75014
Métro: Alésia, Mouton-Duvernet, Gaîté
25 rooms, all with shower or bath and toilet

When I first visited this hotel several years ago, it was my final hotel stop after a long, rainy day, and as I walked I thought, this place is about two blocks east of nowhere, and it better be very, very good. Luckily, the Hôtel de Blois turned out to be a winner in the one-star, budget-hotel sweepstakes, and it still is. A recent change of ownership has improved things greatly—they have toned down the color mixes and removed lots of the ruffles and fluff, but unfortunately kept most of the chenille bedspreads. The still-feminine bedrooms are now coordinated, thankfully displaying little of former rainbow-palette color schemes and garage-sale Gothic furniture. Ask for Room 20, with a double bed, tiny blue-and-pink floral-print wall covering, and a bathroom with new fittings and a shower curtain. Another favorite choice is No. 2, a double, with an antique armoire and a big pink-tiled bathroom. Space is at more of a premium in No. 9, a triple on the front, but it does have a bathroom with a tub and shower. I would not want to stay in No. 3, which has a poor layout due to the way the shower and toilet were squeezed in. A self-service laundromat is right across the street, and if you need a workout, there is a public swimming pool a hundred meters behind the hotel. The hotel's own workout program— climbing from one to five flights of stairs to get to and from your room—may soon be optional: an elevator is planned, but not assured.

Shopaholics take note: You are within a five-minute, bag-toting distance from one of the discount shopping meccas for bargain-loving Parisians: rue d'Alésia (see page 328).

TEL 01-45-40-99-48 **FAX** 01-45-40-45-62 **EMAIL** hoteldeblois@wanadoo.fr
  INTERNET www.hoteldeblois.com
FACILITIES & SERVICES Direct-dial phone, no elevator (5 floors), hair dryer
  available, TV with international reception, office safe (no charge), WiFi
RATES Single 51–56€, double 55–66€ , triple 72€; *taxe de séjour* 0.42€ per
  person, per day **CREDIT CARDS** MC, V
BREAKFAST Continental 6.20€ per person

HÔTEL DELAMBRE ★★★ (17)
35, rue Delambre, 75014
Métro: Montparnasse-Bienvenüe, Vavin, Edgar-Quinet
30 rooms, all with shower or bath and toilet

I continue to be impressed by Patrick Kalmy's Hôtel Delambre, which retains my vote for the smartest rehab effort in the fourteenth arrondissement. A few years ago, he took a dog-eared one-star, where poet André Breton lived in 1921 and Paul Gauguin lived in 1891 (while planning his last trip to Tahiti), and transformed it from stem to stern into a snazzy three-star and—this is important—kept the prices within reason. In cleaning out the debris from the old hotel,

M. Kalmy found some unlikely treasures, which he incorporated nicely in the lobby and breakfast room. In the street-side dining area, he cleverly displays an old metal garden gate, and two original regal columns stand by the elevators.

The rooms are well done in two dominant colors: either red and blue or yellow and blue. Rooms 34 and 40, with white walls and enameled doors with wood detailing, are doubles with a built-in curved desk and an interesting view over a garden to a block of apartments beyond. Number 50, a two-room minisuite that requires climbing seventeen steps, combines the charm of sloping ceilings with smaller windows. The addition of a skylight, good closet space, and a large bathroom make this a popular choice, but not for tall guests. The hotel is within walking distance of the Luxembourg Gardens and Montparnasse. Otherwise, public transportation is easy and close by.

TEL 01-43-20-66-31 **FAX** 01-45-38-91-76 **EMAIL** delambre@club-internet.fr
   INTERNET www.hoteldelambre.com
FACILITIES & SERVICES Air-conditioning, direct-dial phone, elevator (to most
   floors), hair dryer, laundry service, TV with international reception, room
   safe (no charge), WiFi
RATES 1–2 persons 89–93€, suite 156€; *taxe de séjour* included
   CREDIT CARDS AE, MC, V
BREAKFAST Buffet or in-room Continental 10€ per person

HÔTEL DE L'ESPÉRANCE (NO STARS, ¢, 23)
1, rue de Grancey, 75014
Métro: Denfert-Rochereau
17 rooms, 6 with shower, none with toilet

Montparnasse is the neighborhood that made café-hopping famous, so for many there is no need to spend time in, or money on, a hotel room. You will be doing neither at Jackie Lacourarie's useful seventeen-room address, which doesn't pretend to be stylish. It is situated right around the corner from rue Daguerre, a good place to observe the happenings on one of the more active shopping streets in the fourteenth arrondissement. Amenities are lean, but the rooms have double-glazed windows, are *très propre* (very clean), and free of cascading patterns and dizzying color schemes. Jackie bills herself as "the original French mother," which means she will take good care of you during her shift. Her son Laurent, who speaks English, is equally as hospitable. In digs like this, it is always budget-smart to book the cheaper, showerless rooms and use the hall facilities, which in this case are very good. It is also wise to book early, because there is seldom a vacancy.

NOTE: The hotel is closed from August 1 to 15.

TEL 01-43-21-41-04 **FAX** 01-43-22-06-02
   EMAIL hoteldelesperance@hotmail.com
FACILITIES & SERVICES No elevator (2 floors), hair dryer available, French TV,
   office safe (no charge)
RATES Single 28.80€, 1–2 persons 35.20–59€, triple 61€; shower 3.50€; *taxe
   de séjour* 0.20€ per person, per day **CREDIT CARDS** MC, V
BREAKFAST Continental (no croissant) 5.50€ per person

HÔTEL DES BAINS ★ (16)
33, rue Delambre, 75014
Métro: Edgar-Quinet
41 rooms, all with shower or bath and toilet

The Hôtel des Bains is far from the usual lean one-star stopover; consider the formal sitting room, which is decorated with silk flowers in a graceful silver bowl, oriental rugs, and an oval dining table that would easily seat eight. For a one-star, the prices seem high, but for what you get, they are very fair and definitely packed with value. Late risers will appreciate the set-back location from the street . . . all the rooms are quiet, at least for this part of Paris. The rooms aren't big on decorating frills, but they are a quantum leap from the Day-Glo colors and frayed-at-the-edges furnishings one usually contends with in one-star abodes. They come equipped with excellent bathrooms, TVs with international reception, hair dryer, room safe, and the possibility of outside private parking—an unheard-of extra in a one-star hotel.

Even though they lack much storage space, the best deals are the suites, all of which have a bedroom with one large bed and an adjoining room with twin beds. Oddly enough there are no towel racks in some, and when I asked about their absence, I was told the towels were changed daily. Another oddity for some might be the collection of paintings of reclining nude women that hang over the beds and adorn the walls, or in some cases are fashioned into side lights. Number 447 is a two-room selection facing the courtyard. It is open and simply done with hardwood floors, coordinated fabrics, and a corner glass shower in the bathroom. If you are at all claustrophobic, you won't want Suite 227, with only a tiny barred ceiling window in the second bedroom. On the other hand, Suite 772 would easily befit a three- or four-star property. Up a flight of stairs, this two-room suite is amazingly nice, with gray faux-finished beds and cane headboards. Ruby spreads and upholstered chairs match the tassels holding back the embroidered floor-to-ceiling floral print draperies. Each room comes equipped with its own TV, adequate seating, and open closet space. The large granite bathroom has a glass-enclosed stall shower, magnifying mirror, and extra hooks. Some of the doubles are really too small for two, unless you are staying only a night, have very limited luggage, or enjoy very cozy confines with your traveling companion. Better choices are No. 221, overlooking a garden, or No. 71, which can be a double or triple, and is sold as a suite. It is decorated in yellow and has a big bathroom with a glassed-in shower.

TEL 01-43-20-85-27 **FAX** 01-42-79-82-78 **EMAIL** des.bains.hotel@wanadoo.fr
  INTERNET www.hotel-des-bains-montparnasse.com
FACILITIES & SERVICES Air-conditioning, direct-dial phone, elevator (to halfway between floors), hair dryer, parking (14€ per 24 hours), trouser press, TV with international reception, room safe (no charge)
RATES 1–2 persons 82–88€, suite (1–4 persons) 126–141€; baby bed 12€; *taxe de séjour* 0.70–1.40€ per person, per day **CREDIT CARDS** AE, MC, V
BREAKFAST Buffet 8€ per person

HÔTEL L'AIGLON ★★★ (19)
232, boulevard Raspail, 75014
Métro: Raspail; RER Denfert Rochereau
47 rooms, all with shower or bath and toilet

The Hôtel l'Aiglon, now under the umbrella of the Esprit de France hotel group, is a refined choice a quick walk from the Raspail métro stop. A formal tone pervades, from the faux book–lined bar to the traditionally decorated rooms, all of which have been planned with discretion and good taste. Don't miss the original stained-glass windows over the stairway, which takes guests from the ground floor to a formal dining room with large sideboard and mahogany tables covered in starched white linen.

The rooms all face outward, and many have peaceful views over the Cimetière Montparnasse. They are color-coordinated, with textured fabrics, firm mattresses, good closet and luggage space, and bathrooms with windows. The eight suites are dreams come true, especially No. 55 with its soft blue colors. The sitting room is comfortably furnished with a desk, sofa bed, and easy chair, and it has a half bath to one side. Twin beds in the bedroom, with its own balcony, and a double-sink bathroom make up the rest. I also like Room 19, the only one with a kitchenette. It is handsomely done in kelly green and yellow with a pleasant sitting room, a large bedroom with a walk-in closet, and a beautiful bathroom. The advantage of Suite A is that both nicely appointed bedrooms have separate bathrooms, a real bonus for families. In No. 16, bright yellow and green are carried out on the quilted bedspread and curtains. The gray bathroom has gold and beige accents and a floral design in the shower. If you are *tout seul,* it is a perfect choice. Some people may not like the rooms on the top, or sixth, floor because the windows are higher than normal, but I find them quite charming. One of my favorite choices is No. 61. I like the room itself, with a three-drawer chest, a comfortable armchair, and print fabrics, but it is the bathroom that is the real star, with two windows and a view. I am also a fan of No. 67, with its sweeping view of the fourteenth arrondissement.

Other Paris hotels that are part of the Esprit de France hotel group are Hôtel Brighton (see page 71), Hôtel Mansart (see page 77), Hôtel de la Place du Louvre (see page 73), Hôtel des Saints-Pères (see page 177), and Hôtel d'Orsay (see page 179).

TEL 01-43-20-82-42 **FAX** 01-43-20-98-72 **EMAIL** aiglon@espritfrance.com
    INTERNET www.esprit-de-france.com or www.hotel-paris-aiglon.com
FACILITIES & SERVICES Air-conditioning, bar, direct-dial phone, elevator, hair dryer, kitchenette in one suite, laundry service, minibar, private parking (16€ per 24 hours, reserve ahead), TV with international reception, office safe (no charge), WiFi
RATES Single 92–118€, 1–2 persons 138–168€, suite (1–4 persons) 194–249€; apartment (1–4 persons) 250€, 5 persons 265€; extra bed 15€; *taxe de séjour* included **CREDIT CARDS** AE, DC, MC, V
BREAKFAST Buffet 10€, Continental 8€, per person

HÔTEL LENOX MONTPARNASSE ★★★ (18)
15, rue Delambre, 75014
Métro: Vavin, Edgar-Quinet, Montparnasse
52 rooms, all with shower or bath and toilet

The atmosphere is engaging and the clientele an international blend at the Lenox Montparnasse. The collection of furniture suggests Art Deco and the 1930s in both the lobby and large bar to one side. Green plants bring life to the area, beautiful sprays of fresh orchids give it wonderful color, and the ceiling painted like a beautiful cloud-filled Parisian day adds a light touch.

Rooms are nice, with just enough personality to set them apart from other mainstream Montparnasse hotels. Even though the rooms are charming and have all the amenities, some are short on space. If you want more leg room, reserve No. 69, a big twin with a corner sitting room, a tiny fireplace, and a rooftop view. It is softly decorated in blue and light gray. The bathroom has a rolling toiletry cart and blue and green inserts of flowers set against the white-tile walls. Rooms 10 and 14 are standard doubles, but I hope the guests are small people with only hand luggage. The bathroom in No. 10 is adequate, but in No. 14, *c'est trop petite.* That said, either would be just fine for a solo guest. Number 58 is a Club Room, which means it is slightly bigger than a standard room, and the bathroom has a tub. I like its cheery red striped wallpaper and Toile de Jouy animal print fabric. Number 60 is a good-value, twin-bedded suite beautifully done in blue and white with hand-painted window shutters and an old tile heater with a marble top. Seating is nicely arranged around a sofabed and two comfortable reading chairs. The top-floor, two-room suite, with its marble fireplace and clock, period furniture, and geometric upholstery, shows that an eclectic combination of styles and patterns can work if done correctly. Amusing etchings of French ladies of leisure with their dogs or coyly wrapped in fur—and not much else—grace the walls. The narrow bathroom has all the extras, including Roger and Gallet products.

TEL 01-43-35-34-50 **FAX** 01-43-20-46-64 **EMAIL** hotel@
lenoxmontparnasse.com **INTERNET** www.hotellenox.com

FACILITIES & SERVICES Air-conditioning, bar, direct-dial phone, elevator, hair dryer, laundry service, minibar, parking (15€ per 24 hours), robes in suites, room service, flat-screen TV with international reception, room safe (no charge), free WiFi in lobby

RATES 1–2 persons: standard 135–150€, club 170€, junior suite (2–3 persons) 260–290€; *taxe de séjour* included **CREDIT CARDS** AE, DC, MC, V

BREAKFAST Buffet 14€ per person

HÔTEL MONTPARNASSE DAGUERRE ★★★ (21)
94, rue Daguerre, near avenue du Maine, 75014
Métro: Denfert-Rochereau, Gaîté
30 rooms, all with shower or bath and toilet

For a reliable modern stay in this neck of the Paris woods, the Hôtel Montparnasse Daguerre is a top-notch choice. Even though it has recently been bumped up from two to three stars, nothing much has changed, including the prices. Paintings of the *bouquinistes* along the banks of the Seine, some Monet prints, and a mural of the Louvre accent the small sitting room and stone-walled breakfast area. The standard-issue rooms are comfortably furnished and have more than their share of perks, including heated towel racks and WiFi access on the first and second floors. The even-numbered rooms face the street and have showers and more noise. The odd-numbered slots have tubs and are quiet. Those ending in the number three or located on the second and third floors are nonsmoking. No room faces a blank wall. The elevator does not go to the breakfast room and lands between the floors for the rooms, so there will always be a few steps to climb. The best feature of Nos. 501 and 505 are their glassed-in verandas looking toward Montmartre. If these rooms are booked, ask for No. 601, which has some view of the Sacré Coeur, or No. 301, with a pleasant view of the garden. If you want your own little terrace, try Nos. 1 or 2.

TEL 01-43-22-43-54, 01-56-80-25-80 **FAX** 01-43-20-66-84 **EMAIL** hotel daguerre@wanadoo.fr **INTERNET** www.hoteldaguerre.avenueduweb.net

FACILITIES & SERVICES Direct-dial phone, elevator (to half landings), hair dryer, minibar, TV with international reception, room safe (no charge), several floors nonsmoking, free WiFi in portion of hotel

RATES Single 80€, double 90€, suite 125€; extra bed 25€; *taxe de séjour* 1€ per person per day **CREDIT CARDS** AE, DC, MC, V

BREAKFAST Buffet 11€ per person

Fifteenth Arrondissement

LEFT BANK
Parc André Citroën

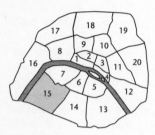

Home to a quarter of a million Parisians, the fifteenth is the biggest arrondissement, but it has few tourist attractions. If you enjoy seeing how the average Parisian lives, this is the perfect vantage point. La Ruche, which means beehive, was designed by Eiffel in 1900 as a wine pavilion. It is now used as artists' studios and occasionally is open to the public. The Parc André Citroën is a futuristic park built with computerized fountains, water jets, and even some green areas.

HOTELS IN THE FIFTEENTH ARRONDISSEMENT
(see map page 230)

(¢) indicates a Cheap Sleep

AU PACIFIC HÔTEL ★★ (¢, 6)
11, rue Fondary, 75015
Métro: Avenue Émile-Zola, Dupleix
57 rooms, all with shower or bath and toilet

This hotel and the Family Hôtel Résidence (a residence hotel, see page 306) are owned by Michèle Lepoutre, a gracious multilingual woman who took them over from her parents and grandmother. Both properties are on the same street in a blue-collar corner of Paris that is within a brisk fifteen-minute walk to the Eiffel Tower. At the Au Pacific, the rooms are sparse and spare with blond furniture and neutral colors. Eight in the back building have balconies, and now all have private facilities and television with French reception. Housekeeping is excellent; you won't see dirt or mold lurking in corners anywhere.

The breakfast room is soberly yet very smartly furnished with the latest Italian designs in wood and chrome. Though amenities and prices are lean, the quality is never compromised. These are great budget sleeps, and euro-conscious, international guests stay here in droves.

TEL 01-45-75-20-49 **FAX** 01-45-77-70-73 **EMAIL** pacifichotel@wanadoo.fr
   INTERNET www.au-pacific-hotel.com
FACILITIES & SERVICES Direct-dial phone, elevator (to most floors), hair dryer, French TV, office safe (no charge)
RATES Single 58€, double 66€; *taxe de séjour* included **CREDIT CARDS** MC, V
BREAKFAST Buffet 6.50€ per person

HÔTEL ALIZÉ GRENELLE TOUR EIFFEL ★★★ (9)
87, avenue Emile-Zola, 75015
Métro: Charles-Michels; RER Javel
50 rooms, all with shower, bath, and toilet

The savings can be 30 percent on the weekends, when the businessmen who stay during the week go home and management is eager to fill the fifty rooms. There's not much going on in the neighborhood, sophistication-wise, but I like it for its reality. This is a typical working-class area where people live, work, take their children to school, visit the pharmacy, buy a bouquet of flowers, and frequent the same café for years. It is not too far from the Eiffel Tower, the Parc André Citroën; if you are a veteran walker, plan on a bracing half hour to UNESCO. The rooms follow the Motel 6 school of decorating, but they are clean, have the usual perks, pleasant colors, and nice bathrooms with plenty of light. The triples are a tight squeeze, so if there are more than two in your party, better sleep somewhere else.

Also under same ownership is Hôtel Beaugrenelle St-Charles (see below).

TEL 01-45-78-08-22 **FAX** 01-40-59-03-06 **EMAIL** info@alizeparis.com
   INTERNET www.hotelbeaugralize.com
FACILITIES & SERVICES Air-conditioning, direct-dial phone, elevator, hair dryer, laundry service, minibar, trouser press, TV with international reception, room safe (3.50€ per day), WiFi
RATES Single 88–110€, double 89–115€; extra bed 33€; *taxe de séjour* included
   CREDIT CARDS AE, DC, MC, V
BREAKFAST Buffet 11€ per person

HÔTEL BEAUGRENELLE ST-CHARLES ★★ (4)
82, rue St-Charles, at place St-Charles, 75015
Métro: Charles-Michels, Dupleix
51 rooms, all with shower or bath and toilet

This hotel is just as unassuming as its neighborhood, which offers a comfortable look at what everyday life is really all about in Paris, outside of the glittery and artsy *quartiers* that draw most visitors. You can spot the hotel from the place St-Charles . . . just look for the red awning and the boxwood bushes framing the entry. The lobby has Art Deco–style leather loveseats and armchairs. A modern breakfast room with black laminated tables and chairs is set apart by a bank of green plants. A glassed-in walkway joins the two buildings that make up the fifty-one-room hotel.

Several ground-floor rooms open onto the garden, and these are some of the best. Three rooms on the sixth floor have balconies and Eiffel Tower views, and one on the back, a single, also has a peek of the Eiffel Tower. All the rooms are small, especially the doubles with a shower, but decent closet space rescues them from feeling too cramped. Light, pastel-colored fabrics and blond furniture lend a modern touch. Peace and quiet prevails at night, as the neighborhood shuts down about 9 or 10 P.M.

NOTE: One of the best Monoprix stores in Paris is right around the corner. See page 362 for a description of this Parisian version of Wal-Mart, Target, and a huge supermarket all rolled into one. Also under same ownership is the nearby Hôtel Alizé Grenelle Tour Eiffel (see page 239).

TEL 01-45-78-61-63 **FAX** 01-45-79-04-38 **EMAIL** info@beaugrenelleparis.com
   INTERNET www.hotelbeaugralize.com
FACILITIES & SERVICES Air-conditioning, direct-dial phone, elevator (to most
   floors), hair dryer, laundry service, minibar, small pets allowed (but not
   left alone in rooms), some trouser presses, TV with international reception,
   room safe (3.50€ per day), WiFi
RATES Single 83–104€, double 84–111€; extra bed 33€; children under 12
   free; pets free; *taxe de séjour* included **CREDIT CARDS** AE, MC, V
BREAKFAST Buffet 11€ per person

HÔTEL DE L'AVRE ★★ (8)
21, rue de l'Avre, 75015
Métro: La Motte Piquet–Grenelle, Avenue Émile-Zola
26 rooms, all with shower or bath and toilet

If you don't require much space and don't mind being somewhat in the boonies, then Bernard Vialette's twenty-six-room Hôtel de l'Avre is a well-priced Great Sleep. The hotel is wrapped around a flowering spring and summer garden, where tables and umbrellas are set out for guests to enjoy breakfast or to relax from the rigors of sight-seeing. The garden-theme rooms are simple, yet a far cry from the standard-issue two-star. Framed prints of herbs and flowers add interest, and primary colors and striped fabrics keep rooms bright and cheerful. Closets are geared for short stays, and bathrooms for fast in-and-out use. Nine overlook the garden (which is at its best in warmer weather); another faces a day-care center. The largest rooms face the street, but this is a residential area, so quiet prevails after the sun sets. Good restaurants are nearby, and one of the biggest and most colorful roving street *marchés* sets up stalls only a block away on boulevard de Grenelle every Wednesday and Sunday morning.

TEL 01-45-75-31-03 **FAX** 01-45-75-63-26 **EMAIL** hotel.delavre@wanadoo.fr
   INTERNET www.hoteldelavre.com
FACILITIES & SERVICES Direct-dial phone, elevator, fans, hair dryer, TV with
   international reception, office safe (no charge), 20 nonsmoking rooms, free
   WiFi

RATES Single 69–79€, double 79–87€, double garden room 90€, garden 114€; extra bed 22€; children under 8 free; *taxe de séj*

CREDIT CARDS AE, DC, MC, V

BREAKFAST Continental 8 € per person

MERCURE PARIS SAINT CHARLES ★★ (5)
37, rue St-Charles, at 36, rue Rouelle, 75015
Métro: Dupleix, Charles-Michels

30 rooms, all with shower or bath and toilet

This hotel belongs to Mercure, which is a mid-priced division of Accor, the largest hotel group in the world. This hotel affiliation resulted in a new facade, new decor, new mattresses, some new bathrooms, special rates for those over fifty-five and two-for-one offers. One important thing has not changed: the warm hospitality that owner Claire Fournerie extends to all her guests. To some, the location might be considered a tourist backwater; for others, it represents a change of pace and is a safe bet for those insisting on peace in noisy Paris. I like it not only because it is well maintained and executed but because it offers a vantage on a calmer day-to-day Parisian life. In the place St-Charles, old men sit quietly under the shade of the chestnut trees reading their newspapers and talking about old times. Pretty young girls with long ribbons and smocked dresses roller-skate along the sidewalks, and matrons walk their little dogs. Hurrying housewives carry brimming shopping baskets from shop to shop picking just the right ingredients for their evening meal. For trips away from the hotel, the métro stop is only a five-minute walk, and the RER Line C to Versailles is close to the Eiffel Tower, both of which are about a fifteen-minute walk if you windowshop along the way.

The hotel is done simply but with good taste and style. Each floor is coordinated in a different color: blue, pink, or yellow. The concise, spotless rooms have country-style, pine built-in furniture and matching draperies and bedspreads. The book-theme lobby overlooks a small garden, which is especially inviting in the spring and summer. Be sure to examine the framed needlepoints hanging here. If you look carefully, you will see one done by every member of the family. One dating from 1907 was made by Mme. Fournerie's grandmother when she was a little girl. Another by the fireplace was done by her brother-in-law, and her son, Vincent, stitched the one hanging by the door when he was eight.

Mme. Fournerie always takes a personal interest in her guests and their well-being, and she would like to know when guests find her through *Great Sleeps Paris,* so please tell her you did.

NOTE: The café/bar/rotisserie/brasserie next door is also owned by Claire and her husband, Martial. They are open all day, weekdays only, but drop in between noon and 2 P.M. for a typical working-class lunch and order the daily special; dinner is served from 7:30 to 10 P.M.

TEL 01-45-79-64-15 **FAX** 01-45-77-21-11 **EMAIL** H1928@accorhotels.com
INTERNET www.accorhotels.com

FACILITIES & SERVICES Air-conditioning, bar (next door), direct-dial phone, elevator, hair dryer, laundry service, minibar, TV with international reception, no safe, free WiFi

RATES Single 87–110€, double 107–131€; extra bed 31€; children under 12 free; seniors pay for a single and are upgraded to a double, and get two breakfasts for the price of one; *taxe de séjour* included **CREDIT CARDS** AE, DC, MC, V

BREAKFAST Buffet 10.50€ per person

PRACTIC HÔTEL (NO STARS, ¢, 10)
20, rue de l'Ingénieur Robert Keller, 75015
Métro: Charles-Michels; RER Javel–André Citroën
38 rooms, 27 with shower or bath and toilet

For a cheap bed in the fifteenth arrondissement, the Practic Hôtel, just behind the Centre Beaugrenelle shopping complex, attracts a loyal band of regulars who are looking to cut accommodation corners in order to enjoy other aspects of their stay in Paris. While it's definitely not a candidate for those who revel in Louis XV or Madame Pompadour surroundings, the hotel displays few of those depressing, exhausted, faded, and snagged interiors that plague many other budget addresses in Paris. You will be welcomed by one of the sweetest receptionists this side of heaven, Mme. Bihan, who has been behind the desk since 1962. The owner of the hotel is Agnes Pouloux, who took over the reigns from her parents and grandparents, who built the hotel. With help and encouragement from her husband, she is slowly improving the hotel by adding bathrooms and following a regular schedule of maintenance.

The entry definitely needs a new look: it's done in dull brown with industrial-strength carpeting, with a vase of flowers and old prints of Paris scattered around. But you don't live in the entry, so just keep going. I am a fan of No. 66, a twin on the back with a corner glass-enclosed shower in a blue-and-beige marble-tiled bathroom. Room 57, coordinated in yellow and blue with a stall shower, sleeps one. Number 59 is a two-room suite (don't forget we are in a no-star here) with blond furniture. One room has twin beds, the other just one twin. The bathroom comes with soap and shampoo and shower doors. What a deal! Eight rooms have courtyard views, but they are not too bad. Breakfast is served in a blue-and-white first-floor dining room and includes cheese, fruit compote, juice, croissants, and bread and jam—an unheard-of spread for a no-star hotel.

NOTE: Great Sleeps Paris readers can get 10 percent off room rates. Shoppers will want to know that one of the best Monoprix stores in Paris is nearby (see page 362).

TEL 01-45-77-70-58 **FAX** 01-40-59-43-75 **EMAIL** hotel.practic.hotel.15E@wanadoo.fr **INTERNET** www.practichotel.fr

FACILITIES & SERVICES Direct-dial phone, elevator, hair dryer available, French TV no safe

RATES 1–2 persons 75€, twin beds 95€, 3–4 persons in the suite 120–140€; extra bed 20€; free public showers; 10% discount for *Great Sleeps Readers*; *taxe de séjour* included **CREDIT CARDS** AE, MC, V

BREAKFAST Continental 8€ per person

Sixteenth Arrondissement

Known as a sedate, posh, and old-moneyed sector, the sixteenth is the home of the BCBG (*bon chic bon genre*) crowd, otherwise known as French yuppies. This is stylish territory, bordered by the Bois de Boulogne and the Seine. Here you will see luxurious apartments along with prostitutes in BMWs on the avenue Foch and at night in the Bois de Boulogne. The Bois de Boulogne has two thousand acres of lakes, gardens, two racetracks, and the Jardin d'Acclimatation, a children's amusement park. Fashionable shops line the unhurried and uncrowded rue de Passy and the avenue Victor-Hugo. The Trocadéro, directly across from the Seine and the Eiffel Tower, is the name

RIGHT BANK
Avenue Foch
Bois de Boulogne
Jardin d'Acclimatation
Maison de Balzac
Marmottan Museum
Musée Guimet
Palais de Chaillot
Passy
Trocadéro

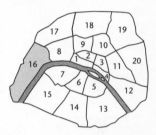

for the gardens around the Palais de Chaillot, an imposing two-winged building that houses four museums. The spectacular view from the steps of the Trocadéro at night, across the Seine to the Eiffel Tower, with the illuminated pools, fountains, and statues between, is one you must not miss. Neither do you want to miss the Marmottan Museum, which houses a magnificent display of Claude Monet's water lily canvases; the Guimet, which has a collection of Asian art; or the Maison de Balzac, the home where Honoré de Balzac lived and worked.

Sixteenth Arrondissement

BOIS

DE

BOULOGNE

Allée de Longchamp

Route

Porte de la Muette

PL. DE COLOMBIE

CARREFOUR DES CASCADES

Boulevard Suchet

Avenue Raphaël

Av. de Ingres

Bd. de Rue

Rue de

Jasmin

R. Jasmin

HIPPODROME D'AUTEUIL

Boulevard Suchet de Montmorency

Bd.

Av. Mozart

Porte d'Auteuil

Avenue de la Porte d'Auteuil

Boulevard

Rue du Château

Avenue Robert Schuman

PARC DES PRINCES

R. C. Farrère

Porte Molitor

d'Auteuil

PL. DE LA PORTE DE D'AUTEUIL

Ⓜ Porte d'Auteuil

Rue d'Auteuil

Ⓜ Michel Ange Auteuil

Église Ⓜ d'Auteuil

Murat

Michel Ange Molitor

Boulevard

Bd. de

Rue Ⓜ Molitor

Michel Ange

Chardon Lagache

Chardon Lagache Ⓜ

Exelmans Ⓜ Exelmans

Rue de

Chardon

Rue de

Versailles

Avenue de

Ⓜ *Métro Station*
● *R.E.R. Station*
500 meters

N

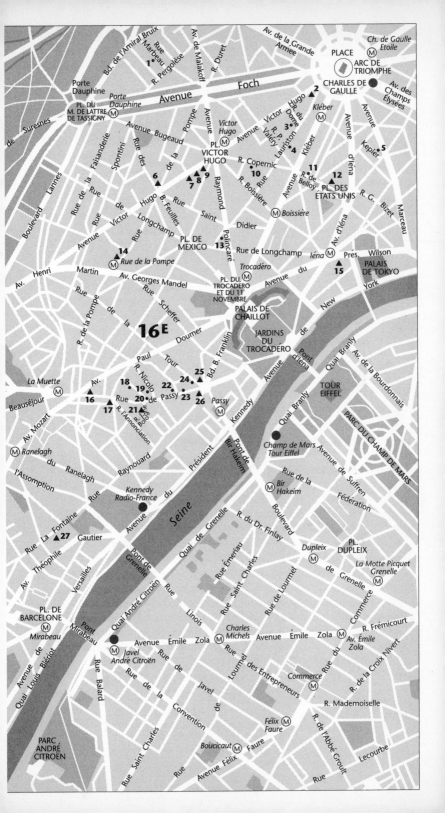

HOTELS IN THE SIXTEENTH ARRONDISSEMENT

OTHER OPTIONS
Camping Out

($) indicates a Big Splurge

BEST WESTERN CHAMPS-ÉLYSÉES ★★★ ($, 4)
51, rue Lauriston, 75016
Métro: Kléber; RER Charles-de-Gaulle-Étoile
46 rooms, all with shower or bath and toilet

The Best Western Champs-Élysées pampers its guests with cleverly laid out rooms and all the electronics you could want, including voice mail, WiFi, and pay-per-view TV with twenty-two channels. The themed, tissue-covered rooms use stripes in various combinations on the baldaquin framing the bed headboards, on the upholstery, and on the tie-back curtains. There is a second maid service in the evenings for bed turndowns and a change of towels. Marble bathrooms have magnifying mirrors, deep tubs, fluffy towels, terrycloth bathrobes, and shelf space. The mirrored, garden breakfast room is noteworthy for its glass ceiling and beautiful silver serving pieces. Beautiful floral arrangements here and in the black-and-white lobby add needed color accents. The location is ideal for anyone going to conferences or trade shows at the Palais des Congrès, or who wants to sample life in a high bourgeoise French neighborhood.

TEL 01-56-26-59-29; toll-free in U.S. and Canada 800-528-1234 (Best Western) **FAX** 01-47-55-81-69 **EMAIL** foch.elysees@wanadoo.fr **INTERNET** www.elysees-foch.com

FACILITIES & SERVICES Air-conditioning, bar, direct-dial phone with voice mail, elevator to half floors in front building, no elevator in second building (3 floors), hair dryer, laundry service, robes, porter, room safe (no charge), TV with international reception and pay-per-view, 10 nonsmoking rooms, WiFi

RATES Single 195€, double 210€, duplex 250€; *taxe de séjour* 1€ per person, per day **CREDIT CARDS** AE, DC, MC,V

BREAKFAST Buffet 14€ per person

HÔTEL AU PALAIS DE CHAILLOT ★★ (13)
35, avenue Raymond Poincaré, 75116
Métro: Trocadéro, Victor-Hugo
28 rooms, all with shower or bath and toilet

For up-to-the-minute appeal in an area not known for budget anything, look no further than Cyrille Penn's hotel, which is nicely situated between the Trocadéro and the Champs-Élysées. The front desk is usually a beehive of activity, with the overworked, multilingual manager trying to do five things at once, resulting in high anxiety for all concerned. However, if you can live with this frenzied approach to customer service, it will be hard to find a better value in the area. The prices are impressive, especially for readers of *Great Sleeps Paris* who, upon mentioning this book, receive a 10 percent discount throughout the year on any Saturday or Sunday, and a whopping 15 percent anytime between July 15 and August 31. Reserve now, and don't forget to say who sent you!

From beginning to end, the hotel is a model of casual French 1930s chic. Two potted trees frame the red awning entrance. To one side is a little summer terrace where breakfast and drinks can be served; otherwise, breakfast takes place in a yellow marbleized room with a half-mirrored wall reflecting five tables and armchairs. The bright bedrooms combine wicker with bold colors and have flashy bathrooms that include tubs and/or showers with corner shelves for shampoo and soap. All doubles face the street. There are five rooms similar in size to No. 34, a junior suite on the back. I like the walk-in closet, the small sitting area with red detailing around the ceiling, and the Dufy print over the bed. These rooms also have twin beds that can be adapted to a king. For the area, it is almost impossible to imagine a better value.

TEL 01-53-70-09-09 **FAX** 01-53-70-09-08 **EMAIL** palaisdechaillot-hotel@ magic.fr **INTERNET** www.palaisdechaillot-hotel.com

FACILITIES & SERVICES Direct-dial phone, elevator (to half landings; a few stairs required), fans in suites, hair dryer, private parking (16€ per day, reserve in advance), room service for drinks, TV with international reception, room safe (no charge)

RATES Single 105€, double 120€, junior suite for 1–3 people 140€; extra bed 20€; children under 5 free; discounts for readers of this guide; *taxe de séjour* 0.68€ per person, per day **CREDIT CARDS** AE, DC, MC, V

BREAKFAST Continental 9€ per person

HÔTEL CHAMBELLAN MORGANE ★★★ (5)
6, rue Kepler, 75116
Métro: George-V; RER Charles-de-Gaulle-Étoile
20 rooms, all with shower or bath and toilet

In 1984, when I began writing my Paris hotel guide, I fell in love with a little hotel in the sixteenth arrondissement called Résidence Morgane. It was run by a petite *grand-mère* who pampered her guests beyond the call of duty. She would make an omelet at midnight, keep your messages, forward your mail, and do your laundry and ironing if asked. When I returned a year later, Madame had left and the hotel had been taken over by a noncaring owner. Five years later, on a hunch, I decided to recheck the hotel, and I am so glad I did. Although Madame had not come back, new owners had masterminded a renovation that turned the hotel into the epitome of three-star elegance and classic luxury. Things have not changed since: the owner and her staff still do their utmost to please their international clientele.

The stage is set by the entrance and lobby, done in yellow and blue with white enamel woodwork and beautifully upholstered Louis XV–style antiques. The only holdover from the past is the old, copper Morgane nameplate by the front doorstep. Well-lighted halls lead to stylishly outfitted bedrooms with silk wall coverings, matching quilted spreads and curtains, a comfortable chair, and efficient mirrored and marbled bathrooms. Light snacks are served in the bar. Lower rates in July and August and on weekends, subject to availability, make this more attractive to a wider audience.

TEL 01-47-20-35-72 **FAX** 01-47-20-95-69 **EMAIL** chambellan.morgane@wanadoo.fr **INTERNET** www.hotel-paris-morgane.com

FACILITIES & SERVICES Air-conditioning, bar serving light snacks, conference room, direct-dial phone, elevator, hair dryer, laundry service, minibar, room service, TV with international reception, office safe (no charge), several nonsmoking rooms, WiFi

RATES 1–2 persons 158–174€; *taxe de séjour* 1€ per person, per day
  CREDIT CARDS AE, DC, MC, V
BREAKFAST Buffet 12€ per person

HÔTEL DE SÉVIGNÉ ★★★ (11)
6, rue de Belloy, 75116
Métro: Bossière, Kléber
30 rooms, all with shower or bath and toilet

"My sole occupation is the immense joy of receiving you into my home." These words, written by the Marquise de Sévigné in a letter to her daughter on February 5, 1674, echo the welcome extended today by the owner of this hotel, Mme. Boileau, and her professionally trained staff.

Who was the Marquise de Sévigné? Marie de Rabutin-Chantal, Marquise de Sévigné (1626–1696), was a prolific letter writer who shed light on the political, social, and literary aristocratic life of high society and the nobility of the seventeenth century during the reign of Louis XIV. Orphaned at an early age, she was educated by her grandmother, who began a convent in Paris. The street, rue de Belloy, was on the edge of the convent's fields. Madame de Sévigné lived an elegant life in castles around France, but from 1677 to 1696, when she was in Paris, she held court in her town house, the Hôtel Carnavalet near the place des Vosges. The building is now a fascinating museum dedicated to the history of Paris from pre-Roman times to the present. Mme. Sévigné's desk and some of her letters are on display at the museum.

The hotel is an excellent three-star value and loaded with extras. The five floors of the hotel are named after people and places of significance in Madame Sévigné's life. The first floor is named after her husband's castle, Les Rochers; the second, Carnavalet, her home in Paris; third, Bourbilly, her grandmother's castle; fourth, Le Comte Roger Bussy-Rabutin, her cousin; and the fifth, Le Château de Grignan, her daughter's castle where Madame died. All thirty rooms are designed to cater to the comfort and well-being of their guests. In each you will find a large desk with both fax and computer connections, balconies on the second and fifth floors, plenty of closet and luggage space, and bathrooms with magnifying mirrors, space for toiletries, and good lighting. The rooms designated *chambres de charme* have all the above plus newer furnishings and a richer color scheme. The hotel is across from the place des États-Unis, a quiet green square only a few minutes from all the pomp and circumstance awaiting you along the Champs-Élysées. Also occupying this prestigious *place* is Baccarat, a magnificent showcase for their reknowned crystal. Aside from visiting the glorious showrooms, don't miss the Philippe Starck–designed restaurant and the unusual ladies room.

TEL 01-47-20-88-90 **FAX** 01-40-70-98-73 **EMAIL** hotel.de.sevigne@wanadoo.fr
   INTERNET www.hotel-sevigne.fr
FACILITIES & SERVICES Air-conditioning, direct-dial phones in rooms and
   bathrooms, elevator, hair dryer, Internet in lobby, laundry service, minibar,
   parking (27€ per day, reserve ahead), TV with international reception and
   pay-per-view channels, room service for light snacks, room safe (no charge),
   1st floor entirely nonsmoking
RATES Single 127–137€, superior for 1–2 persons 148–159€, superior twin
   170€; extra bed 37€; *taxe de séjour* included **CREDIT CARDS** AE, DC, MC, V
BREAKFAST Continental 12€ per person

HÔTEL DU BOIS ★★★ (3)
11, rue du Dome, at 29, avenue Victor-Hugo, 75116
Métro: Kléber; RER Charles-de-Gaulle-Étoile
41 rooms, all with shower or bath and toilet

For a stay on the exclusive avenue Victor-Hugo, just ten boutiques down from the Arc de Triomphe, and a direct RER line to Disneyland Paris from place d'Étoile, many consider the Hôtel du Bois to be a reasonable choice. The entrance to the hotel is in a passageway reached either by steep steps from the avenue Victor Hugo level or on an upper level from rue Lauriston. You will recognize the hotel by the pretty planter boxes under each window. The hotel has been shined, polished, and redone with coordinating rich red floral and checked fabrics, mahogany furniture, and a framed Hôtel du Bois poster and a watercolor painting. The reception and breakfast areas have been refitted, and in the rooms, all the old bathrooms have received quickie facelifts composed of enclosed showers, a shelf for toiletries, and a hook on the back of the door. Rates are reasonable for this high-rent area, and the best choices are the superiors with a bath and shower that face rue du Dome. The standard rooms with a shower are on the back side of both floors of the hotel, and they look onto an ugly, depressing, blank gray wall; those on avenue Victor Hugo will experience some noise. The bottom line: This makes an affordable choice in an otherwise expensive neighborhood, but choose your room carefully.

TEL 01-45-00-31-96 **FAX** 01-45-00-90-05 **EMAIL** reservations@hoteldubois.com
INTERNET www.hoteldubois.com
FACILITIES & SERVICES Direct-dial phone, no elevator (2 floors), fans, hair dryer, minibar, TV with international reception and pay-per-view channels, room safe (no charge), WiFi
RATES 1–2 persons: small room 120€, standard 145€, superior 175€, prestige 225€; extra bed 70€; *taxe de séjour* included **CREDIT CARDS** AE, DC, MC, V
BREAKFAST Buffet 14€ per person

HÔTEL GAVARNI ★★★ (22)
5, rue Gavarni, 75116
Métro: Passy
21 rooms and 4 suites, all with shower or bath and toilet

The Hôtel Gavarni is a textbook example of what an owner with an unlimited budget can do if given the opportunity. The result of a year of hard work and an unimaginable amount of money is this boutique hotel, offering guests a sanctuary of privacy, discretion, and tranquillity in twenty-one rooms and four suites. Guests are first greeted by a dramatic entry mirror, which is composed of nine squares in a floral pattern. Frosted-glass doors lead to the breakfast room, which continues the floral theme on five glass-top tables facing a mirrored buffet and a small garden and veranda beyond. This pretty *bijou* setting is accented by a large canvas of fruits and leaves painted in bold orange, yellow, and burgundy. The reception desk is backed by four large, amusing paintings of ladies who lunch. The hotel and street it is on are named after Gavarni, a nineteenth-century critic and lithographer. Hanging on each floor are one or two of his original signed and numbered lithographs.

The amenities in the suites rival those you would expect to find in a much more expensive property. From the queen-size bed, you can stretch out and watch the enormous plasma television set, which has an LCD screen and DVD player. There is also a remote control panel with which guests can operate all the electrical components of the suite with a flick of a switch or turn of a dial. The Eiffel Suite has a stained-glass ceiling and crystal chandelier in the entryway, which leads to a sitting area with a pair of closets flanking a marble fireplace. The walls and ceiling are hand-detailed; the paintings and prints are of this famous landmark. The views of the Eiffel Tower and the rooftops of Paris are

through windows or from chairs on the balcony. Other suites
the Trocadéro and Vendôme, both junior suites with a courtyard vi...
and Versailles, which can be joined with the deluxe Trianon room to
form a two-room suite. Not everyone is going to check into one of these
suites, but the services and high-quality surroundings continue in the
deluxe and superior rooms, which are personalized and customized
right down to the soap and the matchboxes. Depending on size
and location, many have marble fireplaces, granite bathroom sinks,
draped beds, crystal lights, hand-painted ceilings, large television sets,
and all the necessary technical hookups to stay connected.

TEL 01-45-24-52-82 **FAX** 01-40-50-16-95 **EMAIL** reservation@gavarni.com
INTERNET www.gavarni.com

FACILITIES & SERVICES Air-conditioning, bar, conference room, direct-dial
phone, fax in suites, elevator (to half landings; a few stairs required), hair
dryer, Jacuzzis in suites, laundry service, minibar, room service, TV with
international reception, room safe (no charge), some nonsmoking rooms,
WiFi

RATES Standard single 99–125€, superior (1–2 persons) 145–180€, suites (1–4
persons) 245–340€; *taxe de séjour* included **CREDIT CARDS** AE, DC, MC, V

BREAKFAST Buffet 10€ per person

HÔTEL NICOLO ★★ (19)
3, rue Nicolo, 75116
Métro: Passy, La Muette
28 rooms, all with shower or bath and toilet

Join diplomats visiting the nearby embassies, delegates to the
European Organization for Economic Cooperation and Development,
and other knowledgable travelers by staying at the hidden Hôtel
Nicolo in the center of Passy. Because the hotel is set back off the
street, your room will be blissfully free from the usual symphony
of Parisian street noises. Now, it is even more alluring because the
farsighted owner swept out the funky furnishings, flocked wallpaper,
dated colors, and woebegone bathrooms. He also added a pretty, plant-
filled garden gazebo where guests are invited to sit on warm days. The
results—and the prices—can be summed up in one word: Wow!

The mood suggests the Far East, particularly Indonesia. Check
into No. 5, where the bed is backed by an antique Balinese screen and
the wall is decorated by a colorful parrot print. Green and soft beige
fabrics blend well with the overall Asian feeling in this room. In addition to a chest of drawers, a comfortable armchair, and excellent work
space, you will have a fabulous new bathroom with double sinks and
an Indonesian hand-painted floral frame around the mirror. The Art
Deco Suite, No. 21, sleeps four and is done in yellow with a collection
of parrot prints decorating the walls. A sunken oval bathtub is the
highlight of the lovely bathroom, which also has a colorful painted
Indonesian frame around the mirror. Another two-room suite, No.
32, has a sitting room with a blue leather sofa and armchair and an
antique Indonesian desk. The room overlooks the quiet courtyard,

which is shaded in the spring and summer by a leafy green tree. Red-hot-red is the color of choice in the dramatic No. 11, which has a desk with brass pulls; black, red, and white prints of French villages; and a marvelous tub in the bathroom. Red is also the color of the ornate headboard in No. 24, which has a large framed poster portrait of Brad Pitt, who shares wall space with five yellow birds and two moose prints. Go figure!

TEL 01-42-88-83-40 **FAX** 01-42-24-45-41 **EMAIL** hotel.nicolo@wanadoo.fr
  INTERNET www.123france.com
FACILITIES & SERVICES Direct-dial phone, elevator stops between floors, ceiling fans, hair dryer, private parking (18€ per day, advance reservation only), TV with international reception, room safe (no charge)
RATES Single 117€, double 123–175€, triple 193€, quad 203€; *taxe de séjour* included **CREDIT CARDS** AE, DC, MC, V
BREAKFAST Included

HÔTEL PASSY EIFFEL ★★★ (23)
10, rue de Passy, 75116
Métro: Passy, La Muette
49 rooms, all with shower or bath and toilet

The Hôtel Passy Eiffel, on the main street in Passy, provides a firsthand look at one of Paris's most exclusive neighborhoods, which has some of the best shopping you can find. The hotel's marble-lined foyer and lobby open onto a glassed-in winter garden with six rooms facing it. To one side is the sitting area with a comfortable sofa and small bar. On the other is the breakfast room, where a buffet is served every morning. Wood-beam ceilings add a sense of dimension to the variety of rooms, which are tasteful, clean, and very comfortable with pleasing views. Ten bathrooms boast showers with massage jets. I think Nos. 1, 2, and 7 on the ground floor are very nice. They are viewless but are large enough that you won't feel closed in. Number 57 is a large twin on the back with a big bathroom and lots of space. If you are traveling solo, No. 61, also on the back, has good space, but for a view, balcony, bathtub, and more light, request No. 54. From other top-floor rooms facing rue de Passy, guests can watch the elevator scale the Eiffel Tower as it takes tourists to the top. For breakfast, be sure to sample some of the honey bottled directly from the owner's beehives.

TEL 01-45-25-55-66 **FAX** 01-42-88-89-88 **EMAIL** contact@passyeiffel.com
  INTERNET www.passyeiffel.com
FACILITIES & SERVICES Air-conditioning, bar, direct-dial phone, elevator (to most floors), hair dryer, minibar, TV with international reception, office safe (no charge)
RATES Single 145€, double 155€, triple 175€, suite 225€; *taxe de séjour* included **CREDIT CARDS** AE, DC, MC, V
BREAKFAST Buffet 12€ per person

HÔTEL REGINA DE PASSY ★★★ (24)
6, rue de la Tour, 75116
Métro: Passy
64 rooms, all with shower or bath and toilet

Built in 1930 for the International Exhibition, this hotel is high on the Right Bank of the Seine across from the Eiffel Tower. The almost-grand lobby has a staircase framed by signed stained-glass windows. However, I don't like the public bathroom off the lobby: How dated are swinging louvered bar doors to divide the men's and the women's rooms? Fortunately the hotel rooms have been restyled over time, and they are generally large with geometric prints, chrome-and-leather furniture, and modern bathrooms. Closet and living space is ample. One penthouse apartment and a junior suite, both with private rooftop terraces, boast impressive furnishings, marble bathrooms (one with a sunken tub), small bars, fully equipped kitchens, and enough wardrobe space for most of us to unpack and stay a year. Staff attitude has improved 100 percent.

TEL 01-55-74-75-75 **FAX** 01-40-50-70-62, 01-45-25-23-78
　　EMAIL regina@gofornet.com **INTERNET** www.hotel-paris-passy.com
FACILITIES & SERVICES Air-conditioning, bar, direct-dial phone, elevator, hair
　　dryer, laundry service, minibar, TV with international reception and pay-
　　per-view, room safe (no charge), WiFi
RATES Single 98€, double 135–155€, apartment 192–290€; extra bed 58€;
　　taxe de séjour included **CREDIT CARDS** AE, MC, V
BREAKFAST Buffet 15€, in-room Continental 11€, per person

HÔTEL RÉSIDENCE FOCH ★★★ (1)
10, rue Marbeau, 75116
Métro: Porte Dauphine; RER Porte Maillot, *sortie* (exit) rue Malakoff
25 rooms, all with shower or bath and toilet

This hotel is on a quiet little street in one of Paris's most sought-after residential districts, not too far from Porte Maillot and the Palais de Congrès. It is run by the lovely Nelly Rolland, former owner of the Hôtel Gavarni (see page 250). Nelly is a graduate of the hotel management school in Lausanne, Switzerland, and she is young and full of life and new ideas. Her charm and innate sense of style are evident the minute you meet her, and it is clear they have carried over into her second hotel. The reception, lobby, and bar areas have an open plan layout looking onto a well-tended atrium garden. If your workout routine includes the stairmaster, substitute the stairs here and enjoy a different stained-glass artwork on each level and the hand-painted floral detail along the bright Provençal yellow hallways.

The rooms have character, thanks to decorative color combinations of golden orange, soft green, Williamsburg blue, and white. The traditional furnishings and matching fabric treatments are interspersed with contemporary conveniences such as built-in minibars, good drawer and closet space, and tiled baths with plenty of towels. Some, including the smallest doubles, have tip-of-the-Eiffel-Tower views. All deluxe rooms have queen-size beds; a few have a balcony. I like No. 61 in soft gold tones with interesting neighborhood views from the windows and a hand-painted tiled bath. Blue-and-white Toile de Jouy surrounds guests in No. 71, and gold fish faucets in the bathroom add an exotic touch.

NOTE: At press time Mme. Rolland was in negotiation to buy another hotel. Knowing Nelly, it will be special indeed, so be sure to inquire.

TEL 01-45-00-46-50 **FAX** 01-45-01-98-68 **EMAIL** residence@foch.com
INTERNET www.residencefoch.com
FACILITIES & SERVICES Air-conditioning, bar, direct-dial phone, elevator (to half floor; some stairs required), hair dryer, iron and ironing board, laundry service, minibar, room service, tea & coffee makers, TV with international reception, room safe, (no charge), some nonsmoking rooms, free WiFi
RATES 1–2 persons: standard room 135–150€, deluxe room 160–180€, family room (1–4 persons) 170–250€; *taxe de séjour* included **CREDIT CARDS** AE, DC, MC, V
BREAKFAST Buffet 11€ per person

HÔTEL TROCADÉRO LA TOUR ★★★ (18)
5 bis, rue Massenet, 75116
Métro: Passy, La Muette
41 rooms, all with shower or bath and toilet

For a pleasant stay in Paris on a tranquil street in Passy, I like the formal Trocadéro La Tour, a family-owned hotel since the 1930s. The well-heeled French executive clientele appreciate the serene neighborhood close to the *bon ton* Passy shopping district; the professional services of the uniformed hotel staff—especially Thay, the courteous receptionist who has worked the desk for more than two decades—and, above all, the prices. These travelers know that if the hotel were in a more mainstream location, the prices would be nearly double.

Downstairs, the public rooms are paneled in rich walnut. Soft seating and a small library along one wall create an appealing English intimacy. Morning croissants are served on a year-around glass terrace that is heated in the winter and cooled in the summer. All the comfortable rooms are well furnished and impeccably maintained. Room 70, a corner double, has its own balcony looking out to the Eiffel Tower and La Tour Montparnasse; its walk-in closet is almost as large as some hotel rooms I have stayed in. If traveling alone, request No. 71, a top-floor single with an Eiffel Tower view terrace, or No. 51 with a small balcony, double closet with shelves, and a large bathroom. If quiet and space are top priorities, No. 25, a back sunny twin with two big windows, has a triple-drawer marble dresser, workable desk, three chairs, double luggage rack, and a bathroom with two sinks, a large tub, and oversize towels.

TEL 01-45-24-43-03 **FAX** 01-45-24-41-39 **EMAIL** trocadero-la-tour@magic.fr
INTERNET www.trocadero-la-tour.com
FACILITIES & SERVICES Air-conditioning, bar, 2 conference rooms, direct-dial

phone, elevator, hair dryer, laundry service, minibar, TV with international reception, room safe (no charge), 10 nonsmoking rooms, WiFi

RATES Single 139€, double 159€, triple 179€, junior suite 199€; extra bed 30€; baby bed free; *taxe de séjour* 1€ per person, per day
   CREDIT CARDS AE, DC, MC, V
BREAKFAST Continental 11€ per person

HÔTEL VICTOR HUGO ★★★ (10)
19, rue Copernic, 75116
Métro: Victor-Hugo, Boissière
75 rooms, all with shower or bath and toilet

This hotel has been a stalwart in the sixteenth arrondissement for years. For a long time, it seemed to be resting on its laurels and mired in the past. Not anymore, thanks to the vim, vigor, and vitality of the second generation, who have stepped up to the plate and now are in charge. Frankly, I hardly recognized the place: halls repainted and recarpeted and hung with paintings and art posters. The still spotless and spacious rooms have shed their matronly appearance, especially the fifteen on the sixth and seventh floors, which over-look the vast reservoir behind the hotel. Rooms 75 and 77 are good examples. Both are large doubles with a balcony, reservoir views, and big new bathrooms. Harmonious, pastel colors in cream and rose with lavender accents add to their peaceful ambience. For views of the Eiffel Tower, ask for No. 73, which has four windows and a granite bathroom. Still firmly in place is the very pretty garden breakfast room, with its flagstone floor and fruit-and-vegetable vendor cart, which is used for the buffet. Adding to the outdoor theme are the green lattice walls, Villeroy and Boch fruit-basket china, and Parisian poster–wrapped pillars that look just like those you see on all the city streets. An English club–style bar is lined with books by Victor Hugo and other great French writers. When I inquired about the fabulously kitschy carved Eiffel Tower light on the bar, I was told that *everyone* asks about it . . . and wants one, too. Sorry, this is a one-of-a-kind treasure the owner found in a flea market. Also still very much in evidence is the excellent staff, most of whom have been loyal employees for decades.

TEL 01-45-53-76-01; toll-free in U.S. and Canada (Best Western) 800-528-1234 **FAX** 01-45-53-69-93 **EMAIL** paris@victorhugohotel.com
   INTERNET www.victorhugohotel.com
FACILITIES & SERVICES Air-conditioning, bar, direct-dial phone, elevator, hair dryer, Jacuzzis in some superior rooms, laundry service, minibar, tea- and coffee-makers, robes and slippers in deluxe rooms, TV with international reception and pay-per-view, room safe (no charge), nonsmoking rooms on the 3rd and 7th floors and No. 82, WiFi
RATES Single 150–156€, double standard 170–177€, double superior 190–200€, double deluxe 238–250€, triple 201–214€, suite 330–361€; *taxe de séjour* included **CREDIT CARDS** AE, DC, MC, V
BREAKFAST Buffet 15€, in-room Continental 12€, per person

LE HAMEAU DE PASSY ★★ (20)
48, rue de Passy, 75116
Métro: Passy, La Muette
32 rooms, all with shower or bath and toilet

Sequestered in a garden walkway off the busy rue de Passy, Le Hameau de Passy is a snappy two-star in this posh pocket of Paris, owned by Marianne Daugreilh, a former English teacher, and her family. All the rooms face the garden and are done in the same style, with stark white walls, open closets, soft sheer curtains at the windows, and harmonizing fabrics and carpets. Bathrooms are spotless and offer either an enclosed shower or bathtub/shower combo for the same price. Ground-floor rooms in the three-story buildings have metal security shutters, but I still suggest asking for something on a higher floor. If you are lucky and land in Building 4 (or if you request it when reserving), the elevator takes the strain out of climbing up several flights to your room. Otherwise, in Buildings 1, 2, and 3, you will pay the same price and still have to hike up a winding outdoor metal stairway to get to your room. If this sort of exercise does not bother you, and you want to be only a whisper away from all the great shopping in Passy—including the designer discount and consignment clothing stores along rue de la Tour and rue de la Pompe (see page 332)—then consider this hotel.

TEL 01-42-88-47-55 **FAX** 01-42-30-83-72 **EMAIL** hameau.passy@wanadoo.fr
   INTERNET www.hameaudepassy.com
FACILITIES & SERVICES Direct-dial phone, dogs accepted, elevator (in one
   building only), hair dryer, TV with international reception, room safe (12€
   for entire stay), WiFi
RATES Single 120€, double 132–138€, triple 157€, quad 175€; extra bed for
   children under 10, 11€; dog 7€; *taxe de séjour* 0.78€ per day, per person
   CREDIT CARDS AE, DC, MC, V
BREAKFAST Continental included

Seventeenth Arrondissement

The better half of the seventeenth arrondissement extends west from boulevard Malesherbes to the Arc de Triomphe. To the east and toward Gare St-Lazare, the area is full of questionable characters dealing in the shadier side of life and residentially challenged local *clochards* (transients) relaxing in doorways, guzzling beer or cheap wine; this is the section to avoid. There are many fine hotels in the better section of the arrondissement, and the areas around them are safe. The main attractions are the proximity to

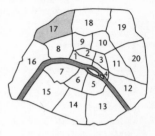

the Champs-Élysées and the Palais des Congrès, a convention center with restaurants, movie theaters, and the pickup and drop-off point for passengers going to and from Roissy–Charles-de-Gaulle Airport. There is also easy access to two RER lines—Line A to Disneyland-Paris and Line C to Versailles—as well as to excellent bus and métro connections to central Paris.

HOTELS IN THE SEVENTEENTH ARRONDISSEMENT

($) indicates a Big Splurge; (¢) indicates a Cheap Sleep

Seventeenth Arrondissement

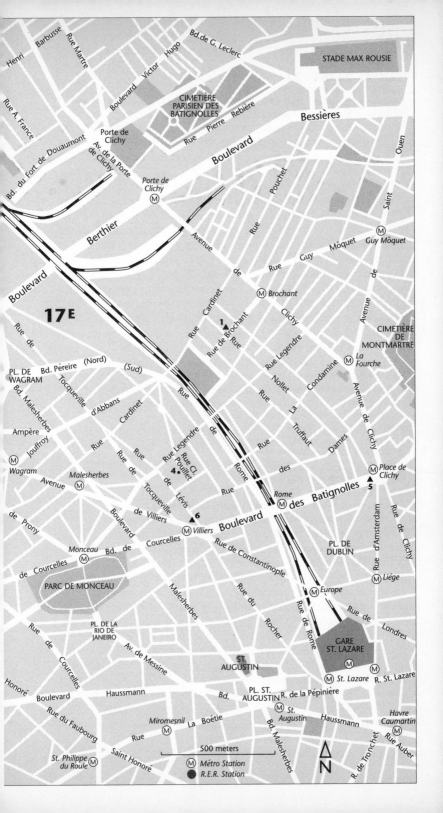

CENTRE VILLE ÉTOILE ★★★ (16)
6, rue des Acacias, 75017
Métro: Argentine; RER Charles-de-Gaulle-Étoile, Neuilly–Port Maillot–Palais des Congrès
16 rooms, all with shower or bath and toilet

Original, smart, and stylish are three words that well describe this Art Deco–inspired hotel close to the Arc de Triomphe and the Champs-Élysées. A three-story glass atrium joins the two buildings, which house only sixteen sleeping slots. An interesting collection of American cartoon prints enlivens the lobby and hallways. I also like the four Alsatian ceramic heaters that help keep the reception warm. The small masculine rooms, which haven't a ruffle in sight, display a judicious use of space and employ hard-edge colors of red, black, blue, and white along with black lacquered furnishings. Tiled and mirrored bathrooms are modern, with adequate shelf space and rolling carts for toiletries and stretch tubs for leisurely bathing. The personable staff goes beyond the call of duty in welcoming guests and pampering them in the evening by closing the curtains, turning down the beds, and putting a chocolate on the pillow. Nonsmokers will be happy to know there are five rooms exclusively reserved for them.

TEL 01-58-05-10-00 **FAX** 01-47-54-93-43 **EMAIL** hcv@centrevillehotels.com
   INTERNET www.centrevillehotels.com
FACILITIES & SERVICES Air-conditioning, direct-dial phone, elevator, hair dryer, laundry service, minibar, robes, TV with international reception, room safe (no charge), 5 nonsmoking rooms, WiFi
RATES Single 130€, double 145–165€; extra bed 25€; *taxe de séjour* 1€ per person, per day **CREDIT CARDS** AE, DC, MC, V
BREAKFAST Continental 11€ per person

HÔTEL ASTRID ★★★ (14)
27, avenue Carnot, 75017
Métro: Argentine; RER Charles-de-Gaulle-Étoile
41 rooms, all with shower or bath and toilet

Florence Guillet heads one of the best family-run hotels in Paris. Started by her grandfather in 1937, the Hôtel Astrid provides comfortable, moderately priced accommodations in this top-drawer part of the city. The colors throughout the hotel are cheerfully appropriate and blend well with the furnishings. All rooms face the street, and each floor has a theme: starting from the top, you have modern painters, then nature and birds, Paris bridges, Impressionists, and old Paris. Two of the nicest bedrooms have small balconies for viewing the Arc de Triomphe. The rooms are upgraded continually, and each one has its own individual ambience. In No. 7, a blue twin with brass beds and a marble fireplace, you have the luxury of a marble bathroom. I also like No. 25, which is done in pastels and has desk and luggage space, two chairs, and a double bed. The spotless bathroom has a stall shower, hooks, and a shelf for toiletries. Room 42, done in florals, and Room 36, a large family room for three, also come with a large tile-and-granite bathroom. I can't find fault with the layout in No. 21, but somehow the muddy brick-colored walls just don't mix well with the rose-colored headboard and dull beige bathroom. On the sixth floor, there are no bathtubs, only enclosed showers, which are excellent.

Finally, the hotel is only about a five-minute walk from the Air France bus stop for Roissy–Charles-de-Gaulle Airport, so if you're traveling light, you can save money on cab fare. Two RER stations are within a five-to-ten-minute walk.

TEL 01-44-09-26-00 **FAX** 01-44-09-26-01 **EMAIL** paris@hotel-astrid.com
   INTERNET www.hotel-astrid.com
FACILITIES & SERVICES Air-conditioning, bar, small conference room (seats
   6–8), direct-dial phone, elevator, hair dryer, laundry service, TV with
   international reception, room safe (no charge), entire hotel nonsmoking,
   WiFi
RATES Single 125€, double 145–158€, triple 175€, quad 186€; *taxe de séjour*
   included **CREDIT CARDS** AE, DC, MC, V
BREAKFAST Buffet 11€ per person

HÔTEL BALMORAL ★★★ (17)
6, rue du Général Lanrezac, off avenue Carnot, 75017
Métro: Argentine; RER Charles-de-Gaulle Étoile
57 rooms, all with shower, bath, and toilet

The Hôtel Balmoral is well located, well run, and well priced.

First, the location. It is a three-minute walk to the métro, RER Line A, and the Air France bus stop for Roissy–Charles-de-Gaulle Airport. You are only minutes away from the Champs-Élysées, boutique shopping along Victor Hugo, or great discount shopping on rue de la Pompe.

Next, guests immediately feel at home in the traditionally decorated rooms with their gracious period furnishings, old-fashioned comforts, wonderful bathrooms, and all the required modern amenities; several rooms are reserved for nonsmoking guests. Business guests will appreciate No. 29, a large double with adequate space to spread out papers, plug in a computer, and work comfortably. Standard twin and double rooms make good use of space and overlook an interior courtyard. If you like being surrounded by a rainbow of colors—that is, flaming pink, yellow-orange, and lavender—check into No. 14, a deluxe double with good closets, a quiet outlook, and a new double-sink bathroom. For more subdued surroundings, check into No. 12 on the front. This is a standard double with a built-in desk, a pair of ducks hanging over the bed, and a trio of floral prints brightening the other walls. Downstairs is a paneled breakfast room with leather hobnail chairs and a red bar with small alcove seating, which seems perfect for a quiet drink or a confidential conversation with someone special.

Finally, the price. This is an area full of three-star hotels that cost twice as much and offer half the comfort and value. The Balmoral wins on all three counts.

TEL 01-43-80-30-50 **FAX** 01-43-80-51-56 **EMAIL** hotel@hotelbalmoral.fr
   INTERNET www.hotel-balmoral.com

FACILITIES & SERVICES Air-conditioning, bar, direct-dial phone, elevator, hair dryer, laundry service, minibar, porter, trouser press, TV with international reception, room safe (no charge), WiFi
RATES Single 117–127€, double 142–157€, triple 167–182€; *taxe de séjour* included **CREDIT CARDS** AE, DC, MC, V
BREAKFAST Continental 10€ per person

HÔTEL BÉLIDOR ★ (¢, 7)
5, rue Bélidor, 75017
Métro: RER Neuilly–Port Maillot–Palais des Congrès
47 rooms, 33 with shower or bath and toilet

No serious economy-minded traveler in Paris can afford to overlook the Bélidor. A stay here provides you with a clean bed in a decent area just around the corner from the Palais des Congrès. It is an old-fashioned sort of hotel that has been in the same family over half a century. Their furniture fills the first of two breakfast rooms; it is the prettiest and is nonsmoking. In the second, there is a marble-and-brick fireplace and an upright piano, and you can smoke, but the ambience just isn't there. The owner is just as sweet as ever, the room colors and patterns are just as mixed, and all the electrical switch boxes are openly displayed over the radiator by the reception desk. The rooms are neat as pins, and those with bathtubs are larger than many two- and three-star rooms costing twice as much. However, if you book a bathless room, plan on sponge bathing because there is no communal *douche* (shower) in this hotel, but there is a WC on every landing. If you can live with this, then please don't let the orange chenille and nontouristy location deter you. After only a ten- or fifteen-minute métro journey, you can be standing under the pyramid at the Louvre, floating down the Seine on a *bateau mouche,* or strolling through the most romantic streets in St-Germain-des-Prés. It is crucial to remember to plan ahead for this one because it is booked weeks in advance all during the year.

NOTE: The RER station at Porte Maillot is enormous, so look for these directions in French for the correct exit: *sorti côté Paris, bd. Gouvion-Saint-Cyr côté impairs.* (In other words, exit on the Paris side of the métro station, on the odd-numbered side of boulevard Gouvion St-Cyr.)

TEL 01-45-74-49-91 **FAX** 01-45-72-54-22
FACILITIES & SERVICES Direct-dial phone, no elevator (5 floors), no communal showers, no TV, office safe (no charge)
RATES 1–2 persons 43–78€; *taxe de séjour* included **CREDIT CARDS** MC, V
BREAKFAST Continental 6€ per person

HÔTEL DE BANVILLE ★★★★ ($, 2)
166, boulevard Berthier, 75017
Métro: Porte-de-Champerret
38 rooms, all with shower or bath and toilet

The classic Hôtel de Banville is my idea of a wonderful, personalized Parisian hotel. It was built in 1928 by architect Jerome Bellat, who designed many of the magnificent buildings for which the seventeenth arrondissement is famous. From the beautiful lobby to the rooms filled with family antiques and heirlooms, you can tell immediately that this is a hotel where the owners know and care very much about what they are doing. The hotel has developed a large following of appreciative international guests who applaud the efforts of owner Mme. Lambert; her daughter, Marianne Lambert-Moreau, who now is at the helm; and their right-hand man, Jean-Pierre, who is also the talented artist who did many of the paintings on display in the hotel. Marianne Lambert-Moreau grew up in the hotel business, and all of her family is involved in the industry in some way. Her background and expertise, combined with her impeccable good taste, are evident everywhere you look. She once told me, "I want this hotel to be like a private house, and I think I have realized my wish." I agree without question, and so do the hotel's devoted guests.

Every time I visit the hotel, I think, this is it. What more can be done to improve on perfection? And each time I find wonderful new additions. On this visit, it was the redecorated reception area, which now has a wood-burning fireplace and a baby grand piano in the center of the marble floor and a teardrop chandelier hanging over it. Every Tuesday evening from 6:30 to 10 P.M., Marianne invites guests to join her around the piano and sing.

A lovely staircase and wide hallways lead to bright red enamel doors with gold fittings and the room number illuminated on the floor. The superior rooms, each with its own name and something outstanding and unique to recommend it, have some of the most beautiful bathrooms in Paris. If someone had told me before I saw these absolutely fabulous bathrooms that an open bathroom (with separate, enclosed toilets, of course) subtly incorporated into the main room itself would work, I would have had my doubts. I can assure you that they work magnificently . . . and I predict once you see these, you will be devising ways to remodel your own.

L'appartement de Marie is a suite aptly subtitled, "an invitation to dream." It is true. I cannot imagine a dream more romantic or wonderful that this fabulous two-room suite, with a wrought-iron canopy bed surrounded in soft, white gauze netting. The large, sunny sitting room, done in contemporary brick and beige colors, has a sweeping view from the Arc de Triomphe to the Tour Montparnasse. If the view does not capture your attention, the imaginative open bathroom surely will. Located within the suite—not behind closed doors—it features a double antique marble sink and huge bathtub, with an enclosed toilet to one side. Honeymooners should reserve the captivating *La Chambre d'Amélie,* where glass doors open onto a terrace filled with sunshine all day long. Seated in a comfortable chair, your vista includes Montmartre, the Eiffel Tower, Arc de Triomphe, Montparnasse, and more. In the open marble bathroom, you can float in the huge footed tub and see the Eiffel Tower. *Théodore de Banville* incorporates wood from country farms to separate the bedroom from its walk-through marble bathroom. Here you see the tip of the Eiffel Tower from your balcony and sleep in a bed covered with a snowy white quilt. *Pastourelle* and *Amélie* are superior rooms. It is impossible to select a favorite, but *Pastourelle,* with its red bathtub on legs, is very appealing. I also like the antique lamps, good desk space, and the red painted-wood backdrop behind the bed. Room 73 has a floral theme. It nicely sleeps three in quilt-covered beds and has a big blue-and-white bathroom with flower accents. Room 74, with an Eiffel Tower view, is a double with gold-trimmed white furnishings. The red-and-white-striped carpet and barely gray wall coverings keep it elegantly casual. For a modern approach to living, book No. 62, done in gray-and-blue stripes. The simple wood headboard matches the bedside tables and desk. The chrome-fitted bathroom has a floating sink, large glass-enclosed shower, and a mirrored black-and-white mosaic-tile bath. Even the smallest room in the hotel, *La Chambre de Julie,* is done with elegance and gentle charm. Even if you do not stay in one of the superior rooms, it would be impossible to be disappointed in any of the rooms or the quality of service and amenities offered in this outstanding hotel.

The hotel is located on a busy boulevard lined with plane trees. The métro is close, and you can take the RER to the Musée d'Orsay and St-Michel or to Versailles. For buses, the No. 92 puts you at Étoile, and the No. 84 drops you at place de la Concorde.

TEL 01-42-67-70-16 **FAX** 01-44-40-42-77 **EMAIL** info@hotelbanville.fr
  INTERNET www.hotelbanville.fr
FACILITIES & SERVICES Air-conditioning, piano-bar, two direct-dial phones
  per room, elevator (to most floors), hair dryer, laundry service, some
  robes and slippers, porter, 24-hour room service for light meals, TV with
  international reception, room safe (no charge), free WiFi in lobby, free
  high-speed Internet in rooms, some nonsmoking rooms
RATES Classic, single 175–205€, double 235€; superior (1–2 persons) 275€;
  suite, *L'Appartement de Marie* 335€; extra bed 20€; dog 5€; *taxe de séjour*
  included **CREDIT CARDS** AE, DC, MC, V
BREAKFAST Buffet 15€ per person

HÔTEL DES DEUX ACACIAS ★★ (12)
28, rue de l'Arc-de-Triomphe, 75017
Métro: Argentine; RER Charles-de-Gaulle-Étoile
31 rooms, all with shower or bath and toilet

Never mind its rather plain atmosphere—this choice will please bean counters wanting to stay within a budget and still be conveniently close to the Champs-Élysées and two convenient RER lines. The hotel is owned by members of the Roubache family, who have improved it gradually since taking over a few years ago from Mme. Delmas—who ran it for seventy years and resisted change with an iron-willed determination. In back of the reception desk you will notice a huge map of the Paris métro system that dates back to the time that Mme. Delmas's parents owned the hotel. Fortunately, the Roubaches kept it for posterity . . . if not for nostalgia.

No one could ever call this modest place modern, but it is improved in almost all respects. Upstairs, new paint, carpets, bedspreads, and redone bathrooms have perked up most of the rooms. Room 12, a frankly feminine roost, is done in soft yellow with a white metal and brass-tipped bed. Room 14 is in desert sand and has lots of closet and shelf space for the price, but it has an older bathroom. Room 18 is a very tight quad, and is better as a triple; it has a new bathroom. The prize for the best remake goes to No. 50, with blue-and-white Toile de Jouy patterned wall covering, white wicker furniture, and a marble sink in the bathroom. Winner of the worst room is No. 20, a double on the back that does have an ample bathroom and sweet, school-girl floral fabrics on the curtains and bed, but a drab view of air-conditioning ducts and tin rooftops. The least-expensive rooms are Nos. 52, 54, 56, and 58. These top-floor perches are not only cheap but sunny and cheerful, with no depressing views. Bathrooms are elfin, but at these rates you are lucky to have a shower and toilet to call your own. On my last visit the upholstery on the sofa in the sitting area adjoining the lobby had improved, and hopefully, the hall carpeting will soon be scheduled for renewal.

NOTE: Enclosed public parking is available across the street.

TEL 01-43-80-01-85 **FAX** 01-40-53-94-62 **EMAIL** hotelacacias@voila.fr
INTERNET www.2acacias.com
FACILITIES & SERVICES Direct-dial phone, elevator, hair dryer available, TV with international reception, office safe (no charge)
RATES 1–2 persons 95–105€, triple 125€, quad 155€; *taxe de séjour* 1€ per person, per day **CREDIT CARDS** AE, MC, V
BREAKFAST Continental 9€ per person, downstairs or in room

HÔTEL EBER MONCEAU ★★★ (9)
18, rue Léon-Jost, 75017
Métro: Courcelles
18 rooms, all with shower or bath and toilet

Travelers longing for peace and quiet have at their disposal a group of French hotels whose owners have taken a vow of silence. The Hôtel Eber Monceau is one of the 275 members of *Relais du Silence,* an association of individually owned hotels dedicated to providing a silent and calm atmosphere where guests can feel at home. The entrance is along a tiled walkway that opens onto a beamed salon centered around a Henri II carved wooden fireplace. To the left of the reception desk is an inviting bar and breakfast area with comfortable armchairs. In back is a green patio, where metal tables and chairs are set out on warm days for al fresco breakfasts.

The rooms tend to be small and are decorated in light beiges with good-looking American art prints and posters on the walls. The family rooms feature not only two rooms but two bathrooms. In Room 55, guests have a lovely terrace that's shaded by an awning in the summer. There is no view, but there is plenty of light . . . and of course, peace and quiet. Number 54, a two-level duplex, can sleep three, but

I think it is better for two. Downstairs there is a sitting room, upstairs a mezzanine bedroom with a sky light and a bathroom with a tub and shower. Many of the hotel's clientele are from the world of fashion and entertainment, not a group known for its introverted behavior. However, owner Jean-Marc Eber and his diligent manager, Martin Duprez, say that those who want nonstop excitement should stay in St-Germain-de-Prés.

You will need public transportation for most things on a tourist agenda, but it might be interesting to walk by 25, rue de Chazelles, about two blocks away, to see where the Statue of Liberty was originally built. A photo of it under construction hangs by the hotel elevator. Also on display around the hotel are photos of the statue in varying stages of development and the signatures of those who attended the completion ceremonies.

M. Eber now runs a second hotel, the Hôtel Eber Mars (see page 183), not far from the Eiffel Tower.

TEL 01-46-22-60-70 **FAX** 01-47-63-01-01 **EMAIL** reservation@ hotelebermonceau.com **INTERNET** www.hotelebermonceau.com

FACILITIES & SERVICES Air-conditioning, bar, direct-dial phone, elevator, hair dryer, laundry service, minibar, room service from area restaurants, TV with international reception, office safe (no charge)

RATES 1–2 persons 140–170€; junior suite (1–2 persons plus 2 children) 240€; duplex 1–2 persons 260€, with terrace 285€; extra bed 25€; *taxe de séjour* included **CREDIT CARDS** AE, DC, MC, V

BREAKFAST Continental served all day 12€ per person

HÔTEL ÉTOILE PÉREIRE ★★★ (3)
146, boulevard Péreire, 75017
Métro: RER Péreire

26 rooms, all with shower or bath and toilet

The Étoile Péreire is a sophisticated hotel offering modern luxury at affordable prices. Occupying a distinctive building that is hard to identify as a hotel, it has benefited from several remodeling projects, and now from a new, enthusiastic owner, Laury Duquesnoy. Unfortunately, this attitude is not always extended by the reception staff, who can be icy and aloof.

The rooms all overlook a courtyard and are individually decorated around a specific color or theme. The result is a mixture of modern touched with the fanciful. The largest selections are the two-story duplexes with air-conditioning, ceiling fans, and skylights. Otherwise, the rooms are very nice but naturally smaller. In No. 205, a double, the green walls and latticework create a gardenlike feeling, and in No. 206, six wild animal prints define the room. No matter where you land, your bathroom will be modern and well supplied with Roger and Gallet products. I did not find it relaxing being surrounded by bubble gum pink walls in No. 406, and ditto for No. 107, enveloping its guests in rose-orange walls. However, they both have good bathrooms and all the comforts.

Breakfasts are served in a half-paneled basement dining room that displays pictures of coffee on one wall and various Provençal *confitures* (jams) on the other. White leatherette seating lines one side of the room and down the center is a communal table with silver leather chairs. Diners have a choice of twenty of the best-quality jams, jellies, or honeys to accompany their croissants and fresh orange or grapefruit juice. If you want more, ham or bacon and eggs are available.

While hardly in the tourist mainstream, the hotel is close to Porte Maillot and the Air France air terminal. A large city park with tennis courts and plenty of picnic benches is across the street, as are several dining favorites listed in *Great Eats Paris*.

TEL 01-42-67-60-00 **FAX** 01-42-67-02-90 **EMAIL** info@etoilepereire.com
  INTERNET www.etoilepereire.com
FACILITIES & SERVICES Air-conditioning in four duplexes, bar, direct-dial phone, elevator, hair dryer, Internet in lobby, laundry service, minibar in most rooms, TV with international reception, room safe (no charge), 3rd floor is nonsmoking, WiFi
RATES Single 130€, double 150€, duplex 205€; *taxe de séjour* included
  CREDIT CARDS AE, DC, MC, V
BREAKFAST Buffet 12€ per person

HÔTEL JARDIN DE VILLIERS ★★★ (4)
18, rue Claude Pouillet, 71017
Métro: Villiers, Malesherbes
26 rooms, all with shower or bath and toilet

After years of keeping my eye on this neglected property, someone has finally turned it into the lovely hotel I always imagined it could be. Several years ago, Pierre Bachy came on board and tastefully overhauled it from top to bottom, creating an intimate and welcoming hotel overlooking a flowered patio. The twenty-six rooms are harmoniously decorated in ruby, gold, and blue, with excellent beds and large-screen televisions. Even though they are a bit dark, I like the red-and-blue rooms on the back overlooking the quiet garden and patio. Ten are nonsmoking, all are Internet friendly, free movies play on the TV every day, and the special prices for *Great Sleeps Paris* readers are simply unbeatable. The stone *cave* breakfast room serves as a changing exhibition gallery for local artists. No, the hotel is not close to the usual Parisian tourist hubs. It is, however, a block or two away from one of the most authentic shopping streets in the *quartier*, rue de Lévis, and within easy jogging or walking distance to the lovely Parc de Monceau.

TEL 01-42-67-15-60 **FAX** 01-42-67-32-11 **EMAIL** hoteljdv@wanadoo.fr
  INTERNET www.jardindevilliers.com
FACILITIES & SERVICES Air-conditioning, direct-dial phone, hair dryer, elevator, free Internet hookup in rooms, laundry service, minibar, TV with international reception and free movies, office safe (no charge)
RATES Special rates for *Great Sleeps Paris* readers: single 100€, double 115€; *taxe de séjour* included **CREDIT CARDS** AE, DC, MC, V
BREAKFAST Continental included

HÔTEL LA RÉGENCE ÉTOILE ★★★ (15)
24, avenue Carnot, 75017
Métro: Argentine; RER Charles-de-Gaulle-Étoile
38 rooms, all with shower or bath and toilet

The hotel is on the jacaranda-lined avenue Carnot, one of the spokes of the famed traffic circle that radiates from the Arc de Triomphe. Because the prices are reasonable for a three-star, it is a good choice if you are a budget-minded business traveler in Paris and your work takes you to La Defense or the Palais des Congrès convention center. In addition, it is dependably decorated, and only a stone's throw or two from the bright lights and crowds along the Champs-Élysées.

A lighted nymphette statue in pristine alabaster greets guests as they enter the Directoire-style sitting area, where comfortable velvet-covered armchairs and sofas flank a marble fireplace. A sparkling mirrored elevator takes you to the predictably acceptable upmarket rooms, which are in yellow and blue. Everything you need is here: air-conditioning, television with CNN, two chairs, a desk, a mirrored armoire, and heated towel racks in a twenty-first-century bathroom. Rooms with balconies on the fifth floors have views of the Arc de Triomphe. Breakfast is served downstairs in a room that has Turner-like murals wrapping around three of the walls, and the glass-top metal tables and chairs have gold-painted bows and garlands.

Also under the same ownership is the Hôtel Montparnasse Daguerre (see page 237).

TEL 01-58-05-42-42 **FAX** 01-47-66-78-86 **EMAIL** hotelregenceetoile@wanadoo.fr **INTERNET** www.hotelregenceetoile.com
FACILITIES & SERVICES Air-conditioning, bar, direct-dial phone, elevator, hair dryer, laundry service, minibar, TV with international reception, room safe (no charge), WiFi
RATES Single 125€, double 165–185€, triple 205€; *taxe de séjour* included
   CREDIT CARDS AE, DC, MC, V
BREAKFAST Buffet or in-room Continental 12€, per person

HÔTEL REGENT'S GARDEN ★★★ ($, 8)
6, rue Pierre-Demours, 75017
Métro: Ternes; RER Charles-de-Gaulle-Étoile (exit rue Carnot)
39 rooms, all with shower or bath and toilet

Originally built by Napoléon III for his personal physician, this building is now a refined garden hotel. Hidden behind a high brick wall, it seems a little far from the center of activity, but in fact, rue Pierre-Demours is only a few minutes' walk from the Champs-Élysées and the Arc de Triomphe.

The rooms offer affordable elegance with a Parisian ambiance of bygone days. They have been redone to reflect their former Second Empire glory and offer combinations of high-ceilings, crystal chandeliers, decorative moldings, marble fireplaces, brass or mahogany bedsteads, floor-to-ceiling mirrors, luxurious fabrics, and authentic period furnishings. Many rooms connect for convenient family use, and several have large walk-in closets with built-in shelves and shoe racks. The bathrooms are luxuriously fitted with terry robes, heated towel racks, scented bubble bath and soaps, and plenty of light and mirrors for applying makeup. Most rooms overlook the garden, which is landscaped with large trees, stone statues, flowering walkways, and a terrace with tables for summer breakfasts or afternoon teas. The fresh flower displays are always beautiful, and the staff helpful and courteous. Everyone who has ever stayed here, myself included, loves it, and you will, too.

NOTE: As of press time, plans were still not finalized for redoing the reception area and the breakfast room. However, whatever changes are made will be positive and only serve to enhance this very special Great Sleep in Paris.

TEL 01-45-74-07-30; toll-free in U.S. and Canada 800-528-1234 (Best Western) **FAX** 01-40-55-01-42 **EMAIL** hotel.regents.garden@wanadoo.fr **INTERNET** www.hotel-paris-garden.com or www.bestwestern.fr

FACILITIES & SERVICES Air-conditioning, bar, direct-dial phone, elevator, hair dryer, parking (13€ per day, on a first-come basis), TV with international reception, room safe (no charge), 2nd floor exclusively nonsmoking, WiFi

RATES Single 189€, double 199–279€; *taxe de séjour* included

   CREDIT CARDS AE, DC, MC, V

BREAKFAST Buffet 13€ per person

HÔTEL RIVIERA ★★ (¢, 11)
55, rue des Acacias, 75017
Métro: Ternes; RER Charles-de-Gaulle-Étoile
26 rooms, all with shower and toilet

The tailored size of the rooms and baths matches the small prices at this little budget jewel, which packs a money-saving punch if you want to stay near the Etoile and the Champs-Élysées. As the manageress said to me, "Our rooms are not big, but they are pretty." How right she is. Four of them face an inside court that has been softened by the addition of a tiny terrace. Three good choices for a contented stay are No. 20, a single on the back; No. 21, a twin with oak built-ins and a wicker chair; and No. 26, a nonsmoking double with a beige-striped bedspread and a mini-bathroom with an enclosed shower. Even though No. 25 is the biggest room and can sleep four in two double beds, the orange walls close it in. Breakfast is served in a little room that overlooks some green plants. Frankly, I would skip the hotel breakfast and instead indulge in pastries from the bakery next door.

Also under the same ownership is the popular Hôtel Saint-Jacques (see page 127).

TEL 01-43-80-45-31 **FAX** 01-40-54-84-08 **EMAIL** hotel.riviera@wanadoo.fr **INTERNET** www.hotelriviera-paris.com

FACILITIES & SERVICES Air-conditioning in most rooms, direct-dial phone, elevator (to half-landings), hair dryer, room safe (no charge), TV with international reception, 10 nonsmoking rooms, WiFi (top three floors)

RATES Single 51–82€, double 72–90€, triple 100–106€, quad 106–115€; *taxe de séjour* included **CREDIT CARDS** AE, MC, V

BREAKFAST Continental 6.50€ per person

ROYAL MAGDA ÉTOILE ★★★ (18)
7, rue Troyon, 75017
Métro: RER Charles-de-Gaulle Étoile
37 room with shower or bath and toilet

Two brothers operated a business that bought, renovated, and subsequently managed hotels for various investors. Finally, they thought . . . enough! And they decided to go into business for themselves. The result is the Royal Magda Étoile, a three-star Great Sleep that has been completely redone in a simple, pleasing style. There are three types of rooms: "Club," with a bathtub and choice of double or twin beds; junior suites, which actually means one large room; and two-room suites suitable for family stays. Even the smallest Club guarantees coordinated surroundings, warm duvets on the beds, adequate work space, and sparkling bathrooms with heated towel racks. In the future is a fitness center, and I am sure more hotels to renovate as well.

TEL 01-47-64-10-19 **FAX** 01-47-64-02-12 **EMAIL** hotelmagda@wanadoo.fr
   INTERNET www.paris-hotel-magda.com
FACILITIES & SERVICES Air-conditioning, bar, direct-dial phone, elevator, hair
   dryer, minibar, room safe (no charge), TV with international reception,
   WiFi in lobby, high speed Internet in rooms
RATES Club (1–2 persons) 150–180€; junior suite (1–3 persons) 260€; suite
   (1–4 persons) 290€; *taxe de sejour* included **CREDIT CARDS** AE, DC, MC, V
BREAKFAST Buffet 14€ per person

Eighteenth Arrondissement

Montmartre is a rambling *quartier* full of contrasts, combining picture-postcard quaintness and razzle-dazzle. It was here that Toulouse-Lautrec drew the cancan girls dancing at the Moulin Rouge, and Picasso and Braque created Cubism at the Bateau-Lavoir on the place Émile Goudeau. The panoramic view from the steps of the Sacré Coeur at dawn or sunset, the many artists, and the intimate village atmosphere that prevails along the narrow streets—

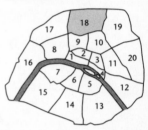

many of which are the same as when Utrillo painted them—continue to evoke the dynamic spirit and colorful past of this vibrant part of Paris, and it is a must-stop for any visitor. A walk down rue Lepic or rue des Abbesses, lined with bars and shops, leads to Pigalle, an area known for its bawdy nightlife. East of Montmartre is La Goutte d'Or, where many North Africans live, and to the north is the famed flea market at Porte de Clignancourt. Abbesses, one of the major métro stops, is one of two remaining métro stations that have their original Guimet-designed glass awning.

($) indicates a Big Splurge; (¢) indicates a Cheap Sleep

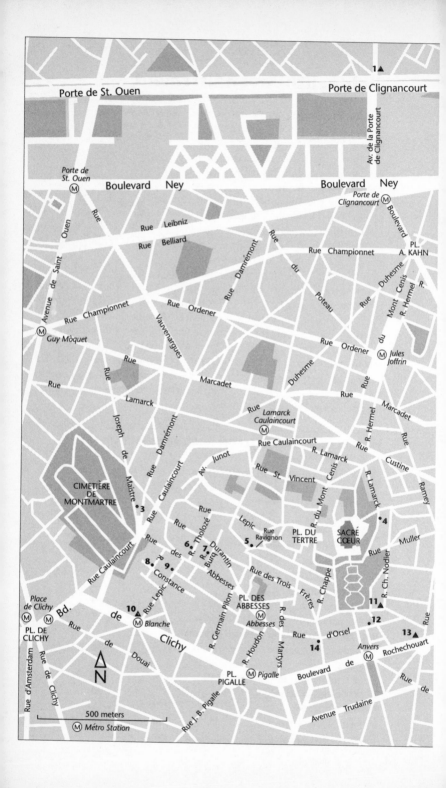

Porte de St. Ouen

Porte de Clignancourt

1 ▲

Av. de la Porte
de Clignancourt

Porte de
St. Ouen Ⓜ

Boulevard Ney

Boulevard Ney

Porte de
Clignancourt Ⓜ

Boulevard

PL.
A. KAHN

Rue Leibniz

Rue Belliard

Rue Championnet

Rue Damrémont

Rue

du

Poteau

Duhesme

Rue

R. Hermel

R.

Rue Championnet

Rue Ordener

Vauvenargues

Mont Cenis

Avenue de Saint Ouen

Rue

Guy Môquet Ⓜ

Rue

Lamarck

Joseph

de

Maistre

Rue

Marcadet

Rue Ordener

Duhesme

Ⓜ Jules
Joffrin

Rue

Rue

Marcadet

Rue Hermel

Rue

Rue

Custine

CIMETIÈRE
DE
MONTMARTRE

Rue Damrémont

Rue Caulaincourt

Av. Junot

Rue

Lamarck
Caulaincourt Ⓜ

Rue Caulaincourt

Rue St. Vincent

R. Lamarck

R. du Mont Cenis

Ramey

R. Lamarck

Rue

Rue Caulaincourt

Rue

des

•3

Rue

R. Tholozé

Durantin

Lepic

Rue
Ravignon

5 •

PL. DU
TERTRE

SACRÉ
CŒUR

•4

Muller

6 • 7 •

8 • •9
Constance

Rue des Abbesses

Rue des Trois

Frères

R. Chappe

Rue

R. Ch. Nodier

11 ▲

10 ▲

Ⓜ Blanche

Rue Lepic

R. Germain Pilon

PL. DES
ABBESSES

Ⓜ Abbesses

R. des Martyrs

•12

Place
de Clichy
Ⓜ

Bd.

Ⓜ

PL. DE
CLICHY

Rue

de

Clichy

R. Houdon

Rue d'Orsel

13 ▲

14 •

Anvers
Ⓜ

Rochechouart

Rue

de

Douai

PL.
PIGALLE

Ⓜ Pigalle

Boulevard de

Rue d'Amsterdam

Rue de Clichy

△
N

Rue I. B. Pigalle

Avenue Trudaine

Rue de

500 meters

Ⓜ Métro Station

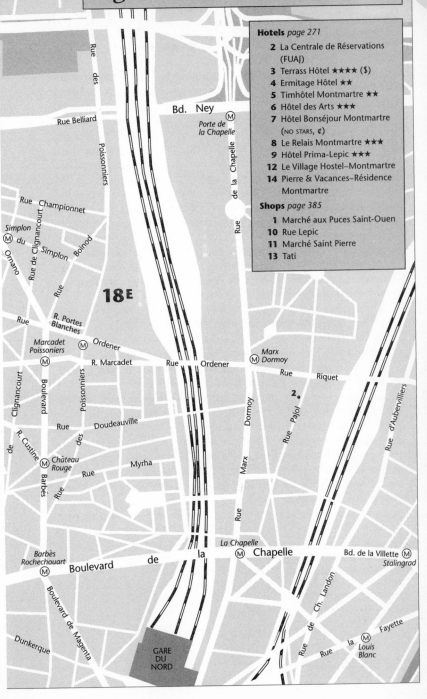

Eighteenth Arrondissement

Hotels *page 271*

- **2** La Centrale de Réservations (FUAJ)
- **3** Terrass Hôtel ★★★★ ($)
- **4** Ermitage Hôtel ★★
- **5** Timhôtel Montmartre ★★
- **6** Hôtel des Arts ★★★
- **7** Hôtel Bonséjour Montmartre (NO STARS, ¢)
- **8** Le Relais Montmartre ★★★
- **9** Hôtel Prima-Lepic ★★★
- **12** Le Village Hostel–Montmartre
- **14** Pierre & Vacances–Résidence Montmartre

Shops *page 385*

- **1** Marché aux Puces Saint-Ouen
- **10** Rue Lepic
- **11** Marché Saint Pierre
- **13** Tati

..GE HÔTEL ★★ (4)
24, rue Lamarck, 75018
Métro: Lamarck-Caulaincourt, or bus No. 80 or No. 85
12 rooms, all with shower or bath and toilet

Close your eyes and imagine waking up in Paris in an antique-filled hotel high atop Montmartre with magical views over the entire city. Sound wonderful? It does, and it is all possible at the Ermitage, a poetic refuge run for many years by the engaging Maggie Canipel and her husband. Now they have retired, and their lovely daughter, Sophie, is in charge. However, Maggie still comes back now and then, and she fills in completely when Sophie and her family go on vacation. In the late 1970s, M. and Mme. Canipel sold everything they had and bought the Ermitage. They updated the plumbing, filled the old mansion with their collection of fine furniture, and began welcoming guests, continually outdoing themselves with their boundless energy and engaging smiles in order to make everyone feel at home. They succeeded beautifully and are now one of the favorite hotels for readers of *Great Sleeps Paris*. If this sounds appealing, book the Ermitage the minute you know the dates for your trip. Bookings are taken *only* over the telephone or by fax.

The rooms are redecorated on a revolving basis, and bathrooms have been upgraded. Any one of the twelve rooms could steal your heart, but my favorites are still Nos. 6 and 10—on the top floor, with tall French windows opening onto the morning sun and views of all Paris—and Nos. 11 and 12, which open onto their terrace garden. Number 2 is beautiful, with a magnificent set of nineteenth-century reproduction Louis XV bedroom furniture: a carved bed, two side tables, and a mirrored armoire. A crystal chandelier completes the picture. True, you need strong legs and lungs to walk up the hill from the métro. However, once there, you will be richly rewarded not only by the warmth and hospitality of Sophie, but by being in the center of one of the most picturesque parts of Paris. You can wander the streets once painted by Utrillo, peek into artists' ateliers, and have your portrait painted by one of the pseudo-artists lining the touristy place du Tertre. Decent restaurants in all price ranges are within easy walking distance (see *Great Eats Paris*).

TEL 01-42-64-79-22 **FAX** 01-42-64-10-33 **INTERNET** www.ermitagesacrecoeur.fr
FACILITIES & SERVICES Direct-dial phone, no elevator (3 floors), hair dryer, no TV, office safe (no charge), entirely nonsmoking hotel
RATES Single 80€, double 92€, triple 118€, quad 140€; *taxe de séjour* included
 CREDIT CARDS None, cash or Euro traveler's check only
BREAKFAST Included, cannot be deducted

HÔTEL BONSÉJOUR MONTMARTRE (NO STARS, ¢, 7)
11, rue Burq, 75018
Métro: Abbesses, Blanche

34 rooms, 18 with shower, none with bath or toilet

Attention, tightwads! If money is your first concern, this old—but very clean—hotel should be one of your first picks. Occupying a hillside corner location, it is well protected from the low life and tourist mania that plagues Montmartre and its underbelly, Pigalle. It is run by Michel Bellart, who checks you in, and his hard-working wife, Amina, who is in charge of housekeeping and looking after their adorable little girl, Miriam. Each year the Bellarts make improvements: this year it was adding wood flooring in all the rooms, repainting a few others, and generally weeding out the mishmash of garage-sale furnishings. The clean rooms appeal to a young, intellectual, and sometimes impoverished crowd of international guests, who cheerfully ignore the lack of high-tech amenities and do not mind using hall facilities, or going to the first-floor communal shower and spending 2€ for a seven-minute wash. The cheapest rooms face walls and are bathless. If you can swing just a little more money, ask for one with a balcony (Nos. 23, 33, 43, or 53, the last of which is the best because it has a nice Parisian view); No. 51, a triple with a tiny peek of the tip of the Sacré Coeur; or No. 55, a double with the same lofty view. The balcony rooms come with double beds. If you need twins, ask for No. 41 on the street, which also has more space and better bedspreads than some others. Breakfast can be part of the plan here, but you can feel more Parisian by walking to one of the many cafés that line rue des Abbesses and rue Lepic.

TEL 01-42-54-22-53 **FAX** 01-42-54-25-92 **EMAIL** hotel-bonsejour-montmartre@wanadoo.fr **INTERNET** www.hotel-bonsejour-montmartre.fr
FACILITIES & SERVICES No elevator (5 floors), office safe (no charge)
RATES Single 32–44€, double 38–48€, triple 60€; extra bed 11€; shower 2€; *taxe de séjour* included **CREDIT CARDS** None, cash only
BREAKFAST Continental 6€ per person

HÔTEL DES ARTS ★★★ (6)
5, rue Tholozé, 75018
Métro: Abbesses, Blanche

50 rooms, all with shower or bath and toilet

The Lameyre family works as an honest, hard-working team, intent on providing good value for money. Heading the welcoming committee is their friendly chocolate-colored Lab, Caramel. The attractively furnished lobby and breakfast rooms are especially well done, with textured walls, fresh flowers, and a growing collection of local artwork depicting scenes and aspects of life in Paris and the village of Montmartre. Paintings of picturesque Montmartre also grace the bedrooms. The rooms are redecorated on a revolving basis using bright colors, good-quality furnishings, and nicely coordinated fabrics. Bathrooms are pristine. If you don't mind walking up a flight of stairs, the sixth-floor rooms have rooftop views of the white tip of Sacré Coeur, and in Nos. 60 and 62, you will see the tip of the Eiffel Tower and La Defense. If stairs don't appeal, request No. 55, a double with built-in closets. It is the smallest room in the hotel, but it has a western exposure with a view of the Eiffel Tower. The street is quiet, so at night you won't be awakened by wild, cruising party animals.

TEL 01-46-06-30-52 **FAX** 01-46-06-10-83 **EMAIL** hotel.arts@wanadoo.fr
  INTERNET www.arts-hotel-paris.com
FACILITIES & SERVICES Direct-dial phone, elevator (to most floors), hair dryer, room safe (no charge), TV with international reception, WiFi
RATES Single 78€, double 92–100€; extra bed for child only 15€; *taxe de séjour* included **CREDIT CARDS** AE, MC, V
BREAKFAST Buffet 9€ per person

HÔTEL PRIMA-LEPIC ★★★ (9)
29, rue Lepic, 75018
Métro: Abbesses, Blanche
38 rooms, all with shower or bath and toilet

Finally, it has been redone. Gone are the dusty ruffles and flourishes that hung in the dark halls, overpowering the worn-out, shabby bedrooms. Thanks to an owner who knows the kind of impression an infusion of euros can make, the hotel is always among my Great Sleeps in Paris. Several features continue to stand out: the original mosaic-tile entryway with its heavily molded ceiling, and the killer, white wrought-iron garden-style chairs and tables in the breakfast area. They are pretty to look at, but ten minutes into your *café au lait* and croissant, you know these chairs were not built for comfort. This is not the case for the bedrooms, which are designated by a photo of a Montmartre landmark on the doors. All chambers are slightly different, but the colors are coordinated, even in the bathrooms, where the floor tiles blend with the colors used in the room. For a view onto the interesting market street, rue Lepic, ask for No. 24, Montmartre; this is done in blue and yellow with a white-dotted swill half-tester over the bed. Several rooms are similar to No. 15, among them Caulaincourt, which has a white bed with gauzy curtains on each side and a balcony large enough for a table and chairs. Number 12, Tholozé, done in lavender with floral lights, has a feminine flair to it. So does No. 43, a back single with floral detailed wall covering that coordinates with a quilted bedspread. Number 27, Sacré Coeur, is a cozy double in yellow and green. There are three suites, but frankly nothing can be done to change their poor layout or the fact that you have to crawl up some steep steps to reach one of them. In the largest, one room has no window, the other exposure is gloomy, and the floors slant. My best advice is to avoid the suites.

TEL 01-46-06-44-64 **FAX** 01-46-06-66-11 **EMAIL** reservations@ hotel-prima-lepic.com **INTERNET** www.hotel-prima-lepic.com

FACILITIES & SERVICES Direct-dial phone, very small dogs accepted (but not left alone in room), elevator (to most floors), hair dryer, luggage room, TV with international reception, room service, room safe (2€ per day), WiFi

RATES Single 104€, double 118–128€, Baldaquin room 157€; apartment, 3 people 182€, 4 people 202€; very small dog free; *taxe de séjour* included

CREDIT CARDS AE, MC, V

BREAKFAST Buffet 11€ per person

LE RELAIS MONTMARTRE ★★★ (8)
6, rue Constance, 75018
Métro: Blanche, Abbesses
26 rooms, all with shower and toilet

Le Relais Montmartre, which opened its doors in December 2005, is a beautiful boutique hotel that displays a refined sense of elegant attitude from top to bottom. Every room is a distinct pleasure, in which the colors are determined by heavy ceiling beams painted in hand-mixed hues of red, soft green, rose, orange, lavender, and yellow. These are then delicately matched with coordinated fabrics and carpets. Even the standard rooms are spacious, with fine-quality bedding on mattresses made from seven layers of foam. The furniture is custom made, interesting pieces of art hang on the walls, and on the desk, a different antique lamp shines brightly. Streamlined baths have all the necessities: magnifying mirrors, heated towel racks, and a welcome basket of toiletries. The arched stone breakfast room is enlivened by the thick red cushions softening yellow metal chairs, and a lovely brass samovar. In warm weather, breakfast is served on a small patio centered by a bubbling fountain. Service is very personalized and matches the high quality of this hotel.

From the hotel you can walk in any direction and see something interesting. You can climb up to Sacré Coeur, or crawl down the hill to Pigalle. For longer trips, jump on the Montmartobus, a minibus service that plies the winding streets snaking around the Butte; it is one of the most pleasurable rides you can take in Paris.

Also under the same management is Hôtel Le Relais Saint-Honoré (see page 75).

TEL 01-70-64-25-25 **FAX** 01-70-64-25-00 **EMAIL** contact@relaismontmartre.fr
   INTERNET www.relaismontmartre.fr

FACILITIES & SERVICES Air-conditioning, direct-dial phone, elevator, hair dryer, laundry service, minibar, private parking, room safe (no charge), flat-screen TV with international reception, free WIFI

RATES 1–2 persons, standard 150€, comfort 170€, superior 190€

CREDIT CARDS AE, DC, MC, V

BREAKFAST Buffet or in-room Continental 12€, per person

TERRASS HÔTEL ★★★★ ($, 3)
12, rue Joseph-de-Maistre, 75018
Métro: Lamarck-Caulaincourt
100 rooms, all with shower or bath and toilet

The Terrass Hôtel on the Butte Montmartre has some of the most spectacular views of Paris. In the summer months, the roof garden on the seventh floor with its panoramic view of the City of Light is the perfect place for a romantic lunch or dinner *à deux*. Otherwise, meals are served in Diapason, a distinctly contemporary dining room with large windows onto the street. Both of these exceptional restaurants are open to both hotel guests and the public. The hotel has been in the same family for four generations, and despite its size, it has an easy atmosphere that recalls the peace of less-turbulent times. The wood-paneled lobby and reception areas are formal but not pretentious. During most of the year, they are enlivened by changing art exhibitions with works by local artists.

The rooms are individually done in the best of traditional taste, and they fall into three categories: standard, deluxe, and junior suite. Some can be called modern, others romantic, and a few fall into the vintage category. All of them benefit from a long list of amenities and four floors are designated as nonsmoking. Naturally, the fifteen view rooms on the fourth through the eighth floors are in great demand, but just because a room is viewless does not mean that it is inferior. Number 704, a deluxe, evokes romance and embodies the phrase "a room with a view." In addition, it has a large bathroom with a corner Jacuzzi. In Number 408, there is a beautiful sunset view over the Cimetiére Montmartre. Room 418 is a perfect Art Deco–inspired choice for the business traveler. In addition to nine feet of glass-topped workspace, there are two leather armchairs, a stepwalking machine, hamam steam shower, and dimmer-switch lights to set whatever mood is called for. Red Japanese screens divide the bedroom from a sitting/office space in No. 603, a junior suite. Red appears again on the suede-covered chairs and on the entry door to the room. In No. 610, the view is not spectacular, but it is there. The room benefits from a dramatic red fabric–covered wall in the sitting area and a small terrace. Number 114, with gray velvet–covered walls, is a standard room with no view, but it has excellent work space and a draped bed.

Under the same ownership are the Artus Hôtel (see page 137), Le Madison Hôtel (see page 164), and the Hôtel Bourgogne & Montana (see page 174).

TEL 01-44-92-34-14 **FAX** 01-42-52-29-11 **EMAIL** reservation@
terrass-hotel.com **INTERNET** www.terrass-hotel.com

FACILITIES & SERVICES Air-conditioning, bar, conference room, direct-dial
phone, elevator (except to top floor), hair dryer, some iron and ironing
boards, some Jacuzzis, laundry service, minibar, magnifying mirror,
concierge and porter, two restaurants (both open to public), room service,
tea & coffee makers, TV with international reception and pay-per-view,
4 nonsmoking floors, WiFi

RATES 1–2 persons: standard 255€, deluxe 300€, junior suite 355€; *taxe de séjour* included **CREDIT CARDS** AE, DC, MC, V
BREAKFAST Buffet or in-room Continental 18€, per person

TIMHÔTEL MONTMARTRE ★★ (5)
11, rue Ravignan, 75018
Métro: Abbesses
60 rooms, all with shower or bath and toilet

The rue Ravignan runs along the place Émile Goudeau. It was here that Picasso, Juan Gris, Modigliani, and others had studios in the Bateau-Lavoir. Picasso arrived at age nineteen and painted the *Demoiselles d'Avignon* (which now hangs in the MoMA in New York). Cubism was also born here. In 1970, the famous landmark burned. This bit of art history trivia leads me to the Timhôtel, which is right on the place Émile Goudeau. Normally, I am not an advocate of any type of chain hotel. However, there are always exceptions, and this is a good one for the views alone. In addition to its historic location, the hotel boasts views of Paris from ten rooms and of Sacré-Coeur in ten more. Each floor is painted yellow, has blue carpeting, and is named after a well-known Montmartre painter. The identical, dormitory-inspired rooms with open closets are hardly candidates for the style-obsessed, so if you don't get one with a view, to put it simply, don't bother hiking the slopes of Montmartre to stay here.

TEL 01-42-55-74-79 **FAX** 01-42-55-71-01 **EMAIL** montmartre@timhotel.fr
INTERNET www.timhotel.fr
FACILITIES & SERVICES Air-conditioning in some rooms, direct-dial phone, elevator, hair dryer, laundry service, small pets accepted (no charge), TV with international reception, office safe (4€ per day), 15 nonsmoking rooms, WiFi in some rooms and lobby
RATES 1–2 persons: standard 135€, superior 150–165€, triple 155–215€, suite 205€; *taxe de séjour* included **CREDIT CARDS** AE, DC, MC, V
BREAKFAST Continental 9€ per person

Other Options

If you are lucky to have lived in Paris,... then wherever you go for the rest of your life, it stays with you, for Paris is a movable feast.

> —*Ernest Hemingway*, A Movable Feast

If hotel life is not for you, there are other reasonable and often quite inexpensive options that make sleeping sense in Paris. For the cheapest choice of all, consider a return to nature—that is, camping, which you can do just outside of Paris in the Bois de Boulogne. For a more total immersion in Parisian life, plan a stay with a French family in a B&B. For one of the most unusual sleeps in Paris, you can live luxuriously on your own private *péniche* (barge) docked on the Seine in the shadow of the Eiffel Tower. If you are a student or can go the hostel route, there are many excellent low-priced accommodations awaiting you. Other cost-saving possibilities are to stay in a residence hotel in a unit with a kitchenette, or to become truly Parisian and rent your own studio or apartment. The benefits of these last two choices are numerous, from having more space to spread out to the adventure of interacting with merchants while shopping for life's necessities in your own Parisian neighborhood.

OTHER OPTIONS

Apartment Rental Agencies

There is something about the rhythm of being in Paris, and there is no city more beautiful. Period.
—*Holly Hunt, interior decorator*

If you want to live in Paris, not just be a visitor during your stay, then the best way to experience Paris *comme les Parisiens* is to rent a short-term apartment. Believe me, once you do it, you will not want to return to the confines of hotel living in the City of Light for any of your future visits. If you are going to be in Paris for more than a few days, extra space begins to matter. Not only does a stay in a Parisian apartment give you more elbow room than a hotel, and for less money in the long run, it makes you feel less frantic about seeing and doing absolutely everything. You are caught up instead with the fun and adventure of exploring and getting to know your own Paris *quartier*, which you will soon come to think of as your own, becoming a little Parisian in the process.

During the years I have researched Paris apartments, I have seen just about every nightmare and little chamber of horrors possible—including total dumps that were filthy, unattractive, and in terrible areas that have absolutely nothing to offer a tourist. Many are operated by huge firms, or are let by absentee owners who are on the scene to collect your money but then vanish, leaving you high and dry when maintenance problems arise, which they generally do. Just as with all of the hotels and shops listed in this book, I have personally visited every apartment agency listed and viewed a large sampling of what they offer before I decided to recommend them to you.

Even though I mention it as the number-one tip in apartment renting, it bears repeating here: If you rent an apartment, be sure you clearly understand the payment, cancellation, and refund policies. It is beyond the scope of *Great Sleeps Paris* to detail the various policies you will encounter, but they are *never* in your favor. Therefore, it is absolutely essential that you purchase cancellation insurance, which is available through many state automobile associations, travel agents, and in some cases, through the apartment agency itself (see "Insurance," page 41). This small investment will pay off tenfold if you have to change dates, cancel altogether, or must suddenly cut short your stay.

Tips on Renting a Paris Apartment

1. Most important: Know the deposit, payment, and cancellation policies, and buy cancellation insurance.

2. Lower rates are always negotiable for longer stays or during slow periods. *Always* ask. Once you determine a guaranteed rate,

find out about extra charges such as linens, cleaning (whether weekly housekeeping service is included or extra, and what the final cleaning fee is), telephone, heating, electricity, high-speed Internet hookup, and so on.

3. A picture is worth a thousand words. Most agencies now have Websites with pictures of their properties. This is fine for a start, but it does not cover all the bases. In addition to photos of the kitchen, bathroom, and storage space, always ask for pictures of the views taken from the windows of the apartments you are considering. You probably don't want to move into your apartment and find that you are facing dull, interior courtyards; ugly, blank walls (which may be what the rental agency means when it says yours is a "quiet, calm, and peaceful address"); or a main thoroughfare with nonstop traffic.

4. Important: Many Paris buildings are undergoing exterior cleaning, painting, and/or extensive renovation. Find out if your apartment is in one of these buildings, which means it will be covered in plastic sheeting and scaffolding, smelling like paint, and essentially crawling with workers—who arrive early, make noise, create dust, and don't care that you can't open the windows, or even see out of them, during what could be months of very disconcerting building noise, repairs, and work. Don't ever believe that an owner "didn't know that work was going to be done." All property owners are not only informed, but assessed for this type of work. While they might not know the exact date for the work to begin, believe me, they know it is going to happen, and they should not attempt to rent the apartment under these very unpleasant circumstances. This is your vacation in Paris . . . not an endurance test.

5. Be *very specific* when stating your needs: size of flat and for what number of occupants; whether you want a stall shower rather than a handheld shower nozzle in a half tub with no shower guard or curtain; and what sort of kitchen equipment you'd like—do you need only a microwave? Do you want pots and pans for major cooking events? Are you only going to drink wine and eat baguettes and French cheese at the dining room table? Inquire about closet space and luggage storage. Don't forget to consider the beds. Will a sofabed do, or does your back demand something better than a folding bed, and if so, will you require a double bed or twin beds?

6. Is a television important for you—one that includes CNN, BBC, and Euro-Sport? Don't discount French TV, as it's a great way to improve your French comprehension. Is there a land-line phone, and how much are calls? Can you make both local and long-distance calls? Is there an answering machine, fax, and Internet hookup?

7. How far is the apartment from your center of interest? Where is the nearest market, laundry and dry cleaner, pharmacy, métro and bus stop, best café, and *pâtisserie?* Ask for a good local map with your address and the nearest métro stop pinpointed on it.

8. Is the apartment suitable for children? Is there a park or playground nearby?

9. Is there an elevator to your apartment? Many buildings in Paris do not have them. While that penthouse apartment with a dynamic view is romantically wonderful, consider carrying groceries, wine and water, shopping purchases, and your luggage up and down. Think about this one carefully...stairs can get to be a problem, fast.

10. Upon arrival, will someone meet you at the apartment and show you the ropes, or are you mailed the keys along with a booklet of instructions on how to make things work in your rental? Or worse yet, do you have to go to an office in Paris to get the keys? This is very important after a long international flight: dragging luggage and tired children through Paris in search of the keys to your Paris kingdom is not an attractive option.

11. What other services does the apartment rental company offer? Ask about drivers; itinerary planning throughout France and in other parts of Europe; ongoing reservations; and air travel arrangements and concierge services in Paris.

12. Check with your homeowner's or renter's insurance policy to see if it covers you for any damage that may occur while you are renting a foreign apartment. Many of these policies do cover you. If so, fax the information to the agency in question. Many times hefty deposits are taken, and unfortunately, you can be blamed for damages caused by another renter. To avoid this, upon arrival, go over the apartment very carefully and point out any damages or potential problems, no matter how small they may seem. When you leave, get a written statement that the apartment was in good condition when you left it.

APARTMENT RENTAL AGENCIES

Bonapart Consulting

Who hasn't dreamed of owning a romantic *pied-á-terre* in Paris, with lovely terrace views and walking distance to all things one thinks of as *trés* Parisian. Making that dream a reality is another matter. For a foreigner, buying property in Paris, or any place in France for that matter, is not simple. Quite the contrary: it can be frought with peril and one of the most hair-tearing, frustrating experiences of a lifetime. I know many who have finally managed to do it and then said, had they known before what lay ahead, never, never would they have even considered it.

But not to worry if you have Susie Hollands and Bonapart Consulting. As Susie says, "I am helping people to make their dream come true."

Susie is a hard-working, dynamic young woman transplanted to Paris from Glasgow, Scotland. She will assist you in every stage of buying a property: from the initial property search, through renovations, to final move-in, and if requested, renting it when you are not here. With Bonapart at your side, you will be shielded from French red-tape nightmares and not fall prey to the pitfalls that are lurking along every step of the way. Her consulting fees consist of an initial amount to open the dosier and conduct the property search, plus a percentage of the purchase price to handle all the other details, so that all you have to do is move in and begin living your dream.

If buying is not on your agenda, but you are planning a stay in Paris on a long-term basis, Susie can also assist you and find the perfect rental, tailoring it to your specific needs. Nothing is too much trouble, from finding schools for your children to opening a bank account so you can easily pay for all of this superb personalized service. Apartment rental fees are paid directly to the owner and start from 1,000€ per month for a studio. However, she also handles a some short-term rentals (two-month minimum); with these, there is no fee for the customer, as her services are paid for by the apartment owner.

TEL 06-17-40-82-04 **EMAIL** susie@bonapartconsulting.com
  INTERNET www.bonapartconsulting.com
RATES Apartment purchase: 1,000€ to open the dossier and conduct the
  property search, plus 2.5% of the purchase price; apartment rental:
  monthly rent is paid directly to the owner and starts from 1,000€ per
  month for a studio; one-time fee for Bonapart's services is 2,000€ for
  long-term rentals. **CREDIT CARDS** MC, V (through PayPal), Euro check,
  bank transfer

CHEZ VOUS
1001 Bridgeway, Suite 245
Sausalito, CA 94965

When renting a Paris apartment, I definitely subscribe to the Chez Vous philosophy: *When you step out the door, you should know you are in Paris!*

Chez Vous apartments offer you an elegant Paris address in several of the best areas of the city, not in marginal, out-of-the-way *quartiers* that some apartment owners or agencies will try to convince you are interesting. None of the apartments are owner-occupied. All are on long-term lease to Chez Vous, who comes in and repaints, redecorates, and fixes what ever is necessary to bring the property up to their exceptionally high standards. All the comforts of home are here: beautifully fitted kitchens, all major appliances, high-speed Internet, cable TV, and DVD and CD players. In Paris they employ a staff to oversee maintenance, decorating, and guest services. Believe me, this is a class act from the get-go.

TEL 415-331-2531 **FAX** 415-331-5296 **EMAIL** bonjour@chezvous.com
  INTERNET www.chezvous.com
RATES From $250 (5-night minimum, starts any day of week); includes
  linens, final cleaning, and all utilities except international telephone calls
  and housekeeping services. Discounts are offered in the winter (with the
  exception of Christmas) and after the 22nd night. **CREDIT CARDS** None,
  U.S. checks only

CHOICEAPART

ChoiceApart offers Website and booking services for top-quality, center-city apartments in five major European cities: Paris, London, Florence, Venice, and Barcelona. These centrally-located, fully-furnished and -equipped rental properties provide clients high standards of style, character, cleanliness and on-site support. All properties are inspected on a regular basis. Full descriptions and clear pictures of the apartments are given on the Website, along with excellent background information on each city.

For Paris, owners Bill and Natalie Cameron Ward offer a number of exceptional apartments in the most desirable parts of the city. A stay in any one of them puts the visitor in an interesting, lively area with excellent access to bus and métro transportation, good restaurants, and wonderful neighborhood shopping. The apartments, which they own or exclusively manage, range in size from a roomy studio to a two-bedroom, two-bathroom apartment sleeping six. Each has its own character, with quality furnishings and coordinated color schemes. Kitchens are fully fitted with everything from a paring knife and an electric tea kettle to a microwave, attractive china, glassware, and cutlery. Most have a washer and dryer and a dishwasher. All have cable TV reception, several have a high-speed Internet connection and DVD or VCR. All prices include utilities (with the exception of the telephone) and housekeeping service after ten days. Bill and Natalie are a charming hands-on team who inspect each property regularly, know the owners, and spare no effort in making their guests feel welcome and at home. All you have to do is arrive with your luggage, settle in, and enjoy home-sweet-home in Paris. There is usually a five-day minimum stay.

TEL Paris: 01-42-21-13-31, 01-6-22-58-45-85; ChoiceApart: toll-free from U.S. 800-224-6113; International 44-871-218-0037 **FAX** 44-207-738-7046 **EMAIL** stay@choiceapart.com **INTERNET** www.choiceapart.com
RATES From $995 per week for a studio to $3,500 per week for a luxury 2-bedroom, 2-bathroom apartment; discounts for stays of 10 days or more, and a special extra 5% discount for *Great Sleeps Paris* readers
  CREDIT CARDS MC, V, or personal checks in dollars, euros, or British pound sterling

COOPER PARIS FLATS/RENTALS IN PARIS

For a romantic stay on either Ile de la Cité or Ile St-Louis, Glenn Cooper is the man to contact. These are stylish apartments he owns, which he has renovated using traditional Parisian furnishings and fabrics. Kitchens are fully loaded, bathrooms modern, and the locations definitely say, "Ah, this is Paris!" He also has a very nice selection of apartments in the historic center, all of which put guests within walking distance to most of the must-sees in Paris. All his apartments include a washer and dryer, cable TV, high-speed Internet, land-line phones with local phone calls included, weekly linen service, and cleaning every two weeks.

Glenn is a smart American businessman who understands what Americans want in terms of amenities and level of service. As a result, his apartments are in great demand. To avoid being disappointed, get your reservation in as far in advance as possible.

TEL 01-42-60-22-98, 06-11-32-60-92; in the U.S. 516-977-3318
  EMAIL cooopergl@gmail.com **INTERNET** www.rentals-paris.com
RATES Studios from 900€ per week; 1-bedroom from 1,000€ per week, 2-bedroom from 1,500€ per week; one-week minimum stay; discounts for longer stays **CREDIT CARDS** MC, V

DE CIRCOURT ASSOCIATES (58)
11, rue Royale, 75008
Métro: Concorde

De Circourt Associates was founded by Claire de Circourt to assist people moving to Paris, either for professional reasons or for a stay of at least two months. Claire de Circourt is a very savvy businesswoman who has lived and worked in New York City, so she knows the type of accommodations and service most Americans expect. Her customer service is superb because she always provides backup, or intermediary help, if any client ever has a problem. She has active computerized listings of over five thousand apartments and homes in Paris, and in the suburbs close to all the international schools, which are updated every fifteen days, plus a dynamic Website. It is also possible to reserve on her Website. Thanks to a sophisticated computerized search system, she or one of her exceptionally competent English-speaking staff will find you the place of your dreams at a price you can afford. Her office can also find an apartment in less than twenty-four hours. As she told me, "Clients can come in the morning, and by evening, have a contract in their pocket." The possibilities range from a romantic, beamed, one-bedroom walkup on Île de la Cité, to a zany artist's studio done in black and white with a bird-shaped chair, to the to-die-for apartment occupied by Robert Altman while he was on location in Paris filming *Prêt à Porter.* It is all up to you and your budget—whatever you want, chances are excellent De Circourt Associates will have it.

TEL 01-43-12-98-00 **FAX** 01-43-12-98-08 **INTERNET** www.homes-paris.com
RATES From 1,000–12,000€ per month; 2-month minimum stay
   CREDIT CARDS AE, MC, V

FRANCE FOR RENT
160 Beaver Street
San Francisco, CA 94114

France for Rent has properties in all price ranges throughout France, but the emphasis is on Paris and Provence. Owner Claude Nederovique, who was born in Avignon, owns more than twenty of the properties, and has stayed in every one he represents. As he says, "We rent what we love."

The Paris apartments are located in the most popular arrondissements and range in size from small studios and beamed Marais apartments to a fabulous town house on the Seine filled with magnificent art and all the latest high-tech gadgetry. All are nonsmoking, have cable television, CD stereo systems, and modern, well-equipped kitchens. Housekeeping service is available on request (extra charge), and some apartments have elevators, air-conditioning, clothes washers, dishwashers, and a high-speed Internet line. Two distinct advantages are that credit cards are accepted and that an English-speaking representative of the company is always on-call twenty-four hours a day in Paris if there are any problems. There is a one-week minimum stay and discounts after stays of two months.

TEL Toll-free in U.S. 866-437-2623; outside U.S. 415-642-1111 **FAX** 805-
649-2689 **EMAIL** info@FranceForRent.com **INTERNET** www.France
ForRent.com or www.ProvenceForRent.com
RATES Small studio from $900 per week; 1-bedroom from $1,300 per week;
2-bedroom from $2,000 per week; 3-bedroom from $2,700 per week;
one-week minimum; 20% discount for stays of 2 months or more
CREDIT CARDS MC, V

GUEST APARTMENT SERVICES PARIS (53)
9, Quai de Bourbon, 75004 (Île St-Louis)
Métro: Pont-Marie

Guest Apartment Services Paris specializes in short-term rentals of
some of the most beautiful Parisian apartments I have seen. In addition, their commitment to service and guest satisfaction is the standard
to which all others aspire. Each apartment, which is exclusive to Guest
Apartment Services Paris, is carefully chosen for its innate charm and
authentic character. All have been decorated in a comfortable Parisian
style with beautiful period furnishings, nicely equipped kitchens, and
modern bathrooms. I can assure you they are wonderful. Nothing is
faded, out-of-date, tasteless, or displays even a hint of that shabby-chic
decor one often finds in French rental properties. All are located either
on the beguiling Île St-Louis or in the Marais around place des Vosges.
Some have quiet garden views; others have sweeping, panoramic
picture-postcard outlooks. From the smallest studio on a quiet courtyard with a lovely magnolia tree to an elegant town house near place
des Vosges, complete with indoor swimming pool and garden—and
the staff to maintain them—you can be assured that Christophe
Chastel and Philippe Pée will provide you with a memorable Parisian
stay. All apartments include weekly housekeeping and linen service
(daily housekeeping service is available), cable television, DVD players, stereo with CD, private telephone, answering machine and fax,
high-speed Internet hookup, and all major appliances. Free baby crib
and highchair are available, as are fans for the apartments that do
not have air-conditioning. The small studios, however, do not have
washers and dryers. Arrangements can be made for airport transfers,
a car and driver during your stay or for trips out of Paris, a personal
chef, babysitting... whatever is needed to enhance your stay. There is
a five-night minimum stay in low season and a one-week minimum
in high season.

To live like a nineteenth-century lord, but with all the comforts of
today, reserve all or part of Philippe and Christophe's elegant manor
home in Normandy, which is about twenty-five minutes by car from
Honfleur and Deauville. However, once you arrive at this beautiful,
restored home, you may never want to leave. The property is situated
in a private park, with its own swimming pool, walking paths, and
lovely garden. Bicycles are available for further excursions. The inside
has been totally renovated and now sleeps up to eight in three suites
with ensuite bathrooms. All are attractively furnished with French
pieces Christophe began collecting when he was fifteen years old.

TEL 01-44-07-06-20, 06-80-63-19-95 (cell phone) **FAX** 01-46-33-37-73
   EMAIL info@guestapartment.fr **INTERNET** www.guestapartment.com
RATES Per day: from 150€ for small studio; 570€ for luxurious apartment
   on Île St-Louis; for town house 1,520€; one- to two-week minimum,
   depending on season; Manor House: rates vary and are quoted on request
   CREDIT CARDS MC, V

HAVEN IN PARIS

   American Erica Berman and her French partner, Alain, are young,
artistic, energetic, and full of good ideas. They have purchased and
totally renovated a roster of smart, uncluttered accommodations that
will appeal to anyone the minute they step in the front door. Being
American, Erica knows the expectations of her compatriots and has
designed the apartments to appeal to her many American visitors.
She and Alain use simple colors, sprinkle the rooms with antiques,
and fit the kitchens and baths to American standards. Erica and Alain
live in Paris and are always accessible to their clients. Upon arrival
they meet you on-site and provide you with the necessary details,
and they are available during your stay 24/7 to make sure you feel at
home. The apartments all have telephones, cable television, washer
and dryer, dishwasher, microwave or oven (or both), stereo system, and
an Internet hookup. Also available are short-term rentals in Provence.
See the Website for details.

TEL 01-42-28-32-34, 06-10-28-26-06; in U.S. 978-405-9420
   FAX in U.S. 480-275-3419 **EMAIL** info@haveninparis.com
   INTERNET www.haveninparis.com
RATES From $700 per week; discounts for stays over 2 weeks; last-minute
   specials on Website **CREDIT CARDS** MC, V; checks in U.S. dollars

HISTORIC RENTALS
100 W. Kennedy Boulevard, No. 260
Tampa, FL 33602

   George Hamilton owns beautiful studio and one- to three-
bedroom apartments in Paris that he and his French partner, Jean-
Pierre Durousselau, have completely restored. Two are located in the
fifth arrondissement near the Panthéon, another is on rue des Rosiers
in the Jewish Quarter in the Marais, two are near Montparnasse, and
a three-bedroom site is near the Opéra. When I saw them, I thought
they didn't look like rentals; they looked and felt like lovely homes.
   All are decorated with charming furnishings, quality fabrics, and
great attention to detail. Kitchens and bathrooms are small but completely up-to-date. The bedrooms have a king-size bed, and there is
another comfortable couch in the living room that converts to a single
bed with a trundle bed. There are plenty of electrical outlets suitable
for plugging in laptops, and always a comfortable work space with
good lighting. These two features may sound routine, but let me assure
you they are not. I cannot tell you the number of nice apartments and
hotels in Paris with little or no work space, and plugs so far away that
several extension cords snaking across the room are required. Thirty

days before arrival, guests receive a concierge book filled with the particular apartment's details plus many helpful hints. Cable television, hair dryer, high-speed Internet, fans, and utilities are included, along with weekly cleaning and linen changes. None of the apartments are located above the second floor, and all are absolutely nonsmoking. You may start your stay on any day of the week; there is a one-week minimum; and discounts are given for longer stays.

If your travels are taking you to Annecy, which is a picturesque town on a lake in the French Alps, ask about their apartment venture located in the town's historic center. In addition, there are three wonderful properties in the heart of Provence. For something closer to home, George has eight apartments in the heart of the French Quarter in New Orleans, all fully furnished with air-conditioning, telephone, television, and parking.

TEL Toll-free in U.S. 800-537-5408; outside U.S. 813-765-4701
   EMAIL inquiries@historicrentals.com **INTERNET** www.historicrentals.com
RATES Per week: studio $700–$800, 1-bedroom $850–$1,100, 3-bedroom
   $1,700–$2,200; one-week minimum stay; discounts for multiple weeks or
   in low season. See Website for properties outside Paris.
   CREDIT CARDS MC, V

KUDETA HOME (9)
22, rue Rambuteau, 75003
Métro: Rambuteau

Stéphane Martin was once the marketing manager for Galeries Lafayette, and Pierre Filliole was involved in international banking and finance. A few years ago they decided to change careers and entered the short-term apartment-rental business. They now own or manage forty-five attractive studios and apartments geared to all types of budgets. For the seriously budget-minded, they have several modestly priced studios in the Marais and around rue Montorgueil, the colorful shopping street near Les Halles. These are both very trendy areas, full of bars, restaurants, and a fascinating blend of fashionistas. While these studios are definitely budget in size and require some stair climbing, they have a certain simple charm . . . think Ikea accented with a smattering of beams, an antique door, or lovely mirror, plus nice curtains, hardwood floors, and little kitchenettes. These studios are available for stays of five nights, one week, one month, or more. If you need more space, consider a one- or two-bedroom apartment that has all the bells and whistles, plus quality furnishings and a wonderful atmosphere that invites you to move right in and begin your life as a temporary Parisian. All properties have cable television, phones, high-speed Internet, hair dryers, and a lovely welcome by Stéphane and Pierre, who remain on-call throughout your stay. The more expensive apartments also include stereos, fax line, answering machine, and housekeepers on request. Depending on location, there will be a washer and dryer and dishwasher, and some with an elevator. Options include cell phone and laptop rental and airport transfers.

TEL Cell: Stéphane 06-72-72-10-42, Pierre 06-63-06-74-39
　FAX 01-44-78-06-76 **EMAIL** contact@kudeta-home.com
　INTERNET www.kudeta-home.com
RATES Per week: small studios 480–800€; 1-bedroom 690–1,200€;
　2-bedroom 800–1,200€; lower rates for stays of 3 months or more
　CREDIT CARDS MC, V

PANACHE
141 South Main Street
Cohasset, MA 02025

Connie Afshar specializes in excellent short-term apartment rent-als in Paris that are centrally located in the Marais, Île St-Louis, Île de la Cité, les Halles, and near the Louvre. They range from basic-budget to lovely and lavish, and they are equipped accordingly. It all depends on your pocketbook and your needs. Properties are inspected regularly, and detailed descriptions and pictures are available on the Website. In addition to securing your perfect Parisian apartment, Connie and her resourceful staff can help with travel arrangements, engage a chef to prepare your meals, or book you into other properties they have throughout France or in Venice, London, and Scotland.

TEL 781-383-6006 **FAX** 781-383-6087 **EMAIL** info@panacherental.com
　INTERNET www.panacherental.com or www.oneworld-travel.com
RATES $170–750 per night; lower rates for stays over 1 week
　CREDIT CARDS Depends on apartment; otherwise, cash or check

PARIS HOLIDAY APARTMENTS

John Knutson's goal is "to ensure your holiday stay in Paris is as enjoyable and exciting as you expect and deserve." Because he owns most of the impressive apartments he rents, there is seldom a middle-man, so his prices are very competitive. As a result, his apartments are so popular that it is vital to reserve at least three months in advance to get the location you want. His Website is particularily well laid out and easy to use. Apartment amenities vary, but all are nonsmok-ing and have washers and dryers, cable TV, hair dryer, and land-line telephone with free outgoing local calls. None are air-conditioned or have a safe. There is a four-night minimum stay and discounts for stays over three weeks.

TEL 01-40-13-97-55 **FAX** 01-40-41-06-04 **EMAIL** parisholidayapts@noos.fr
　INTERNET www.parisholidayapts.com
RATES From 95€ per night for a small studio to 185€ per night for a
　2-bedroom **CREDIT CARDS** MC, V (through PayPal); otherwise, cash or
　U.S. dollar check

PERFECTLY PARIS

Perfectly Paris is an umbrella company representing a group of independent owners in and around Montmartre who want to share their exceptional apartments with you. Don't worry...these are not any old hovels an owner decided to rent while they left town on their own vacation. Indeed not! Each one has been personally selected by

Gail Boisclair because it has met her rigorous requirement that it provide all you need to have a perfectly Parisian living experience. The furnishings and appointments are beautiful, the bathrooms up-to-date, kitchens are very well equipped, and you can rest assured that there will be none of the owner's belongings sharing your space. Because the apartments are in Montmartre, there will be some walking required, and much of it uphill. But the views are spectacular, and the streets are lined with pretty buildings and interesting boutique shopping. Look on the positive side: this exercise permits extra indulgences at the many *patisseries,* restaurants, and interesting cafés that Montmartre is famous for.

Car pickup can be arranged from the airports; guests are met upon arrival at the apartment, and there is always someone on call around the clock should any need arise. There are discounts on stays of two weeks or more.

TEL 01-44-92-00-84; cell 06-77-06-85-87 **EMAIL** gail@perfectlyparis.com
INTERNET www.perfectlyparis.com
RATES From 650€ per week for smallest apartment to 1,350€ a week for 3-bedroom **CREDIT CARDS** MC, V (through PayPal); or U.S., euro, or Canadian check or cash

RENDEZ-VOUS À PARIS LLC

Katrine Grillard has a roster of twenty-five or more marvelous apartments that she manages exclusively. It is easy to see why they are always full. Leaving nothing to chance, Katrine has personally decorated each property in her own tasteful French style, and they are all lovely. I can additionally assure you without question that these are dynamite apartments in locations that every visitor clamors to be in: Île St-Louis, St-Germain-des-Prés, and near Alma in the eighth. The apartments range in size from one to four bedrooms, and always the bedrooms are on the back, away from early-morning and late-night street noise. They have cable television (where possible), stereo music systems, telephones with answering machines, high-speed Internet, washers and dryers, and dishwashers. Housekeeping services are available on request, or are included for stays of over one month. The kitchens are fitted with matching china, nice glassware and cutlery, good cooking facilities, and proper stoves and ovens in addition to microwaves. The availability of air-conditioning and elevators depends on the building, its age, and location.

TEL 06-15-26-30-04 **FAX** 01-56-24-19-06 **EMAIL** rendez-vousaparis@ club-internet.fr **INTERNET** www.rendez-vousaparis.com
RATES From 175–400€ per night, 3,000–6,000€ per month; 4-night minimum stay; lower rates for longer stays and in low season
  CREDIT CARDS None, payment in U.S. dollars, euros, or bank transfer

RENTVILLAS.COM
700 East Main Street
Ventura, CA 93001

Rentvillas.com has an enviable track record of being one of the most customer-focused rental companies in the industry. Founded by Suzanne Pidduck, it has grown from covering only Italian properties to being a thoroughly computerized operation with properties all over Europe, including Paris and the French countryside. Everyone on staff has extensive travel experience and many are multilingual. You will be matched with a travel advisor who has expertise in your area of interest.

TEL 805-641-1650, toll-free in U.S. 800-726-6702 **FAX** 805-641-1630
    EMAIL suzanne@rentvillas.com **INTERNET** www.rentvillas.com
RATES From $781 per month; 1-week minimum; no Sun arrivals
    CREDIT CARDS MC, V

ROTHRAY (20)
10, rue Nicolas-Flamel, 75004
Métro: Châtelet

It is an undisputed fact that RothRay apartments are some of the most popular in Paris. This opinion is shared not only by all of their loyal and contented clients but by most of the competition. I absolutely agree—after one stay, I vowed to always let competent Ray Lampard and his capable partner, Roth, arrange my living accommodations anytime I am in Paris. The problem is that their apartments are always full, usually a year in advance!

Some short-term private apartment rentals in Paris can be potluck affairs: you find unwelcome surprises on arrival, and during your stay you must contend with strange decor, varying amenities and levels of cleanliness, and haphazard services by the agency in charge, which shows little interest in you after they have your money . . . up front. You will find none of these problems in any RothRay apartment, which are located in interesting *quartiers* that put picturesque Paris at your fingertips. After a few days you will discover what fun it is to actually be a part of Paris, and you'll probably spend a good deal of your time trying to make more permanent arrangements or planning your return.

RothRay's well-equipped properties have cable television, stereo systems, telephones with answering machines, washers, some dishwashers, and kitchens fitted with china, crystal, and cooking utensils. You can only fully appreciate the quality of their kitchens if you have ever tried to prepare a meal in a French closet-style kitchen with a mishmash of "rental" pots and pans and chipped, unmatched dishes for serving. Weekly housekeeping service, linen changes, and a refrigerator stocked upon arrival with fruit juices, champagne, and beer are all included. Both Roth and Ray are available in Paris for problem-solving around the clock. This is an important point: you are not dealing with a local representative of the person or company you rented from. With

RothRay you are dealing with the two people who are the property owners and who are in charge of, and responsible for, everything, and they pride themselves on a very high level of around-the-clock guest satisfaction. As one guest happily told me, "There is RothRay, and then everyone else, just trying to catch up." How very true that is. RothRay apartments are in such demand that they are booked usually a year in advance, so please make your reservation the minute you know your dates in Paris. There is a seven-day minimum, and they prefer one-month rentals.

Exclusive for readers of *Great Sleeps Paris:* When reserving a RothRay apartment, *Great Sleeps Paris* readers who mention the book will get a complimentary taxi ride from the airport. They will be personally welcomed by Ray Lampard at their apartment and reimbursed for the taxi trip. Just be sure to save your receipt.

TEL 01-48-87-13-37 **FAX** 01-42-78-17-72 **EMAIL** rothray@online.fr
   INTERNET www.rothray.com
RATES 90–190€ per day. Prices vary by size, location, and length of stay.
   7-day minimum stay; stays of 1 month or more preferred. Monthly rates
   are 25–30% less on a daily basis. **CREDIT CARDS** None; cash or personal
   checks in your currency.

SAINT-LOUIS MARAIS RÉSIDENCE (49)
1, rue Charles V, 75004
Métro: St-Paul

The stunning Saint-Louis Marais Résidence apartments evoke a lovely feeling of Paris, thanks not only to their A+ locations but to their classic French style. There is no question: these are some of the best in Paris and at the best prices. What you can save by staying here versus in a luxury hotel will easily allow you to book an extra week and still have money left over.

The dozen or so studios and apartments are managed by Jean-Michel Tournou, who is also the director of Hôtel Saint-Louis Marais (see page 104), Hôtel Saint-Louis Bastille (see page 220), and Hôtel Saint-Louis Opéra (see page 211). There is a one-week minimum stay, and of course, the longer the stay, the better the rate. All of the apartments are on pretty courtyards; none face noisy streets. They are kept in excellent condition: no peeling paint or cloths tossed over a chair to hide its many spots. Half have elevators, but the others, with one exception, are on the first or second floor. Most have air-conditioning, WiFi, dishwashers, and washers and dryers. The bathrooms and kitchens are excellent. Twice weekly maid service is included, as is cable television, CD players, and telephones.

TEL 01-48-87-87-04 **FAX** 01-48-87-33-26 **EMAIL** slmarais@noos.fr
   INTERNET www.saintlouismarais.com
RATES From 90–400€ per day; one-week minimum stay (start any day of the
   week); discounts for stays over 2 weeks **CREDIT CARDS** AE, DC, MC, V

Bed and Breakfast in a Private Home

If you want to get up close and personal with the Parisians, staying in a bed and breakfast in a private home is the way to go. I cannot imagine a better way to personalize a stay and learn more about the French culture in general and life in Paris in particular.

BED AND BREAKFAST IN A PRIVATE HOME

ALCÔVE & AGAPES, LE BED & BREAKFAST À PARIS

Françoise Foret has developed a roster of over eighty Parisian hosts who offer bed-and-breakfast accommodations in their homes, which range from Haussmann apartments, private mansions, and artists' workshops to lively family homes. As she puts it, "Alcôve & Agapes can offer guest rooms that cater to the businessperson, please the budget-conscious, and charm the first-class traveler."

Françoise personally visits every home at least once a year to ensure that her standards of cleanliness and comfort are being met. All are located in Paris and are within walking distance to a métro. The majority are nonsmoking. Her hosts range in age from twenty-five to sixty-five years and usually speak fluent English. Some homes have shared bathrooms and/or toilets, have adored family pets, are up a few flights of stairs, or have strictly residential locations. Others are deluxe in every way and are in the most desirable tourist areas. To avoid any unpleasant surprises, Françoise provides detailed descriptions and photos, which are available on the Website or can be sent to prospective guests. Taking the guesswork out of selecting the right B&B, these fact sheets provide details about the host, home, bedroom, neighborhood, distance from tourist sites, and directions on how to get there. She also has a list of services that are available to guests, including airport pickup and delivery, massages, cooking lessons, and private guides. Whatever your bottom line, Françoise says, "We take great care to ensure a pleasant stay in the City of Light and trust that you will be among our many satisfied guests who arrive as clients and leave as friends."

TEL 01-44-85-06-05 **FAX** 01-44-85-06-14 **EMAIL** info@bed-and-breakfast-in-paris.com **INTERNET** www.bed-and-breakfast-in-paris.com
RATES 1–2 people 75–175€ per night, depending on accommodation
  CREDIT CARDS V only for B&B fee; rentals take euros only, paid to host upon arrival

GOOD MORNING PARIS (36)
43, Lacepede, 75005
Métro: Place Monge

Christine Bokobza spent twenty years traveling the world and staying in B&Bs along the way. When she settled in Paris, she wanted to enable visitors to have the type of personal accommodation that would allow them to get to know locals on a deeper level. The result is Good Morning Paris, which provides one hundred B&B choices ranging from a simple room with a shared bath to an apartment filled with decades of family mementos, to a knockout one-bedroom choice in the heart of the Latin Quarter. A few of her locations have kitchens where guests can prepare their own breakfast; otherwise, in true B&B fashion, you have breakfast with your hosts. All the bedrooms are nonsmoking, but policies for the remainder of the house depend on the hosts. All of her hosts speak English and are eager to help their guests enjoy Paris to the fullest.

TEL 01-47-07-28-29 **FAX** 01-47-07-44-45 **EMAIL** info@goodmorningparis.fr
INTERNET www.goodmorningparis.fr
RATES Single: shared bath 54€, private bath 64€, private bath in "charm & character" B&B 94€; double: shared bath 66€, private bath 76€, private bath in "charm & character" B&B 106€; extra person 18€
CREDIT CARDS AE, MC, V

LE MARAIS HOUSE

Le Marais House is a fifteenth-century town house on the edge of the Marais, just down from the oldest house in Paris, which was built in 1407 by the chemist Nicolas Flamel, who inspired J. K. Rowling's *Harry Potter* stories. This very special home is so exclusive and private that there is no address, no name outside, and no keys. Entry is by secret code only. The house is owned by Yann Gabriel Hentschke, a successful businessman who lived in New York for many years and then in a chateau in Touraine. When he decided to move his young son and business interests to Paris, he wanted to re-create the ambience of his chateau. After extensive searching, he found this property, which had been, among other things, a factory making glass signs and a café.

Yann's motto may be "Too much is never enough," but it still took great vision to turn the delapidated interior into the elegant five-suite town house it is today. During nine months of hard work, he and his decorator meticulously created the fabulous rooms, filling them with museum-quality furnishings and creating mahogany-paneled bathrooms with fittings from C. P. Hart in London. Nine fireplaces were added; thick carved doors brought in to hide the elevator; floors were made from seventeenth-century stones from the Loire Valley and fifteenth-century stones from a monestery in Burgandy. Bevilacqua fabrics from Venice were used in one of the suites; magnificent velvets, damasks, and fabrics from Brunschwig & Fils in others. A glass-floored, plant-filled atrium forms the bridge between two sections of the house. Breakfast is served in a beautiful vaulted dining room that is ten meters under the building. Guests are always invited to sit by the fire in the living room and enjoy an afternoon cup of tea or a drink before dinner. The suites, one of which has its own balcony, can be booked independently, or the house can be reserved in its entirety for small and elegent gatherings, including candlelight dinners and photo shoots. Yann is always on hand to greet his guests and see to their every need. Assisting him in these efforts are Vendôme and Bonheur, a pair of friendly chocolate Labs.

TEL 01-42-74-61-36; cell 06-16-23-39-90 **EMAIL** info@maraishouse.com
   INTERNET www.maraishouse.com

FACILITIES & SERVICES Elevator to most parts of the house (some steps required), hair dryer, minibar, sauna, TV with international reception, entirely nonsmoking.

RATES 1–2 people 225€ per night; entire house 3,000€ per night
   CREDIT CARDS MC, V for deposit only; cash or traveler's checks in euros

Boat on the Seine

BATEAU SYMPATICO (6)
Port du Suffren, 75007
Métro: Bir Hakeim; RER Champ-de-Mars–Tour Eiffel

Bob Abrams's love of boats is evident the minute you step off the *quai* along the Seine and into his meticulously restored *peniche* (barge). He has spent upwards of twenty years on the project, and the results are remarkable. The main part of the boat consists of one great room (800 square feet!), trimmed in highly polished wood with gleaming brass fittings. It is furnished with a leather settee, comfortable chairs, a dining table and chairs, and some of the many fascinating objects he has collected during his years of globetrotting. To stay connected with the outside world, you will have a telephone, Internet connection, and television with a VCR (all utilities except the telephone are included in the rate). There is a king-size bed, plus a trundle bed suitable for a child. However, no children under ten are accepted, and neither are smokers or animals.

Hardly a galley, the kitchen is big enough for you to cook your Christmas goose in the oven and prepare all the side dishes on the four-burner stove. Of course, the kitchen is equipped with all the pots, pans, and necessary implements to do it in great style. For simple heating and eating, there is a microwave. The large bathroom has a shower and a washer and dryer. If you are here in the warm months, you will be able to relax on the deck in a lounge chair and watch all the activities taking place along this interesting part of the Seine. And you'll be right under the shadow of the Eiffel Tower and only a three-minute walk from a métro stop. For a different, very memorable time in Paris, a stay on the romantic *Bateau Sympatico* will be impossible to top.

TEL & FAX 01-47-53-02-7 **EMAIL** enquiries@quai48parisvacation.com
INTERNET www.quai48parisvacation.com
RATES 2 people $1,820 per week; extra person 16€ per day (maximum of 2 extra people); 1-week minimum from May–Aug; lower rates for longer stays; 30% supplement for Christmas through New Year's; reservations required **CREDIT CARDS** None; cash, bank transfer, or traveler's check in U.S. dollars

Camping Out

LES CAMPINGS DU BOIS DE BOULOGNE
Allée du Bord de l'Eau, Bois de Boulogne, 75016
Métro: Porte-Maillot, then take camp shuttle bus or public bus No. 244

Coleman stoves, tents, inflatable mattresses, and citronella candles may not be on everyone's packing list for a trip to Paris, but they might be on yours if you are a camper. Yes, it is possible to pitch a tent in Paris! Les Campings in the Bois de Boulogne is next to the Seine on the far edge of the park and provides the only true rustic opportunity for those who like to pitch a tent under the stars. Geared to students and hearty international travelers, or those with RVs, the campground is located four kilometers away from the nearest métro, making it almost essential that you have your own set of wheels. Otherwise, there is a camp bus, but its schedule may not match yours, and then you'll be forced to walk. At the campground, there's a convenience store, hot showers, a coin-operated washer and dryer, and a restaurant. The office is open from 7 A.M. until 10 P.M. and accepts no reservations for campsites, but it will accept them for RV bookings and large camping groups. Everything is always on a first-come, first-served basis.

NOTE: To reach the campground from the Porte-Maillot métro station, exit the station at sortie André Maurois and take a shuttle bus, which runs April to October every half hour during much of the day (but not between noon and 6 P.M.) and some of the night; it's free in July and August. Alternatively, take public bus No. 244 from the Porte-Maillot métro station, get off at route des Moulins, and walk down the path to the right. Do not follow misleading signs to the left on the main road.

TEL 01-45-24-30-00 **FAX** 01-42-24-42-95 **EMAIL** paris@campingparis.fr
INTERNET www.campingparis.fr

FACILITIES & SERVICES Open year-round, convenience store, coin-operated washers and dryers, information office, free hot showers, shuttle bus service, and restaurant from April to October

RATES All rates are per night: 1–2 persons, no car, tent site without electricity 17€, with electricity 19€; with car, tent site without electricity 28€; with electricity 35€; RV (camper van) site with electricity and water hookups 35€. Mobile home rental (including electricity & water) for 2–4 people 75–95€ per night. Lower rates Sept–June; *taxe de séjour* on all rates 0.20€ per person, per day **CREDIT CARDS** AE, MC, V

Hostels

Hostels appeal to travelers with youth on their side and wanderlust in their hearts. Only one of the hostels listed here has an age limit, but otherwise, they all follow the same general guidelines: shared rooms, public facilities, lockouts in the afternoon, and sometimes a sheaf of other rules and restrictions regarding drinking, smoking, guests, curfews, and so on. However, they often make up in camaraderie what they lack in luxury, and you are almost certain to meet like-minded budget travelers who will be more than willing to share their tales of Parisian adventures.

If you are serious about hostelling, then you should consider becoming a member of Hostelling International/American Youth Hostel (HI/AYH), which runs 4,500 hostels in seventy countries. There is no age limit (13 percent of members are senior citizens), and they offer other services as well. If you are not already a member when you arrive at an affiliated hostel, you will be charged a supplement per night for six nights, which will then qualify you as a member. Auberge Jules Ferry is the best located HI hostel in Paris. For general information on Hostelling International and a list of their other Paris hostels, see La Centrale de Réservations or log onto their Website, www.hiayh.org.

HOSTELS

ALOHA HOSTEL (13)
1, rue Borromée, 75015
Métro: Volontaires
60 beds, 2 rooms with showers, none with toilets

Two brothers own the Aloha Hostel and four other hostels in Paris: Le Village Hostel–Montmartre, 3 Ducks Hostel, Woodstock Hostel, and Young & Happy Hostel. In addition, they operate a bottom-of-the-barrel budget hotel that I do not include because, in my opinion, the neighborhood is not safe after dark and the desk staff is creepy.

While each hostel they run has its own personality, all have many similarities in rates, services, and amenities. Unless otherwise stated, the following information applies to all five hostels. They are open year-round, but during the summer high-season between April and October, all stays are generally limited to two weeks. There is no age limit for guests. Every day there is a cleaning lockout between 11 A.M. and 5 P.M. and a strict 2 A.M. curfew, though reception is open daily from 8 A.M. to 2 A.M. No booze, no refunds, no smoking in the rooms, and please do not call the receptionist "ma'am." No credit cards are accepted—it is euro cash or euro traveler's checks only. There are lower rates in winter from November through March. Breakfast—which consists of bread, and coffee, tea, or hot chocolate—is included, and so are showers and the *taxe de séjour*. If you do not BYO sheets and towels, count on spending around 3€ plus a 7€ deposit for sheets and 2€ plus 2€ deposit for a towel. You can surf the Internet or send and receive emails for a nominal charge. There are kitchen privileges, a TV in the lounge, and always a friendly atmosphere and helpful, English-speaking staff. Extensions must be made by 9:30 P.M. the day before. There are strict, and costly, cancellation policies: read the fine print!

At the Aloha Hostel in particular, guests can mingle in the backpack-laden reception area, comparing cheap travel tips. Rooms have benefited from a redecoration project; beams have been added and so have new showers. There are no singles. The working-class neighborhood is full of supermarkets, bakeries, banks, and other survival-type shopping. Otherwise, it's at least twenty minutes to tourist destinations.

TEL 01-42-73-03-03 **FAX** 01-42-73-14-14 **EMAIL** friends@aloha.fr
    INTERNET www.aloha.fr
FACILITIES & SERVICES Communal kitchen, no elevator (3 floors), Internet in lounge, luggage room (unlocked), no lockers, nightly movies, showers on every floor, safe in office (no charge), no smoking in rooms
RATES Double room 26€, dorm (4–8 people) 23€ per person; showers free; *taxe de séjour* included **CREDIT CARDS** Only to secure reservation; otherwise, euro cash or traveler's checks only
BREAKFAST Included

AUBERGE INTERNATIONAL DES JEUNES (19)
10, rue Trousseau, 75011
Métro: Ledru-Rollin
190 beds

It is clean, you can book ahead, and you can pay by credit card. When you arrive, you will have a spartan clean room that is shared by two to four people. Rooms for four have private facilities. Sinks are in all the other rooms, while toilets and free showers are in the hall. There is no curfew, no age limit, and no ban on groups, but you will have to observe a cleaning lockout from 10 A.M. to 3 P.M.

TEL 01-47-00-62-00 **FAX** 01-47-00-33-16 **INTERNET** www.aijparis.com
FACILITIES & SERVICES No elevator (4 floors), Internet in lounge, locked luggage area, office safe (no charge), no smoking or booze allowed
RATES March–Oct 15€ per person; Nov–Feb 14€ per person; towel rental 1€; *taxe de séjour* included **CREDIT CARDS** AE, MC, V
BREAKFAST Continental included

AUBERGE JULES FERRY (2)
8, boulevard Jules Ferry, 75011
Métro: République
99 beds

No curfew, no age limit, no reservations for four to six people, no groups, and no stays over one week in this sanctioned Hostelling International choice near place de la République. An International Youth Hostel Card is required. Rooms sleep from two to six, and the price includes breakfast, showers, and sheets. No towels are provided. Cleaning lockout is from noon to 2:00 P.M.; the office is open 24/7.

TEL 01-43-57-55-60 **FAX** 01-43-14-82-09 **EMAIL** auberge@micronet.fr
INTERNET www.fuaj.org
FACILITIES & SERVICES Elevator, Internet in lounge, lockers (BYO locks), microwave, communal refrigerator, coin-operated washer and dryer
RATES 20€ per person; small lockers free, large lockers 1.55€ per day; *taxe de séjour* included **CREDIT CARDS** MC, V
BREAKFAST Included

LA CENTRALE DE RÉSERVATIONS (FUAJ; 2)
27, rue Pajol, 75018
Métro: Marx-Dormoy

La Centrale de Réservations (FUAJ), run by Hostelling International, is a good place to go to get a cheap student bed in Paris, or anywhere else in Europe. Membership in Hostelling International is required; when purchased in the United States, it costs around $14 if you are twenty-six years old or younger, or around $20 if you are over twenty-six. If you buy your card in France, it will cost more. Cards are good for one year from date of purchase. A trip to one of their Paris offices will provide you with a same-day reservation in any of their affiliated hostels or budget hotels. Not only can you book a bed, but you can make ongoing travel arrangements by bus, boat, or air; book tours to other parts of the world; or nail down an excursion in Paris.

There will be a reservation fee, payable at the time of booking, but it is deducted from the cost of your bed. The office is open Monday to Friday from 9:30 A.M. to 5 P.M., Saturday 10 A.M. to 4 P.M.

TEL 01-44-89-87-27 **FAX** 01-44-89-87-10/49 **INTERNET** www.fuaj.org
RATES 21€ per person in dorms; showers free; rental towels 3€; sheets 3€; *taxe de séjour* 1€ per person, per day; requires HI membership
   CREDIT CARDS MC, V
BREAKFAST Included

LE VILLAGE HOSTEL–MONTMARTRE (12)
20, rue d'Orsel, 75018
Métro: Anvers
75 beds in rooms for 2–6 persons, all with shower and toilet

At this hostel, all the rooms have private facilities, and six rooms (Nos. 201, 205, 302, 305, 401, and 406) have views of Sacré Coeur and the gardens surrounding it. If these rooms are not available, you can enjoy the view from the small hostel terrace. The hostel is on a street lined with fabric shops, and the famed bargain-bin department store Tati is at the corner. Montmartre can be fun if you don't mind the hikes around the *butte,* and if you revel in the laid-back party atmosphere that permeates the more tourist-saturated parts of this special area of Paris. The good news for party animals is that there is no curfew at this hostel. For a complete description, see Aloha Hostel (page 301).

TEL 01-42-64-22-02 **FAX** 01-42-64-22-04 **INTERNET** www.villagehostel.fr
FACILITIES & SERVICES Elevator, hair dryer, kitchen privileges, luggage room, TV with international reception in lounge, office safe (no charge), no smoking in rooms, WiFi in lounge
RATES Double 57€ (includes sheets), dorm (4–6 people) 23€ per person, triple 25€ per person; sheets 2.50€, towels 1€ **CREDIT CARDS** Only to secure reservation; otherwise, euro cash or traveler's checks only
BREAKFAST Included

3 DUCKS HOSTEL (12)
6, place Étienne Pernet, 75015
Métro: Félix-Faure, Commerce
70 beds in shared rooms; 6 rooms also have showers only

This youthful hangout is not the sort of place moms and dads would check into—nor is it one you would want them to check out on your behalf. Its rugged appeal draws backpackers and other wanderers who value camaraderie along with wild and ribald fun over esthetics or a peaceful night's rest. The relaxed management provides cooking facilities, hot showers, a TV in a casual bar with cheap beer and wine, and rooms for two, three, or four persons. There are no lockers, only a storage room. The reception and bar are open all day. The lockout is from noon to 4 P.M., but there is a shower, bathroom, and kitchen open during this time. There is no curfew. For a complete description, see Aloha Hostel (page 301).

NOTE: 3 Ducks Hostel is on the right side of Jean Baptiste de Grenelle Church, at the end of rue de Commerce.

TEL 01-48-42-04-05 **FAX** 01-48-42-99-99 **INTERNET** www.3ducks.fr
FACILITIES & SERVICES Bar with beer and wine, no elevator (3 floors), kitchen privileges, French TV in bar, office safe (no charge), WiFi in lounge
RATES Double 26€ per person, dorms (4–10 people) 23€ per person
   CREDIT CARDS Only to secure reservation; otherwise, euro cash or traveler's checks only
BREAKFAST Included

WOODSTOCK HOSTEL (3)
48, rue Rodier, 75009
Métro: Anvers, Poissonnière
75 beds

Woodstock Hostel is about a ten-minute walk from the Gare du Nord and Gare de l'Est train stations and across the street from a pretty park where you can enjoy a picnic lunch or watch children playing. Also close by are bakeries, a grocery, and a laundromat. Even though it is close to Pigalle and all the sleaze of that area, the hostel is in a safe pocket. But do be aware that the Anvers métro station is not considered safe at night. For a complete description, see Aloha Hostel (page 301).

TEL 01-48-78-87-76 **FAX** 01-48-78-01-63 **INTERNET** www.woodstock.fr
FACILITIES & SERVICES No elevator (3 floors), Internet in lounge, kitchen privileges, office safe (no charge)
RATES Double 24€ per person, dorms (4–6 people) 21€ per person
   CREDIT CARDS Only to secure reservation; otherwise, euro cash or traveler's checks only
BREAKFAST Included

YOUNG & HAPPY (Y & H) HOSTEL (34)
80, rue Mouffetard, 75005
Métro: Place Monge, Censier-Daubenton
65 beds

The Young & Happy Hostel is so named because it's friendly and everyone who stays here has such a good time. It is located on rue Mouffetard, a famous *marché* street with loads of cheap eats—everything from crêpes and croissants to pizza slices and dripping Greek sandwiches. It is also close to the Latin Quarter. You can reserve with a one-night advance deposit, or arrive when they open and hope for the best. Lockout is from 11 A.M. to 4 P.M., and curfew is at 2 A.M. For a complete description, see Aloha Hostel (page 301).

TEL 01-47-07-47-07 **FAX** 01-47-07-22-24 **INTERNET** www.youngandhappy.fr
FACILITIES & SERVICES No elevator (4 floors), Internet in lounge, kitchen privileges, French TV in lounge, office safe (no charge)
RATES Double 26€ per person, dorms (3–8 people) 23€ per person
   CREDIT CARDS Only to secure reservation; otherwise, euro cash or traveler's checks only
BREAKFAST Included

Residence Hotels

Residence hotels are a popular concept because they combine many of the services and amenities you find in regular hotels with the advantages of having your own apartment. They generally come with a fully-equipped kitchen, are usually roomier, have more closet space than most deluxe hotel rooms, and often include some sort of housekeeping service. They are nice options for business travelers staying for longer periods of time who still want the services of a hotel. It is important to note that they bear absolutely no resemblance to the down-and-out accommodations that often go by the name "residence hotels" in the States.

Residence hotels in France can choose whether or not to apply for a star rating, and many do not. If a place listed below possesses no stars, that does not mean it is a "no star"; it could be luxurious and expensive—it just doesn't have the stars to prove it.

RESIDENCE HOTELS

($) indicates a Big Splurge

CENTRE PARISIEN DE ZEN (22)
35, rue de Lyon, 75012
Métro: Gare de Lyon, Bastille
5 studios, 1 one-bedroom apartment, all with kitchenettes

Peace and serenity are the by-words of this calming alternative to a stressful hotel stay. Grazyna and Jacob Perl, both Polish and both Zen masters, have opened five studio apartments, a one-bedroom apartment, and a meditation center in an old school building. When I first heard about it, I definitely had my doubts. Once I saw the amazingly low prices for the sparkling clean, whitewashed, wood-floor studios surrounding a leafy, cobbled courtyard, I was ready to check in. Each bright, sunny, Ikea-furnished unit sleeps two on a good mattress with an orthopedic pillow (on request) and a duvet cover. In addition to a private bath and shower, there is a kitchen corner with two burners, refrigerator, sink, and all the utensils and dishes you will need. With one exception (No. 24), closet and drawer space is certainly adequate. A telephone, cable television, and WiFi insure you will stay connected. Nice touches include Grazyna's framed paintings and a few paperback books. Once-a-week housekeeping service and linen change is included. The meditation room is open to everyone, and the friendly dogs, Anouk and Taylor, are never too busy for a friendly pat on the head.

The neighborhood is a ten-minute walk from the Bastille, and the Marais and place des Vosges are a twenty-minute stroll. If you are a night owl, there is the fun and frivolity along rue de Lappe and rue de la Roquette. On Thursday and Sunday there is a huge open-air market at Bastille, and plenty of little food shops are nearby. A minimum stay of one week is required, and longer stays are welcomed. No smoking is allowed, and neither are shoes.

TEL 01-44-87-08-13 **FAX** 01-44-87-09-07 **EMAIL** maisonzen@ pariszencenter.com **INTERNET** www.maisonzen.com

FACILITIES & SERVICES Air-conditioning, direct-dial phone with free local calls, no elevator (3 floors), hair-dryer, meditation room, cable TV, office safe (no charge), no smoking allowed, WiFi

RATES Per week: studio, single/double 385/490€; 1-bedroom apartment, single/double 455/560€; *taxe de séjour* included **CREDIT CARDS** None, cash only

BREAKFAST Not served

FAMILY HÔTEL RÉSIDENCE (7)
23, rue Fondary, 75015
Métro: Dupleix, Avenue Émile-Zola, La Motte Picquet–Grenelle
21 studios, all with kitchenette, shower, and toilet

These plain-as-could-be studios in the middle of the working-class fifteenth arrondissement put the B in "basic." The twenty-one bargain sites are geared for economizers who are in for the long haul and want only a clean place to cook, eat, sleep, and take a shower, and nothing more. Fifteen have TV; some have sofabeds, and others proper double or twin beds. The low-maintenance floors are white tile, bathrooms are reminiscent of train compartments, and the closets are designed for those who travel light and never shop. The colors match and so does the simple furniture. Kitchens are stocked with the barest essentials to prepare simple meals. There are two burners for cooking, but no microwave or oven. The units are kept clean, thanks to the housekeepers who swoop through three times a week. The operation is owned and run by Au Pacific Hôtel (see page 238) down the street, where you pick up your keys and pay your bill.

TEL 01-43-92-42-42 (9 A.M.–7 P.M. daily) **FAX** 01-45-77-70-73 **EMAIL** pacifichotel@wanadoo.fr **INTERNET** www.familyresidence75.com

FACILITIES & SERVICES Direct-dial phone with separate line for each studio, elevator, kitchenettes, housekeeping service, TV with international reception (in most rooms), office safe at Pacific Hôtel (no charge), Internet in rooms

RATES Single 41€ (sofabed, no TV); 1–2 persons 48€ (double sofabed, no TV), 66–74€ (double or twin beds, TV); triple 81€ (double and single

beds, TV); 20% discount after 7 nights, 30% discount after 15 nights;
all utilities, except phone, included; *taxe de séjour* included
CREDIT CARDS MC, V
BREAKFAST 7€, available at Au Pacific Hôtel

HOME PLAZZA: LE PATIO SAINT-ANTOINE AND LES JARDINS DU MARAIS

The two Home Plazza hotels are in the eleventh arrondissement,
a part of Paris that once was a tourist wilderness and now is close to
the thick of things. They both are in lovely garden settings and offer
guest rooms or suites with fitted kitchenettes in a universally modern
style that suits both professional and family stays. While the Art
Deco–inspired Les Jardins du Marais has the edge in location, history,
and amenities, the smaller Le Patio Saint-Antoine is less impersonal
and sterile. At both, impressive discounts can be negotiated during
the low season and for longer stays, but during the fashion shows, the
Paris Air Show, and any other internationally publicized events or
conferences, there are serious supplements.

LE PATIO SAINT-ANTOINE ★★★ ($, 20)
289 bis, rue du Faubourg St-Antoine, 75011
Métro: Nation, Faidherbe-Chaligny
89 guest rooms and suites, all with equipped kitchenettes

From a security standpoint, I would avoid the rooms on the garden level. For most people staying at Le Patio Saint-Antoine, public
transportation would be easier than walking to the closest tourist
attractions in and around the Marais.

TEL 01-40-21-22-23 (reservations), 01-40-09-40-00 **FAX** 01-40-09-11-55
    EMAIL resabastille@homeplazza.com **INTERNET** www.homeplazza.com
FACILITIES & SERVICES Air-conditioning (portable unit), conference room,
    direct-dial phone, elevator to most rooms, hair dryer, laundry service,
    parking (23€ per day), TV with international reception and pay-per-view,
    room safe (no charge), guest computer in lobby, 1 floor nonsmoking
RATES Single 230€, double 250–295€, junior suite (3–6 persons) 465–725€;
    extra bed 46€; free baby cot; *taxe de séjour* included **CREDIT CARDS** AE,
    DC, MC, V
BREAKFAST American buffet 18€ per person, 12€ for children under 14

LES JARDINS DU MARAIS ★★★★ ($, 11)
74, rue Amelot, 75011
Métro: St-Sébastien–Froissart, Chemin Vert
265 guest rooms and suites, some with equipped kitchenettes

History buffs will be interested to know that the "Eiffel" building
at Les Jardins du Marais was once Gustave Eiffel's workshop, and is
now a designated Parisian historical monument. From the doorstep
of Les Jardins du Marais, it is an easy walk to place des Vosges, the
Bastille, and the Musée National Picasso.

TEL 01-40-21-20-00 **FAX** 01-47-00-82-40 **EMAIL** resabastille@
    homeplazza.com **INTERNET** www.homeplazza.com

FACILITIES & SERVICES Air-conditioning, airport transfers (50€), bar, business center, conference room, direct-dial phone, elevator, fitness center, hair dryer, 10 rooms handicapped-accessible, Internet access, iron, laundry service, luggage storage, complimentary newspapers, parking (23€ per day), restaurant, TV with international reception and pay-per-view, room safe (no charge), several nonsmoking floors
RATES 1–2 people 350–395€; junior suite (1–4 people) 600–700€; *taxe de séjour* included **CREDIT CARDS** AE, DC, MC,V
BREAKFAST American buffet 20€ per person

HÔTEL RÉSIDENCE DES ARTS ($, 28)
14, rue Gît-le-Coeur, 75006
Métro: Odéon, St-Michel; RER St-Michel–Notre-Dame
2 double rooms (no kitchens), 6 suites with kitchens

If you are looking for the ease of independent living combined with the full services of a hotel, the posh Résidence des Arts is for you. Pivotally located in the very core of St-Germain-des-Prés, the fifteenth-century private residence hotel offers two beautiful rooms and six suites, each combining luxurious touches and individual service. In all of the units, there is a private telephone line, cable television, Internet connection, and air-conditioning. One benefit of the deluxe rooms and suites is that they can be combined into large two-bedroom apartments, which is convenient for families.

TEL 01-55-42-71-11 **FAX** 01-55-42-71-00 **EMAIL** resa@residencedesarts.org
INTERNET www.arts-residence-paris.com
FACILITIES & SERVICES Air-conditioning, direct-dial phone with private line, hair dryer, elevator to half-floor, daily housekeeping service, daily towel and linen change, kitchen with microwave in suites, laundry service, TV with international reception, room safe (no charge), free WiFi
RATES Standard room (1–2 persons) 135–190€; suite for 1–2 persons 205–280€, 3–4 persons 220–300€; connecting suites for up to 4 adults and 2 children 340–490€; *taxe de séjour* included **CREDIT CARDS** AE, DC, MC, V
BREAKFAST Continental 10€ per person

LIBERTEL RÉSIDENCE–VILLA DAUBENTON (39)
34, rue de l'Arbalète, 75005
Métro: Censier-Daubenton
16 studios and apartments

From a day-to-day living standpoint, the location is interesting because it is within easy walking distance to rue Mouffetard, one of the most famous market streets on the Left Bank, and the roving market at place Monge, where stalls are set up on Wednesday, Friday, and Sunday mornings. Walkers will enjoy strolling through the nearby Jardin des Plants or Jardin du Luxembourg. The accommodations are exceptional. There are only three per floor, so that alone is a plus. All of them, including the studios, have enough room, excellent bathrooms, and good closet space. Two one-bedroom units have a private terrace, and No. 601, an airy two-level duplex, has two terraces. The color of choice is blue, which can be a bit tiring, but you are not moving in forever . . . just a week or two. Daily housekeeping service is included.

TEL 01-55-43-25-50 **FAX** 01-55-43-81-40 **EMAIL** residencevilladaubenton@ regetel.com **INTERNET** www.regetel.com

FACILITIES & SERVICES Direct-dial phone, elevator, hair dryer, equipped kitchen, laundry services, parking (15€ per day), TV with international reception, office safe (no charge), Internet in lobby

RATES Studios (1–2 persons) 180€; apartments (1–4 persons) 230€; duplex (1–6 persons) 275€; *taxe de séjour* included **CREDIT CARDS** AE, DC, MC, V

BREAKFAST Continental 10€ per person

PIERRE & VACANCES–RÉSIDENCE MONTMARTRE (14)
10, place Charles Dullin, 75018
Métro: Abbesses, Anvers
76 studios and apartments

Pierre & Vacances is a large company that has many vacation-residence hotels throughout France, plus two in Rome. This Paris property is located on a quiet cul-de-sac in Montmartre. Staying anywhere in Montmartre will require walking up and down hills, but the payoff is the villagelike community and all the picturesque little streets and alleyways you will discover in your travels. Thanks to a recent facelift that involved painting and recarpeting, this once worn-out establishment has improved. Unfortunately, this has not extended to the lobby and reception, which have had the same ugly black leather sofas for years. The impersonal yellow, blue, and white accommodations are spacious and simply furnished in wash-and-wipe white laminate. Most units have a microwave, all have a dishwasher and weekly housekeeping service. Frankly, it is not my first choice, but it is a good fall-back address to remember if you like Montmarte.

TEL 01-45-58-87-00 (reservations), 01-42-57-14-55 **FAX** 01-45-57-28-43 (reservations), 01-42-54-48-87 **EMAIL** montmartre@pierre-vacances.fr **INTERNET** www.pierrevacances-city.com

FACILITIES & SERVICES Direct-dial phone, elevator, equipped kitchens, some with dishwashers, laundry services, private parking, TV with international reception, office safe (no charge)

RATES Studio (1–4 persons) 117–151€; apartments (2–6 persons) 183–231€; parking (20€ per day, 80€ per week); 10% discount after 8 days, 20% discount after 31 days; *taxe de séjour* 1€ per person, per day **CREDIT CARDS** AE, DC, MC, V

BREAKFAST In-room Continental 9€ per person

RÉSIDENCE HÔTEL DES TROIS POUSSINS ★★★ (5)
15, rue Clauzel, 75009
Métro: St-Georges
19 studios with kitchens, 16 hotel rooms, all with bath or shower and toilet

In its former life, the Résidence Hôtel des Trois Poussins was a fleabag bunker for young, hard-partying backpackers who were more interested in the earthly activities around Pigalle than in a decent place to stay. To say the place has been renovated is an injustice. It has been totally transformed and is now a very smart-looking address geared toward a discriminating clientele who are accustomed to the better things in life. The hotel is a combination of regular hotel rooms and studios with kitchenettes, allowing you to choose whichever style of accommodation suits your needs. Finally, its location in a small, nice neighborhood enclave is light-years away in spirit from the seamier neighborhood next to it.

Everything in the hotel has been well conceived, from the small, fitted kitchens, to the coordinated checks and prints that decorate the pretty rooms, to the garden where summer breakfasts are served. Many of the sixth-floor rooms have views that stretch from the Panthéon and Notre Dame to L'Église Notre Dame de Lorette. One of the most popular, especially for honeymooners, is No. 603, which has large windows encompassing this wide view and a lovely new bathroom. Those on the fourth floor are bathed in sunshine. The staff has a sense of what personal service is . . . and they deliver it. Nearby is an interesting market street, and you are within brisk walking distance to Montmartre. Special rates during the low season and for stays that include Friday, Saturday, and Sunday nights are available on request.

TEL 01-53-32-81-81 **FAX** 01-53-32-81-82 **EMAIL** h3p@les3poussins.com
  INTERNET www.les3poussins.com
FACILITIES & SERVICES Air-conditioning, direct-dial phone, elevator, hair
  dryer, 2 handicapped-accessible rooms, daily housekeeping service,
  kitchens in studios, laundry service, flat-screen TV with international
  reception, room safe (no charge), 10 nonsmoking rooms, WiFi
RATES Hotel single 143€, double 158–193€, triple or quad 228€; studio
  with kitchenette 15€ supplement per day; extra bed 30€; seasonal &
  weekend discounts; *taxe de séjour* 1€ per person, per day
  CREDIT CARDS AE, MC, V
BREAKFAST Buffet 12€ per person

Student Accommodations

There are more than ten thousand student beds in Paris. The following list of both public and private sources offers help in finding low-cost student accommodations year-round. Most places have a minimum stay in the summer, and curfews are not uncommon. All will give you the rules of the road before you get your bed, so there will be no excuses for improper conduct or pleading ignorance. It is critically important to remember that often only cash is accepted, and that most times you must either be an enrolled student or within a certain age bracket.

Any student can take advantage of the French government–run and –subsidized student lodgings as well as a wide range of other student discounts. To qualify for the *tarif étudiant,* you are required to show proof of full-time student status, in addition to your university or college ID, or if you are not a student, prove you are between the ages of twelve and twenty-five. The best way to show this additional proof is with the International Student Identity Card (ISIC; www.isic.org) or with the Go-25 card (if you are between twelve and twenty-five years old and not a student). Both cards entitle you to savings on selected museum entry fees, film and theater tickets, transportation costs, meals at certain student dining halls, and of course, lodgings. Teachers can get some of the same discounts and all of the benefits by purchasing the International Teacher Identity Card (ITIC). In the United States the cards cost around $25, require a one-inch-size passport photo and are available through STA (for details, visit www.statravel.com). In Paris, the card can be issued at the centrally located OTU Voyage and at the CROUS office: 39, avenue Georges-Bernanos, 5th; Métro: Port-Royal; Tel: 01-40-51-36-00; Open: Monday to Friday 9 A.M. to 4:30 P.M. In addition, an ISIC card will save on airfares, transportation, attractions, and accommodations in more than 106 countries. It also provides users with a twenty-four-hour emergency help line and worldwide voice mail, fax messaging, and phone-card service through its ISIConnect feature. It is an unbelievable bargain. If you send for the card, allow three weeks; if you go to your local office, it will be issued on the spot.

STUDENT ACCOMMODATIONS

BUREAU DES VOYAGES DE LA JEUNESSE (BVJ)
Paris/Louvre location (53)
20, rue Jean-Jacques Rousseau, 75001
Métro: Louvre-Rivoli
150 beds, none with shower, bath, or toilet

Quartier Latin location (18)
44, rue des Bernardins, 75005
Métro: Maubert-Mutualité
100 beds, all rooms with shower, none with bath or toilet

There are 250 beds for young people (ages eighteen to thirty-five) available in the heart of Paris, either on the Right Bank near the Louvre (called Paris/Louvre) or on the Left Bank in the Latin Quarter (at Quartier Latin). Most of the clientele travel light with only a backpack and don't mind sharing dorm rooms with up to eight other weary travelers. The good news: The prices are reasonable; there are some single and double accommodations in addition to the shared dorm rooms (for up to eight); and there is no daytime lockout or midnight curfew. The key is to land in a room with as few roommates as possible. The hall showers are free at Paris/Louvre, but at Quartier Latin, all rooms have a shower. No towels or soap are provided at either location; lockers cost 2€ per opening and are worth it. During high season, individual travelers usually need a two- or three-day advance reservation, but groups should always reserve as far ahead as possible. The type of room cannot be guaranteed, but you don't have to pay for it until you see it upon arrival. There is a maximum one-week stay, with extensions only if space is available.

TEL Paris/Louvre: 01-53-00-90-90; Quartier Latin: 01-43-29-34-80; Group reservations: 01-53-00-90-95 **FAX** 01-53-00-90-91 **EMAIL** bvj@wanadoo.fr **INTERNET** www.bvjhotel.com

FACILITIES & SERVICES No elevator at Quartier Latin (6 floors), Internet in lobby and TV at Quartier Latin, no safe, no smoking allowed at either location, free sheets, towels for sale (3.50€)

RATES All rates are per person. Louvre: double 29€, 4-bed dorm 26€. Quartier Latin: single 36€, 2–4 beds 29€, 5–10 beds 22€; *taxe de séjour* included **CREDIT CARDS** None

BREAKFAST Continental included

CROUS ACADÉMIE DE PARIS (41)
39, avenue Georges-Bernanos, 75005
Métro: RER Line B Port-Royal

CROUS plays a vital role in the life of a student in Paris. This organization is in charge of all University of Paris student residences, and it offers beds during the French university vacation and a listing of short-term student foyers. It's the clearinghouse for foreign-student grants and operates student cafeterias providing students with inexpensive meals in its Restos-U (see *Great Eats Paris*). It is also a source of cheap trips and discount tickets for theater and cultural events, and the ISIC card is sold here. The address above is the main office where you should start your search, whether it be for meal tickets, a bed for your stay, or a trip outside of Paris. English is spoken most of the time.

TEL 01-40-51-36-00, 01-40-51-55-55 **FAX** 01-40-51-36-99
  INTERNET www.crous-paris.fr
OPEN Mon–Fri 9 A.M. –4:30 P.M.

MAISON INTERNATIONALE DE LA JEUNESSE ET DES ÉTUDIANTS (MIJE, 45)
6, rue de Fourcy, 75004
Métro: St-Paul

MIJE offers some of the best student beds in Paris in two converted seventeenth-century historic mansions and a former convent. Each room holds from two to ten people; all rooms have a sink and shower. The address given above (Le Fourcy) is also the main office where all reservations are made. There is also a dining room here that is open to anyone staying in the three hostels. Sheets are provided, but no towels or soap. There is a 2.50€ one-year membership fee, the maximum stay is seven nights, and no one over thirty is accepted. No smoking or booze is allowed, and there is a room lockout from noon to 3 P.M., and a 1 A.M. curfew. Advanced reservations by telephone only are accepted a week before arrival; two months ahead via the Internet. They do not accept reservations by fax.

NOTE: The other two locations are Fauconnier, 11, rue Fauconnier (4th), Métro: St-Paul; and Maubuisson, 12, rue des Barres (4th), Métro: Hôtel-de-Ville.

TEL 01-42-74-23-45 **FAX** 01-40-27-81-64 **INTERNET** www.mije.com
FACILITIES & SERVICES Elevator (Fourcy), Internet at Fourcy and Fauconnier, restaurant at Fourcy, office safe (no charge for groups, individuals pay 1€ for the key)
RATES All rates are per person: single 46€, double 34€, triple 30€, quad 28€, dorm (5–10 persons) 29€; restaurant, lunch or dinner 11€, three courses; *taxe de séjour* included **CREDIT CARDS** None, euro cash or traveler's checks only
BREAKFAST Included

OTU VOYAGE (13)
119, rue St-Martin, Parvis de Beaubourg, 75004
Métro: Rambuteau

Located across the square from the Centre Georges Pompidou (Beaubourg), OTU provides discount travel help and information on accommodations, travel, and many other related items of interest to anyone ages eighteen to thirty. Office hours are Monday to Friday 9:30 A.M. to 6:30 P.M., Saturday 10 A.M. to 5 P.M. They also sell the student ISIC cards and teacher ITIC cards, which every student or teacher should have in their possession (see page 311).

TEL 01-40-29-12-22 **FAX** 01-40-29-12-20 **EMAIL** paris.beaubourg@otu.fr
  INTERNET www.otu.fr
CREDIT CARDS MC, V

Shopping: Great Chic

Paris is wrenchingly beautiful, and so are many of its people. If you use your eyes and take in everything, you can learn more about true style in a weekend than in a lifetime's perusal of fashion magazines.
—*Lucia Van der Post*

A museum is a museum, but a bargain is forever. . . .
—*Suzy K. Gershman,* Born to Shop Paris

Paris is a shopper's dream world. Even those who claim to dislike shopping are bound to be attracted by the unending selection of shops with beautiful window displays. The haute couture, open-air *marchés* overflowing with beautiful foods, extravagant toy shops, and the dazzling displays of jewelry, antiques, and collectibles tempt everyone from the serious buyer to the casual browser. There has always been something very stylish about the French. Just the addition of the word French to everyday objects such as jeans, silk, perfume, bread, wine, cheese, and toast lifts them out of the ordinary. For many of us, going to Paris is a dream come true, but it isn't quite enough. . . . We want to bring something of Paris home with us. However, satisfying this desire doesn't come cheap. Indeed, a recent study showed Paris to be the most expensive city in Europe for buying clothes and shoes. What are we to do—those of us who cannot afford to pay the astronomically high prices that come with such glorious merchandise? Become a Parisian smart shopper.

After you have been in Paris for a day or so, you will realize that style counts: the French do not just get dressed—they get turned out, many in *couturière* battle dress, with the emphasis on quality, not quantity. You will no doubt wonder how a modest shop clerk manages to look so elegant, considering his or her low wages and the high price tags for clothing. The answer is simple: savvy Parisian shoppers know where to go for the best quality and value, and they seldom pay full price.

Shopping the secondhand clothing stores was once reserved for a minority who seldom admitted it, but this has now become a mainstream activity in Paris. Paying less has been given a new cachet. Determined discount bounty hunters shop with a vengeance for vintage clothing, which has become so "in" that designers base entire collections on specific retro looks. As a lifelong, dedicated discount shopper with a black belt in the art, I know that bargain shopping of any kind can be both frustrating and exhausting—until the moment you find that fabulous designer suit in your size and favorite color for half price. Any type of discount shopping in Paris takes a good eye, limitless patience, endurance, and comfortable shoes. In Paris, of all places, it should be more than just a quest to track down the cheapest items available. . . . It should be fun. Finding something *très à la mode* at below retail in Paris is not *that* difficult once you know how, and that is what this chapter will help you to do: transform your T-shirt into a significant outfit, with just the right pair of pants, a sassy jacket, and perfect accessories for the moment—all for reduced prices and, more importantly, for less than you would pay at home.

With all discount shopping, especially in clothing stores, the selections will vary from day to day and season to season. Shops also come and go. What is here today and very "in" may be gone tomorrow. The comfort of the customer is seldom a top priority if you are on the designer discount beat. As a result, many of these places do not have proper dressing rooms, most are jammed with merchandise, there is limited individual attention, and in many cases, only fragmented English is spoken. And never mind the ice-maiden *vendeuse* who has an innate knack for sizing you up and pricing everything you are wearing in one glance. Believe me, it is all worth it because nothing is more satisfying than being clad in designer labels at knockdown prices.

In addition to leading you to fabulous discount clothing buys, this chapter guides you to a gamut of great shopping: from the best English-language bookstores, children's toys and clothes, cosmetics, kitchen supplies, and jewelry to flea and antique markets, produce markets, gourmet stores, museum shops, historic passages, and department stores. Armed with "Great Chic," you are bound to find great gifts and clothes, save money, and come home with unique discoveries your friends will die over. *Bon chance!* And please, if you uncover something wonderful, let me know.

Tips for Great Shopping

> Nobody who has not lived in Paris can appreciate the unique savor of that word *femmes*.
>
> —*Arnold Bennett,* Paris Nights *(1913)*

> If there is a city that seems profoundly feminine, it is Paris . . . There is a sense, soft as a sigh, that women are the very sum of the place.
>
> —*Catherine Calvert*

1. Know the prices at home so you will be able to spot a bargain in Paris when you see it. Carry a calculator to be sure you are getting the bargain you think you are.

2. Form is very important for the French. When you enter a shop, you will be greeted with *Bonjour, Madame* or *Monsieur,* and when you leave, *Au revoir, Madame* (or *Monsieur*), *merci.*

Please respond in kind, with *Bonjour, Mademoiselle*, and so on. It is considered extremely bad form not to acknowledge the salespeople when entering or leaving a store.

3. If you like something, can afford it, and can get it home, buy it when you see it. If you wait until later, it probably will not be there when you go back, and then you will see it when you get home for twice the price.

4. Look for these signs in the windows—they mean lower prices:

Soldes	a sale in progress
Fin de Séries	end of collection
Dégriffés	labels cut out
Stock	overstock
Dépot Vente	resale
Fripes	used clothing
Troc, brocante	secondhand

5. Seldom in small shops will you be able to return something, and if you manage to do so, the hassle will probably not be worth it. To avoid this time-consuming headache, be sure when you buy something from a small shopkeeper that it does not have flaws, that it fits, and that it's what you want. However, most major department stores, chain stores (including Monoprix), and fashion boutiques will accept returns for full refund if you present the item and receipt within thirty days of the purchase date.

6. If you have a consumer complaint with a shop or store, write to Direction Départmentale de la Concurrence, de la Consommation, et la Repression des Fraudes, 8, rue Froissart, 75153 Paris (Tel: 01-40-27-16-00; Mon–Fri 9 A.M.–noon, 2–5:30 P.M.). This office is in the Ministry of Finance. Be sure to include an explanation, copies of your receipt, and any correspondence you have had with the seller.

7. Never change money at a shop. The rate will not be in your favor. Go instead to a bank or ATM, or use a credit card.

8. If you are shopping at one of the flea markets, you can definitely bargain. The asking price is not the price you are expected to pay. You should be able to get the price down by 15 to 30 percent. Also, bring cash: you cannot bargain with plastic, and most sellers do not take credit cards anyway.

9. Pharmacies are marked with a green cross on a white background. They are the places to go if you need a prescription filled or advice on cold remedies. In addition, many pharmacies also carry excellent hair and skin products that you never see at home. But everyday toiletries and basic cosmetics will be cheaper

in supermarkets, parapharmacies, or at Monoprix. And remember, if you shop at one of the major department stores, you get an automatic 10 percent discount even if you purchase only a lipstick (see 11 below).

10. Pack an empty, soft-folding suitcase in your luggage so you can transport your treasures without the extra bother and expense of mailing. An extra bag on an airline (over the limit of two, plus a carry-on) will cost around $125, and that will be less than you will have to pay the store, Federal Express, or UPS to have it sent, never mind the time and hassle to pack and get your items there. That said, if you do have a major department store mail your packages, the *détaxe* is automatically deducted from the total price, so that could be an incentive (See "Getting It All Home," page 323).

11. Be sure to get the 10 percent discount card issued to all foreigners who shop at the major department stores (with the exception of Bon Marché and Monoprix). If you add this savings to the *détaxe* (which is 13 percent), the savings can be considerable (see "Department Stores," page 321).

12. If you are eligible for a tax refund, take the time to fill out the *détaxe* form, and remember to turn it into the customs officials at the airport before you relinquish your luggage or go through customs or passport control (see "Tax Refund: *Détaxe,*" page 319).

13. The French government sets the dates in early January and July for the eagerly awaited sales (*soldes*). The savings can be up to 75 percent, if you wait to the end of the sale period and are lucky enough to find something that is not in a hideous color or terribly shopworn. The best strategy is to preshop, spotting what you want to purchase, and then get into battle dress and go for it the first day of the sale. Early discounts are from 10 to 25 percent, and if you are shopping at Galeries Lafayette or Printemps, don't forget to show your 10 percent discount card, which kicks in on top of sale prices (see page 322).

14. When returning to the United States, remember these points when going through customs:

    • You and every member of your family, regardless of age, can bring back $800 worth of purchases duty-free. Books are duty-free. Family members can pool their duty-free purchases (see "Customs," page 320).

    • Don't cheat, don't smuggle, and above all, don't carry drugs.

    • Be nice.

Shopping Hours

Generally speaking, shopping hours are Monday through Saturday from 9:30 or 10 A.M. to 7 P.M. Large department stores are open later one night a week. Small shops sometimes close for lunch, and often for all or part of August. Food markets are usually open Sunday morning but closed on Monday. With the exception of the heavily touristed areas, all stores are closed on Sunday and major holidays.

Size Conversion Charts

Many French off-the-rack manufacturers have their own cuts, and sizes are not always uniform. Whenever possible, it is important to try on clothing before you buy. However, that is not always possible, so bring your measurements and carry a tape measure showing both inches and centimeters. Be careful with men's shirt sleeves, as the length is not always given; be prepared to measure. Table and bed linen sizes are also different from those in the States.

Women's dresses: To change French dress sizes to U.S. sizes, subtract 28 from the French dress size. To change U.S. dress sizes to French, add 28 to the U.S. dress size.

French	32	34	36	38	40	42	44
U.S.	4	6	8	10	12	14	16

Women's sweaters and blouses: To change French sizes to U.S., subtract 8 from the French blouse or sweater size. To change U.S. sizes to French, add 8 to the U.S. size.

French	38	40	42	44	46	48	50
U.S.	30	32	34	36	38	40	42

Men's suits: To change French suit sizes to U.S. sizes, subtract 10 from the French suit size. To change U.S. suit sizes to French, add 10 to the U.S. size.

French	46	48	50	52	54	56	58
U.S.	36	38	40	42	44	46	48

Men's shirts: To change French shirt sizes to U.S., subtract 8 from the French size and divide by 2. To change U.S. shirt sizes to French, multiply the U.S. size by 2 and add 8.

French	36	37	38	39	40	41	42	43
U.S.	14	14.5	15	15.5	16	16.5	17	17.5

Women's shoes: To change French shoe sizes to U.S., subtract 32 from the French size. To change U.S. shoe sizes to French, add 32 to the U.S. shoe size.

French	36	37	38	39	40	41
U.S.	5	6	7	8	9	10

Men's shoes:

French	39½	41	42	43	44½	46	47
U.S.	7	8	9	10	11	12	13

Children's clothing: French children's clothes are sized according to the child's age. Look for the abbreviations "m" and "a," which stand for month and year (in French, "m" stands for *mois,* or "month," and "a" stands for *ans,* or "years"). Thus, *2m* means two months, *16m* means sixteen months, *2a* means two years, *6a* means six years, and so on.

Children's Shoes

French	24	25	27	28	29	30
U. S.	8	9	10	11	12	13

Tax Refund: *Détaxe*

Every non–European Union resident spending six months or less in France is entitled to a 12 to 14 percent *détaxe* (tax rebate) for minimum purchases of 175€ made on the same day in the same store. In smaller shops you usually must ask for the form, but in the big department stores, you can get it from the Tax Refund Desk. You must always present your passport for identification. If shopping with a friend, combine your purchases to reach the total and share the proceeds when they arrive. You and the store representative fill out the simple paperwork. At your point of exit from France, or another European Union country, present your tax refund forms and have your purchases ready for inspection at the customs office in the last country you visit in the European Union. At the airport, look for the window that says *douane de détaxe* and allow an extra half hour to accomplish the mission. After having customs stamp the forms, you must send back the pink form(s) in the self-addressed, stamped envelope given to you by the store at the time of purchase. There is usually a mailbox next to the customs office. You have three months following the month you made your purchases to do this. That's it.

On the *détaxe* form, you will be asked to state whether you want the refund mailed to you in a euro check or to have it credited to your credit card. Obtaining your refund by check is not recommended because it is hard to deal with in the United States and getting it can take forever. Ask for the rebate on your credit card—your credit card company will credit the refund to you in U.S. dollars. Expect a delay of two to three months. For items shipped directly from the store, the *détaxe* is automatically deducted without any paperwork. Yes, it all does take some extra time and effort, but the savings do add up, so persevere.

If you are shopping in an airport duty-free shop, the price will already reflect a 13 percent *detaxe* discount.

NOTE: The *détaxe* does not apply for services, food, drink, medicine, unset gems, antiques, works of art, automobiles or their parts, or commercial purchases.

Customs

Each U.S. citizen, even a week-old baby, is entitled to bring back $800 worth of duty-free goods acquired abroad. Families can pool their duty-free purchases, so you can use what your spouse and children do not. After the $800 point, there will be a duty charged. Have your receipts ready and make sure they coincide with what you filled out on the landing card. Don't cheat or lie, as you will invariably be caught. If that happens, you and your luggage will undergo exhaustive searches, and that will just be for openers. Any purchase worth less than $100 can be shipped back to the States as an unsolicited gift and is considered duty-free, and it does not count in your $800 limit. You can send as many of these unsolicited gifts as you wish, but only one unsolicited gift per person for each mailing, and don't mail anything to yourself. If your package worth exceeds $100, you will pay duty.

Antiques must be over one hundred years old to be duty-free.

A work of art is duty-free, and it does not matter when it was created or who the artist was.

If you have expensive cameras, piles of imported luggage, fancy watches, or valuable jewelry, carry the receipts for them, or you could be questioned about them and even end up paying duty on them.

Finally, it's simply a fact of customs: people who look like hippies get stopped and have their bags searched. The same goes for bejeweled and bedecked women wrapped in full-length furs and carrying expensive designer luggage.

For more information on U.S. Customs rules and regulations, go online or send for the free brochure *Know Before You Go,* available from the Department of the Treasury, U.S. Customs Service, 1300 Pennsylvania Avenue, NW, Washington, D.C., 20229; 202-927-1700 or 202-354-1000; www.cbp.gov.

Consignment Shops: *Dépôts-Ventes*

Consignment shops sell previously owned items at a fraction of original cost. Some people balk at the idea of wearing "used" clothing, but try to shed this reluctance. Keep in mind that many of the items are barely worn; they are being consigned so that their owner will have more money to spend in the designer boutiques . . . only to recycle them again after one wearing. In Paris, it is considered very fashionable to resurrect something from oblivion and incorporate it into your wardrobe, or to outsmart retail buyers by finding a fabulous Armani suit for a fraction of what they paid for it. Believe me, this is big business in Paris, and you would be surprised at the number of very sophisticated and well-known fellow bargain-inspired shoppers you may recognize standing next to you searching the racks for just the perfect "previously owned" outfit.

For a complete list of all the consignment shops in this book, see page 396.

Department Stores

Bargain shoppers take note: Most of the department stores will issue a 10 percent discount shopping card upon presentation of your passport. The card is valid for items *without* a red dot. Just go to the Welcome Desk; someone who speaks English will be there to issue you the card. When paying, you may have to go to a special *caisse* (a cashier's desk) to pay, and then take your paid receipt back to the department where you initially found the item. It's a bit of a drag . . . but it is 10 percent, and that can add up. The major exceptions are Franck et Fils, Monoprix, and Bon Marché.

On top of that, don't forget that you will qualify for the 12 to 14 percent *détaxe* if you spend 175€ in the same store. Unfortunately, that amount is not cumulative over several shopping trips; it is per day. But if you plan accordingly and combine it with your 10 percent discount card, you can save 23 percent. Keep this in mind especially if you are shopping for items that may be sold elsewhere in Paris in specialty boutiques. For example, many Americans have a love affair with Mephisto and Arche shoes, and know that they are cheaper in Paris. Galeries Lafayette carries these shoes . . . so, why buy them someplace else if you can buy them here and save an additional 10 percent plus the *détaxe*?

For a complete list of all the department stores in this book, see page 396.

Designer Discount Boutiques

Anyone can pay retail. . . . It takes talent, dedication, and hard work to get a good deal.

—*Diana Withee, art historian and veteran shopper*

These boutiques sell designer label stock at well below the retail prices you will pay elsewhere in Paris for exactly the same items, but you will be looking at last season's collections. Sometimes the labels have been cut out.

For a complete list of all the designer discount boutiques in this book, see page 396.

DISCOUNT SHOPPING MALL: LA VALLÉE OUTLET SHOPPING VILLAGE
3 cours de la Garonne, 77700 Serris, Marne-la-Vallée

For a total immersion in discount shopping, go to La Vallée Outlet Shopping Village, a very posh outlet shopping mall open seven days a week and a forty-five-minute RER ride from Paris. For the nonshoppers in your party, Paris Disney is only a five-minute RER ride from the discount mall, and even closer is the Sealife Aquarium next door. An on-call shuttle service is available to and from Disney hotels and the Val d'Europe RER station.

The shops are well laid out on a winding walkway that is designed to look like a provincial market town. The list of designers represented is impressive, and so are the discounts: at least 30 percent for openers, and in some cases, up to 50 or 60 percent. Okay, so the items are last season or end of stock, but there are plenty of classic staples from names we all love: Kenzo, Versace, Givenchy, Max Mara, Charles Jourdain, Reebok, Calvin Klein, Diesel, Jean-Charles de Castelbajac, Prada, Christian Lacroix, and many more. Don't forget to get the *détaxe* on purchases that total over 175€ made in the same store (see "Tax Refund: *Détaxe*," page 319). Go on a weekday and you will have the shops and the salespeople almost to yourself. There are no restaurants here, but there are nice bathrooms and a play area for children. In the regular-price mall next door, there are plenty of places to eat, the Sealife Aquarium, as well as an immense Auchan *hypermarché* with thirty checkout stands.

How to get there: Take the RER A line that goes direct to Val d'Europe in direction Disney Paris. On the train platform, look for the light that is on next to Val d'Europe. This is the train you want (that is your stop). Before leaving the station at Val d'Europe, check on the return train times for Paris. When you leave the train station, walk through the mall (Commercial Centre Val d'Europe) to the outlet center, which is at the end. There is also a Cityrama shuttle bus from Paris going on Tuesday, Thursday, and Sunday; call 01-44-55-60-00 for information and reservations.

TEL 01-60-42-35-00 **INTERNET** www.lavalleevillage.com
CREDIT CARDS Depends on shop, but usually MC, V
OPEN Mon–Sat 10 A.M.–7 P.M. (to 8 P.M. from May 20–Sept), Sun 11 A.M.–7 P.M. (hours can vary slightly)

Sales: *Soldes*

During most of the year, when you venture into one of the designer shops, they are quiet enough for you to hear the rustle of money being spent by the wealthy customers. However, we less-affluent mortals also have a chance in these stores. It is hard to imagine the U.S. government dictating to stores the dates on which they can hold sales . . . but that is exactly what happens in France. As it now stands, during the first three weeks in January and six weeks beginning the last week of June through July, the French *ministre de shopping* has declared that *toute* Paris will be on sale. In addition, Galeries Lafayette, Printemps, and many other large department stores have special offers throughout the rest of the year. But the real bargains are found during the January and July sales, when the crowds of shoppers move with dizzying swiftness, all zeroing in on the considerable savings. If you can brave these shopping pros, this is the time to go to the designer boutiques and pick up a little number for about one-third the U.S. retail price. In October and March, Hèrmes has its annual sales. The line forms the night before, with shoppers eager to pay 50 percent less for the famous signature scarves (currently retailing for over $250), ties, leather goods, and conservative line of clothing. Of course there are lines and crowds, but this sale is a must for Hèrmes fans. For the exact sale dates, watch the billboards in the métro stations, scan newspaper ads, or call 01-40-27-16-00.

Getting It All Home

I recommend taking an extra fold-up suitcase to hold any purchases you make. This way, you can take your purchases with you on the plane, they arrive when you do, and at worst, you have to pay the extra bag charge of around $125. If you buy such a suitcase in Paris, you get to keep the bag for the next trip. Some stores, including the major department stores, will ship items. Otherwise, you have three options, two of which will cost about the same as the extra bag on the airplane, maybe more, and all three will entail work on your part. These options are Federal Express, UPS, and the French post office. But do you really want to carry heavy boxes (or the contents that need packing) through several métro changes or in a taxi, wasting time you could be doing more shopping? Of course not. Put everything in your fold-up bag and take it on the plane.

FEDERAL EXPRESS
63, boulevard Haussmann, 75009
Métro: Havre-Caumartin

The folks at FedEx speak English, have boxes, and will pick up your parcels (3€ extra). All packages have tracking numbers. Their prices are very expensive and are based on weight, contents, and destination, but they do include the box. As an example: 10kg costs 150€; 25kg costs 240€.

TEL 08-00-12-38-00 **INTERNET** www.fedex.com/fr
CREDIT CARDS AE, MC, V
OPEN Mon–Fri 9 A.M.–7:30 P.M., Sat 9 A.M.–5:30 P.M.

UPS
Corner rue Réaumur & rue Montmartre, 75002
Métro: Sentier

The folks at UPS also speak English, have shipping boxes, tracking numbers, and prices based on weight, contents, and destination. They also have a free pick-up service. However, their rates are even higher than Fedex.

TEL 0800-877-877 **INTERNET** www.ups.com
CREDIT CARDS MC, V
OPEN Mon–Fri 11 A.M.–8:30 P.M.

POST OFFICE (PTT)

Post offices (*bureaux de poste*) are in every *quartier*. The best one in Paris is the main post office at 52, rue du Louvre, 75001, Métro: Louvre-Rivoli, Tel: 01-40-28-76-00. It is open 24 hours a day, 365 days a year; it is the only post office in France with these hours. At all post offices, you can purchase boxes in various sizes. There are two types: one marked Chronopost for mailing within France, and another marked Colissimo, which you will need if you are sending items to the U.S. The price of the box includes the postage, and while there is no weight limit, the boxes are not designed to hold more than 8 kilos (17 pounds). Figure around 38€ for the largest box. The hours at all other post offices are Mon–Fri 8 A.M.–7 P.M., and Sat 8 A.M.–noon. Plan on standing in line at least thirty minutes.

Shopping Areas

PLACE DES VICTOIRES, 75001 (31; see map page 66)
Métro: Étienne-Marcel, Palais-Royal–Musée du Louvre

This is a smart shopping section nestled behind Palais-Royal. After going around the place des Victoires, branch out down the side streets. This is an area of many fashion innovators and well worth serious time just to see what you will be wearing two years from now. The prices are not bargains unless you happen to hit a sale.

PLACE VENDÔME, 75001 (13; see map page 66)
Métro: Tuileries, Opéra

Cartier, Van Cleef & Arpels, Trussardi, Bulgari, and international banks cater to the needs of the guests at the Hôtel Ritz around place Vendôme. Rue de la Paix leads from place Vendôme to boulevard Haussmann, home of two major department stores: Printemps and Galeries Lafayette.

RUE ST-HONORÉ & FAUBOURG ST-HONORÉ, 75001, 75008 (9, see map page 66; 56, see map page 192)
Métro: Tuileries, Concorde, Madeleine

Some of the most exclusive and expensive shopping opportunities in Paris are along this gold-plated stretch of real estate. Face the Madeleine Church, and rue St-Honoré will be to your right, rue Faubourg St-Honoré to your left.

MARAIS AND PLACE DES VOSGES, 75003 and 75004 (16 and 42; see map page 86)
Métro: St-Paul

The Marais is the oldest *quartier* in Paris. The kosher food shops along rue des Rosiers, the trendy boutiques along rue Francs Bourgeois, the menswear shops lining the rue de Turenne, and the avant-garde designers make shopping in the Marais an excellent adventure. The place des Vosges, which Henri IV had constructed between 1605 and 1612, was the first planned square to be built in Paris. Today, the symmetrical, soft-pink stone square made up of thirty-six slate-roof town homes is lovely. Be sure to include a stroll through the shops and galleries in the stone arcades and sit in one of the cafés. Most of the shops along Francs Bourgeois and in the place des Vosges are open on Sunday.

VILLAGE ST-PAUL, RUE ST-PAUL, AND RUE DU PONT LOUIS PHILIPPE, 75004 (51; see map page 86)
Métro: St-Paul

The Village St-Paul is a collective name for the fifty or more antique and *brocante* dealers who line rue St-Paul and the courtyard squares surrounding it. It's a favorite Sunday destination for many Parisians because the shops are all open. One of my favorites is Baïkal at 24, rue St-Paul (01-42-74-73-39; www.baikal.fr). This interesting shop, run by Michael Monlaü and his partner, Thierry de la Salmoniere, specializes in Asian artifacts and antiques. For almost seventy years, the shop was a local bar run by the same woman and by her parents before that. When Michael and Thierry took it over, they saved and restored the old bar and countertop, which had stood in the same place for a century. For all those years, the locals spent part of their lives here and left part of their souls, leaning against the bar and tossing down their daily quotas. Today it's still in the middle of the shop. The bar is not for sale, but everything else is.

On the rue du Pont Louis Philippe, you will find calligraphy and paper shops, stores selling perfumed candles, and a few unusual clothing boutiques.

ST-GERMAIN-DES-PRÉS, 75006 (22; see map page 134)
Métro: St-Germain-des-Prés

Sensational shopping can be found on the rue de Sèvres, rue Bonaparte, rue du Four, rue St-Sulpice, rue Jacob, rue de Saints-Pères, rue du Dragon, rue de Grenelle, rue du Bac, and the rue de Seine, to mention only a few of the streets that line this *quartier,* which is literally packed with fashion boutiques, antique shops, art galleries, bookshops, and the magnificent Le Bon Marché department store. In fact, if you have only a short time to devote to shopping and browsing, this is where you should go.

CHAMPS-ÉLYSÉES, 75008 (19; see map page 192)
Métro: Charles-de-Gaulle-Étoile

The Champs-Élysées is enjoying a renaissance for shopping and entertainment. There are still waves of tourists (300,000 per day) flowing up one side and down the other of the most famous avenue in the world. Now, in addition to the movie theaters, airline offices, banks, car dealers, fast-food outlets, minimalls, and outdoor cafés—all charging top prices for everything—fashion boutiques and multipurpose stores are making their presence known. The Virgin Megastore, Séphora cosmetics and perfume supermarket, and the Peugeot showroom (redone by Sir Terence Conran into a design and dining space) are only a few of the blockbuster addresses Parisians are flocking to.

Also very much on the shopping scene is Le Drugstore (near the Arc de Triomphe) and the fabulous multistory Louis Vuiton store at 101 avenue des Champs-Élysées.

No one said anything about bargains, either in food, goods, or drink, but a stroll along the Champs-Élysées, some window-shopping, and sipping a drink at a café, all the while engaging in fascinating people-watching, is one of the must-dos of Paris and is now more enjoyable than ever. For further information consult www.champs-elysees.org. Please beware: Pickpockets continue to work both sides of the street and they are pros . . . watch out!

RUE ROYALE, 75008 (57; see map page 192)
Métro: Concorde, Madeleine

Rue Royale runs from the place de la Concorde to the Madeleine Church. It is a short stretch but packed with shopping treasures that are not only *très chic,* but *très cher.* In addition to admiring the window displays, be sure to stop at Ladurée, which opened on rue Royale in 1862. Ladurée is credited with inventing the macaroon, and theirs are without question the best. Obviously, Parisians agree—3,000 are sold daily. Be sure to wander into the pedestrian passages that flow off of rue Royale—the glass-roofed Galerie de la Madeleine, the Galerie Royale, and Le Village Royale—for elegantly magical shopping. Along one side of the church is a colorful flower market, and lining the streets behind it are the finest gourmet shops in the city.

THE GOLDEN TRIANGLE, 75008 (see map page 192)
Métro: Alma-Marceau

When cost is not an object, come to the Golden Triangle (*Le Triangle d'Or*), which is formed by Avenue George-V, avenue Marceau, avenue Montaigne, and rue François 1er. For window-shopping and dreaming of the highest order, these four premier shopping streets are to designer fashion and haute couture what the Louvre is to priceless art. The boutiques and shops are not to be missed, even if you only stroll by the elegant window displays.

RUE DE PASSY AND AVENUE VICTOR HUGO, 75016 (26 and 2; see map page 244)
Métro: Passy, Victor Hugo

Walking down either of these streets in the sixteenth arrondissement will give you an idea of how the upper-middle-class live in Paris. You will see few tourists, no razor-shaved haircuts, and certainly no hawkers waving T-shirts or plastic replicas of the Eiffel Tower. This is the land of the BCBGs (French yuppies), old money, and tradition. There are several cafés if someone in your party would rather sit and have a beer while watching the world wander by.

Discount Shopping Streets

Just as Paris has its high-priced shopping streets, it also has its discount shopping streets. No dedicated discount shopper will want to miss a trip to one of these streets where, if you are lucky, you will bring home something marvelous that your friends would kill for . . . even at three times the price you paid. Finding the perfect outfit, pair of shoes, or great handbag takes time and energy, not to say patience. Don't try to squeeze this type of shopping in . . . allow time and leave nonshopping pals at the hotel.

Note that most shops will take Visa or MasterCard, not American Express or Diners Club. Hours vary with each shop; however, in general stores are open Monday 2 to 7 P.M., and Tuesday to Saturday 10 A.M. to 7 P.M.

RUE ST-PLACIDE, 75006 (51; see map page 134)
Métro: Sèvres-Babylone
Bargain fever has hit Paris in a cluster of boutiques along rue St-Placide. Start at Bon Marché department store and work both sides of the street. This can be frustrating if the crowds are out in force, especially at lunchtime when the office workers surge through and on Saturday when housewives bring *les enfants* in bulky strollers and make the pilgrimage. Best buys are in casual sportswear and teenage "must-haves" of the moment. There are no top-name designers, but everything is *au courant*. Windows are often more appealing than the stuffy, cramped interiors, where merchandize is dumped into bins or loaded onto racks. Sharpen your elbows for this—and watch your handbag carefully.

RUE ST-DOMINIQUE, 75007 (3; see map page 170)
Métro: Latour-Maubourg
It isn't as good as it used to be, but along rue St-Dominique from avenue Bosquet to boulevard de Latour-Maubourg, shops sell clothing for men, women, and children from designer *dégriffés* (labels cut out) to last season's T-shirts. Affordable.

Rue de Paradis, 75010
Métro: Château d'Eau, Gare de l'Est
This was once considered the best area in Paris for china and crystal, in one crowded shop after another. However, since Baccarat moved to the sixteenth (see page 381), it seems to have lost some of its luster. However, if you are interested in serious china and crystal shopping, it is definitely a place to check out and comparison shop, in addition to the major department stores. Worthwhile stops are at La Maison de la Porcelaine at 21, rue de Paradis, with over a hundred thousand items of Limoges porcelain in stock; and Limoges Unic, 34 and 58 rue de Paradis. Staff in all shops speak English, the *détaxe* is available, and they ship.

RUE D'ALÉSIA, 75014 (27; see map page 230)
Métro: Alésia

Both sides of rue d'Alésia are home to an assortment of outlet shops carrying last season's lines of designers, some of whom you have heard of and some you never will. The best line of attack is to go up one side and down the other to get an overview, and then come back to those that seem promising. The worst time to go is on Saturday. Some of the better shops are the following: SR (Sonya Rykiel), No. 110 and No. 64; Dorotennis Stock (Dorothée Bis), No. 74; Evolutif: Georges Rech, Kenzo, YSL, Givenchy, Armani, all for men, No. 98; Tout Compte Fait, No. 103; Jacadi, No. 116; Cacharel, No. 114; Café Cotton, No. 115; Chevignon, No. 124; LA City, No. 113; Urban Kids, No. 82; and two Monoprix stores with regular prices.

NOTE: The numbering system is crazy, but these are close.

Passages

Long before anyone heard of shopping malls, Paris had galleries and *passages*—skylighted, decorated, tiled, and beautiful. Built in the early nineteenth century for wealthy shoppers, they are a reflection of the prosperity and flamboyance of the Belle Epoque era. Tucked away off major commercial streets, mainly in the second and ninth arrondissements, they are easy to miss if you are not looking for them. Unfortunately, in a few, commercialism has taken over and there are some low-end shops. On the other hand, the occupants of the spaces come and go, and it is still fun to stroll through one or two if only to see a sampling of the old-fashioned shops selling handmade dolls, fancy pipes, old books, 78RPM records, model trains, and toys.

In general, you can count on most shops being open Monday afternoon to Saturday 10 A.M. to 7 P.M.

GALERIE VÉRO-DODAT (52; see map page 66)
19, rue Jean-Jacques Rousseau & 2, rue du Bouloi, 75001
Métro: Palais-Royal–Musée du Louvre

This Empire-style passage opened in 1826 and has an ornate interior with facades of dark wood and a black-and-white mosaic-tile floor. There are some interesting shops, including an old toy shop, but my favorite is Anne Galerie, where the owner sells her beautiful handmade scarves and magnificent shawls. They are truly works of art.

CREDIT CARDS MC, V
OPEN Mon–Sat 11 A.M.–6 P.M.; some shops close in Aug

GALERIE VIVIENNE (29; see map page 66)
4, rue des Petits-Champs; 5, rue de la Banque; and 6, rue Vivienne 75002
Métro: Bourse

The most beautiful passage of all opened in 1823. The stunning shops reflect their elegant surroundings. While here, be sure to stop at Lucien Legrand, a famous wine shop that now serves light lunches, or have tea at the popular Á Priori-Thé (see *Great Eats Paris*).

PASSAGE DES PANORAMAS (3; see map page 66)
10, rue Saint-Marc & 11, boulevard Montmartre, 75002
Métro: Grands Boulevards

One of the oldest, dating from 1800, it was build by American James Thayer. Its name is taken from the *panoramas* (painted frescoes) of Rome, Jerusalem, London, Athens, and other world capitals. The most interesting things to see here are the old-fashioned stationery store, stamp and coin dealers, and the shop selling old postcards. There are numerous restaurants, one resembling the interior of a train car.

PASSAGE DU GRAND-CERF (38; see map page 66)
145, rue Saint-Denis, or 10, rue Dussouds, 75002
Métro: Étienne-Marcel

Paved in marble, the passage has a high glass roof, wrought-iron walkways, and wood-framed windows in shops devoted to contemporary design.

PASSAGE JOUFFROY (17; see map page 192)
10–12, boulevard Montmartre & 9, rue de la Grange-Batelière, 75009
Métro: Grands Boulevards

Built in 1846, this was the first passage to be heated. It also contains the Hôtel Chopin (see page 208) and the Musée Grevin, the hundred-year-old Paris wax museum inspired by Madame Tussaud's in London. I love the shop called Pain d'Épices at Nos. 29–33. If you are a dollhouse lover, this shop is required. Not only do they have dollhouse furnishings down to the underwear the inhabitants wear and the miniature table settings they use, but accessories you assemble and paint. Also here are puppets galore and everything you need to put on a great show, DIY crafts, reproduction French household items, and pretty Christmas ornaments (in season only).

PASSAGE VERDEAU (15; see map page 192)
31 bis, rue du Faubourg-Montmartre & 6, rue de la Grange-Batelière, 75009
Métro: Richelieu-Drouot, Grands Boulevards

Shops have been here since 1847, and some of the merchandise in the collectibles shops looks it; check out books, old prints, old postcards, a shop selling vintage cameras, and another devoted to embroidery.

Shopping Malls

Indoor shopping complexes are popping up all over Paris. They are not my favorite shopping venues, but if you need several items and only have a short time to shop, they are useful.

FORUM DES HALLES (54; see map page 66)
rue Pierre Lescott (main entry), 75001
Métro: Les Halles, Étienne-Marcel

This is the result of filling the hole left after the wholesale food market Les Halles was moved to Rungis. Forum des Halles is the largest commercial project in France, and the largest métro station in the world lies under it. But please be careful: this is not considered a safe place to wander late at night. When it opened, the multilevel complex attracted forty million shoppers a year. On the weekend, it feels as though half of them are either milling around outside or roaming the mall inside. Even though the area has lost its original allure, those youthful in mind, body, and spirit still gravitate to this covered shopping wonderland to check out the general scene, cruise the shops, eat in the fast-food joints, hang out in FNAC (see page 370), and try the hair salons offering sculpted cuts, intricate extensions or dye jobs in glowing pink, green, or yellow. If you don't feel like doing any of the above, you can watch a film in the Cine Cité multiplex (which has over thirty theaters), swim in the public swimming pool, or just hang out and enjoy the fauna and flora as it walks by.

NOTE: Forum des Halles is scheduled for massive renovations, but probably hard hats will not be needed anytime soon. No two planners or architects can agree on anything, thus the project is mired in a controversial stalemate with no hints of resolution.

TEL 01-40-39-38-74
CREDIT CARDS Depends on shop, but usually MC, V
OPEN Mon–Sat 10:30 A.M.–7:30 P.M. for the shops; daily 10 A.M.–1:30 A.M. for films

LA GALERIE DU CARROUSEL DU LOUVRE (51; see map page 66)
99, rue de Rivoli, 75001
Metro: Palais-Royal–Museé du Louvre

Combine your visit to the Louvre with a shopping stroll through thirty-five or more tempting shops, which range from Limoges and Lalique to a Virgin Megastore, and from clothing boutiques to tourist kitsch and a post office. . . . You name it, and they have it. One of the best all-purpose shopping destinations in Paris, and it is open on Sunday! See *Great Eats Paris* for details on La Galerie du Carrousel du Louvre food court.

TEL 01-43-16-47-15 **INTERNET** www.lecarrouseldulouvre.com
CREDIT CARDS Depends on shop, but always MC, V
OPEN Daily 10 A.M.–8 P.M.

LE MARCHÉ SAINT GERMAIN (40; see map page 134)
Entrances on rue Lobineau, rue Fléiabien, rue Clément, rue Mabillon, 75006
Métro: Odéon

In addition to a section devoted to food stalls, this small, enclosed mall has all the usual mall shopping adventures and offers liquid sustenance in a popular Irish pub. On Saturday, outside and under the arches, sellers set up makeshift stalls. Be sure to see the one selling hand-smocked children's clothes at cut-rate prices. Look carefully before you buy: these are made in the Philippines, and the quality of workmanship varies.

CREDIT CARDS Depends on shop
OPEN Food stalls Tues–Sat 8 A.M.–1:30 P.M., 4–8 P.M., Sun 8 A.M.–1 P.M.; shops Mon–Sat 10 A.M.–8 P.M.

GALERIE 3 QUARTIERS (55; see map page 192)
23, boulevard de la Madeleine, 75008
Métro: Madeleine

At this shopping mall you'll find seventy-five boutiques and a sports store to behold. Prices are high, but stroll through anyway to get an idea of how much you will save by shopping at the other shops listed in this book. The quality is better than at Forum des Halles, but the spirit is really dead.

TEL 01-42-97-80-12
CREDIT CARDS Depends on boutique, but usually MC, V
OPEN Mon–Sat 10 A.M.–7 P.M.

BERCY VILLAGE
9, Cour St-Emilion, 75012
Métro: Cour St-Emilion

Shopping, entertainment, bars, banks, and restaurants in an American-like mall that pulls in the crowds, especially on the weekends. What to expect? Everything from a huge pet store selling live animals and guppies to a beautiful garden shop, houseware warehouse, computer store, three-level sport fishing store, movie multiplex, and much more. It is probably more of a unique experience for Parisians than for Americans, but it is interesting to see what Parisians think is so *branché.*

NOTE: When you are here, you are two métro stops away from the François Mitterrand Bibliothèque Nationale, quai François-Mauriac; Métro: Bibliothèque or Quai de la Gare. This was Mitterrand's final project, but it was completed after his death. The library has over ten million books and enough space for three thousand people (to use the library you must be over eighteen years old). It's open Tues–Sat 10 A.M.–8 P.M., Sun noon–7 P.M.

TEL Not available **INTERNET** www.bercyvillage.com
CREDIT CARDS Depends on store, generally MC, V
OPEN Shops, daily 11 A.M.–9 P.M., restaurants close at 2 A.M.

MAINE-MONTPARNASSE (14; see map page 230)
Tour, Maine-Montparnasse, 75014
Métro: Montparnasse-Bienvenüe

Round up the usual chain stores, stick them in a mundane indoor mall at the Montparnasse-Bienvenüe métro station, and you have this shopping mall. It does have a small Galeries Lafayette, but it is certainly not worth a special trip. If you are here, fine; otherwise, never mind.

TEL Not available
CREDIT CARDS MC, V (depends on store)
OPEN Mon–Sat 10 A.M.–7 P.M. (stores may vary)

PASSY PLAZA (21; see map page 244)
Corner rue Jean Bologne and rue de Passy, 75016
Métro: Passy, La Muette

This shopping mall has middle-of-the-road boutiques with lots of clothes for the junior set or for something to knock around in and still feel fashionable. Also a very good supermarket, Inno.

CREDIT CARDS MC, V (depends on shop)
OPEN Shops Mon–Sat 10 A.M.–7:30 P.M.; supermarket Mon–Sat 9 A.M.–8 P.M.

Store Listings by Arrondissement

FIRST ARRONDISSEMENT (see map page 66)

ARCHE (57)
13, rue des Innocents, 75001
Métro: Châtelet (exit Place Ste-Opportune)

Arche shoes are some of the most comfortable I have ever worn, and they seem to last forever. This French shoe concept has four elements: color, comfort, style, and material. The colors are great and reflect the latest trends in twenty-five new colors each season. The comfort goes without saying. Style . . . well, you can't help but love something this comfortable. And finally, material: Arche shoes are made from the softest leathers and nubucks, and the soles are 100% natural latex from the Hevea tree in tropical Asia. In addition to another shop in the first arrondissement (at 11, boulevard Madeleine), there are several other locations in Paris as well as outlets in Galeries Lafayette (see page 375) and Bon Marché (see page 367).

TEL 01-45-08-19-45 **INTERNET** www.arche-shoes.com
CREDIT CARDS AE, MC, V
OPEN Mon–Sat 10 A.M.–7 P.M.

BABY TUILERIES (17)
326, rue St-Honoré, 75001
Metro: Tuileries

For five decades *mamans* and *grande-mères* have been outfitting their children in the absolutely adorable fashions found in this beguiling boutique. If you can't find the outfit of your dreams for your little one here . . . I give up! Prices? Don't ask. Whatever you select will pay for itself many times over as one of your family heirlooms.

TEL 01-42-60-42-59 **INTERNET** wwww.baby-tuileries.com
CREDIT CARDS AE, DC, MC, V
OPEN Mon–Sat 10 A.M.–7 P.M.

BOUTIQUE CHANTAL THOMASS (22)
211, rue St-Honoré, 75001
Métro: Tuileries

If your lingerie wardrobe could use a shot of va-va-voom, the Boutique Chantal Thomass is the place to start your search. The two-level boutique, next to Colette (see page 335), has been designed to resemble a seductive French boudoir. Decorated in shades of pink and violet downstairs, and soft peach up the winding staircase to the first level, it sells naughty-but-nice, oh-so-sexy French underwear, silky negligées, real corsets, fantasy stockings, garterbelts, and feathery things to warm you for an evening in or out. If you are into vintage, don't miss the collection on the first floor.

TEL 01-42-60-40-56
CREDIT CARDS AE, DC, MC, V
OPEN Mon–Sat 11 A.M.–7 P.M. **CLOSED** 10 days mid-Aug

BOUTIQUE PARIS-MUSÉES (54)
Forum des Halles, 1, rue Pierre Lescott, 75001
Métro: Les Halles

There are three of these museum boutiques in Paris offering reproductions of items from the various permanent collections of the city's big museums. This boutique specializes in contemporary design reproductions, the other two in classic. Here you will find a wonderful selection of jewelry and household goods. Though the address is Forum des Halles, it is located on your left as you enter the Forum from rue Pierre Lescott.

The other two locations are in the third and fourth arrondissements (see pages 345 and 349).

TEL 01-40-26-56-65
CREDIT CARDS AE, V
OPEN Mon 2–7 P.M., Tues–Sat 10:30 A.M.–7 P.M.

CATHERINE PERFUMES AND COSMETICS (16)
7, rue de Castiglione, 75001
Métro: Tuileries

Jacques Levy, his wife, and their two daughters run this boutique. They offer an excellent selection of perfumes, cosmetics, scarves, hair ornaments, jewelry, and ties. They speak English and don't employ "hard sell" tactics. To begin, you will receive a tax-free price of 20 to 25 percent off on anything in the shop, even a simple comb and brush or powder compact. If you purchase over 175€ worth of merchandise, you get the original 20 to 25 percent off plus the 13 percent *détaxe*, which translates into a savings of up to 38 percent. If you are a collector of old perfumes, talk with Jacques, who has an excellent selection of hard-to-find scents. For mail orders, which you can do by fax, the same discounts are offered.

TEL 01-42-61-02-89 **FAX** 01-42-61-02-35
CREDIT CARDS MC, V
OPEN Mon 11 A.M.–7 P.M., Tues–Sat 9:30 A.M.–7 P.M.; **CLOSED** Aug 15–31, 1 week after Jan 15

COLETTE (21)
213, rue St-Honoré, 75001
Métro: Tuileries

Colette bills itself as a *styledesignartfood* concept store. It continues to be one of the "hot" addresses in Paris, but frankly I think it is a shopping experience best characterized as "boutique chic meets designer kitsch at rip-off prices," which the customer is supposed to consider *la dernière cri* in cutting-edge fashion and minimalistic accessories. A band of ohhh so cool *vendeuses,* dressed in skin-tight designer (of course!) jeans and spray-on sleeveless T-shirts, or slender young men with attitude and all-black clothing, cruise the aisles trying to look busy. Models wander around dressed in over-the-top outfits no one would ever wear . . . even if they could afford them. Big, burly, muscle-flexing bouncers man the doors, scowling at anything they don't like, including this writer, who was literally thrown out of the store twice: once for shooting a photo and again for taking notes. The shop has three levels. Downstairs is a stylized food and designer water bar with prices as high as the noses of the diners and drinkers. Go to Colette, don't miss it in fact, because it is the city's only Museum of the Outrageous. Just remember: look, buy if you must, but don't take photos or notes.

TEL 01-55-35-33-90 **FAX** 01-55-35-33-99 **INTERNET** www.colette.fr
CREDIT CARDS AE, DC, MC, V
OPEN Mon–Sat 10:30 A.M.–7:30 P.M.

DEHILLERIN (42)
18–20 rue Coquillière and 51, rue Jean-Jacques Rousseau, 75001
Métro: Louvre-Rivoli, Les Halles

Since 1820, the Dehillerin family has been supplying chefs and serious cooks with every utensil and cooking accessory needed to create the perfect dish. The selection is vast, and should you forget something, they have an English catalog and will ship. This is a must for anyone who loves to spend time in the kitchen.

TEL 01-42-36-53-13 **FAX** 01-42-36-54-80 **EMAIL** www.e-dehillerin@
wanadoo.fr **INTERNET** www.e-dehillerin.fr or www.dehillerin.com
CREDIT CARDS MC, V
OPEN Mon 9 A.M.–12:30 P.M., 2–6 P.M.; Tues–Sat 9 A.M.–6 P.M.

DU PAREIL AU MÊME (54)
Forum des Halles, Niveau 2 (second level), 75001
Métro: Les Halles

Finally, adorable French children's clothing we all can afford. If you have shopped for children in Paris before, you know how prohibitive the prices are . . . a little play outfit could cost $100, and a tiny bikini, $50. Take heart, and take your credit card to this mecca for mommies: Du Pareil au Même. If you have anyone on your list between the ages of one and twelve, you absolutely must include one of these shops on your Paris A-list of things to do. At last count, there were twenty shops well-positioned throughout Paris. There are also shops in every major French city. You can shop with Du Pareil au Même online and have your purchases sent. This is a major breakthrough in French merchandising for children, and it has captured everyone's attention. Don't miss it. Consult their Website, or pick up a card, which lists all of their many locations throughout Paris and France.

TEL 01-40-13-95-29 **INTERNET** www.dpam.fr
CREDIT CARDS AE, MC, V
OPEN Generally Mon–Sat 10 A.M.–7 P.M.; hours vary slightly at each location

DU PAREIL AU MÊME BÉBÉ (63)
1, rue Saint-Denis, corner avenue Victoria, 75001
Métro: Châtelet

Du Pareil au Même has created a shop exclusively for babies, with numerous locations around Paris. The discount clothing for the tiny ones is just as adorable as what the other stores sell for the older children. This one is not far from the Du Pareil au Même in Forum des Halles.

TEL 01-42-36-26-53 **INTERNET** www.dpam.com
CREDIT CARDS AE, MC, V
OPEN Generally Mon–Sat 10 A.M.–7:30 P.M.; hours vary slightly at each location

GALIGNANI (19)
224, rue de Rivoli, 75001
Métro: Tuileries

Galignani has the distinction of being the first English language bookstore established on the continent of Europe. It has everything book lovers want in a quality bookstore, including a knowledgeable staff willing to assist. Galignani is known for its fine selection of decorative art books and for filling worldwide special mail orders.

TEL 01-42-60-76-07 **FAX** 01-42-86-91-31 **EMAIL** galignani@wanadoo.fr
CREDIT CARDS MC, V
OPEN Mon–Sat 10 A.M.–7 P.M.

JEAN-PAUL HÉVIN (24)
231, rue Saint-Honoré, 75001
Métro: Tuileries

If chocolate is your passion, a visit to Jean-Paul Hévin's chocolate boutique and tearoom is required anytime you are in Paris. The shop window seduces the chocolate lover with a precise, almost museum-like display of chocolates and chocolate fantasies. Up the steep steps is the tearoom, where you can order hot food, but instead, save every calorie for one of the forty types of chocolate or for a slice of cake or a pastry dessert and a pot of steaming aromatic tea. Two other Paris locations are at 3, rue Vavin in the sixth arrondissement, and at 23 bis, avenue de la Motte-Picquet in the seventh, but they do not have tearooms. Or, order Hévin chocolates online.

TEL 01-55-35-35-96 **INTERNET** www.jphevin.com
CREDIT CARDS AE, DC, MC, V
OPEN Mon–Sat: chocolate boutique 10 A.M.–7:30 P.M.; tearoom for lunch noon–3 P.M., for tea 3–7 P.M. **CLOSED** Sun; holidays, Aug

LA DAME BLANCHE (48)
186, rue de Rivoli, 75001
Métro: Palais-Royal–Musée du Louvre

You will soon become dizzy and confused walking along the tourist trail that leads from place de la Concorde down rue de Rivoli. The area has one of the highest concentrations of tourist merchandise in the city. You know the type: plastic Eiffel Towers, T-shirts with the Mona Lisa and a smart remark, gaudy scarves, and wild ties your husband would blush wearing. However, dedicated shop hounds know that with a little digging, treasures are here. Where? At Michael and Suzanne's La Dame Blanche, which was started by their mother in 1969 as a small glove boutique. The windows of their side-by-side shops are jam-packed with Limoges boxes that collectors will go mad over, Le Faïence de Quimper, leather gloves, authentic French berets, small and large tapestries, and more. Do not let this confusing clutter deter you from exploring one of the best shops along this stretch. Not only is the selection good, so are the prices. If you want a special Limoges box, ask Michael and he can have it made for you. Both Michael and Suzanne speak English, offer excellent service, and are delightful besides. They ship worldwide. Don't forget to fill out the paperwork for the *détaxe* if you spend 175€ or more.

TEL 01-42-96-31-56 **FAX** 01-42-96-02-11
CREDIT CARDS AE, DC, MC, V
OPEN Mon–Sat 10 A.M.–6:30 P.M.

LA DROGUERIE (43)
9–11, rue du Jour, 75001
Métro: Les Halles (exit Turbigo-Rambuteau)

It doesn't look like much when you walk by it, but once inside, it is an Ali Baba's cave of glorious ribbons, yarn, trim, buttons, feathers, and glitter, plus the glue to put it all together. If you are into jewelry making, beading, knitting, making your own purses—or any other creative DIY hobby—you will love this treasure trove. Do yourself a favor and try to avoid coming on Saturday, when they are absolutely swamped with eager customers.

TEL 01-45-08-93-27 **FAX** 01-42-36-30-80
CREDIT CARDS MC, V
OPEN Mon 2–6:45 P.M., Tues–Sat 10:30 A.M.–6:45 P.M.

LAVINIA (7)
3, boulevard de la Madeleine, 75001
Métro: Madeleine

Welcome to one of the world's biggest wine shops, where over 6,000 bottles of wines and spirits are sold by the glass, bottle, or case in this multilevel, 16,000-square-foot *supermarché* of wines. Not only that, there is an eighty-seat restaurant (reservations essential), a tasting bar, wine accessory boutique, and a friendly multilingual staff to help you spend money on interesting wines from around the world. To encourage as much tasting and ultimately buying as possible, wine served at the bar or table is the same price as on the store shelf. Special wine tastings and theme events (conducted in French) are scheduled throughtout the year.

TEL 01-42-97-20-20 **EMAIL** laviniafrance@lavinia.fr **INTERNET** www.lavinia.fr
CREDIT CARDS AE, DC, MC, V

OPEN Wine store: Mon–Fri 10 A.M.–8 P.M., Sat 9 A.M.–8 P.M.; restaurant: Mon–Sat noon–3 P.M.; tasting bar: Mon–Sat 3–8 P.M. **CLOSED** Sun; holidays, NAC

LE CÈDRE ROUGE (61)
22, avenue Victoria, 75001
Métro: Châtelet

Le Cèdre Rouge has several Paris stores selling elegant home and garden decor and accessories. Most of what you see, you will not be able to take home, but you can always take new ideas with you, or perhaps a pretty pillow or set of unusual table linens.

TEL 01-42-33-71-05 **INTERNET** www.lecedrerouge.com
CREDIT CARDS AE, MC, V
OPEN Mon 1–7 P.M., Tues–Fri 10:45 A.M.–7 P.M., Sat 10:15 A.M.–7 P.M.

LE LOUVRE DES ANTIQUAIRES (49)
2, place du Palais-Royal, 75001
Métro: Palais-Royal–Musée du Louvre

Here you will find more than two hundred dealers selling antiques from all over the world, and at world-class prices. Each piece comes with a certificate of guarantee. You don't have to buy, but it is interesting to see such a concentration of magnificent, museum-quality antiques.

TEL 01-42-97-27-00 **INTERNET** www.louvre-antiquaires.com
CREDIT CARDS Varies, but generally MC, V
OPEN Tues–Sun 11 A.M.–7 P.M. **CLOSED** Sun–Mon, Aug, all holidays

LE PRINCE JARDINIER (28)
117–121 Jardins du Palais Royal, Arcade Valois, 75001
Métro: Palais-Royal–Musée du Louvre

The Palais Royal gardens are known and loved as some of the most beautiful in Paris. Now, in addition to admiring the palace built by Cardinal Richelieu in 1632, you have another enchanted garden to visit. Prince Louis-Albert de Broglie, a young Paris banker, has opened Le Prince Jardinier, a charming garden boutique along the arcades of the Palais Royal. Not only does he sell seeds and spades, he has hand-crafted garden tools, brass buckets, stainless-steel watering cans, and tools that fit into custom-made aprons and sacks. The shop also has a line of exclusive garden attire for the stylish gardener—aprons, bags, hats, smocks, and coats—along with plants, herbal teas, and spices. One titled customer has found Prince Broglie's wares irresistible, and he uses them on his Highgrove estate. Who? Prince Charles.

TEL 01-42-60-37-13 **INTERNET** www.princejardinier.fr
CREDIT CARDS MC, V
OPEN Mon–Sat 10:30 A.M.–7 P.M. **CLOSED** Mon–Wed 1–2 P.M.

LES ARTS DÉCORATIFS (50)
107, rue de Rivoli, 75001
Métro: Palais-Royal, Musée du Louvre

Three rooms of stunning gifts, books, postcards, and paper products. There's something for everyone on your shopping list, including yourself.

TEL 01-42-60-64-94 **FAX** 01-42-96-13-18 **EMAIL** artcodif@wanadoo.fr
CREDIT CARDS MC, V
OPEN Tue–Fri 11 A.M.–6 P.M., Sat–Sun 10 A.M.–6 P.M.

L'ESPACE CRÉATEURS (54)
Forum des Halles, Niveau 1, (first level), Porte Berger (Berger Gate)
Entrance on rue Pierre Lescot or rue Berger, 75001
Métro: Les Halles

Fifty young designers have joined forces to display their creations in the Forum des Halles. Aimed at a young, buff, fashion-conscious audience, this is the place to check out what new talent is around and to spot who has an edge on the future.

TEL 06-21-02-69-65
CREDIT CARDS Depends on designer
OPEN Mon–Sat 11 A.M.–7 P.M.

MADELIOS (6)
23, boulevard de la Madeleine, 75001
Métro: Madeleine

Madelios is a megastore for men featuring top brand names. The store offers a 10 percent discount on purchases, as well as an immediate 15 percent tax refund (in cash or on your credit card) after you spend 175€ in the store.

TEL 01-53-45-00-00 **INTERNET** www.madelios.com
CREDIT CARDS AE, DC, MC, V
OPEN Mon–Sat 10 A.M.–7 P.M.

MARÉCHAL (18)
232, rue de Rivoli, 75001
Métro: Tuileries

If you cannot find a Limoges box here to suit you, they will have one custom designed for you and shipped anywhere you like. In addition to their fabulous selection of well-displayed Limoges boxes, they have a good selection of quality Paris souvenirs. They also have a shipping and a mail-order service.

TEL 01-42-60-71-83 **FAX** 01-42-60-33-76 **EMAIL** marechalparis@wanadoo.fr
INTERNET www.limogesmarechal.com
CREDIT CARDS AE, MC, V
OPEN Daily 10:30 A.M.–6:30 P.M.

OLIVER B (46)
21, rue Pierre Lescot, 75001
Métro: Étienne-Marcel, Les Halles

At Oliver B you will find inexpensive separates that are easy to wear and cheap enough to toss out after a season or two. Lots of sizes and nothing too far out. The clothes are poorly displayed, but at least they are organized by color. Don't expect much help from the bored (and often smoking) sales babes. The store has good sales in January and July and periodic mark-downs the rest of the year.

TEL 01-40-27-27-27
CREDIT CARDS MC, V
OPEN Mon–Sat 11A.M.–7 P.M.

PLAQUES ET POTS (58)
12, rue de la Ferronnerie, 75001
Métro: Châtelet, Les Halles

Whatever sign you want, it is here. If not, one can be customized to your specifications and shipped to your address. You can either buy a Parisian street sign with the name already on it (such as, Champs-Élysées), or for something more unique, have your own street name painted on one of the blue-and-green Paris street signs. Going a step further, you can have signs personalized with the name of your house and so on. . . . Let your imagination be your guide. There is also a selection of handmade pottery, but frankly, the best buys here are the signs.

TEL & FAX 01-42-36-21-72 **INTERNET** www.plaquesetpots.fr
CREDIT CARDS MC, V
OPEN Mon–Sat 10 A.M.–6 P.M. **CLOSED** first 2 weeks of Aug

SCOOTER (45)
10, rue de Turbigo, 75001
Métro: Étienne-Marcel

Scooter specializes in jewelry, accessories, and clothing of the moment that are young, fun, and wearable. They have several locations, but this is the main boutique.

TEL 01-45-08-50-54 **INTERNET** www.scooter-paris.com
CREDIT CARDS MC, V
OPEN Mon 2–7 P.M., Tues–Sat 11 A.M.–7 P.M.

W. H. SMITH (15)
248, rue de Rivoli, corner rue Cambon, 75001
Métro: Concorde

If you forgot to bring along a book to read, long for an English-language magazine, or need a travel guide (especially one on Paris or France), W. H. Smith will come to your rescue. The British-based bookstore has two floors filled to the brim with English-language books, newspapers, magazines, and videos. It also has a wonderful travel book section that stocks the books in the *Great Sleeps* and *Great Eats* series.

TEL 01-44-77-88-99 **EMAIL** whsmith.france@wanadoo.fr
  INTERNET www.whsmith.fr
CREDIT CARDS AE, MC, V
OPEN Mon–Sat 9 A.M.–7:30 P.M., Sun 1–7:30 P.M.

SECOND ARRONDISSEMENT (see map page 66)
Shops

A. SIMON (32)
52 & 48, rue Montmartre, 75002
Métro: Étienne-Marcel

Calling all chefs, gourmets, and gourmands—whether past, present, or budding—as well as anyone with a love of cooking and good food. For one hundred years, A. Simon occupied the corner of 36, rue Étienne Marcel. When their lease ran out, they had to move to smaller quarters in two shops on rue Montmartre. At the two side-by-side A. Simon shops, you will still find all the French cooking and dining essentials you will ever need. With its broad inventory of cooking utensils of every known type and variety and its fascinating array of tableware, this is the Rolls Royce in its field. Prices are geared for the volume buyer, but anyone is welcome, and you will be graciously treated whether you outfit a restaurant or buy a tiny *pichet* for your *vin du table*.

TEL 01-42-33-71-65 **EMAIL** simon.sa@wanadoo.fr
  INTERNET www.simon-a.com
CREDIT CARDS AE, MC, V
OPEN Mon 1:30–6:30 P.M., Tues–Sat 9 A.M.–6:30 P.M.

ANTHONY PETO (33)
56, rue Tiquetonne, 75002
Métro: Étienne-Marcel

Hats off to these fabulous *chapeaux*! I love hats and wear them often, especially when traveling. Anthony Peto runs his hat shop in conjunction with Marie Mercié, who has her own location and her own hats in the sixth arrondissement (see page 362). Between the two stores, their hats run the gamut from frankly fanciful to downright sane and sensible. If you need a hat for any occasion, or, like me, just enjoy wearing—or admiring—them, please make a point of seeing some of the best hats in Paris. Anthony's shop is geared for men, though he carries some unisex hats. I like his summer Panama hats that you can roll up in your suitcase; they just pop back into shape when ready to wear. The service is exceptionally helpful.

TEL 01-40-26-60-68 **FAX** 01-40-26-38-01 **EMAIL** peto@wanadoo.fr
CREDIT CARDS AE, MC, V
OPEN Mon–Sat 11 A.M.–7 P.M. **CLOSED** Middle of Aug

BRENTANO'S (12)
37, avenue de l'Opéra, 75002
Métro: Opéra

This shop has two levels of books as well as a wide selection of stationery and greeting cards, all in English.

TEL 01-42-61-52-50 **INTERNET** www.brentanos.fr
CREDIT CARDS AE, MC, V
OPEN Mon–Sat 10 A.M.–7:30 P.M.

DEBAUVE & GALLAIS (1)
33, rue Vivienne, 75002
Métro: Bourse

For details about this famous chocolate maker and supplier to the kings of France since 1800, please see page 366. All other information is the same.

TEL 01-40-39-05-50
OPEN Mon–Sat 9 A.M.–6:30 P.M.

ET VOUS STOCK (40)
17, rue de Turbigo, 75002
Métro: Étienne-Marcel

They offer up to 50 percent off on the simply styled Et Vous brand of men's and women's clothing and accessories, which almost anyone can wear.

TEL 01-40-13-04-12 **FAX** 01-40-13-01-39
CREDIT CARDS AE, MC, V
OPEN Mon–Sat noon–7 P.M.

EXPLORA (37)
46, rue Tiquetonne, 75002
Métro: Étienne-Marcel

I was first drawn to this beautifully colored line of clothing and accessories—geared toward active, eclectic women—before I knew about the store. The Explora line is designed in Paris and uses only high-quality fabrics such as pima cotton, cashmere, and alpaca. You will see the Explora label in Vogue magazine and Le Bon Marché department store in Paris, and in Henri Bendel in the United States, but for the best selection and prices, come to the source. The *détaxe* starts after 175€.

TEL 01-40-41-00-33 **FAX** 01-42-33-79-96 **EMAIL** expl46@aol.com
    INTERNET www.explora-paris.com
CREDIT CARDS AE, MC, V
OPEN Mon–Fri 10 A.M.–2 P.M., 3–7 P.M., Sat 2–7 P.M. **CLOSED** 2 weeks in Aug

LOLLIPOPS (34)
60, rue Tiquetonne, 75002
Métro: Étienne-Marcel

Fantasy accessories with the emphasis on glam, glitter, and great fun for the young at heart from nine to ninety. Several locations in Paris, including boutiques on rue Dragon (6th), rue de Rossiers (4th), and in the Les Halles behemoth, Galeries Lafayette, and Printemps.

TEL 01-42-33-15-72 **INTERNET** www.lollipops.fr
CREDIT CARDS AE, MC, V
OPEN Mon–Sat 11 A.M.–7:30 P.M. **CLOSED** 1 week in Aug

STOCK KOOKAÏ (30)
82, rue Réaumur, at rue St-Denis, 75002
Métro: Réaumur-Sebastapol

There are Kookaï boutiques worldwide, but this is the only show-room partially devoted to permanent sale items from the line. There are two sections, with the newer, regularly priced clothing toward the back. You can tell which section is which easily: the clothing in front is last season's collection, and it is where fellow savvy shoppers are plying the goods. Dressing rooms are minuscule, and there is only a communal mirror.

TEL 01-45-08-93-69 **INTERNET** www.kookai.fr
CREDIT CARDS AE, DC, MC, V
OPEN Mon–Sat 10 A.M.–7:30 P.M.

VILLAGE JOUÉ CLUB–LA PASSION DE JOUET (4)
3–5, boulevard des Italiens, 75002
Métro: Richelieu-Drouot

If it is on the toy market, chances are you will find it in this two-level mall devoted exclusively to toys that appeal to the child in all of us. In addition to all the toys, educational and creative learning games, dolls, stuffed animals, and art supplies, there is a children's *coiffeur,* a one-hour photo service, party area, and pleasant red-vested sales personnel to guide you through this wonderland, the biggest in Paris.

TEL 01-53-45-41-41 **INTERNET** www.joueclub.fr
CREDIT CARDS AE, MC, V
OPEN Mon–Sat 10 A.M.–8 P.M.

WOLFF ET DESCOURTIS (29)
Galerie Vivienne, 18
6, rue Vivienne, 4, rue des Petits-Champs, 75002
Métro: Bourse, Pyramides

The family-owned Wolff et Descourtis sells luxurious handmade shawls and scarves using timeless mixes of fabrics, designs, and colors. The quality is exquisite in these one-of-a-kind pieces of art, which you will never find elsewhere.

TEL 01-42-61-80-84 **FAX** 01-42-97-46-65
CREDIT CARDS MC, V
OPEN Mon–Fri 11 A.M.–7 P.M., Sat 2–7 P.M.

THIRD ARRONDISSEMENT (see map page 86)
Shops

BOUTIQUE PARIS-MUSÉES (28)
Musée Carnavalet, 23, rue de Sévigné, 75003
Métro: St-Paul

Inside Musée Carnavalet, which explores the history of Paris, this shop specializes in books. For a full description of this museum shop, see page 335.

TEL None
CREDIT CARDS MC, V
OPEN Tues–Sat 11 A.M.–1:30 P.M., 2:30–7 P.M., Sun 11 A.M.–7 P.M.
    CLOSED Mon

DOT–DIFFUSION D'OBJETS DE TABLE (7)
47, rue de Saintonge, 75003
Métro: Filles-du-Calvaire, République

I love this store. You will, too, if you are a *devotée* of French bistro ware, unusual glass and crystal pieces, vintage children's books, enamel boxes, and wooden kitchen utensils, all gathered together under one roof. Garage sale and flea market addicts won't want to miss the basement, which is literally piled to the ceiling with things that have not sold upstairs. There is absolutely no order to the basement, but the good part is that everything in this dugout is half price. I suggest that you wear old clothes, bring a pair of rubber gloves, and have a great time digging. Chances are great you will find something you must have. Email them if you want to be on their mailing list, and check out their Website to order online. But above all, visit them the next time you are in Paris. The staff is as much fun as the store.

TEL 01-40-29-90-34 **EMAIL** dot.bon@wanadoo.fr
INTERNET www.dot-france.com
CREDIT CARDS AE, MC, V (after 40€)
OPEN Mon–Fri 9 A.M.–6 P.M. **CLOSED** Sat–Sun, holidays, Aug (call to check)

GOUMANYAT ET SON ROYAUME (6)
3, rue Charles-François Dupuis, at rue de la Corderie, 75003
Métro: Temple, République

The catalog says it all: "Goumanyat is a rediscovery of the pleasures of taste and the taste of pleasures . . . a rich and thrilling adventure for you and your guests."

For seven generations the Thiercelin family has searched the globe for the finest spices, essential oils, exotic herbs, and fine food products. It all began in 1809, when they specialized in buying natural saffron, which they still sell in its purest form. Today the store is mecca for serious chefs who want the best in unusual herbs and spices, plus jam, honey, mustard, natural vinegar, or flavored salt and sugar. Sniffing, tasting, and enjoying are all encouraged. Three-hour cooking classes are held using ingredients available here.

TEL 01-44-78-96-74 **FAX** 01-44-78-96-75 **INTERNET** www.goumanyat.com
CREDIT CARDS AE, DC, MC, V
OPEN Tue–Fri 2–7 P.M., Sat 11 A.M. –7 P.M. **CLOSED** Sun, Mon, holidays,
2 weeks in Aug

LAURENT GUILLOT (15)
48, rue de Turenne, 75003
Métro: Chemin Vert

Laurent Guillot's crystal and Plexiglas jewelry trimmed in gold and silver appears on the pages of *Elle, Vogue,* and almost every other fashion magazine on the stands. He also supplies many of the top-name designers with jewelry used during the Paris fashion shows. This is his display/boutique in Paris, and it is worth seeing if you like beautifully handcrafted, contemporary jewelry at surprisingly reasonable prices.

NOTE: Rue de Turenne is lined with men's clothing stores.

TEL 01-48-87-87-69 **EMAIL** l.guillot.pa@infonie.fr
INTERNET www.laurentguillot.com
CREDIT CARDS MC, V
OPEN Mon–Sat 11 A.M.–12:30 P.M., 1:30–6:45 P.M.

L'HABILLEUR (10)
44, rue de Poitou, 75003
Métro: St-Sébastien Froissart

Two rooms with cutting edge French and Italian clothes for men and women at 50 percent off from Helmut Lang, Plein Sud, Roberto Collina, Isimiaki, and more. All are leftovers from last season's collections, mixed in with some catwalk outfits and a few shoes.

TEL 01-48-87-77-12
CREDIT CARDS DC, MC, V
OPEN Mon–Sat noon–8 P.M.

PATYKA (12)
14, rue Rambuteau, 75003
Métro: Rambuteau

Founded in Budapest in 1922, the Patyka line of handmade beauty products is made from pure plant extracts and natural ingredients. Based on a desire to live in harmony with nature, Patyka does not use synthetic materials that are harmful to you or the environment. This is a small, independent company of European artisans and aromatherapists who believe in a world where simplicity and quality are one. I am a committed admirer of their certified organic line of cosmetics, perfumes, creams, and oils, their beautifully scented candles, and their relaxing bath products. Shipping is available. They also have outlets at Printemps and Bon Marché.

TEL 01-40-29-49-49 **FAX** 01-44-54-02-52 **EMAIL** patyka@patyka.com
  INTERNET www.patyka.com
CREDIT CARDS MC, V
OPEN Mon, Thur–Sat noon–8 P.M., Sun noon–7 P.M.

TATI (4)
174, rue du Temple, 75003
Métro: Temple, République,

Attention, shoppers! If you love swap meets, garage sales, and basement fire sales, then Tati is for you. The crowds are impossible, especially on Saturday, but for truly amazing bargains hidden among some real junk, join the diverse crowd at Tati. Prices defy the competition on stock that ranges from bridal wear to linen slacks, cheap silk shirts, cheaper shoes, baby gear, and kitchen equipment. Be sure to check each item carefully because quality control is not a priority when this much volume is concerned. While here, save a few minutes to check out the Monoprix around the corner. If you buy more than you can carry on this shopping spree, there is a luggage store at 178, rue du Temple, with a supply of cheap bags on wheels.

TEL Not available
CREDIT CARDS MC, V
OPEN Mon–Fri 9:30 A.M.–7 P.M., Sat 10 A.M.–7:30 P.M.

FOURTH ARRONDISSEMENT (see map page 86)

A LA BONNE RENOMMEE (26)
26, rue Vieille du Temple, 75004
Métro: St-Paul

A la Bonne Renommee became famous for its multifabric and multicolored handbags. Now they have expanded into men's and women's clothing and accessories, both for wearing and using in the home. Some of the colors and fabric mixes leave me wondering, and so do most of the prices, but if you can find something you like on sale, it will be a good buy . . . and will probably last a long time.

TEL 01-42-72-03-86 **FAX** 01-42-72-32-02 **EMAIL** a.la.bonne.renommee@
wanadoo.fr **INTERNET** www.labonnerenommee.com
CREDIT CARDS AE, MC, V
OPEN Mon–Sat 11 A.M.–7 P.M., Sun 2–7 P.M.

BHV–BAZAR DE L'HÔTEL DE VILLE (29)
52–64, rue de Rivoli, 75004
Métro: Hôtel-de-Ville

This is a shopping experience no do-it-yourselfer should miss, except on Saturday when an estimated twenty-five thousand shoppers stream through the store. BHV (pronounced bay-ashe-vey) is famous for its basement hardware department, which is a Parisian DIY experience in itself—with vast kitchen and automotive sections, not to mention paints, electrical supplies, and a series of DIY classes. While in the basement, don't miss seeing the Bricolo Café, which looks like a 1920 garage. The food is quite ordinary, but it is okay for a coffee or cold drink. The rest of the multilevel store is ho-hum—not very exciting *or* stylish. The store offers a 10 percent discount for non-EU citizens, but they are not going to make it easy. To get the discount card, you must go up to the seventh floor, through several doors, wander down empty corridors until you find the "welcome" desk and face a grumpy staff who must see your passport before they dole out the discount cards that are valid for only one day. Really, some welcome. This takes the booby prize for customer service and convenience. The store also grants a 12 percent *détaxe* when purchases total 175€ or more.

TEL 01-42-74-90-00 **INTERNET** www.bhv.fr
CREDIT CARDS AE, MC, V
OPEN Mon–Tues, Thur, Sat 9:30 A.M.–7:30 P.M., Wed & Fri 9:30 A.M.–9 P.M.

BISCUIT (48)
15, rue Beautreillis, 75004
Métro: St-Paul, Bastille

I found Michiko and her children's *dépôt vent* and design boutique just a week after she opened. Now she has added women's clothing in small sizes (36–40) and accessories. I must say I am still very impressed with the quality and condition of the formerly owned clothes she stocks. Her clothing sizes for children are from newborn to twelve years. Prices are tempting, and it will be hard to leave without buying something you and your children or grandchildren will love. While you are here, you can't miss the black-and-white photo of her daughter that hangs on one wall. It was taken by her husband, who is a fashion photographer.

TEL 01-42-71-43-73
OPEN Mon–Tues, Thur–Fri 1–7 P.M., Sat 3–7 P.M.
CREDIT CARDS MC, V

BOUTIQUE PARIS-MUSÉES (27)
29 bis, rue des Francs-Bourgeois, 75004
Métro: St-Paul

For a description of this museum store, see page 335.

TEL 01-42-74-13-02
OPEN Mon 2–7 P.M., Tues–Sat 11 A.M.–1 P.M., 2–7 P.M., Sun noon–7 P.M.

C & P (44)
16, rue du Pont Louis-Philippe, 75004
Métro: Pont-Marie, St-Paul

Marie Chaumette and Patrick Poirier (C & P) design fluid, wearable clothing that never seems to go out of style. These are the clothes you always reach for in your closet when you are dressing for the day or packing for a trip. The colors are simple: black, blue, gray, beige, and white. Fabrics are excellent and the prices affordable when you think how long you are going to enjoy the outfit.

TEL 01-42-74-22-34 **EMAIL** patrickpoirier75@free.net
CREDIT CARDS MC, V
OPEN Mon 2–7 P.M., Tues–Sat 11 A.M.–7 P.M.

FAÏENCERIES DE QUIMPER (17)
84, rue St-Martin, 75004
Métro: Hôtel de Ville, Rambuteau

Here you can find everything for the Quimper collector, including paper napkins, Christmas ornaments, linens, and numbers or name tiles for your home. The display is excellent, and so is the friendly sales staff. They will ship.

TEL 01-42-71-93-03 **EMAIL** boutique.paris@hb-henriot.com
    INTERNET www.hb-henriot.com
CREDIT CARDS AE, MC, V
OPEN Mon–Sat 11 A.M.–7 P.M.

L'ÉCRITOIRE (18)
61, rue Saint-Martin, 75004
Métro: Châtelet, Hôtel de Ville

For over thirty years, this has been a delightful destination for inks, inkpots, fountain pens, journals and diaries, pretty papers, and greeting cards destined to please anyone who still remembers the postman.

TEL 01-42-78-01-18
CREDIT CARDS MC, V
OPEN Mon–Sat 11 A.M.–7 P.M., Sun (in Dec only) 1–7 P.M.

LIBRAIRIE ULYSSE (58)
26, rue Saint-Louis en L'Ile, 74004
Métro: Pont Marie

Catherine Domain spent ten years traveling nonstop around the world before she returned to Paris and opened this travel bookshop, which when it opened was the first of its kind anywhere. Now almost forty years later, her travel enthusiasm has not waned, and she still takes time every year to sail the Pacific and to tend to her other bookshop in the Basque region of France. Clearly travel and books are in her blood. One of her grandfathers circumnavigated the world; the other had a prosperous bookshop.

The Librairie Ulysse is a fascinating treasure trove of more than twenty thousand new and used travel books and maps on countless destinations. You can also order obscure or out-of-print books, sell your travel-inspired books (either in person or by correspondence), or just stop by to talk with English-speaking Catherine, who is one of the most knowledgeable travelers and booksellers you will ever meet.

TEL 01-43-25-17-35; cell 06-27-15-34-67 **FAX** 01-43-29-52-10
    EMAIL ulysse@ulysse.fr **INTERNET** www.ulysse.fr
CREDIT CARDS None, euros only
OPEN Tues–Fri 2–8 P.M.; call to check if closed in Aug

L'OCCITANE
17, rue des Francs-Bourgeois, 75004 (37)
18, place des Vosges, 75004 (38)
55, rue St-Louis-en-l'Île, 75004 (57)
Métro: St-Paul, Pont-Marie

For the best in natural, vegetable-based cosmetics, go to L'Occitane. All the products are from Provence and include cosmetics, essential oils, soaps, creams, perfumes, and bath accessories. It is worth a trip to any of their shops just to smell the aromas and admire the beautiful displays. Whatever you buy will be beautifully gift-wrapped. These three shops in the fourth arrondissement are my favorites, but there are branches all over Paris. At last count, the company had shops in Europe, the United States, Mexico, Asia, the Middle East, Oceania, and Africa. But you are lucky . . . the prices in France are less than elsewhere. These three branches are open on Sunday, as is the L'Occitane in the first arrondissement in the La Galerie du Carrousel du Louvre shopping mall (see page 330), and I've noted several other convenient L'Occitanes throughout the shopping chapter.

TEL 01-42-77-96-67 (rue des Francs Bourgeois); 01-42-72-60-36 (place des Vosges); 01-40-46-81-71 (l'Île St-Louis) **INTERNET** www.loccitane.com
CREDIT CARDS MC, V
OPEN The hours may vary slightly in each shop, but generally they are Mon–Sat 11:30 A.M.–7:30 P.M., Sun 10:30 A.M.–7 P.M. Most of the shops close an hour for lunch.

MARIAGE FRÈRES (24)
30–32, rue de Bourg-Tibourg, 75004
Métro: Hôtel de Ville, St-Paul

No serious tea lover can afford to miss the Tiffany of tearooms in Paris: Mariage Frères, which for more than 145 years has been dedicated to the art of tea drinking. Over 500 teas from thirty-five countries are prepared in these world-famous shops by master tea makers who still do everything by hand, including carefully cutting and stitching each tea bag out of tissue or muslin. While nothing beats enjoying a lovely pastry and a sublime cup of tea in this civilized establishment, adjoining each tearoom is a wonderful tea boutique. The one here houses a small tea museum, and there is a *comptoir* (tea shop) across the street. Other locations include 13, rue des Grands-Augustins in the sixth; 260, rue du Faubourg St-Honoré in the eighth; and in Bon Marché and Printemps department stores.

TEL 01-42-72-28-11 **INTERNET** www.mariagefreres.com
CREDIT CARDS AE, MC, V
OPEN Daily: lunch noon–6:30 P.M., afternoon tea 3–6:30 P.M., tea boutique and tea museum 10:30 A.M.–7:30 P.M. **CLOSED** Never

MATIÈRE PREMIÈRE (36)
12, rue de Sévigné, 75004
Métro: St-Paul

Baubles, bangles, and beads—either assemble your own or buy ready-made necklaces, earrings, and pins at decent prices.

TEL 01-42-78-40-87 **EMAIL** matierepremiere@wanadoo.fr
INTERNET www.matierepremiere.fr
CREDIT CARDS MC, V
OPEN Mon–Sat 11 A.M.–7:30 P.M., Sun 3–7 P.M.

PWS–PRICES WITHOUT SURPRISE (35)
13, rue de Sévigné, 75004
Métro: St-Paul

Owner Claude Windisch got the idea for his discount store after visiting the United States and seeing all the cut-price stores. Although he has some women's apparel, he is better with men's. He stocks everything for the man in your life, from top-name (Louis Feraud, Cerruti) to no-name designer clothing. Prices are 20 percent off the marked prices on this season's clothing. He does not stock last year's collections. If you spend 175€, you will qualify for a 15 percent discount on the marked price, plus another 15 percent for the *détaxe*. Manager Myriam Benarroche speaks English and is very helpful.

NOTE: The shop is in a courtyard. Look for the PWS flag hanging next to the archway on the street that leads to the courtyard.

TEL 01-44-54-09-09 **EMAIL** claude@parispws.com
INTERNET www.parispws.com
CREDIT CARDS MC, V
OPEN Mon 2–7 P.M., Tues–Sat 10 A.M.–7 P.M.

THE RED WHEELBARROW BOOKSTORE (50)
22, rue St-Paul, 75004
Métro: St-Paul, Bastille, Sully-Morland

Penelope Fletcher-Le Masson and Abigail Altman own and run this charming Anglophone bookstore. Their stock is excellent, especially in children's books and contemporary literature. They are both young, enthusiastic, and consummate booksellers who are passionate and extremely knowledgeable about their profession.

TEL 01-48-04-75-08 **EMAIL** good.reading@wanadoo.fr
INTERNET www.theredwheelbarrow.com
CREDIT CARDS MC, V
OPEN Mon–Sat 10 A.M.–7 P.M., Sun noon–7 P.M.

SIDNEY CARRON (14)
37, rue des Archives, 75004
Métro: Hôtel de Ville, Rambuteau

The window displays of unusual jewelry caught my eye . . . and then I looked at the prices charged by this talented designer in his workshop/boutique. For the beautifully crafted silver and gold jewelry, the prices are excellent. Carron also makes jewelry for the Salvador Dali Museum in Montmartre (11, rue Poulbot, 75018).

He is also a very enthusiastic collector, especially of American designs from the thirties and forties and parts of airplanes. You can see some of his collection displayed in his shop: an Eames chair, a piece of wing support from the Concorde, and propellers and panels from other planes. When I was last there, he told me he was planning to build his own airplane, because now, "I am old enough to have time."

TEL 01-48-87-27-70 **FAX** 01-48-87-32-77 **EMAIL** sidneycarron@carronsidney.fr
CREDIT CARDS None, cash only
OPEN Mon–Fri 9:30 A.M.–7:30 P.M., Sat 11 A.M.–7:30 P.M. **CLOSED** Aug, holidays

STOCK GRIFFES (25)
17, rue Vieille du Temple, 75004
Métro: St-Paul

It is not my first choice for low-cost duds, but if you are nearby and swing through, you might get lucky.

TEL 01-48-04-82-34
CREDIT CARDS MC, V
OPEN Tues–Sat 10:30 A.M.–7:30 P.M.

UN CHIEN DANS LE MARAIS (33)
35 bis, rue du Roi de Sicile, 75004
Métro: Hôtel-de-Ville

Un Chien dans le Marais is *le ne plus ultra* of Parisian doggie boutiques offering, and I quote, "many high-quality items that will excite both you and your dog." Of course they carry a large line of collars, leads, food, treats, and toys. However, if they don't have the glam-goods in stock you are looking for, never fear. . . . They have catalogs where you can order Dog Fashion Apparel that will make you and Fifi or Jacques the absolute fashion envy of all the other owners and dogs in your neighborhood. These slick catalogs offer dapper dogs modeling sweaters galore, little tartan skirts, houndstooth coats with matching carrying cases, diva tutus, jogging suits, princess padded coats . . . even pajamas and wedding outfits. Don't ever think you can stop with only one or two drop-dead outfits. *Mais non!* You must accessorize, and of course the catalogs have a complete line of actual jewelry for your dog, in addition to traditional leads and collars, bejeweled or not.

Whether you have pets at home or not, this boutique is a hoot!

TEL 01-42-74-30-06 **EMAIL** contact@unchiendanslemarais.com
   INTERNET www.unchiendanslemarais.com
CREDIT CARDS AE, MC, V
OPEN Daily 11 A.M.–8 P.M.

FIFTH ARRONDISSEMENT (see map page 108)

THE ABBEY BOOKSHOP (9)
29, rue de la Parcheminerie, 75005
Métro: St-Michel, Cluny–La Sorbonne

Canadian Brian Spence stocks new and used English books. He also takes special orders, will ship, and holds literary events in his bookshop near the Cluny Museum. Once a month a book club meets (discussion are in English), and on Sunday, he leads hiking trips to the countryside. Check his Website for the events schedule, or email him and ask to be put on the activities list.

TEL 01-46-33-16-24 **FAX** 01-46-33-03-33 **EMAIL** abbeybookshop@wanadoo.fr
   INTERNET www.abbeybookshop.net
CREDIT CARDS AE, MC, V
OPEN Mon–Sat 10 A.M.–7 P.M., sometimes also on Sun **CLOSED** 1 week Aug
   (dates vary)

AU VIEUX CAMPEUR (13)
48, rue des Écoles, 75005
Métro: Maubert-Mutualité

Outdoor enthusiasts and sports-minded people must make a pilgrimage to one of the nineteen stores under the Au Vieux Campeur umbrella. If it has to do with the outdoors or sports, they stock it and probably in several brands and models. Drop into their main store at the above address and pick up a sheet (which includes a map) that gives the addresses of their other stores, all located within a few blocks of each other between rue des Écoles and boulevard St-Germain. Avoid Saturday, when the crowds are so lethal you cannot get down the aisles.

TEL 01-53-10-48-48 **INTERNET** www.auvieuxcampeur.fr
CREDIT CARDS AE, DC, MC, V
OPEN Mon–Fri 11 A.M.–7:30 P.M., Thur until 9 P.M., Sat 10 A.M.–7:30 P.M.

DIPTYQUE (17)
34, boulevard St-Germain, 75005
Métro: Maubert-Mutualité

Join Puff Daddy, Elton John, and scores of other celebrities who light scented candles from Diptyque. The seven-ounce glass containers hold every wonderful scent you have heard of . . . and plenty you haven't. Traditionalists can buy rose, lilac, cinnamon, or hyacinth, but why not experiment with something unusual: fig tree, newly mown hay, Mexican orange blossom, or myrrh? Room sprays that match the candle scents enhance the experience. Go one step further and wear a matching *eau de toilette* in the same fragrance. Don't leave without a bottle of *vinaigre de toilette*. Based on a nineteenth-century recipe using plants, woods, and spices, this elixir has many uses. In the bath it revives and refreshes; as an aftershave or face spray, it tones and refreshes; and a capful in a bowl of boiling water will remove cooking and tobacco smells from a room. Loyalists know to stock up on their favorite Diptyque products in Paris. For instance, a perfumed candle sells in Paris for 55€ ($65). Buy it in London and you will spend £38 (about $70) or in New York for $70. One candle lasts fifty hours.

TEL 01-43-26-45-27 **EMAIL** diptyue@diptyqueparis.com **INTERNET**
www.diptyque.com
CREDIT CARDS AE, MC, V
OPEN Mon–Sat 10 A.M.–7 P.M.

LA TUILE À LOUP (38)
35, rue Daubenton, 75005
Métro: Censier-Daubenton

Marie-France and Michel Joblin-Dépalle stock regional tableware, housewares, and linens from all over France. True, most of the pieces are heavy and probably too bulky for a suitcase, but they will insure and ship your purchases.

TEL 01-47-07-28-90 **FAX** 01-43-36-40-95 **EMAIL** tuilealoup@aol.com
INTERNET www.latuilealoup.com
CREDIT CARDS MC, V
OPEN Mon 1–7 P.M., Tues–Sat 10:30 A.M.–7 P.M. **CLOSED** Aug (dates vary)

LE ROUVRAY (6)
3, rue de la Bucherie, 75005
Métro: Maubert-Mutualité, St-Michel

Le Rouvray's motto says it all: "We speak patchwork fluently." This is a wonderful shop if you sew and love homespun fabrics. The shop stocks two thousand fabrics featuring Provençal prints and Toiles de Jouy, offers classes, and fills mail orders. In addition, they will sell you all the supplies you need to create your own work of art.

TEL 01-43-25-00-45 **FAX** 01-55-42-02-61 **EMAIL** lerouvray@easyconnect.fr
INTERNET www.lerouvray.com
CREDIT CARDS MC, V
OPEN Tues–Sat 10 A.M.–6:30 P.M. **CLOSED** Last two weeks of Aug

L'OCCITANE (37)
130, rue Mouffetard, 75005
Métro: Monge

Natural cosmetics and body products. For a complete description, see page 351.

TEL 01-43-31-98-12
OPEN Tues–Sat 9:30 A.M.–1:30 P.M., 3 P.M.–7:30 P.M., Sun 9:30 A.M.–1:30 P.M.

SIMON (32)
56, boulevard Saint-Michel, 75005
Métro: Luxembourg

The business card of this wonderfully old-fashioned shop states it is *Le Spécialist du parapluie et de la canne:* The Specialist for umbrellas and canes. From the frilly and fanciful, to the useful and utilitarian, if it is an umbrella or walking cane you want, this *is* the place to come. Prices range from a modest 15€ to a whopping 400€ for one of their exclusive umbrella designs. They will also repair broken unbrellas.

TEL 01-43-54-12-04 **EMAIL** parapluies-simon@wanadoo.fr
CREDIT CARDS AE, MC, V
OPEN Mon–Sat 10 A.M.–7 P.M.

SIXTH ARRONDISSEMENT (see map page 134)
Shops

ARCHE (32)
21, rue du Dragon, 75006
Métro: St-Germain-des-Prés

For details about these comfortable, long-lasting shoes, see page 334. All other information is the same.

TEL 01-42-22-54-75

BOIS DE ROSE (9)
30, rue Dauphine, 75006
Métro: Odéon, Pont Neuf

Bois de Rose stocks the prettiest hand-smocked clothes for the little fashion plates in your life, whether they are only three months or twelve years old. The clothes are probably more suited to girls, especially the adorable dresses with frilly socks and headbands to match.

TEL & FAX 01-40-46-04-24 **INTERNET** www.boisderose.fr.vu
CREDIT CARDS AE, DC, MC, V
OPEN Mon–Sat 10:30 A.M.–7 P.M.

BOUTIQUE DU CAFÉ DE FLORE (10)
26, rue Saint Benoit, 75006
Métro: St-Germain-des-Prés

Café Flore is one of the most famous cafés in Paris. The historic watering hole was once the meeting place of the Lost Generation, and it still attracts would-be intellectuals to its weekly Monday night play readings and first Wednesday of the month philosophy dicussions, both in English (starting at 8 P.M.). The food is mediocre and overpriced, and so is the coffee, but never mind. You are here for nostalgia and great Parisian people-watching. If you want to take home an interesting Parisian souvenir, you can buy any piece of china or glassware used in the café at their boutique around the corner. I like the green-and-white signature cocktail napkins and the little jam and sugar dishes, which are easy to pack and great reminders of a trip to Paris. If the boutique is closed, which it frequently is, the china is sold at the cash register in the café.

TEL 01-45-44-33-40 **INTERNET** www.cafe-de-flore.com
CREDIT CARDS AE, DC, MC, V (16€ minimum)
OPEN Tues–Sat 11 A.M.–2 P.M., 3–8 P.M. **CLOSED** First 3 weeks in Aug

CARTES D'ART (20)
9, rue du Dragon, 75006
Métro: St-Germain-des-Prés

Most of the postcards are printed exclusively for Cartes d'Art. You will see their designs all over town, but here is the source for their whimsical takes on Paris life, her monuments, and places of interest. They also stock literally thousands of other postcards, all arranged by type. In addition, you will find greeting cards and other stationery products that make nice gifts or souvenirs for yourself. If you don't see what you want, just ask and they probably have it someplace.

TEL 01-42-22-86-15 **EMAIL** cartesdart@easynet.fr
CREDIT CARDS AE, DC, MC, V
OPEN Mon–Sat 11 A.M.–7 P.M.

CHERCHEMINIPPES (62)
109, rue du Cherche-Midi, 75006
Métro: Duroc

Between street Nos. 102 and 124, rue de Cherche-Midi, Chercheminippes has five *dépôt vents* selling previously owned clothing for men, women, and children, plus toys and decorative items. I think the most interesting shop is the *Décoration* shop at 109, which has lots of little things for less than 10€.

TEL 01-42-22-45-23
CREDIT CARDS MC, V (26€ minimum)
OPEN Mon–Sat 10:30 A.M.–7 P.M. **CLOSED** July 15–Aug 22 (dates can vary)

CHRISTIAN LU (60)
86, rue de Vaugirard, 75006
Métro: St-Placide, Rennes

Christian Lu designs and makes all the silks you see in her colorful shop and often waits on you herself. Everything is made in China, but the quality and craftsmanship are very high. She has large, hand-rolled scarves; mix-and-match skirts, blouses, jackets and trousers; and some dresses. The scarves make great gifts. Everything is hand washable.

TEL 01-45-44-93-37 **FAX** 01-42-21-04-72
CREDIT CARDS MC, V
OPEN Mon–Sat 10:30 A.M.–7 P.M. **CLOSED** middle 2 weeks of Aug

DÉPÔT–VENTE DE BUCI (14)
4, rue de Bourbon-le-Château, off rue de Buci, 75006
Métro: Mabillon

These two side-by-side boutiques run by a mother and daughter team are well worth a few moments if you like being clad in Chanel, Hèrmes, YSL, Dior, Fendi, and Louis Vuitton, but don't want to pay the asking prices in their boutiques. One side is definitely more *haute* and vintage than the other, but all the previously owned clothes, accessories, and housewares are in good condition. This is a very popular shopping destination for many style mavens in the tony sixth. Note that the vintage side is closed between 1 and 2 P.M.

TEL 01-46-34-45-05 (clothing, accessories); 01-46-34-28-28 (vintage)
CREDIT CARDS AE, MC, V
OPEN Tues–Sat 11 A.M.–7:30 P.M. **CLOSED** Aug 10–15

DU PAREIL AU MÊME (53)
7, 14 & 34, Rue St-Placide, 75006
Métro: St-Placide

For a description of these well-priced children's clothing stores, see page 336. All other information is the same.

TEL 01-45-44-04-40

DU PAREIL AU MÊME (23)
168, boulevard Saint-Germain, 75006
Métro: St-Germain-des-Prés

For a description of this children's clothing store, see page 336.

TEL 01-46-33-87-85

DU PAREIL AU MÊME BÉBÉ (66)
17, Rue Vavin, 75006
Métro: Vavin

For a description of this baby clothing store, see page 337.

TEL 01-43-54-12-34

FLAMANT (11)
8, rue Furstemberg & 8, rue de l'Abbaye, 75006
Métro: St-Germain-des-Pres

Flamant is a world-class theme park showcasing the latest in home accessories, gourmet treats, candies, and books on gardening and design. Everything is targeted to the elegant shopper with impeccable tastes who is prepared to give a real workout to a credit card. The trendy gathering rooms meander from one high-ticket display to another, offering a mother lode of stylish ideas. Should you need strength to carry on, lunch is served from noon to 3 P.M., and tea until 6:30 P.M.

TEL 01-56-81-12-40 **FAX** 01-56-81-12-4 **EMAIL** flamant.paris@flamant.com
INTERNET www.flamant.com
CREDIT CARDS MC, V
OPEN Mon noon–7 P.M., Tue–Sat 10:30 A.M.–7 P.M.

GALERIE DOCUMENTS (8)
53, rue de Seine, 75006
Métro: Mabillon

Mireille Romand, the great-great granddaughter of the founder, is keeping the tradition of selling original posters, all with historic interest and value. She also has a fascinating collection of framed advertisements, theater programs, illustrated menus, and sheet music. The prices start around 25€. They are easy and light to carry with you, or she will wrap and ship your purchases.

TEL 01-43-54-50-68 **FAX** 01-43-29-10-25 **EMAIL** gal.documents@easynet.fr
CREDIT CARDS MC, V
OPEN Mon 2:30–7 P.M., Tues–Sat 10:30–7 P.M. **CLOSED** Aug (dates vary)

GILBERT JOSEPH PAPETERIE (38)
30, boulevard St-Michel, 75006
Métro: St-Michel

Gilbert Joseph is omnipresent in this part of Paris. What started out as a bookstore over a hundred years ago has grown into a conglomerate of stores selling books, videos, CDs, art supplies, and every type of stationery known to civilized humanity. The bookstores are not of as much interest to most visiting shoppers as this stationery store, where the merchandise is spread out over three floors.

TEL 01-44-41-88-66
CREDIT CARDS MC, V
OPEN Mon–Sat 9:30 A.M.–7:30 P.M. **CLOSED** Jan, dates vary

GRAPHIGRO (64)
55, rue St-Placide, 75006
Métro: St-Placide

No artist should miss this emporium dedicated to the needs of artists of all types and levels of ability.

TEL 01-53-63-60-00 **INTERNET** www.graphigro.com
CREDIT CARDS MC, V
OPEN Mon–Sat 10 A.M.–7 P.M.

HUILERIE ARTISANALE J. LEBLANC ET FILS (7)
6, rue Jacob, 75006
Métro: St-Germain-des-Prés

Four generations of the J. Leblanc family have been making a variety of exceptional oils that range from first cold pressed, extra-virgin olive oil to hazelnut, walnut, pistachio, pecan, almond, and peanut oils. Unfortunately, they do not ship, but a small bottle of one of their distinctive oils won't weigh too much in a carry-on bag.

TEL & FAX 01-46-34-61-55 **EMAIL** j.leblanc@huile-leblanc.com
    INTERNET www.huile-leblanc.com
CREDIT CARDS None, cash only
OPEN Mon 2–7 P.M., Tues–Fri noon–7 P.M., Sat 10 A.M.–7 P.M.
    CLOSED 15 days in mid-Aug

LA CIE DE PROVENCE (70)
5, rue Bréa, 75006
Métro: Vavin

Savon de Marseille is one of the most well-known French soaps. In their only Parisian boutique, you can indulge in a wide variety of their bath and body care products geared to pamper and please.

TEL 01-43-26-39-53 **FAX** 01-43-54-08-12 **EMAIL** lcdp@free.fr
    INTERNET www.lcdpmarseille.com
CREDIT CARDS AE, MC, V
OPEN Mon–Sat 10:30–2 P.M., 3–7:30 P.M.

LA DERNIÈRE GOUTTE (13)
6, rue de Bourbon-le-Château, near rue de Buci, 75006
Métro: St-Germain-des-Prés

Juan Sanchez is the multidimensional American owner of this wine shop near the St-Germain-des-Prés Church and the famous Les Deux Magots café. He features lesser-known estate-bottled regional French wines at prices that are 30 to 40 percent less than you would pay elsewhere. Tastings are usually held on Saturday, and often the winemaker is present to talk about his wines. If you are close by, stop in, have a taste, and you will probably leave with several bottles to sample in Paris or to take home. If you are buying in bulk, Juan has a delivery service within Paris.

TEL 01-43-29-11-62 **FAX** 01-46-34-63-41 **EMAIL** goutte@club-internet.fr
CREDIT CARDS AE, MC, V
OPEN Mon 4–8:30 P.M.; Tues–Fri 10 A.M.–1:30 P.M., 3–8:30 P.M.;
    Sat 10 A.M.–8:30 P.M.; Sun 11 A.M.–7 P.M.

LA FROMAGERIE (25)
64, rue de Seine, 75006
Métro: Mabillon, St-Germain-des-Prés

France reportedly produces over four hundred varieties of cheese, a fact that can be overwhelming to anyone used to only Roquefort, Cheddar, and Swiss. While you won't find all four hundred at La Fromagerie, you can still sample over a hundred varieties of seasonal French cheeses, which you can buy to take with you or eat here over lunch or dinner with a nice glass of wine. The owners are passionate about their cheeses and consider it their mission to help you discover new types. This you will most certainly do, and your prize finds can be vacuum packed for transport back home.

TEL 01-43-26-50-31
CREDIT CARDS AE, DC, MC, V
OPEN Tues–Thur: lunch 10 A.M.–3 P.M., dinner 5–8:30 P.M.; Fri–Sat 10 A.M.–
    8 P.M.; Sun: store only 10 A.M.–1:30 P.M. **CLOSED** Sun food service, Mon;
    15 days mid-Aug

LES OLIVADES (41)
95, rue de Seine, 75006
Métro: Odéon

Les Olivades celebrates the textile traditions of Provence in a wide range of products designed to decorate you and your home to reflect the warm colors of the south of France. The quality is excellent and the prices below the competition across the street at Souleiado (see page 364). Home decor is sold at 1, rue de Tournon, just a block away.

TEL 01-56-24-29-19 **FAX** 01-56-24-36-26 **INTERNET** www.les-olivades.com
CREDIT CARDS AE, MC, V
OPEN Mon 1–7 P.M., Tues–Sat 10 A.M.–1 P.M., 2–7 P.M.

L'OCCITANE (67)
26, rue Vavin, 75006
Métro: Vavin

For a description of this store selling natural cosmetics and body products, see page 351.

TEL 01-43-25-07-71
OPEN Mon–Thur 10 A.M.–2:15 P.M., 3:30–7 P.M.; Sat 10:30–7:15 P.M.
  CLOSED Sun

MARIE MERCIÉ (43)
23, rue St-Sulpice, 75006
Métro: Odéon, St-Sulpice

The Marie Mercié hat shop is run in conjunction with the Anthony Peto *chapelier* in the second arrondissement (see page 343). In addition to everyday *chapeaux*, Marie makes theatrical hats exclusively for women, and her creations are almost museum quality—suitable for a day at Ascot, the wardrobe department of a film studio, or the most elaborate fashion event imaginable. She will also do custom orders. Unfortunately, customer service often does not match the dazzle and style of the hats in this shop. Depending on the mood of the *vendeuse,* the welcome will range from aloof and cool to skillfully ignoring your presence. This nose-in-the-air attitude is definitely not present at Anthony Peto's shop.

TEL 01-43-26-45-83 **FAX** 01-40-26-38-01
CREDIT CARDS AE, DC, MC, V
OPEN Mon–Sat 11 A.M.–7 P.M. **CLOSED** middle of Aug

MONOPRIX (21)
50, rue de Rennes, 75006
Métro: St-Germain-des-Prés

A complete renovation has transformed this once grubby Monoprix into a contemporary shopping experience, befitting its neighbor, Emporio Armani (which occupies the corner location we all knew and loved as Le Drug Store). Upstairs is a small women's ready-to-wear department. Downstairs has an enormous grocery, deli, health bar with soup and fruit juice, a bar and café, bakery, and sushi stand where you can eat in or take out. You'll almost forget this is a Monoprix . . . until it's time to check out, and then you'll be snaked behind ten or fifteen other frustrated customers waiting for their turn to pay. Some things never change, and the lines at Monoprix are one of them.

Monoprix stores are all over Paris. Another central location is in the eighth arrondissement (see page 372).

TEL 01-45-48-18-08
CREDIT CARDS AE, MC, V
OPEN Mon–Sat 9 A.M.–9:50 P.M.

PETIT FAUNE (3)
33, rue Jacob, 75006
Métro: St-Germain-des-Prés

For the most adorable classic French baby and children's clothing (birth to eight years), do not miss this beguiling shop. Prices are high, that is true. But I think the clothes are worth the money because of the quality and fine workmanship, and they wear like iron. Look at it this way: These are investment purchases for both the present and future generations of children in your family. In January and July, they have super sales. There is a second location at 13, rue Mézières, 75006 (Métro: St-Sulpice; 01-42-22-63-69).

TEL 01-42-60-80-72 **EMAIL** contact@petitfaune.com **INTERNET**
www.petitfaune.com
CREDIT CARDS AE, MC, V
OPEN Mon–Sat 10 A.M.–7 P.M. **CLOSED** 2 weeks mid-Aug

PIERRE FREY (12)
1–2, rue de Fürstenberg, 75006
Métro: St-Germain-des-Prés

Pierre Frey was founded in 1935 in Paris. Since then, the company has become synonymous with the finest in French home furnishing fabrics and home accessories. There are shops worldwide, but it is always special to visit the source, which includes several shops next to each other. There is another accessories boutique at 22, rue Royale, 75008 (01-49-26-04-77).

TEL 01-46-33-73-00 **INTERNET** www.pierrefrey.com
CREDIT CARDS AE, MC, V
OPEN Mon–Sat 10 A.M.–6:30 P.M. **CLOSED** Aug 8–20 (dates can vary)

THE SAN FRANCISCO BOOK COMPANY (46)
17, rue Monsieur-le-Prince, 75006
Métro: Odéon

Believe it or not, the clutter at this second-hand, English-language book store is organized. The books on the floor are waiting for shelf space on the shelves. Those already on the shelves are alphabetically stacked two deep according to type, so finding something you are looking for literally resembles looking for a needle in a haystack. Then again, if you don't want to pay retail, it sometimes takes a little extra effort, and you will expend it here. Actually, it is a nice place to while away an hour or so just rummaging, and the good news is that you will usually run across something of interest. After finishing reading what you bought, bring it back and exchange it for cash or credit on future purchases.

TEL 01-43-29-15-70 **FAX** 01-43-29-52-48 **INTERNET**
    www.sanfranciscobooksparis.com
CREDIT CARDS MC, V
OPEN Mon–Sat 11 A.M.–9 P.M. (Thur until 8 P.M.), Sun 2–7:30 P.M.

SCOOTER (31)
19, rue du Dragon, 75006
Métro: St-Germain-des-Prés

This is a smaller branch, selling jewelry, a few handbags, and some clothing. For a complete description, see page 341.

TEL 01-45-49-48-28

SOULEIADO (42)
78, rue de Siene, 75006
Metro: Odéon, Mabillon

For beautiful prints and products from Provence, Souleiado is the name everyone knows. No one said anything about it being cheap, but the quality is superb and the selection runs all the way from a lavender sachet to outfitting your entire home and wardrobe á la Souleiado.

TEL 01-43-54-62-25 **FAX** 01-44-07-33-81 **EMAIL** paris@souleiado.com
    INTERNET www.souleiado.com
CREDIT CARDS AE, DC, MC, V
OPEN Mon 10:30 A.M.–1 P.M., 2–7 P.M., Tues–Sat 10:30 A.M.–7 P.M.

TOUT COMPTE FAIT . . . (54)
31, rue St-Placide, 75006
Métro: St-Placide

For trendy French children's clothes that don't cost an arm and a leg, Tout Compte Fait runs a close second to Du Pareil au Même (see page 336). Their stores are all over Paris (see pages 377 and 384).

TEL 01-42-22-45-64 **INTERNET** www.toutcomptefait.com
CREDIT CARDS MC, V
OPEN Mon–Sat 10 A.M.–7 P.M.

SEVENTH ARRONDISSEMENT (see map page 170)

Shops

AU NOM DE LA ROSE (30)
46, rue du Bac, 75007
Métro: Rue du Bac

Everything is coming up roses at this colorful boutique devoted to the rose. I like the rose petal bubble bath, the perfumed candles, and the rose syrup to drink with champagne. These are only a few of the multitude of rose-inspired temptations: scarves, sachets, jam, hats, handbags, perfume, Limoges china, and more. Oh, yes, they do sell beautiful fresh roses. This is the only shop with a boutique. The original shop is at 4, rue de Tournon (75006), and there are branches throughout Paris that are easily recognizable by the rose petals strewn on the sidewalk in front of the shops.

TEL 01-42-22-22-12 **INTERNET** www.aunomdelarose.com
CREDIT CARDS AE, MC, V
OPEN Flower shop Mon–Sat 9 A.M.–9 P.M., boutique Mon–Sat 10 A.M.–7 P.M.;
Sun (this location only) 9 A.M.–2 P.M. **CLOSED** 2 weeks mid-Aug (dates vary)

BONPOINT (21)
42, rue de l'Université, 75007
Métro: Rue du Bac

If you can afford to shop at Bonpoint for your children's clothes, then you don't need this book, since this is probably the most expensive store for outfitting babies and children in Paris. However, this Bonpoint discounts last season's collections and anything else the other stores can't sell. While it still doesn't qualify as cheap, the quality is superb, and the clothes last for generations. They offer even better prices during the sales in January and at the end of June.

TEL 01-40-20-10-55 **INTERNET** www.bonpoint.com
CREDIT CARDS AE, MC, V
OPEN Mon–Sat 10:30 A.M.–6:30 P.M. **CLOSED** 3 weeks in Aug (dates vary)

BONTON (31)
82, rue de Grenelle, 75007
Métro: Rue du Bac

Bonton stocks the latest trends in children's clothing from birth to ten years. The displays are great, and so are the clothes, which are hardly bargains, but your child will stand out with *panache* in a Bonton outfit. There is also a *coiffeur* ready to style the locks of the entire family.

TEL 01-44-39-09-20
CREDIT CARDS AE, MC, V
OPEN Mon--Sat 10 A.M.–7 P.M.

CINÉ-IMAGES (34)
68, rue de Babylone, 75007
Métro: St-François Xaviér

Ciné-Images, the oldest film poster gallery in Europe, stocks a mind-boggling eight thousand original European and American film posters dating from the origin of cinema in 1895 through the 1980s. Also available are books about film posters. The shop is directly across the street from La Pagode, one of the most famous cinemas in Paris.

TEL & FAX 01-45-51-27-50 **EMAIL** cine-images2@noos.fr
INTERNET www.cine-images.com
CREDIT CARDS MC, V
OPEN Tues–Fri 10 A.M.–1 P.M., 2–7 P.M., Sat 2–7 P.M.

DEBAUVE & GALLAIS (24)
30, rue des Saints Pères, 75007
Métro: St-Germain-des-Prés

Debauve & Gallais, founded in 1800, are the oldest makers of chocolate in Paris. And are they popular! In its two shops, Parisians spend over 2.5 million euros annually on thirty tons of chocolate. Only the highest quality, pure ingredients are used, along with the best cocoa beans from around the world. Discerning gourmet chocolate lovers owe themselves a visit to this beautiful shop, which is listed as a national public monument. The chocolates are magnificently displayed on a half-moon carved-wood counter that has been in place since 1819. If you can't wait until your next trip to Paris for one of their divine chocolates, you can shop online and have yours delivered via Federal Express to your door. The other shop is in the second arrondissement (see page 343).

TEL 01-45-48-54-67 **FAX** 01-45-48-21-78 **EMAIL** info@debauve-et-gallis.com
INTERNET www.debauve-et-gallais.com
CREDIT CARDS AE, MC, V
OPEN Mon–Sat 9 A.M.–7 P.M.

LE BON MARCHÉ AND LA GRANDE ÉPICERIE DE PARIS (35)
24, rue de Sèvres, at rue du Bac, 75007
Métro: Sèvres-Babylone

The first department store in Paris, and still my favorite, this showplace store has balustrades and balconies designed by Gustave Eiffel. It is Paris's premier department store, combining the elegant and the practical, and it is easy to manage. To make several purchases anywhere in the store and not have to carry them, ask at any information desk for a purchase booklet. Your selections are noted in the book and taken to the third floor, where you can make just one payment and do the *détaxe*. The only drawback at Le Bon Marché is that they do not offer a 10 percent discount to foreigners, but they do have a 12 percent *détaxe* after 175€.

La Grande Épicerie de Paris is a gourmet *supermarché* to behold, with over thirty thousand items in stock, not counting the five thousand bottles of wine. There is also a *pâtisserie, boulangerie, traiteur* (deli), and restaurant upstairs. Even if you never cook, it is a fabulous feast for the eyes (see *Great Eats Paris*).

TEL 01-44-39-80-00, customer service 01-44-39-82-80
CREDIT CARDS AE, DC, MC, V **INTERNET** www.lebonmarche.fr
OPEN Department store: Mon–Tues, Wed, Fri 9:30 A.M.–7 P.M.,
Thur 10 A.M.–9 P.M., Sat 9:30 A.M.–8 P.M.; food store:
Mon–Sat 8:30 A.M.–9 P.M.

L'OCCITANE (32)
90, rue du Bac, 75007
Métro: Rue du Bac

For a description of this shop selling natural cosmetics and body products, see page 351. All other information is the same.

TEL 01-42-22-55-28

MAÎTRE PARFUMEUR ET GANTIER (28)
84, bis rue de Grenelle, 75007
Métro: Rue du Bac

The fragrance themes alone inspire mystery and romance: For women, seductive scents with names like Les Fleurs Divines, Les Symphonies Légères, l'Invitation au Voyage. For the man in your life, who could resist the scent called Les Caprices du Dandy? To keep your home smelling sensuous, there are special ambience sprays, scented oils, and candles. My favorite gift from this shop is a perfumed pillow to put into a pair of gloves, which revives a seventeenth-century practice when ladies came to perfume salons in order to perfume their gloves and wigs and to practice the art of conversation. There are other locations at 5, rue des Capucines (75001), and at Printemps de la Maison on boulevard Haussemann (75009).

TEL 01-45-44-61-57 **INTERNET** www.maitre-parfumeur-et-gantier.com
CREDIT CARDS AE, MC, V
OPEN Mon–Sat 10:30–6:30 P.M.

RICHART (18)
258, boulevard St-Germain, 75007
Métro: Assemblée Nationale, Solférino

Richart is known for pleasing both the palate and the eye, combining the taste and aroma of pure chocolate with visually stunning presentations of magnificent seasonal collections of chocolate. Flavors range from floral and fruity to herbacious and spicy. One of their best-sellers is a sack of nine milk or dark chocolate salty butter caramels. To promote the love of chocolate in children, each year the family-owned company asks three thousand children from around the world to "design something delicious in your favorite color." The winners get prize money for their schools, and their designs used in that year's collections. There are outlets worldwide, but this is the only one in Paris.

TEL 01-45-55-66-00 **FAX** 01-47-53-72-72
    EMAIL paris-stgermain@richart.com **INTERNET** www.richart.com
CREDIT CARDS MC, V
OPEN Mon–Sat 10 A.M.–7 P.M.

EIGHTH ARRONDISSEMENT (see map page 192)
Shops

Shopping Areas

Passages and Shopping Malls

ALLIX (50)
6, rue de Surène, 75008
Métro: Madeleine

Aline Rodriguez sells unusual handbags that are sold throughout the world at three or four times the prices you will pay here. She also stocks selected items of jewelry. The merchandise is very well displayed, and English is spoken.

TEL 01-42-65-10-79
CREDIT CARDS MC, V
OPEN Mon–Fri 11 A.M.–2:30 P.M., 3:30–6:30 P.M. **CLOSED** Middle 15 days of
  Aug

ANNA LOWE (39)
104, rue du Faubourg du St-Honorè, 75008
Métro: Miromesnil, St-Philippe-du-Roule

Anna Lowe is one of the best designer discount stores in Paris. The location is great, next door to the famous Hôtel Bristol and in the midst of many top fashion houses and designers. You will find all the top-name French and Italian designers, including Chanel, and a fabulous selection of evening wear at reduced prices. All labels are left in, everything is new end-of-season or factory closeouts. There are sensational July and mid-December sales and fast alterations.

TEL 01-42-66-11-32, 01-40-06-02-42 **FAX** 01-40-06-00-53
  EMAIL annaloweparis@aol.com **INTERNET** www.annaloweparis.com
CREDIT CARDS AE, DC, MC, V
OPEN Mon–Sat 10 A.M.–7 P.M.

ARCHE (18)
237, rue du Faubourg Saint-Honoré, 75008
Métro: Ternes

For a description of this excellent brand of French footwear, see page 334. All other information is the same.

TEL 01-42-27-88-46

FAUCHON (52)
30, place de la Madeleine, 75008
Métro: Madeleine

Even though it is not at all what it once was, Fauchon is still to grocery shopping what the Ritz is to hotels. A trip to the famed shop and amazing *charcuterie* epitomizes gourmet grocery shopping. A jar of *herbes de provence,* fancy honey, exotic jam, or a tin of cookies with the Fauchon label is a very much appreciated gift.

TEL 01-47-42-60-11
CREDIT CARDS AE, DC, MC, V
OPEN Mon–Sat 9:30 A.M.–8 P.M.

FNAC (27)
74, avenue des Champs-Élysées (in Galerie du Claridge), 75008
Métro: George V

FNAC is the place to go for a wide range of music and tickets to whatever is playing. You can either stand in line for hours to book concert seats or log onto their Website. FNAC also sells books (in French, naturally), computers, stereos, mobile telephones, photography equipment, and videos. There are branches in Forum des Halles (75001); in Montparnasse at 136, rue de Rennes (75006); near Opéra at 24, boulevard des Italiens (75009); at Saint-Lazare, 109, rue Saint-Lazare (75009); and Bastille (music only) at 4, place de la Bastille (75012); hours at these locations are generally 10 A.M.–9:30 P.M.

TEL 01-53-53-64-64 **INTERNET** www.fnac.com
CREDIT CARDS AE, MC, V
OPEN Mon–Sat 10 A.M.–midnight, Sun noon–midnight

HEDIARD (51)
21, place de la Madeleine, 75008
Métro: Madeleine

Hediard has several other luscious gourmet food locations, but this is its first, anchoring an entire corner of the gourmet food strip surrounding the Madeleine Church. It offers a true feast for the eyes, and it stocks everything a foodie could dream of finding under one roof: smoked salmon from Norway; a tin of beluga caviar (100g, 424€); their own brand of spices, herbs, jams and jellies, and *foie gras d'oie* (228€ per kilo); unblemished fresh fruits and vegetables from around the world; wine, coffee, tea, and much more. If you don't feel in the mood to cook yourself, they have complete meals at the ready, and the perfect wines to accompany them. Upstairs is a restaurant serving coffee from Monday to Friday, lunch and tea Monday to Saturday, and dinner Monday to Friday. For a meal, do make a reservation. There is another branch in the eighth on avenue Georges V, and one in the seventh behind Le Bon Marché department store on rue du Bac.

TEL 01-43-12-88-88, restaurant reservations 01-43-12-88-99
INTERNET www.hediard.fr
CREDIT CARDS AE, DC, MC, V
OPEN Mon–Sat 9 A.M.–9 P.M., Sun (Dec only) 10 A.M.–8 P.M.

KIOSQUE THÉÂTRE (53)
15, place de la Madeleine, 75008
Métro: Madeleine

This is where you can stand in a long line to buy same-day tickets for participating theatrical, dance, circus performances, and some special events for 50 percent off (plus a 3 percent commission per ticket).

TEL Not available
CREDIT CARDS None, cash only
OPEN Tues–Sat 12:30–7:45 P.M., Sun 12:30–3:45 P.M.

L'OCCITANE (25)
Galerie des Champs Élysées, 84, avenue Champs-Élysées, 75008
Métro: Franklin-D-Roosevelt

This l'Occitane is open daily from 11 A.M.–9 P.M. For a description, see page 351.

TEL Not available

MAILLE (54)
6, place de la Madeleine, 75008
Métro: Madeleine

The Maille boutique is devoted to products from the best and most famous name in mustards and vinegars. There are over thirty varieties, many of which are attractively gift packaged with recipes included (in French, but if you speak any French, simple enough to follow). In addition, the boutique stocks vinegars, oils, herbs, mustard pots, pickles, and olives. Prices start as low as 3.81€, and the more unusual mustard varieties make great gifts. They also pump two types of fresh mustard (white wine and a fruity chablis) into a pot that you buy, and top it off with a cork. When the mustard is gone, bring the pot and the cork back, and you only pay for the fresh mustard. They do mail orders.

TEL 01-40-15-06-00 **FAX** 01-40-15-06-11 **EMAIL** am-parisboutique@
  unilever.com
CREDIT CARDS MC, V (15€ minimum)
OPEN Mon–Sat 10 A.M.–7 P.M.

MAXIM'S (59)
5, rue Royale, 75008
Métro: Concorde, Madeleine

Maxim's is synonymous with over-the-top glamour, moneyed moguls, and the best that excess can offer. Located a few steps from the famed restaurant is this boutique selling everything with the Maxim's stamp of approval proudly displayed. I have to give master merchandiser Pierre Cardin (who is now the owner at the helm of the Maxim's enterprises) credit for having something for all budgets. Prices start at 0.50€ for a book of matches and continue on to 5€ to 10€ for their signature pasta, more for a jar of colorful cooked veggies. Not interested in matches or food? Okay, there are pens, watches, a menu from the restaurant (7.50€), jams, jellies, teas, coffees, and a 47€ apron to wear while you heat up that pasta. You can also buy crockery from the restaurant, reproduction Art Nouveau lamps, candles, and champagne buckets. You name it, and Maxim's has it covered.

If you are interested in Art Nouveau, don't miss taking the tour of La Collection 1900 de Pierre Cardin, where you will see Cardin's fabulous collection of 550 Art Nouveau masterpieces. For details, see page 32.

TEL 01-47-42-88-46 **EMAIL** boutique.maxims@freesurf.fr
  INTERNET www.boutique-maxims.com
CREDIT CARDS AE, DC, MC, V
OPEN Mon–Sat 10 A.M.–6:30 P.M.

MISS "GRIFFES" (38)
19, rue de Penthièvre, 75008
Métro: Miromesnil

The shop has been in business for more than a half century, and it is now run by its third owner, Mme. Vincent, who has been here for more than twenty years. I think it is one of the best in the hunt for discount women's clothing, shoes, handbags, and accessories from all the top names, including Chanel, Armani, Ungaro, and Valentino. Prices are high at first glance, but not when you consider what you would pay retail in the boutiques. Also available are prototype collections of last season's models, a few of Mme. Vincent's own designs, and wonderful custom-made blazers. Free alterations are ready in two days. *Great Sleeps Paris* readers receive a 20 percent discount.

TEL 01-42-65-10-00
CREDIT CARDS AE, DC, MC, V
OPEN Mon–Sat 11 A.M.–7 P.M. **CLOSED** Middle 2 weeks in Aug

MONOPRIX (28)
60, avenue des Champs-Élysées, at rue La Boétie, 75008
Métro: Franklin-D-Roosevelt

If you are a Kmart or Target shopper, you will be a Monoprix shopper in Paris. Stores dot the landscape and vary in size and atmosphere, but this is the one that has the longest hours and is the one most tourists will see. All Monoprix stores are good to keep in mind for quick-fix cosmetic buys (including Bourjois, which all smart discount shoppers know is the prototype for Chanel and is sold at a fraction of the cost of the designer brand), cotton underwear, fashion accessories of the moment, toothbrushes, and housewares. Here there is a basement grocery, and thousands of other daily shoppers in addition to you. Because of the inadequate ratio of cash registers to shoppers, you may feel as if you are in the checkout line behind them all.

Another good location is on rue de Rennes in the sixth arrondissement (see page 362).

TEL 01-42-25-27-60
CREDIT CARDS AE, MC, V
OPEN Mon–Sat 9 A.M.–midnight

PUBLICISDRUGSTORE (20)
131–133, avenue des Champs-Élysées, 75008
Métro: Charles-de-Gaulle Étoile

This is some drugstore!

Yes, there is a small, multilingual staffed pharmacy buried in the back, but that is not the *raison d'etre* here. You name it, they have it in this trendorama for fashion wannabes. There is a café, high-priced restaurant and cinemas, two bookstores with international titles, a huge news kiosk, wines and spirits, a deli, and the latest in women's bathrooms.

TEL 01-44-43-79-00 **INTERNET** www.publicisdrugstore.com
CREDIT CARDS AE, DC, MC, V
OPEN Mon–Fri 8 A.M.–midnight, Sat–Sun 10 A.M.–midnight

SCARLETT (33)
10, rue Clément-Marot, at 31, avenue de Montaigne, 75008
Métro: Alma

For vintage to vamp from 1900 to now, Scarlett is a virtual clothing museum that carries all the big names: Chanel, Hermès, Louis Vuitton, Balenciaga, Dior, YVS, Prada, and Bottega Veneta. Other locations are at 3, rue Chambiges, 5, rue Boccador, and in a tent at the Porte de Vanves Marché aux Puces (flea market).

TEL & FAX 01-56-89-03-00 **INTERNET** www.scarlett.fr
CREDIT CARDS AE, MC, V
OPEN Mon–Fri 11 A.M.–7 P.M., Sat 2–7 P.M.

SEPHORA (26)
70, avenue des Champs-Élysées, 75008
Métro: Georges-V

Bouncers guard the front doors of the Champs-Élysées Sephora, probably to try to stem the virtual sea of people who stream through here to revel in the absolutely mind-boggling collection of cosmetics, perfumes, and miscellaneous beauty accessories. All the big name lines are here, including Bourjois (the prototype for Chanel). There is a special room for customers to test makeup under lighting conditions from day to night. Perfumes are arranged in alphabetical order, and as you walk in, there is a circular booth where you can sample many of the scents. There is an immediate 15 percent tax refund to your credit card after spending 175€. Sephora is now opening in the States, so it may not be the experience it once was, but if you are near this flagship store, take a look. There are Sephoras all over Paris; the one on rue de Passy in the sixteenth is also a good one (see page 383).

TEL 01-53-93-22-50 **INTERNET** www.sephora.com
CREDIT CARDS AE, MC, V
OPEN Daily 10 A.M.–midnight

VIRGIN MEGASTORE (29)
52–60, avenue des Champs-Élysées, 75008
Métro: Franklin-D-Roosevelt

Go to the top-floor café for the dazzling view, and then work your way down through an equally dazzling stock of CDs and videos. There is a branch at the La Galerie du Carrousel du Louvre (see page 330).

TEL 01-49-53-50-00
CREDIT CARDS AE, MC, V
OPEN Mon–Sat 10 A.M.–midnight, Sun noon–midnight

NINTH ARRONDISSEMENT (see map page 192)

À LA MÈRE DE FAMILLE (13)
35, rue du Faubourg Montmartre, 75009
Métro: Le Peletier

Even if you don't have a sweet tooth, À la Mère de Famille is worth the trip just to admire the beautiful displays of chocolates and regional candies in this original shop, which dates back to 1761. It is owned by a family as sweet as their wares. They are always helpful and cheerful, whether you are buying an expensive gift box of their own chocolates, a kilo of the special ginger cake, some of the beautiful marzipan creations, or merely an assortment of dried fruits. There are several other locations, including two in the seventh (at 47, rue Cler, and 39, rue du Cherche Midi) and one in the seventeenth (at 107, rue Jouffroy d'Abbans).

TEL 01-47-70-83-69
CREDIT CARDS AE, MC, V
OPEN Mon–Sat: 9:30 A.M.–8 P.M.; Sun: 10 A.M.–1 P.M. **CLOSED** Aug (dates vary)

ANNEXE DES CRÉATEURS (49)
19, rue Godot-de-Mauroy, 75009
Métro: Madeleine

There are two shops next to each other, one has last season's collection of name designers; the other is for sportswear and separates. They also have hats, jewelry, coats, bags, and wedding gowns. Labels are left in. If you can't get to Paris, visit the Website and order online. Prices are 30 to 60 percent off retail.

TEL 01-42-65-46-40 **INTERNET** www.annexedescreateurs.com
CREDIT CARDS AE, MC, V
OPEN Tues–Sat 11A.M.–7 P.M. **CLOSED** Mon, Aug (dates vary)

GALERIES LAFAYETTE (12)
40, boulevard Haussmann, 75009
Métro: Chaussée d'Antin–La Fayette, Havre Caumartin

Galeries Lafayette carries the top names in fashion, featuring seventy-five thousand brand names, including their own label, all laid out in 110 departments. It also boasts a record number of daily shoppers. More than a hundred thousand people per day stream through their Haussmann store (more at Christmas and during *Les Soldes*), and of course, they want you to be one of them during your Parisian stay. In addition to a huge perfume and cosmetic section, and the top names in French fashion, they have everything else you can imagine—including a one-hour photo service, *bureau de change*, car park, restaurants (including McDonald's in the toy department, naturally), travel and theater agencies, and a watch and shoe repair department. Across the street in the old Marks & Spencer building is Lafayette Maison with every possible pot, pan, dish, and home decorating accessory known to civilization. Gourmets and gourmands will want to visit their grocery department (Lafayette Gourmet), which is inspirational: its dazzling array of delicacies features everything a gastronome could possibly want, including food stations where you can stop for a plate of just-made pasta, a sampling of sushi, a quick cappuccino, or a pastry (see *Great Eats Paris*), or contemplate which of the sixty types of cigars to buy. Even dedicated noncooks will want to see this beautiful section of Galeries Lafayette.

TEL 01-42-82-34-56, fashion-show reservation 01-42-82-30-85
   FAX 01-42-82-80-18 **INTERNET** www.galerieslafayette.com
CREDIT CARDS AE, MC, V
OPEN Mon–Sat 9:30 A.M.–7:30 P.M., Thur till 9 P.M.

LOUIS PION (44)
9, rue Auber, 75009
Metro: Opéra

Fashion and fun watches for everyone on your list at prices starting at 10€ for an alarm clock and 20€ for a watch. There are several locations throughout Paris.

TEL 01-42-65-40-33 **FAX** 01-42-65-00-46 **INTERNET** www.louis-pion.fr
CREDIT CARDS AE, DC, MC, V
OPEN Mon–Sat 9:30 A.M.–7 P.M.

MUSÉE DE LA PARFUMERIE FRAGONARD (43)
9, rue Scribe, 75009
Métro: Opéra

In the museum you will see displays showing the perfume-making process according to Fragonard and a collection of their perfume bottles. This part is free; then you exit through the boutique, where a patient multilingual sales force is available to help you decide on just the right fragrance. I think the best buy is the box of five perfumes, which you can divide into five separate gifts. It isn't all perfume. The boutique stocks beautifully packaged soaps, cosmetics, and candles. If you are having trouble making up your mind, remember the words of Coco Chanel, who quoted Paul Éluard, a poet friend of Picasso: "A woman who doesn't perfume herself has no future!"

Note that the museum closes half an hour before the boutique does.

TEL 01-47-42-04-56 **INTERNET** www.fragonard.com
CREDIT CARDS AE, DC, MC, V
OPEN Boutique: from mid-March–Oct, Mon–Sun 9 A.M.–6 P.M.; from Oct–mid-March, Mon–Sat 9:30 A.M.–4 P.M.

PRINTEMPS (11)
64, boulevard Haussmann, 75009
Métro: Havre-Caumartin

This is known as "The Most Parisian Department Store." Famous designer boutiques, a separate men's store, and an excellent leather and cosmetic department are on the ground floor. Also, there's a fabulous umbrella section, which sells thirty thousand *parapluies* per year! The shoe department is excellent, with over forty-one different brands on display. Ask about the shopping booklet, which lets you shop the store and pay only once. Personal shoppers are available, as is a beauty institute, theater and concert reservations, a travel agency, and branches of Mariage Frères and Ladurée. Don't miss the beautiful views of Paris from a window perch in the cafeteria or outdoor terrace on the top floor; have a coffee if you must while you're here, but don't waste time or money on the dismal food.

TEL 01-42-82-50-00 **INTERNET** www.printemps.com
CREDIT CARDS AE, DC, MC, V
OPEN Mon–Sat 9:30 A.M.–7 P.M., Thur till 10 P.M.

SULMACO (14)
13, rue de Trévise, 75009
Métro: Grands Boulevards

English-speaking owner Philippe Madar offers an excellent selection of designer men's fashions and accessories at below retail. In addition to off-the-rack clothing, it is possible to order custom-made clothes and shoes dyed in the color of your choice (300–450€ per pair). The detail in the double-lined tailor-made suits, some in cashmere, is superb. Ready-made suits start around 450€, and *sur mesure* (tailor-made), with your initials inside, begin around 1,200€. These are good prices when you consider you can deduct the 13 percent *détaxe* after spending 175€. Two master tailors are employed to do alterations, which are included in the price of the garment (except during sales). Tailor-made suits are guaranteed ready in five weeks for a first fitting, and delivery in the next three days. If a French tailor-made suit appeals to you, make Sulmaco your first shopping stop in

Paris. Sales are generally held at the end of December and January and during the first part of July (dates vary).

TEL 01-48-24-89-00 **EMAIL** sulmaco@noos.fr
CREDIT CARDS AE, DC, MC, V
OPEN Mon–Sat 10:30 A.M.–7 P.M.; in Aug, Mon–Sat noon–6:30 P.M.
    CLOSED Middle 10 days of Aug

TOUT COMPTE FAIT . . . (9)
62, rue de la Chaussée d'Antin, 75009
Métro: Chaussée d'Antin–La Fayette
    For a description of this children's store, see page 364.

TEL 01-48-74-16-54

ELEVENTH ARRONDISSEMENT (see map page 214)

ALLICANTE (16)
26, boulevard Beaumarchais, 75011
Métro: Bastille, Chemin Vert
    Allicante specializes in oils from France, but it also carries oils from Italy, Greece, Spain, Portugal, Algeria, Israel, and Tunisia, all bottled on site by the grower. The selection is daunting, but you can sample to your heart's content before deciding which to buy. Not all the oils are olive—you can sample and purchase sesame, raisin, or pistachio oil, aromatic oils, essential oils, and therapeutic oils. It is quite an interesting learning and tasting experience. No shipping.

TEL 01-43-55-13-02 **EMAIL** allicantehuilerie@wanadoo.fr **INTERNET**
    www.allicante-huilerie.com
CREDIT CARDS AE, DC, MC, V
OPEN Mon–Sat 10 A.M.–7:30 P.M.

ANNE WILLI (18)
13, rue Keller, 75011
Métro: Ledru-Rollin, Bastille
    Anne Willi is a talented young designer who makes and sells her line of clothes for active young women in this workshop and boutique. Her clothing is not expensive. Many of the separates are reversible, which makes mixing and matching an easy way to maximize an outfit. After the birth of her child, she added a limited amount of baby clothes.

TEL 01-48-06-74-06 **FAX** 01-48-06-74-04 **EMAIL** info@annewilli.com
INTERNET www.annewilli.com
CREDIT CARDS MC, V
OPEN Mon 2–8 P.M., Tues–Sat 11:30 A.M.–8 P.M. **CLOSED** 2 weeks in Aug

TWELFTH ARRONDISSEMENT (see map page 214)

BETTY (21)
10, place d'Aligre, 75012
Métro: Ledru-Rollin

Betty is not worth a separate journey, but it is worth a quick look. Probably the best time to check Betty is early Sunday morning; combine it with a trip to the flea market at place d'Aligre (see page 386). Upstairs they say they have last season's designer labels, but not many on most top-ten lists. The prices are low, and if you want something French and don't care about famous designer labels, you might find this interesting.

TEL 01-43-07-40-64
CREDIT CARDS MC, V
OPEN Tues, Wed, Fri, Sun 9 A.M.–12:30 P.M., Thur & Sat 9 A.M.–12:30 P.M.,
2:30–7 P.M.

VIADUC DES ARTS (23)
9–129, avenue Daumesnil, 75012
Métro: Ledru-Rollin, Gare de Lyon

The railway tracks on top of the stone viaduct carried the suburban railway from Bastille. Now the vaulted archways are enclosed and house a variety of artists' workshops, galleries, boutiques, and a restaurant. The rail tracks have been replaced by a walkway with trees and gardens that goes all the way to the Bois de Vincennes.

TEL Not available **INTERNET** www.viaduc-des-arts.com
CREDIT CARDS Depends on shop
OPEN Tues–Sat noon–7 P.M., Sun 11 A.M.–7 P.M. (some stores may differ)

FOURTEENTH ARRONDISSEMENT (see map page 230)

ARCHE (25)
60, avenue Général Leclerc 75014
Métro: Mouton Duvernet

This is another branch of the popular Arche shoes. For details, see page 334. All information is the same.

DIVINE (22)
39, rue Daguerre, 75014
Métro: Denfert-Rochereau

Hats, berets, bonnets, scarves, and gloves for men and women are piled high in this shop. When I asked, "How many hats do you have?" the answer was, "Too many to count!" When you go, you will believe it.

TEL 01-43-22-28-10
CREDIT CARDS MC, V
OPEN Tues–Sat 10:30 A.M.–1 P.M., 3–7:30 P.M.

GALERIES LAFAYETTE (14)
Centre Commercial Montparnasse (Tour Montparnasse Complex)
22, rue du Départ, 75014
Métro: Montparnasse-Bienvenüe

This location is rather boring and limited compared to the flagship main store. For a complete description, see page 375.

TEL 01-45-38-52-87
OPEN Mon–Sat 9:45 A.M.–7:30 P.M.

LA BOUTIQUE DE L'ARTISANAT MONASTIQUE (20)
68 bis, avenue Denfert-Rochereau, 75014
Métro: Denfert-Rochereau

Doting *grand-mères,* beware! What a find for adorable children's clothing (including christening outfits that are destined to become family heirlooms) and layettes. The shop seems to go on forever, but everywhere you look you find lovely handicrafts, new and antique embroidered linens and laces, cosmetics, food products, and beautiful robes and nightgowns . . . all made by French monks and nuns in 360 convents and monasteries throughout France. The quality is beautiful, and whatever you buy will show the name of the convent or monastery where it was made, and it will be hand-signed by the sister or monk who made it. A volunteer staff of 121 sweet, gray-haired lady volunteers graciously assist you, wrap your purchase, and take your money. Even if you only buy a candle or a bar of soap, it is worth a visit. There are other boutique locations throughout France.

TEL 01-43-35-15-76 **EMAIL** monastic.secretariat@wanadoo.fr
CREDIT CARDS MC, V
OPEN Mon–Fri noon–6:30 P.M., Sat 2–7 P.M. **CLOSED** holidays, last week of July, and Aug

---

FIFTEENTH ARRONDISSEMENT (see map page 230)

MON BON CHIEN (11)
12 rue de Mademoiselle, 75015
Métro: Commerce

As anyone who has spent even a little time Paris knows, dogs are treated royally. They are often far more welcome in public places, especially restaurants, than children. Now pampered pooches have their own *pâtisserie* (the first canine pastry shop in Europe, in fact) courtesy of Harriet Sternstein, an American entrepreneur from Seattle. Some dogs bring their owners two or three times a day for the wholesome sugar-, salt-, and additive-free, slow-baked cookie treats flavored with foie gras, peanut butter, bacon, chicken, garlic and cheese, BBQ beef, banana walnut, and oatmeal cranberry. Older dogs opt for the easier to chew pupcake, with a paw print on top. Is it Fifi's or Jacques' birthday? Order a large cookie in the shape of a bone or a personalized cake. And please, don't worry a moment about what your dog will wear to the party! At Mon Bon Chien, the well dressed dog living in Paris will find sweatshirts, bathrobes, hats and custom-made raincoats, bed, and travel bags. To complete the experience, book a shampoo, cut, and blow-dry for your canine pal in the Grooming salon.

Ah, yes . . . it's still a dog's life in Paris.

TEL 01-48-28-40-12 **INTERNET** www.mon-bon-chien.com
CREDIT CARDS MC, V
OPEN Tues–Sat: 10:30 A.M.–8 P.M. **CLOSED** Mon, Sun; Aug

SIXTEENTH ARRONDISSEMENT (see map page 244)

BACCARAT (12)
11, place des États-Unis, 75016
Métro: Iéna

The famous French crystal maker has moved its headquarters from the blue-collar tenth to this former *hôtel particulière* in the prestigious sixteenth arrondissement.

The Philippe Starck–designed crystal palace serves as a glittering showcase and historical archive for the crystal maker's designs, which are, of course, all for sale. In addition to the awe-inspiring, sparkling display of crystal, there is a very expensive restaurant and a spectacular glass-and-stone bathroom. There is a 7€ entrance fee.

TEL 01-40-22-11-00 **INTERNET** www.baccarat.fr
CREDIT CARDS AE, DC, MC, V
OPEN Mon–Sat 10 A.M.–7 P.M.; restaurant Mon–Sat noon–10 P.M.

DÉPÔT–VENTE DE PASSY (25)
14–16, rue de la Tour, 75116
Métro: Passy

This is one of the best consignment shops, offering a great selection of clothing in mint condition featuring all the biggies for women, from Chanel and Hermès accessories to Dior, Gucci, and Prada. It has a nice staff, fair prices of two-thirds off regular retail, and good dressing rooms. This is one of the favorites of smart French discount denizens.

TEL 01-45-20-95-21
CREDIT CARDS AE, MC, V
OPEN Mon 2–7 P.M., Tues–Sat 10:30 A.M.–7 P.M. **CLOSED** Aug

DU PAREIL AU MÊME (8)
97, avenue Victor Hugo, 75116
Métro: Victor-Hugo

For a description of this children's clothing store, see page 336.

TEL 01-47-37-06-31

FRANCK ET FILS (16)
80, rue de Passy, 75116
Métro: La Muette, Passy

This small, elegant department store sells traditional clothing to the women of Passy, one of Paris's most expensive neighborhoods. The store has all the high-quality designers, including Chanel, and an excellent lingerie and hat department. And it is easily manageable. There is a café on the top floor, but the food is definitely not up to the high-class surroundings. You can do better eating almost anyplace else.

TEL 01-44-14-38-00
CREDIT CARDS AE, DC, MC, V
OPEN Mon–Sat 10 A.M.–7 P.M.

L'AFFAIR D'UN SOIR (6)
147, rue de la Pompe, 75116
Métro: Victor-Hugo

The shop is located in one of the most expensive neighborhoods of Paris, so this tells you another secret of the well-dressed French woman—maybe she leases! If you have been invited to the Élysée Palace and "haven't a thing to wear," don't worry, call L'Affair d'Un Soir for your dress-rental appointment. For female soirée-goers, silk dresses, ball gowns, hats, and elegant accessories are available. They will also rent just one necklace, or a hat, if that is all you need to complete an ensemble. For men, tuxedos and everything to go with them are also here. Sophie de Mestier designs two original collections each year that she rents to her elegant clientele. Many customers rent an outfit and cannot bear to part with it, so they end up buying it. Prices for rentals are between 180€ and 250€ (300–500€ for wedding dresses), plus a deposit of 500€ (and up) depending on the garment. Cleaning and alterations are included.

TEL 01-47-27-37-50 **FAX** 01-47-27-04-52 **INTERNET** www.laffairedunsoir.com
CREDIT CARDS MC, V
OPEN Mon 2–7 P.M., Tues–Sat 10:30 A.M.–7 P.M.

L'OCCITANE (9)
109, Avenue Victor Hugo, 75116
Métro: Victor-Hugo

For a description, see page 351.

TEL Not available
OPEN Mon–Sat 10:30 A.M.–2 P.M., 3–7 P.M.

ORPHELINS–APPRENTIS D'AUTEUIL (27)
40, rue La Fontaine, 75016
Métro: Jasmin

This is admittedly not for everyone, but it's a don't-miss, off-beat shopping venue if you like poking around thrift shops. Plus, a portion of all sales is donated to benefit a nearby children's home. You never know what you will find, from furs to housewares, but it is worth a look if this type of shopping experience is your bag. Sales are held the three Saturdays before Christmas.

TEL Not available
CREDIT CARDS None
OPEN Mon–Fri 9 A.M.–6:30 P.M.; also the first Sat of the month 9:30 A.M.–12:30 P.M., 1:30–6:30 P.M.

RÉCIPROQUE (14)
88, 89, 92, 93, 95, 97, 101, 123, rue de la Pompe, 75116
Métro: Rue de la Pompe

Réciproque is the largest consignment shop in Paris. It is the *grande dame* of formerly worn designer fashions, which are sold for a fraction of their original retail price and displayed in a series of shops. It has everything from gifts and antiques to estate jewelry, shoes, bags, clothes, furs, evening wear, and men's clothing. The sheer volume is staggering, so allow plenty of time if this type of *haute* thrift shopping is your *forte*. Sales are held in January, July, and August. Look for the orange signs indicating their shops along rue de la Pompe. The staff can be helpful.

TEL 01-47-04-30-28 (main office) **INTERNET** www.reciproque.fr
CREDIT CARDS AE, MC, V
OPEN Tues–Fri 11 A.M.–7 P.M., Sat 10:30 A.M.–7:30 P.M.

SEPHORA (17)
50, rue de Passy, 75116
Métro: Passy

For a complete description of this cosmetics and perfume wonderland, see page 373.

TEL Not available
OPEN Mon–Sat 9:30 A.M.–7:30 P.M.

TOUT COMPTE FAIT . . . (7)
115, avenue Victor Hugo, 75116
Métro: Victor-Hugo

For a description of this children's clothing store, see page 364.

TEL 01-47-55-63-36

SEVENTEENTH ARRONDISSEMENT (see map page 258)
Shops

ACCESSORIES À SOIE (13)
21, rue des Acacias, 75017
Métro: Argentine, Charles-de-Gaulle-Étoile

Scarves by Nina Ricci, YSL, pretty silk sweaters, belts, ties, and shirts for the man in your life—all at discount prices. The scarves are beautifully wrapped in the designer box they came in. Ask about their special by-invitation-only sales.

TEL 01-42-27-78-77
CREDIT CARDS AE, DC, MC, V
OPEN Tues–Sat noon–7:30 P.M.

L'ATELIER DE MAÏTÉ (1)
8, rue de Brochant, 75017
Métro: Brochante

Well-loved *poupées* (dolls) and teddy bears and their clothes are bought, sold, and restored with love and expertise by the devoted artisan, who has been in this tiny shop for a quarter century. From Saturday to Monday, she is at the Saint-Ouen flea market (see page 387) at stand Maïté "Poupées," No. 198, on the 1er étage sur la place (at 140, rue des Rosiers) in the Marché Dauphine, which is one of the markets within the huge Marché aux Puces Saint-Ouen.

TEL Shop 01-42-63-23-93; flea market 01-40-11-17-73
CREDIT CARDS V
OPEN Shop Tues–Sat 2–7 P.M.; flea market Sat–Mon 10 A.M.–6 P.M.

EIGHTEENTH ARRONDISSEMENT (see map page 272)

MARCHÉ SAINT PIERRE (11)
2–5 rue Charles-Nodier and 1, place St-Pierre, 75018
Métro: Anvers

Every Parisian interior designer knows this is the only place to come for wonderful fabrics and trimmings in all types, sizes, and price ranges. All the shops are centered around rue Charles-Nodier and place St-Pierre. At Dreyfus, 2, rue Charles-Nodier, you will find discounted bolts of fabric; at Tissues Reine, 5, place St-Pierre, silks and luxury fabrics are sold; and at Moline, 1, place St-Pierre, you have upholstery.

TEL Dreyfus 01-46-06-92-25; Tissues Reine 01-46-06-02-31;
    Moline 01-46-06-14-66
CREDIT CARDS MC, V
OPEN Depends on store, but generally Mon 2–6 P.M., Tues–Sat 10 A.M.–6 P.M.

TATI (13)
4–30, boulevard de Rochechouart, 75018
Métro: Barbès-Rochechouart, Anvers

For a complete description of this department store, see page 347. At this location, watch out for pickpockets, especially children.

TEL 01-55-29-50-00

Flea Markets: Les Marchés aux Puces

What to do on a Saturday or Sunday morning? Go early to the flea market. Wear old clothes and comfortable shoes, beware of pickpockets, and bring cash. You will have a good time even if you don't buy a thing. The days of finding a fabulous antique for a few euros are gone, but you will probably find a keepsake or two. If you have nothing special on your list, just people-watch; the wildlife at the *puces* beats that at the zoo.

FLEA MARKETS: LES MARCHÉS AUX PUCES

MARCHÉ D'ALIGRE (24; see map page 214)
Place d'Aligre, 75012
Métro: Ledru-Rollin

Marché d'Aligre is an Arab-influenced market with bottom-of-the-barrel prices. That's also where most of the quality is, especially for the produce. Wear a concealed money belt and go on a Sunday morning when it is really jumping. Prowl through the little shops, which have the lowest prices on baskets, tea glasses, *couscousières*, teapots, and Middle Eastern kitsch. You can bargain a little and probably save 30 or 40 percent over what you would pay in an uptown shop. In the center of it all is a small flea market selling little junky objects, antique buttons, bric-a-brac, and tacky clothes. Fashion mavens might want to swing through Betty, a designer discount shop that at times has something interesting (see page 328).

OPEN Tues–Sun 7:30 A.M.–1 P.M.

MARCHÉ DE VANVES (28; see map page 230)
Avenue Georges-Lafenestre, 75014
Métro: Porte de Vanves

This is a good place for small antiques and collectibles that tuck easily into a suitcase. Start by walking along avenue Marc-Sangier, and in a morning you will be able to browse and bargain your way through it and come away with a treasure or two. The locals know to come way before noon, when most of the serious sellers fold up their stalls. Every Sunday morning from March to October, the Square Georges-Lafenestre is an open-air art gallery where you can buy directly from the artists.

OPEN Sat–Sun stands on avenue Marc-Sangnier from 7:30 A.M.–1 P.M.; on avenue Georges-Lafenestre until 6 P.M.

MARCHÉ AUX PUCES SAINT-OUEN (1; see map page 272)
Avenue Michelet at rue des Rosiers, 75018
Métro: Porte de Clignancourt

Marché aux Puces Saint-Ouen is the largest flea and antique market in the world—too big to conquer in only a day. More than 11 million bargain hunters come every year, making this the number four tourist site in France. There are over twenty-five hundred dealers here set up in permanent shops. Once you get past the piles of jeans and the Indians selling cheap beads, head for the Marché Biron on the corner of 85, rue des Rosiers. It has the most expensive sellers, but it's the most serious for furniture and art. The Paul Bert Marché, at 110, rue des Rosiers, and 18, rue Paul Bert, has an unusual collection of Art Deco pieces and antiques from the late 1890s. The Marché Jules-Valles at 7, rue Jules-Valles, has the least expensive items, and lots of 1920s and 1930s lace and postcards. For vintage clothing, the Marché Malik at 53, rue Jules-Valles, is the place. Bring cash, expect to bargain, and wear a money belt. Pickpockets are pros here.

NOTE: When you exit the métro station, simply head north, following the crowds and the signs, to find the flea market. Cross boulevard Ney onto avenue de la Porte de Clignancourt, and you can't miss it.

INTERNET www.antikita.com
OPEN Sat 8 or 9 A.M.–6 P.M., Sun–Mon 10 or 11 A.M.–6 P.M.

MARCHÉ DE MONTREUIL
Place de la Porte de Montreuil, 75020
Métro: Porte de Montreuil

The huge market begins once you get through the long line of vendors hawking cheap trash on the bridge, but even then, you will wonder why you came. It's all basically cheap junk of little value or interest for most of us—and I recommend skipping it, unless, of course, you are looking for tools, domestic appliances, or beat-up furniture.

OPEN Sat–Mon 9 A.M.–5 P.M.

Art & Craft Markets

BASTILLE (13; see map page 214)
Place de la Bastille and boulevard Richard Lenoir, 75011
Métro: Bastille, Richard Lenoir

Two hundred and sixty artists exhibit and sell their work every Saturday along boulevard Richard Lenoir. Quality varies and so do the artists.

CREDIT CARDS Depends on the artist
OPEN Sat 10 A.M.–7 P.M.

MONTPARNASSE (15; see map page 230)
Montparnasse, Boulevard Edgar Quinet, 75014
Métro: Edgar Quinet

This Sunday gathering of 120 artists exhibiting and selling their work is similar to the Saturday gathering on boulevard Richard Lenoir. As usual, quality and substance varies with the artists.

CREDIT CARDS Depends on the artist
OPEN Sun 9 A.M.–7 P.M.

Food Shopping Streets and Outdoor Roving Markets

> **Paris in the early morning has a cheerful, bustling aspect—a promise of things to come.**
> —*Nancy Mitford,* The Pursuit of Love

There are two types of markets in Paris (in addition to the growing number of *supermarchés*): *rue commerçantes*—stationary indoor/outdoor markets along certain streets that are open six days a week, including Sunday morning, but not on Monday—and the *marchés volants*—outdoor roving markets of independent merchants who move from one neighborhood to another on Tuesday to Sunday mornings only, seldom in the afternoon. A visit to one of these markets provides a real look at an old, unchanging way of Parisian daily life. When you go, take your camera, don't touch the merchandise, and watch your wallet. I guarantee you that a trip or two to a Paris market will spoil you for your hometown supermarket. In Paris markets, fruits and vegetables of every variety are arranged with the skill and precision usually reserved for fine jewelry store windows. Equal care and attention is given to the displays of meats, fish, cheese, and fresh flowers. Everyone has a favorite vendor for each item on their shopping list, and vendors respond with very personal service. It is not unusual for a fruit seller to ask you not only what day you want to eat your melon or peaches, but at what time, and to select the fruit accordingly. A few favorites are listed here.

Food Shopping Streets: *Rues Commerçantes*

Generally, these are open Tuesday to Sunday 8:30 A.M. to 1 P.M. and 4:30 to 7 P.M. They are closed Monday all day and Sunday afternoon.

RUE MONTORGUEIL, 75002 (36; see map page 66)
Métro: Étienne-Marcel, Sentier

Rue Montorgueil is crowded with dogs, children, motor scooters, and people of all ages and persuasions, who create a great, lively Parisian ambience on one of the best shopping streets in Paris. The street is lined with three supermarkets, seven *boulangeries/pâtisseries,* two produce stands, two ice cream shops, meat (including horse) markets, fishmongers, cheese and wine shops, an Italian *traiteur,* two florists, pharmacies, cleaners, phone and photo shops, a hardware store, a natural food store, restaurants, bars and cafés galore, and a four-star hotel.

OPEN Except for the bakeries, most of the food shops are open Tues–Sat 8:30 A.M.–7 P.M., Sun 8:30 A.M.–1 P.M. **CLOSED** Mon

RUE MOUFFETARD, 75005 (40; see map page 108)
Métro: Censier-Daubenton, Place Monge

This is one of the most photographed and colorful street markets in Paris, but the quality is sometimes suspect and the prices tend to be high. The best times to experience the market street is on Saturday and Sunday mornings.

RUE DE BUCI 75006 (15; see map page 134)
Métro: Odéon

Rue de Buci is a far cry from what it was a few years ago when it was a loud and lively street market. Now, an impersonal *supermarché* has eclipsed the street vendors, but there are still interesting food shops, a wonderful *fromagerie,* a flower shop, a fruit and vegetable stand, and several bakeries to meet most shopping needs. Before or after shopping, it is sociologically interesting to sit at one of the outdoor cafés and watch the crowd.

RUE CLER, 75007 (11; see map page 170)
Métro: École-Militaire

This is the gathering place for aristocratic shoppers in the tony seventh arrondissement, but frankly, the quality has slipped, and the prices have gone up.

RUE D'ALIGRE, 75012 (24; see map page 214)
Métro: Ledru-Rollin

The street stalls are open only in the morning, selling an amazing array of North African and Caribbean produce and fruit in addition to seasonal French produce. Prices are low and quality varies. For an even more ethnic shopping experience, browse through the shops that line both sides of rue d'Aligre. The covered market on place d'Aligre is open in the afternoon. On Sunday morning there is a flea market on place d'Aligre with stalls selling mostly *junque.* There may be a hidden treasure, but I have never thought it was worth the digging. If you like wonderful, whole grain, organic breads, join the queue at Moisan, 5, place d'Aligre (01-43-45-46-60). Moisan is open Tues–Sat 7 A.M.–1:30 P.M., 3–8 P.M., Sun 7 A.M.–2 P.M.

RUE DAGUERRE, 75014 (24; see map page 230)
Métro: Denfert-Rochereau

Here you'll find lots of cafés filled with people-watchers, a Monoprix on the corner, and markets with good-quality products at fair prices.

RUE DU COMMERCE, 75015 (3; see map page 230)
Métro: Commerce, La Motte-Picquet–Grenelle

This provides an interesting look at blue-collar Paris.

RUE DE LÉVIS, 75017 (6; see map page 258)
Métro: Villiers

There is plenty here to tempt you—from bakeries and wine shops to a Monoprix.

RUE PONCELET, 75017 (10; see map page 258)
Métro: Ternes

This is a popular shopping destination with good cheese shops and colorful food hawkers.

RUE LEPIC, 75018 (10; see map page 272)
Métro: Abbesses, Blanche

This runs up the hill from boulevard de Clichy and merges into the heart of this side of the Butte Montmartre.

Outdoor Roving Food Markets: *Marchés Volants*

These are open on the days listed, unless otherwise noted, from 8 A.M. to 1:30 P.M. A few *quartiers* are experimenting with evening markets, which run from around 3 P.M. to 8 P.M. At the markets, look for the sign *producteur,* which usually hangs along the back of the stall. It means the merchant is selling foods or products he or she grew or produced, and the quality is usually better.

MARCHÉ RUE MONTMARTRE (44; see map page 66)
Rue Montmartre, near Eglise St-Eustache, 75001
Métro: Etienne-Marcel

There is a large organic stand, a florist, another selling wines from small producers, a *chèvre* cheese stand, and two stalls dishing up fresh paella and aromatic roast chickens.

OPEN Thur 3–8 P.M., Sun 8 A.M.–1 P.M.

MARCHÉ ST-HONORÉ (14; see map page 66)
Place du Marché St-Honoré, 75001
Métro: Tuileries

Small but good quality, befitting the classy neighborhood.

OPEN Wed 3–8 P.M., Sat 8 A.M.–1 P.M.

MARCHÉ PLACE BAUDOYER (31; see map page 86)
Place Baudoyer, off rue de Rivoli, 75004
Métro: Hôtel de Ville

This is another afternoon market held in Paris. The location is central, but the stands are few. However, prices are competitive, and there are several above-average stalls including one selling plants and flowers, another stirring a huge dish of paella, and another hawking hot and cold *charcuterie*.

OPEN Wed 3–8 P.M., Sat 7–2:30 P.M.

MARCHÉ CARMES (12; see map page 108)
Place Maubert, 75005
Métro: Maubert-Mutualité

This market is small with the usual food stalls, but also those selling foie gras, spices, a variety of olive oils and balsamic vinegar, clothing, rugs, quilts, Provençal prints, as well as a Senegalese merchant selling African art. Thursday is the best day for non-food items.

OPEN Tues, Thur, Sat 8 A.M.–1 P.M.

MARCHÉ MONGE (35; see map page 108)
Place Monge, 75005
Métro: Place Monge

This market is smaller than most, so it's easy to look it all over before deciding what looks the best. Friday is the best day for non-food items.

OPEN Wed, Fri, Sun 8 A.M.–1 P.M.

MARCHÉ RASPAIL (52; see map page 134)
Boulevard Raspail, between rue du Cherche-Midi and rue de Rennes, 75006
Métro: Rennes, Sèvres-Babylone

On Sunday the bio-products are from local growers and producers offering excellent organic fruits and veggies, even sulfate-free wines. If you are a health foodie, you will love it.

OPEN Tues & Fri (non-organic), Sun (organic), 9 A.M.–1 P.M.

MARCHÉ SAXE-BRETEUIL (36; see map page 170)
Avenue de Saxe, from place de Breteuil to place de Fontenoy, 75007
Métro: Sèvres-Lecourbe, Segur

This is one of the best in Paris. The Eiffel Tower serves as a beacon between the lines of food sellers. What a great photo op!

OPEN Thur, Sat

MARCHÉ RICHARD-LENOIR (17; see map page 214)
Boulevard Richard-Lenoir, at rue Amelot, 75011
Métro: Bastille, Richard-Lenoir

Not far from the Bastille, enormous, and very local.

OPEN Thur, Sun

MARCHÉ DUPLEIX (2; see map page 230)
Boulevard du Grenelle, between rue de Lourmel and rue de Commerce, 75015
Métro: Dupleix, La Motte-Piquet–Grenelle

This is considered a very good roving market in Paris because it's so big and has everything, and it's well worth an hour or so on a Sunday morning. In addition to food, you can buy suitcases, smocked dresses, violins, and much more. Despite its proximity to the Eiffel Tower, it's not touristy; in fact, Parisians love to live in the fifteenth arrondissement simply because of this market.

OPEN Wed, Sun

MARCHÉ COURS DE LA REINE (15; see map page 244)
Avenue du Président Wilson, 75016
Métro: Alma Marceau, Iéna

Big, beautiful with lots of luxurious foodstuffs befitting the exclusive neighborhood.

OPEN Wed, Sat

MARCHÉ DES BATIGNOLLES (5; see map page 258)
Boulevard des Batignolles, between rue de Rome and place de Clichy, 75017
Métro: Place Clichy, Rome

On Saturday, stalls sell organic products directly from the growers. Look for the sweet woman selling crêpes made to order.

OPEN Sat

A Shopper's Glossary

These are a few words and phrases to help you during your shopping adventures. For a larger glossary, see page 400.

How much? How many?	*Combien?*
How much does this cost?	*Ça coute combien?*
Do you have a smaller/larger size?	*Auriez-vous la taille plus petit/plus grande*
I am a size 36.	*Je fait un 36.*
I would like	*Je voudrais*
May I try this on?	*Est-ce-que je pourrais essayer cet article?*
I will take it.	*Je le prends.*
Do you accept credit cards?	*Acceptez-vous les cartes decrédit?*
Do you ship to the U.S.?	*Est-ce que vous envoyez au Etats-Unis?*
alteration(s)	*retouche(s)*
apron	*tablier*
belt	*ceinture*
blue cotton worker's uniform	*bleus de travail*
cash	*espèces*
bottle (perfume)	*flacon*
boxer shorts	*caleçons*
chef's hat	*toque*
closed	*fermé*
coat	*manteau*
department store	*magasin*
do-it-yourselfers	*bricoleurs*
dolls	*poupées*
down comforter	*duvet*
dress	*robe*
dressing gown, robe	*peignoir*
dressmaker	*couturière*
end of the collection	*fin de series*
expensive custom-made designer clothing	*haute couture*
fashion designer	*couturier*
first floor above ground (second floor in U.S.)	*premier étage*
flea market	*marché aux puces*
French cuff(s)	*manchette(s)*
glove	*gant*
good deal	*bonne affair*
ground floor (first floor in U.S.)	*rez-de-chausée*

hand-painted pottery	*faïence*
in style	*à la mode*
labels cut out	*dégriffés*
large department store	*grand magasin*
market	*marché*
MasterCard charge card	*Eurocard*
open	*ouvert*
overstock	*stock*
pants	*pantalons*
perfume store	*parfumerie*
poster	*affiche*
purse	*sac*
ready-to-wear	*prêt-a-porter*
resale consignment shop	*dépôt vente*
sales	*soldes*
scarf	*écharpe*
second-hand clothes (à la thrift shops)	*fripes*
second-hand dealer	*brocanteur*
shoes	*chaussures*
size	*taille*
skirt	*jupe*
stockings	*bas*
sweater	*pull*
tax refund	*détaxe*
tie	*cravate*
Visa charge card	*Carte Bleu*
workshop	*atelier*

Shops by Type

Glossary of French Words and Phrases

The French are surprisingly tolerant of foreigners who make an attempt to speak a few words. If you combine that with a smile and some sign language, and liberal use of *Madame* and *Monsieur, s'il vous plaît,* and *merci beaucoup,* you will be surprised how far you will get. Before your trip, buy some French language tapes or check them out from the library, and listen to them whenever you can. You will be amazed at how much you will absorb. For a list of shopping terms, see page 393.

At the Hotel

a room for one/two persons	*une chambre pour une/deux personnes*
a double bed	*un lit double, un grand lit*
twin beds	*deux lits*
a room with an extra bed	*une chambre avec un lit supplémentaire*
a room with running water and bidet	*une chambre avec cabinet de toilette*
a room with shower and toilet	*une chambre avec douche et WC*
a room with bath and toilet	*une chambre avec salle de bain et WC*
for one/two/three nights	*pour une/deux/troix nuits*
suite	*appartment*
two-level suite	*duplex*
a room on the courtyard	*une chambre sur la cour*
a room over the street	*une chambre sur la rue*
ground floor	*rez-de-chaussée*
first floor	*premier étage*
second floor	*deuxième étage*
sixth floor	*seizième étage*
with a view	*avec vue*
quiet	*calme*
noisy	*bruyant*
breakfast included	*le petit déjeuner compris*
I would like breakfast.	*Je voudrais prendre le petit déjeuner.*
I do not want breakfast.	*Je ne veux pas de petit déjeuner.*
air-conditioning	*climatisé*
blankets	*couvertures*
elevator, lift	*ascenseur*
heat	*chauffage*
to iron	*repasser*

key	*clef*
to do laundry	*faire la lessive*
pillow	*oreiller*
sheets	*draps*

Emergencies

police	*police*
Stop!	*Arrêtez!*
help/help me!	*Au secours!/Aidez-moi!*
Leave me alone.	*Laissez-moi tranquille.*
I am sick.	*Je suis malade.*
Call a doctor.	*Appelez un médecin.*
in case of emergency	*en cas d'urgence*
hospital	*l'hôpital*
drugstore	*pharmacie*
prescription	*ordonnance*
medicine	*médicament*
aspirin	*aspirine*

General Phrases

yes/no	*oui/non*
okay	*d'accord*
please	*s'il vous plaît*
thank you (very much)	*merci (beaucoup)*
You are welcome.	*De rien.*
excuse me	*excusez-moi, pardon*
I am very sorry.	*Désolé(e).*
Sir, Mr.	*Monsieur*
Madame, Mrs.	*Madame*
Miss	*Mademoiselle*
good morning,	*bonjour*
good afternoon, hello	
good evening, goodbye	*bonsoir, au revoir*
Hi (familiar)	*salut*
How are you?	*Comment allez-vous? Vous allez bien?*
How is it going?	*Comment ça va?/Ça va? (familiar)*
Fine, thank you, and you?	*Très bien, merci, et vous?*
What is your name?	*Comment vous appellez-vous?*
My name is . . .	*Je m'appelle . . .*
At what time?	*À quelle heure?*
Who is calling?	*C'est de la part de qui?*
hold the line (telephone)	*ne quittez pas*
good/well/bad/badly	*bon (bonne)/bien/mauvais(e)/mal*
small/big	*petit(e)/grand(e)*
beautiful	*beau/belle*

expensive/cheap	*cher/pas cher*
free (without charge)	*gratuit*
free (unoccupied)	*libre*
and/or	*et/ou*
with/without	*avec/sans*
because	*parce que*
a little/a lot	*un peu/beaucoup*
hot/cold	*chaud/froid*

Getting Around

Do you speak English?	*Parlez-vous anglais?*
I don't speak French.	*Je ne parle pas français.*
I don't understand.	*Je ne comprends pas.*
Speak more slowly, please.	*Parlez plus lentement, s'il vous plait.*
I am American/British.	*Je suis Américain(e)/Anglais(e).*
Where is the nearest métro?	*Où est le métro le plus proche?*
When is the next train for...?	*C'est quand le prochain train pour...?*
I want to get off at...	*Je voudrais descendre à...*
ticket	*billet*
far/near	*loin/pas loin*
street	*la rue*
street map	*le plan*
road map	*la carte*
Where are the toilets?	*Où sont les toilettes?*
What is it?	*Qu'est-ce que c'est?*
who	*qui*
what	*quoi*
where	*oú*
when	*quand*
why	*pourquoi*
which	*quel*
how	*comment*
here/there	*ici/là*
right/left	*à droit/à gauche*
straight ahead	*tout droit*
red/green stoplight	*feu rouge/vert*
far/near	*loin/pas loin*
to cross	*traverser*
How much/ how many?	*Combien?*
How much does it cost?	*C'est combien?/Ça coûte combien?*
Do you take credit cards?	*Est-ce que vous acceptez les cartes de crédit?*
I would like...	*Je voudrais...*
I am going...	*Je vais...*
It is/It is not	*C'est/Ce n'est pas*

Places

airport	*l'aéroport*
bank	*banque*
basement	*sous-sol*
bookstore	*librairie*
bridge	*pont*
bus stop	*l'arrêt de bus*
church	*église*
city hall	*hôtel de ville*
department store	*grand magasin*
district, neighborhood	*quartier*
garden	*jardin*
laundromat	*laverie*
market	*marché*
museum	*musée*
post office (stamp)	*la poste (timbre)*
private home	*hôtel particuliere*
street	*rue*
subway	*métro*
ticket office	*vente de billets*
tobacconist	*tabac*
train station/railway/platform	*gare/chemin de fer/quai*

Signs

caisse	cashier
complet	full (restaurant or hotel)
défense de fumer, nonfumer	no smoking
entrée/sortie	entrance/exit
fermeture annuelle	annual closing
hors service/en panne	out of order
interdit/sens interdit	forbidden/no entry
ouvert/fermé	open/closed
stationnement interdit	no parking
tous les jours	daily
zone piétonne	pedestrian zone

Time

What time is it?	*Quelle heure est-il?*
At what time?	*A quelle heure?*
What time does the train leave?	*Le train part à quelle heure?*
today/yesterday/tomorrow	*aujourd'hui/hier/demain*
this morning	*ce matin*
this afternoon	*cet après-midi*
tonight	*ce soir*
daily	*tous les jours*

Days

Sunday	*dimanche*
Monday	*lundi*
Tuesday	*mardi*
Wednesday	*mercredi*
Thursday	*jeudi*
Friday	*vendredi*
Saturday	*samedi*

Months

January	*janvier*
February	*fevrier*
March	*mars*
April	*avril*
May	*mai*
June	*juin*
July	*juillet*
August	*août*
September	*septembre*
October	*octobre*
November	*novembre*
December	*decembre*

Seasons

spring	*printemps*
summer	*été*
autumn	*automne*
winter	*hiver*

Numbers

0	*zéro*
1	*un, une*
2	*deux*
3	*trois*
4	*quatre*
5	*cinq*
6	*six*
7	*sept*
8	*huit*
9	*neuf*
10	*dix*
11	*onze*
12	*douze*
13	*treize*
14	*quatorze*
15	*quinze*

16	*seize*
17	*dix-sept*
18	*dix-huit*
19	*dix-neuf*
20	*vingt*
21	*vingt-et-un*
22	*vingt-deux*
30	*trente*
40	*quarante*
50	*cinquante*
60	*soixante*
70	*soixante-dix*
80	*quatre-vingts*
90	*quatre-vingt-dix*
100	*cent*
1,000	*mille*
1,000,000	*million*
first	*premier*
second	*deuxième*
third	*troisième*
fourth	*quatrième*
fifth	*cinquième*
sixth	*sixième*
seventh	*septième*
eighth	*huitième*
ninth	*neuvième*
tenth	*dixième*
twentieth	*vingtième*
one-hundredth	*centième*

Colors

black	*noir*
blue	*bleu*
brown	*marron/brun*
green	*vert*
orange	*orange*
pink	*rose*
purple	*violet*
red	*rouge*
white	*blanc*
yellow	*jaune*

Index of Accommodations

Index of Shops